*A Quick Guide to the Fundamentals*

# An Introduction to

# INDIAN BANKING & PAYMENT SYSTEMS

**Battula Vijay Kiran**
M.Tech., M.B.A., Ph.D.

**Prof. A. Narasimha Rao**
M.Com., M.B.A., Ph.D., FCMA
DCMS, College of Arts and Commerce, Andhra University

NOTION PRESS

# NOTION PRESS

India. Singapore. Malaysia.

ISBN 979-8-895446-37-9 (Paper Back)
ISBN 979-8-895446-39-3 (Hard Cover)

*This book is dedicated to the memory of my late grandfather,
P. Krishna Murthy.*

# Contents

# Preface

India's banking system and payment and settlement systems form the foundation of the country's financial infrastructure. Understanding how these systems function, interact, and evolve is essential for students, professionals, researchers, and anyone interested in the financial sector.

This book provides a concise introduction to the fundamentals of Indian banking and payment systems. It traces the evolution and structure of the banking sector, explains the major payment and settlement mechanisms, examines traditional banking services, and explores the growing role of technology in financial services. The book also discusses digital transformation, financial inclusion, the interrelationship between banks and payment systems, and emerging trends that are likely to shape the future of the sector.

While banking and payment systems are often studied separately, they are closely interconnected. Developments in one area frequently influence the other, collectively shaping the movement of money, financial stability, and economic growth. By presenting these subjects in a straightforward and accessible manner, this book aims to help readers develop a clear understanding of the concepts, institutions, technologies, and processes that underpin India's financial ecosystem.

**Readers are requested to carefully read the "Note to Readers" that follows, as it contains important information regarding the scope, limitations, and intended use of this book.**

***Note to Readers:*** This book was written with the objective of providing a simple and accessible introduction to the fundamentals of India's banking system and payment and settlement systems. The idea emerged during the author's academic and research journey, where it was observed that many learners, particularly students and newcomers to the subject, often find it difficult to understand how banking institutions, payment systems, technology, regulation, and financial inclusion initiatives are interconnected. This book represents an honest effort to present these topics in a structured and reader-friendly manner.

**The information presented in this book has been compiled, reviewed, and updated up to late 2024.** While every reasonable effort has been made to ensure accuracy, clarity, and reliability, **this book may still contain inadvertent errors, omissions, outdated information, simplifications, or differing interpretations that may have escaped the author's attention despite careful review.** Banking, payment systems, technology, regulations, and financial products continue to evolve rapidly, and developments occurring after the period covered by this book may not be reflected herein.

**Readers are strongly encouraged not to treat every statement, example, opinion, interpretation, or explanation contained in this book as a final or unquestionable authority.** Rather, this book should be viewed as a **foundational and directional guide** designed to help readers develop an overall understanding of the subject before progressing to specialised textbooks, official publications, regulatory documents, academic literature, and professional resources.

**After completing the book, readers are sincerely encouraged to revisit important concepts, facts, regulations, statistics, technological developments, and policy matters through official sources such as the Reserve Bank of India, National Payments Corporation of India, Government of India publications, regulatory notifications, statutes, circulars, annual reports, and other authoritative references.** Such independent verification will not only help identify any inaccuracies that may remain but will also deepen the reader's knowledge and understanding of the subject far beyond what any introductory guide can provide.

This book does not claim to be exhaustive, comprehensive, or free from error. Its purpose is to simplify complex subjects, provide direction for further learning, and encourage readers to explore the Indian banking and payment ecosystem with greater confidence and curiosity.

**The supervising professor's contribution was limited to guidance on general academic writing and textbook preparation. The selection of content, interpretations, explanations, examples, conclusions, and any errors or omissions that may remain are solely the responsibility of the author and should not be attributed to the supervising professor.**

**BATTULA VIJAY KIRAN**

# Acknowledgments

The creation of this book has been shaped by the insights, guidance, and unwavering support of many remarkable individuals. It is a privilege to acknowledge and express my deepest gratitude to them.

In front, my heartfelt appreciation goes to Prof. A. Narasimha Rao, M.Com., M.B.A., Ph.D., FCMA, who, as both a co-author and the Research Director and Principal of the College of Arts and Commerce, has was involved in the development of this book. His consistent encouragement, valuable insights, and unrelenting guidance have been major throughout our collaboration. Prof. Rao's expertise and enthusiasm have profoundly influenced our work, providing both direction and inspiration, making this endeavor a truly rewarding experience.

I owe a special debt of gratitude to all the educators who have been instrumental in my academic journey. Their dedication and knowledge have been a basis of my growth, offering invaluable lessons and perspectives that greatly contributed to this work. Their mentorship has been a beacon, guiding me through the intricacies of this field.

I am eternally grateful to my parents, Sri. B. Sivanandam and Smt. Bhavani, for their unconditional love and unwavering belief in me. Their support has been a driving force throughout this journey. I also wish to acknowledge the support of my siblings and relatives, whose encouragement has been a steady source of strength.

I dedicate this book to the memory of my late grandfather, P. Krishna Murthy, Retd. Civil Engineer, Indian Railways. His principles and legacy have been a guiding force and a constant source of inspiration throughout my life.


**BATTULA VIJAY KIRAN**

# Chapter 1
# Overview of the Indian Banking System

## 1.1 Evolution and History

The evolution of Indian banking is a captivating narrative that spans millennia, reflecting the country's rich cultural heritage and economic development. From the ancient practices of indigenous bankers and temple banking to the organized systems of merchant guilds, the history of banking in India is marked by advance and adaptation. This journey through time reveals how these early forms of banking laid the groundwork for the sophisticated financial systems we see today.

### 1.1.1 Ancient and Medieval Banking Practices

Long before the establishment of modern banking institutions, India had a well-developed financial system that catered to the needs of its diverse population. These early practices were deeply embedded in the social and economic fabric of the time, providing necessary financial services to traders, farmers, and the general populace. The ancient and medieval banking practices in India were not just economic activities; they were central to the community's social structure and cultural norms.

**Indigenous Banking Systems**

The indigenous banking systems in ancient India were characterized by their informal yet highly effective nature. These systems were based on personal relationships, trust, and community networks, providing many financial services, including moneylending, trade finance, and currency exchange.

***Shroffs and Sahukars***

Shroffs and sahukars were the foundation of India's indigenous banking system. Shroffs, often referred to as the money changers of their time, contributed to supporting trade across regions. They were experts in assessing the value of different currencies and provided important services in currency exchange. The role of shroffs was important in a period where different regions used different forms of currency, and there was no standardized monetary system. They not only facilitated local trade but also enabled international commerce by exchanging foreign currencies, thus acting as a bridge between local and global markets.

Sahukars, on the other hand, were akin to modern-day bankers. They were typically wealthy merchants who provided loans to traders, artisans, and farmers. The lending practices of sahukars were based on personal relationships and mutual trust. Unlike modern banks, which rely heavily on formal documentation, sahukars often extended credit based on verbal agreements or simple promissory notes. These moneylenders operated with a high degree of flexibility, adjusting their terms and conditions to suit the needs of their clients. The interest rates charged by sahukars varied, often depending on the borrower's creditworthiness and the nature of the collateral offered, which could range from land to personal belongings. The records maintained by shroffs and sahukars, known as "bahi-khatas," were meticulous. These ledgers contained detailed accounts of transactions, debts, and credits, often written in indigenous languages and scripts. The trust in these records was so strong that they were frequently used as evidence in legal disputes. The operations of shroffs and sahukars extended beyond simple financial transactions; they often acted as advisors and intermediaries in trade and legal matters. Their deep understanding of the local economy and community dynamics enabled them to assess risks and manage their lending portfolios effectively.

### Hundi System

The hundi system was another aspect of indigenous banking in ancient India. Hundis were negotiable instruments used for the transfer of money and goods, serving a function similar to modern-day bills of exchange or promissory notes. This system was particularly useful in a vast country like India, where physical transportation of cash was risky and cumbersome. There were many types of hundis, each designed to meet specific financial needs. For instance, a "darshani hundi" was payable on demand, while a "muddati hundi" had a specified maturity date. These instruments were used extensively by merchants and traders for credit transactions and remittances. A typical hundi transaction involved a drawer (the issuer of the hundi), a drawee (the party to whom the payment was to be made), and a payee (the recipient of the payment). The drawer would issue the hundi, promising to pay the specified amount either on demand or at a future date. The payee could then use the hundi as a form of payment or endorse it to another party.

One of the remarkable features of the hundi system was its flexibility and adaptability. Hundis could be transferred by endorsement, making them a versatile tool for business transactions. They were widely accepted across different regions, and their validity was based on the reputation and creditworthiness of the issuer. This made hundis a needed instrument for trade, as they facilitated transactions without the need for immediate cash payment. The system operated largely on trust, and any breach of trust could severely damage a trader's reputation. The hundi system also had a well-developed network of brokers and agents who helped negotiate and settle hundis. These intermediaries charged a commission for their services, which was a common practice in the financial ecosystem of the time. The widespread use of hundis contributed considerably to the growth of commerce and trade in ancient India, allowing merchants to engage in large-scale transactions with relative ease and security.

### Temple Banking

Temple banking was a part of the ancient Indian financial system. Temples were not only places of worship but also notable economic centers that contributed to the community's financial life. They accumulated vast amounts of wealth through donations, offerings, and revenues from temple-owned lands. This wealth was managed by temple authorities and used for several economic activities, including lending and investment.

Temples provided loans to individuals and businesses at relatively low-interest rates compared to private moneylenders. These loans were often extended for agricultural purposes, trade, and even social functions like weddings. The interest earned on these loans contributed to the temple's income, which was used for maintenance, religious activities, and social welfare. The records of these transactions were meticulously kept, often inscribed on temple walls or recorded in palm-leaf manuscripts. These records ensured transparency and accountability, which were central for maintaining the temple's reputation and trustworthiness. Apart from lending, temples also offered safekeeping services. People could deposit their money and valuables in the temple, confident in the security provided by the sacred nature of the place. The temples issued receipts for these deposits, which could be redeemed at any time. This practice made temples an early form of banking institution, providing services similar to modern-day safe deposit boxes and vaults.

Temple banking extended beyond mere financial transactions; it was also a means of social welfare. Temples often funded public works such as the construction of roads, wells, and irrigation systems, contributing to the community's overall development. They also was involved in disaster relief, providing food and shelter during famines and other crises. The moral and religious authority of the temple ensured that loans were repaid, as defaulting on a temple loan was considered a sin and could lead to social ostracism. The economic influence of temples was not limited to the local community; it extended to regional and even international trade. Temples owned land and engaged in commercial ventures, including agriculture, trade, and shipping. They employed a large number of people, from priests and workers to artisans and traders, making them marked employers in the economy. The wealth generated by temples often translated into political power, allowing them to support or oppose local rulers and participate in governance.

### Merchant Guilds and Banking

Merchant guilds, known as srenis in ancient India, were organized associations of traders and artisans who came together to protect their economic interests and regulate trade. These guilds were more than just trade associations; they were multifaceted institutions that helped with the economic, social, and political life of the time.

One of the functions of merchant guilds was to provide credit and financial services to their members. Guilds maintained common funds, which were used to offer loans to members for trade, production, and other purposes. These loans were typically provided at favorable terms, as the guild aimed to support the economic prosperity of its members. The funds for these loans came from membership fees, fines, and a portion of the profits earned by members. The guilds also acted as guarantors for their members, providing a collective guarantee for the repayment of loans. This system not only facilitated trade but also reduced the risk for individual traders.

Merchant guilds factored into the development of trade networks. They established and maintained trade routes, negotiated trade agreements, and standardized weights and measures. The guilds provided infrastructure, such as warehouses and transport facilities, which were necessary for the effective movement of goods. The collective strength of the guilds allowed them to exert considerable influence over market conditions, control prices, and prevent unfair competition. They also regulated the quality of goods, guaranteeing that products met certain standards, which helped build trust among consumers. In addition to their economic functions, merchant guilds had a social and political dimension. They provided social security to their members, including pensions, medical aid, and support during times of distress. The guilds also contributed to community life, sponsoring religious and cultural activities. Politically, guilds wielded considerable influence, often acting as advisors to local rulers and participating in governance. They could mobilize resources and support for political causes, making them a major force in the local power structure.

The banking practices associated with merchant guilds were instrumental in enabling trade and economic growth. The guilds provided a structured and reliable system for financial transactions, reducing the risks associated with commerce. The regulations and codes of conduct established by the guilds ensured ethical business practices, encouraging a stable and trustworthy business environment. The legacy of merchant guilds and their banking functions can still be seen today in the continued importance of trade associations and cooperatives in India's economic life. The ancient and medieval banking practices in India laid the foundation for the country's modern financial system. From the shroffs and sahukars who provided important financial services, to the hundi system that facilitated trade across regions, and the temple banking and merchant guilds that played roles in economic and social life, these early systems were essential to the development of commerce and trade in India. They not only met the financial needs of their time but also fostered trust and stability in economic transactions. The practices and principles established during these periods continue to influence India's banking sector, reflecting the country's rich cultural and economic heritage.

The legacy of ancient and medieval banking practices in India, including the influential role of merchant guilds, laid a strong foundation for the country's financial system. However, as India moved into the modern era, particularly in the post-independence period, the banking sector faced new challenges and opportunities. The nationalization of banks in 1969 and 1980 aimed to address some of these challenges, but by the late 1980s, it became clear that more broad reforms were needed. The year 1991 was a major moment in India's economic history. The country faced a severe balance of payments crisis, with foreign exchange reserves dwindling to critically low levels, barely enough to cover a few weeks of imports. Inflation was soaring, and India was on the brink of defaulting on its external debt obligations. This economic crisis served as a catalyst for wide-ranging reforms across a number of sectors, with banking leading the way.

In response to this crisis, the government, led by Prime Minister P.V. Narasimha Rao and Finance Minister Manmohan Singh, introduced a series of bold economic liberalization policies. These policies marked India's shift from a largely closed, socialist-style economy to a more open, market-oriented one. The banking sector, being the backbone of the economy, was a main focus of these reforms. The 1991 banking reforms were part of this larger economic overhaul and marked a paradigm shift in the Indian financial sector. They aimed to transform banking from a heavily regulated, public-sector dominated industry to a more dynamic, competitive, and quick system, capable of supporting India's new economic direction. These reforms were multifaceted, addressing aspects of banking operations. One of the most notable changes was the deregulation of interest rates. Prior to 1991, interest rates were largely controlled by the Reserve Bank of India (RBI), reminiscent of the guild-like control over economic activities in earlier times. The reforms allowed banks greater autonomy in setting their own interest rates for deposits and loans, introducing market-driven pricing of financial products.

Just as merchant guilds once regulated entry into trade, the banking sector had been tightly controlled by the government. The 1991 reforms changed this by opening the doors to private sector banks, ending the long-standing monopoly of public sector banks. This infusion of competition brought about a renaissance in banking services, with new entrants introducing new products, improved customer service, and advanced technology. The reforms also addressed the geographical reach of banking services, reminiscent of how merchant guilds established trade networks. The relaxation of branch licensing policies allowed banks more freedom to open branches, especially in underserved areas. This expansion of the banking network was involved in extending formal banking services to a larger section of the population, improving financial inclusion in a way that echoed the community-oriented approach of ancient guilds.

In terms of financial stability and transparency, the reforms introduced prudential norms for asset classification, income recognition, and provisioning. These measures aimed to improve the financial health of banks and align Indian banking practices with international standards. Banks were required to maintain higher capital adequacy ratios and disclose their non-performing assets, improving transparency in the sector. This focus on stability and trust echoed the role that merchant guilds once played in securing ethical business practices and building trust in commercial transactions. The reforms also initiated a gradual reduction in the statutory liquidity ratio (SLR) and cash reserve ratio (CRR) which are explained in the coming sections, freeing up more funds for banks to lend. This move was designed to stimulate economic growth by increasing the availability of credit, much like how merchant guilds once provided credit to support trade and production. The 1991 reforms included measures to recapitalize public sector banks, which had been burdened with non-performing assets. This recapitalization was important in safeguarding the stability of the banking system during the transition period.

These full reforms set the stage for the modernization of India's banking sector, leading to increased effectiveness, improved financial intermediation, and better allocation of resources in the economy. While the challenges and opportunities faced by the banking sector in 1991 were different from those of ancient times, the fundamental goals of easing trade, supporting economic growth, and providing financial stability remained constant. The 1991 reforms represented a modern reinterpretation of these age-old banking principles, adapting them to the needs of a rapidly globalizing economy and pulling India back from the brink of an economic crisis.

## 1.2 Structure and Types of Banks

Banking is a fundamental pillar of the global financial system, supporting economic activities and catering to diverse financial needs. The banking sector encompasses a broad set of services and institutions, each designed to address specific client requirements, from individual consumers to large corporations and governments. Here are the types of banking, each contributing to the economy:

### *Retail Banking:*

Retail banking, often referred to as consumer banking, focuses on providing financial services to individual customers. This sector includes all sorts of products such as savings accounts, checking accounts, personal loans, mortgages, credit cards, and debit cards. These services are designed to meet the everyday financial needs of individuals, allowing them to manage their finances, borrow money, and make payments. Another aspect of retail banking is community banking, which is provided by local banks that tailor their services to meet the needs of their community. Community banks often emphasize personal relationships with customers and focus on supporting small businesses and local development, offering personalized service that larger banks may not provide.

***Commercial Banking:***

Commercial banking is centered around providing services to businesses and corporations, addressing their financial needs through many specialized products. Corporate banking, a component of commercial banking, offers a range of services to businesses, including business loans, asset management, real estate financing, trade finance, and treasury services. These services are needed for businesses to manage their day-to-day operations, finance growth, and handle their financial transactions effectively. Another facet of commercial banking is merchant banking, which caters to the needs of large enterprises and high-net-worth individuals. Merchant banks provide specialized services such as underwriting, loan syndication, and financial advisory, helping businesses to raise capital, manage large-scale financial operations, and receive expert financial guidance.

***Investment Banking:***

Investment banking involves a span of services related to capital markets, where the primary focus is on helping companies and governments raise capital by underwriting new debt and equity securities. Investment banks also contribute to enabling mergers and acquisitions, providing strategic advice and helping to arrange the financing necessary for such deals. They engage in market making, trading of derivatives, and managing the issuance of new securities. Investment banking is central to the financial markets, as it helps channel funds from investors to entities that need capital for expansion, investment, or other purposes.

***Wholesale Banking:***

Wholesale banking provides services to large institutions and corporate clients, typically offering financial products and services on a large scale. These services include large-scale deposits, foreign exchange transactions, bulk cash management, and institutional lending. Unlike retail banking, which deals with individual customers, wholesale banking focuses on the needs of corporations, government agencies, and other large entities, offering tailored solutions to manage marked financial operations.

***Islamic Banking:***

Islamic banking operates in accordance with Sharia (Islamic law), which sets specific guidelines for financial transactions. This form of banking prohibits the charging or paying of interest (riba) and investing in businesses that provide goods or services considered contrary to Islamic principles, such as those involving alcohol or gambling. Islamic banking focuses on profit-sharing and joint venture approaches, where both the bank and its customers share the risks and rewards of investments. This ethical and equitable approach to banking has attracted a substantial following, especially in Muslim-majority countries, and has led to the growth of a global Islamic finance industry.

### *Online Banking:*

Online banking, also known as internet banking, enables customers to access many banking services through the internet. Customers can perform several financial transactions, such as transferring money, paying bills, checking account balances, and applying for loans, all from the convenience of their computers or mobile devices. Online banking has transformed the way people interact with their banks, offering greater flexibility and convenience by eliminating the need to visit physical bank branches.

### *Mobile Banking:*

Mobile banking takes the convenience of online banking a step further by providing banking services directly through mobile devices. With mobile banking apps, customers can manage their finances on the go, accessing their accounts, transferring funds, paying bills, and even depositing checks using their smartphones or tablets. This form of banking has gained popularity due to its accessibility and ease of use, allowing customers to conduct financial transactions anytime and anywhere.

### *Central Banking:*

Central banking refers to the operations of national banks that provide financial and banking services for a country's government and commercial banking system. Central banks, such as the Federal Reserve in the United States or the European Central Bank in the Eurozone, are responsible for managing a nation's currency, monetary policy, and interest rates. They are involved in maintaining economic stability by regulating money supply, setting interest rates, and overseeing the banking industry to guarantee financial stability and protect the economy from systemic risks.

### *Shadow Banking:*

Shadow banking refers to non-bank financial intermediaries that provide services similar to those offered by traditional commercial banks but operate outside the conventional regulatory framework. Entities in the shadow banking system, such as hedge funds, private equity funds, and other non-bank financial institutions, engage in activities like lending, credit intermediation, and asset management without being subject to the same oversight as traditional banks. While shadow banking can increase access to credit and contribute to financial development, it also poses potential risks due to its lack of regulation and transparency.

### Cooperative Banking:

Cooperative banking is based on the principles of cooperative ownership, where the banks are owned and operated by their members, who are also their customers. These banks, such as credit unions, are established to meet the financial needs of their members rather than to maximize profits. Cooperative banks offer a range of retail banking services, including savings accounts, loans, and financial planning, and they typically focus on promoting a strong relationship with their members. Because they are member-owned, cooperative banks often provide more favorable terms and conditions than traditional banks, and they reinvest profits into the community or return them to members in the form of dividends.

### Development Banking:

Development banking involves institutions that provide financial support for economic development projects, particularly in sectors like infrastructure, agriculture, and industry. These banks often work in developing countries, offering long-term financing for projects that promote sustainable economic growth. Development banks help with addressing financial gaps in sectors that are critical for a country's development but may be underserved by traditional financial institutions. They often collaborate with governments, international organizations, and private entities to fund projects that contribute to economic development and social progress.

### Universal Banking:

Universal banking refers to a complete form of banking that combines both commercial and investment services under one roof. Universal banks offer a broad set of financial services to all types of clients, from individuals to large corporations. These banks can engage in a variety of activities, such as taking deposits, making loans, underwriting securities, providing investment advisory services, and offering asset management. The universal banking model allows for greater flexibility and speed, enabling banks to meet the diverse needs of their customers through a single institution.

***Offshore Banking:***

Offshore banking involves banking services provided by banks located outside the depositor's home country, often in jurisdictions known for favorable tax treatment and banking regulations. Offshore banking is commonly used for purposes such as asset protection, tax optimization, and confidentiality. These banks offer services like international investment opportunities, foreign currency accounts, and cross-border financial transactions, making them attractive to individuals and businesses looking to manage their wealth internationally. Offshore banking can provide advantages such as reduced tax liability, privacy, and access to global markets, but it also requires handling complex regulatory environments and potential legal implications.

***Rural Banking:***

Rural banking focuses on providing financial services to people in rural and semi-urban areas, often with an emphasis on agricultural financing and the development of rural economies. Rural banks offer a range of services tailored to the needs of farmers, small businesses, and rural communities, including crop loans, microfinance, savings accounts, and remittance services. These banks factor into improving financial inclusion by extending banking facilities to underserved regions, helping to promote economic development and reduce poverty in rural areas. Rural banking initiatives often involve partnerships between government agencies, development organizations, and private banks to create accessible financial products and services that support the livelihoods of rural populations.

Each type of banking serves distinct purposes and caters to different segments of the market, contributing to the overall stability and functionality of the financial system. Understanding these a number of banking types is important for making informed financial decisions and effectively managing the complex world of finance. The structure of the banking system in India reflects the country's diverse economic sector and its evolving financial needs. The system comprises a variety of institutions, each serving different segments of the economy, from the Reserve Bank of India, which acts as the central authority, to commercial banks, cooperative banks, and other specialized financial institutions. This thorough structure guarantees that financial services are accessible to all sections of society, supporting both economic growth and social development. In this section, we will explore the structure and types of banks in India, beginning with the role of the Reserve Bank of India (RBI).

## 1.2.1 Reserve Bank of India

The Reserve Bank of India (RBI) stands at the apex of India's banking system. Established in 1935, the RBI has helped with shaping the country's monetary and financial policies. As India's central bank, it is responsible for maintaining monetary stability, regulating the financial system, and guaranteeing the smooth functioning of the payment and settlement systems. The RBI's functions and powers are defined by the Reserve Bank of India Act, 1934, and the Banking Regulation Act, 1949. Over the decades, the RBI has evolved to meet the changing needs of the economy, adapting its policies and frameworks to address new challenges and opportunities.

### *Functions and Powers*

The RBI's functions and powers are extensive, covering all sorts of activities that are critical to the functioning of India's economy. At its core, the RBI is tasked with formulating and implementing monetary policy, managing the country's foreign exchange reserves, and supervising the financial sector. These responsibilities make the RBI a player in India's economic policy framework.

### *Organizational Structure*

The organizational structure of the RBI is designed to support its diverse functions and responsibilities. The central bank operates through a well-defined hierarchy, with its headquarters in Mumbai and regional offices across the country. The RBI's governance structure includes the Central Board of Directors, which is the highest decision-making body.

***Central Board of Directors:*** The Central Board of Directors is composed of the Governor, who serves as the chief executive officer of the RBI, and four Deputy Governors. The Governor is appointed by the Government of India and holds a tenure that typically lasts for three years, which can be extended. The Deputy Governors are also appointed by the government and are responsible for specific areas of the RBI's operations, such as monetary policy, banking regulation, financial markets, and foreign exchange management.

In addition to the Governor and Deputy Governors, the Central Board includes non-executive directors appointed by the government. These directors represent sectors of the economy, including industry, agriculture, and finance. The Board also includes a representative from the Ministry of

Finance. The Central Board meets regularly to discuss and decide on primary policy matters, including monetary policy, regulatory issues, and the RBI's budget and accounts.

***Departments and Divisions:*** The RBI's operations are organized into several departments and divisions, each responsible for specific functions. Principal departments include the Monetary Policy Department, which formulates and implements monetary policy; the Department of Regulation, which oversees the regulation of banks and NBFCs; the Department of Supervision, which conducts inspections and audits; and the Department of Economic and Policy Research, which provides economic analysis and research support. Other important departments include the Department of Currency Management, which handles the issuance and distribution of currency, and the Financial Markets Department, which oversees the functioning of money and foreign exchange markets.

The RBI also has several specialized divisions and units, such as the Financial Inclusion and Development Department, which promotes financial inclusion; the Payment and Settlement Systems Department, which regulates payment systems; and the International Department, which manages foreign exchange reserves and external relations.

***Regional Offices and Subsidiaries:*** The RBI operates through a network of regional offices and branches across India. These regional offices contribute to implementing the RBI's policies at the local level and in maintaining close contact with banks and financial institutions in their respective regions. The RBI also has several wholly owned subsidiaries, including the Deposit Insurance and Credit Guarantee Corporation (DICGC), which provides deposit insurance; and the Bharatiya Reserve Bank Note Mudran Private Limited (BRBNMPL), which prints currency notes.

### Monetary Policy Framework

The monetary policy framework of the RBI is designed to achieve its objectives of price stability, financial stability, and economic growth. The framework has evolved over time to incorporate best practices and to respond to changing economic conditions.

***Inflation Targeting:*** Since 2016, the RBI has adopted an inflation-targeting framework, with the objective of maintaining price stability. Under this framework, the RBI aims to keep the Consumer Price Index (CPI) inflation within a target range of 4% ± 2%. The adoption of inflation targeting has brought greater clarity and transparency to the RBI's monetary policy, helping to anchor inflation expectations and improve the credibility of the central bank.

***Monetary Policy Committee (MPC):*** The RBI's monetary policy decisions are made by the Monetary Policy Committee (MPC), which was established in 2016. The MPC consists of six members: the Governor (who serves as the Chairperson), the Deputy Governor in charge of monetary policy, one officer of the RBI nominated by the Central Board, and three external members appointed by the Government of India. The MPC meets at least four times a year to review economic and financial conditions and to decide on the appropriate monetary policy stance. The decisions of the MPC are based on a majority vote, and the RBI is required to publish the minutes of the MPC meetings, including the individual voting records, to secure transparency.

***Policy Instruments:*** The RBI uses a variety of policy instruments to implement its monetary policy. The instruments include:

***Repo Rate:*** The rate at which the RBI lends to commercial banks. Changes in the repo rate influence the cost of borrowing for banks, which in turn affects the lending and borrowing rates in the economy.

***Reverse Repo Rate:*** The rate at which the RBI borrows from commercial banks. It serves as a tool for absorbing excess liquidity from the banking system.

***Cash Reserve Ratio (CRR):*** The proportion of a bank's total deposits that must be kept as reserves with the RBI. Changes in the CRR affect the amount of funds available for lending.

***Statutory Liquidity Ratio (SLR):*** The proportion of a bank's total deposits that must be invested in government securities. The SLR secures that banks maintain a minimum level of safe and liquid assets.

***Open Market Operations (OMOs):*** The RBI's buying and selling of government securities in the open market to control the money supply and liquidity conditions.

***Marginal Standing Facility (MSF):*** A facility that allows banks to borrow overnight from the RBI against government securities. The MSF rate is typically higher than the repo rate and serves as a penalty rate for banks.

***Liquidity Management:*** The RBI actively manages liquidity conditions in the banking system to safeguard that there is adequate liquidity to support economic activity, while also preventing excess liquidity that could lead to inflationary pressures. The RBI uses tools, including OMOs, CRR adjustments, and the MSF, to manage liquidity. The central bank also conducts regular market operations, such as the issuance of government securities and the management of short-term money market rates, to achieve its liquidity objectives.

***Communication and Transparency:*** The RBI places a strong emphasis on communication and transparency in its monetary policy framework. The central bank publishes regular reports, including the Monetary Policy Report, the Financial Stability Report, and the Annual Report, to provide insights into its policy decisions and the economic outlook. The RBI also engages with the public, financial markets, and other stakeholders through press conferences, speeches, and consultations.

The Reserve Bank of India contributes to the structure and functioning of India's banking system. Its functions and powers, organizational structure, and monetary policy framework are critical to maintaining monetary stability, regulating the financial sector, and supporting the country's economic development. As the Indian economy continues to evolve, the RBI's role as the central bank and financial regulator will remain central in securing a stable and resilient financial system.

## 1.2.2 Commercial Banks

Commercial banks form the backbone of the Indian financial system, providing a span of banking services to individuals, businesses, and the government. They are involved in the economy by accepting deposits, extending credit, easing transactions, and supporting the overall financial infrastructure. In India, commercial banks can be broadly categorized into Public Sector Banks (PSBs), Private Sector Banks, Foreign Banks, and Regional Rural Banks (RRBs). Each category has its characteristics and contributions to the banking sector.

***Public Sector Banks***

Public Sector Banks (PSBs) are a dominant force in India's banking environment. These banks are owned and operated by the government, and their objective is to serve the public interest by promoting economic development and financial inclusion. PSBs account for a major share of the total assets and deposits in the Indian banking system, reflecting their extensive reach and influence.

*State Bank of India and Associates*

The State Bank of India (SBI) is the largest public sector bank in India and one of the oldest, with its origins tracing back to the Bank of Calcutta, established in 1806. In 1955, the government nationalized the Imperial Bank of India and renamed it the State Bank of India. Over the years, SBI has grown to become a financial behemoth, offering a broad range of banking services, including retail banking, corporate banking, international banking, and treasury operations. SBI has several associate banks that were once independent entities but have since been merged with the parent bank to simplify operations and strengthen productivity. The most notable of these mergers occurred in 2017 when SBI consolidated five of its associate banks and the Bharatiya Mahila Bank, notably increasing its size and market share. This merger created a unified banking entity with a vast network of branches and ATMs across the country, making SBI one of the largest employers in the financial sector. As a public sector bank, SBI is involved in implementing government policies and schemes. It is heavily involved in priority sector lending, which includes providing credit to agriculture, small and medium enterprises (SMEs), and economically weaker sections of society. SBI also participates in many government initiatives, such as the Pradhan Mantri Jan Dhan Yojana (PMJDY), which aims to promote financial inclusion by opening zero-balance accounts for unbanked individuals. SBI offers a range of digital banking services, including internet banking, mobile banking, and digital wallets, to cater to the evolving needs of its customers.

## Nationalized Banks

Apart from SBI and its associates, India's public sector banking system includes several nationalized banks. These banks were privately owned before being nationalized by the government in two phases: the first in 1969 and the second in 1980. The nationalization of banks was a strategic move to make certain that banking services were accessible to a broader population, particularly in rural and underserved areas, and to align the banking sector with the country's socio-economic development goals. The first phase of nationalization in 1969 saw the government take control of 14 major commercial banks, each with deposits exceeding Rs. 50 crores. The second phase in 1980 brought six more banks under government ownership. These nationalized banks were tasked with promoting financial inclusion, supporting agriculture and small industries, and providing credit to priority sectors. They also was involved in channeling credit to strategic industries and sectors identified by the government as necessary for national development.

Nationalized banks in India include prominent names such as Punjab National Bank (PNB), Bank of Baroda (BoB), Canara Bank, Union Bank of India, and Indian Bank. These banks have extensive branch networks and offer many services, including personal banking, corporate banking, international banking, and treasury operations. They are also involved in implementing several government welfare schemes, such as the MUDRA (Micro Units Development and Refinance Agency) scheme, which provides financial support to micro and small enterprises. Nationalized banks have been instrumental in promoting rural banking and financial literacy. They have established specialized branches, such as rural and agricultural branches, to cater to the specific needs of rural customers. These banks also participate in financial literacy programs and initiatives to educate the public about banking services, savings, investments, and credit management. In recent years, nationalized banks have also embraced digital transformation, offering online and mobile banking services to boost customer convenience and accessibility.

### Private Sector Banks

Private sector banks in India are characterized by their ownership structure, where private entities, individuals, and institutional investors hold considerable stakes. These banks operate on a profit-oriented model, focusing on providing smooth and customer-centric services. Private sector banks are further classified into old private sector banks and new private sector banks, each with distinct characteristics and histories.

### Old Private Sector Banks

Old private sector banks are those that have been in existence since before the liberalization of the Indian economy in the early 1990s. These banks have a long history of serving specific communities and regions, and they have traditionally focused on niche markets. Examples of old private sector banks include Federal Bank, Karur Vysya Bank, and South Indian Bank. These banks have a strong regional presence and have built deep-rooted relationships with their customers. They have traditionally catered to the banking needs of specific communities, such as traders, agriculturists, and small businesses. Despite their relatively smaller size compared to public sector banks, old private sector banks have carved out a niche for themselves by offering personalized services and maintaining strong customer loyalty.

In recent years, old private sector banks have undergone notable transformations to remain competitive in the evolving banking field. They have embraced technology and digital banking solutions, expanded their product offerings, and diversified their customer base. Many of these banks have also ventured into new areas, such as wealth management, insurance, and investment banking, to increase their revenue streams and profitability.

### New Private Sector Banks

New private sector banks emerged in India following the liberalization of the economy in the early 1990s. The government and the Reserve Bank of India (RBI) initiated a series of reforms to encourage the entry of private players into the banking sector, with the goal of strengthening competition, effectiveness, and breakthrough. The licensing of new private sector banks marked a marked shift in India's banking sector, as it allowed for greater participation from private and foreign investors. Prominent new private sector banks include HDFC Bank, ICICI Bank, Axis Bank, and Kotak Mahindra Bank. These banks quickly gained prominence due to their customer-centric approach, novel products and services, and advanced technology infrastructure. They focused on retail banking, offering a broad set of services such as savings accounts, loans, credit cards, and digital banking solutions.

New private sector banks have been leading digital transformation in the Indian banking sector. They have leveraged technology to offer smooth and convenient banking experiences, including internet banking, mobile banking, and contactless payments. These banks have also introduced fresh financial products, such as instant loans, digital wallets, and investment platforms, catering to the diverse needs of their customers. The success of new private sector banks can be attributed to their agility, customer focus, and ability to adapt to changing market dynamics. They have been able to attract a younger and tech-savvy customer base, offering personalized services and advanced digital solutions. The competition from new private sector banks has also prompted public sector banks and old private sector banks to modernize their operations and improve their service offerings.

### Foreign Banks

Foreign banks have a substantial presence in India, bringing global expertise, advanced technology, and best practices to the country's banking sector. These banks operate through branches or wholly-owned subsidiaries and primarily cater to multinational corporations, large Indian businesses, and high-net-worth individuals. Foreign banks offer all sorts of services, including corporate banking, trade finance, investment banking, and wealth management. Some of the prominent foreign banks operating in India include Citibank, HSBC, Standard Chartered Bank, and Deutsche Bank. These banks have a strong presence in major Indian cities and offer specialized services to meet the needs of their corporate and institutional clients. Foreign banks help with supporting international trade and investment, providing foreign exchange services, and offering cross-border payment solutions. Foreign banks are known for their expertise in handling complex financial transactions and providing customized solutions to their clients. They offer a range of products, including syndicated loans, structured finance, treasury services, and investment advisory services. Foreign banks also provide access to global financial markets, enabling Indian businesses to raise capital and invest internationally. The presence of foreign banks in India has contributed to the modernization of the country's banking sector. They have introduced global best practices, advanced risk management techniques, and new financial products. Foreign banks have also factored into boosting competition in the banking sector, prompting domestic banks to improve their services and adopt international standards.

### 1.2.3 Regional Rural Banks

Regional Rural Banks (RRBs) were established in 1975 with the objective of providing credit and other financial services to the rural population, particularly small and marginal farmers, agricultural laborers, artisans, and rural entrepreneurs. RRBs were created as a unique banking model, combining the local knowledge and reach of cooperative banks with the professional management and operational speed of commercial banks. RRBs are structured as joint ventures between the central government, state governments, and sponsoring commercial banks. The central government holds a 50% stake in RRBs, while the state governments and sponsoring banks hold 15% and 35% stakes, respectively. This ownership structure safeguards that RRBs have a strong governance framework and access to capital and expertise from their sponsoring banks.

The primary focus of RRBs is on providing financial services to the rural and semi-rural population. They offer a range of banking products, including savings accounts, fixed deposits, loans, and remittance services. RRBs are known for their extensive branch network in rural areas, making them a necessary channel for delivering banking services to remote and underserved regions.

## 1.2.4 Cooperative Banks

Cooperative banks in India are financial institutions that are owned and operated by their members, who are typically local residents, small business owners, or farmers. These banks operate on a cooperative basis, prioritizing the welfare of their members over profit maximization. Cooperative banks factor into promoting financial inclusion and providing affordable banking services to underserved communities. They are governed by the Cooperative Societies Act, which sets the legal framework for their operations.

### *Urban Cooperative Banks*

Urban Cooperative Banks (UCBs) primarily serve the banking needs of urban and semi-urban areas. They cater to small businesses, retail traders, professionals, and individuals. UCBs offer a span of financial services, including deposit accounts, loans, and remittance services. They are particularly known for providing credit to small-scale industries, self-employed individuals, and small traders who may not have easy access to traditional commercial banks. UCBs are classified into two categories based on the area of operation: scheduled and non-scheduled banks. Scheduled UCBs are included in the Second Schedule of the Reserve Bank of India Act, 1934, and have access to certain privileges, such as borrowing from the RBI. Non-scheduled UCBs do not have these privileges but still provide important banking services to their members.

The governance of UCBs involves a board of directors elected by the members, who are also the owners of the bank. The board is responsible for making policy decisions and overseeing the bank's operations. UCBs operate on democratic principles, with each member having one vote, regardless of the number of shares held. This structure guarantees that the interests of all members are represented fairly. UCBs contribute to the local economy by providing financial support to small and medium enterprises (SMEs) and promoting entrepreneurship. They also contribute to social and community development by financing local projects and initiatives.

### *Rural Cooperative Credit Structure*

The Rural Cooperative Credit Structure in India consists of a three-tiered system designed to provide credit and financial services to the rural population. This structure includes Primary Agricultural Credit Societies (PACS) at the grassroots level, District Central Cooperative Banks (DCCBs) at the district level, and State Cooperative Banks (SCBs) at the state level. These institutions work together to deliver affordable credit to farmers, rural artisans, and other rural residents.

**Primary Agricultural Credit Societies (PACS)** are the foundation of the rural cooperative credit structure. They operate at the village level and provide short-term and medium-term credit to their members. PACS are member-owned and typically consist of local farmers and villagers. They offer a range of financial services, including crop loans, input financing, and consumer loans. PACS are involved in promoting agricultural productivity by providing timely and accessible credit to farmers.

**District Central Cooperative Banks (DCCBs)** serve as intermediaries between PACS and the higher tiers of the cooperative banking system. They provide financial and technical assistance to PACS and guarantee the flow of credit from SCBs to the grassroots level. DCCBs also offer banking services to cooperative societies and individual members within the district. They mobilize deposits and provide loans for a number of agricultural and rural activities.

*State Cooperative Banks (SCBs)* operate at the state level and serve as the apex institutions in the rural cooperative credit structure. They coordinate the activities of DCCBs and PACS and enable the distribution of funds to lower-tier institutions. SCBs also contribute to implementing state-level agricultural and rural development policies. They provide refinancing facilities, technical support, and training to DCCBs and PACS. The rural cooperative credit structure is designed to meet the diverse financial needs of the rural population, including small and marginal farmers, landless laborers, and rural entrepreneurs. It promotes self-reliance, mutual aid, and community development. Despite facing challenges such as limited financial resources, governance issues, and operational inefficiencies, the cooperative credit structure remains a component of India's rural economy. It continues to help with promoting agricultural growth, reducing rural poverty, and improving financial inclusion.

### 1.2.5 Development Banks

Development banks in India factor into promoting economic growth, industrial development, and regional integration. Unlike commercial banks, which primarily focus on short-term credit, development banks specialize in providing long-term financing for projects that have considerable developmental impacts but may not yield immediate financial returns. These banks are instrumental in supporting sectors that are critical for the country's economic and social progress, including agriculture, small and medium enterprises (SMEs), housing, and exports. The following sections provide an in-depth overview of development banks in India: NABARD, SIDBI, NHB, and EXIM Bank.

### *NABARD*

The National Bank for Agriculture and Rural Development (NABARD) was established in 1982 through the merger of the Agricultural Refinance and Development Corporation (ARDC) and the Agricultural Credit Department of the Reserve Bank of India (RBI). NABARD was created with the mandate to promote sustainable and equitable agriculture and rural development in India. It acts as the apex institution for financing, overseeing, and regulating the flow of credit to the agricultural sector, rural industries, and other economic activities in rural areas.

NABARD's functions include:

- **Refinancing:** NABARD provides refinancing facilities to cooperative banks, regional rural banks (RRBs), and other financial institutions involved in extending credit to agriculture and rural sectors. This refinancing helps in the disbursement of short-term, medium-term, and long-term loans for crop production, animal husbandry, fisheries, forestry, and other rural activities.

- **Development and Promotional Activities:** NABARD is actively involved in developmental and promotional activities aimed at strengthening agricultural productivity and rural prosperity. It supports initiatives, such as the Watershed Development Program, Tribal Development Program, and Self-Help Group (SHG) movement. These programs focus on sustainable agricultural practices, water conservation, and financial inclusion, respectively.

- **Infrastructure Development:** NABARD helps with the development of rural infrastructure, including roads, bridges, irrigation systems, and storage facilities. It provides funds to state governments and other agencies for implementing infrastructure projects that improve the quality of life in rural areas and ease economic activities.

- **Financial Inclusion:** NABARD has been ahead in promoting financial inclusion in India. It supports the establishment of rural financial institutions, such as RRBs and cooperative banks, and encourages the adoption of technology-driven banking solutions. NABARD also oversees the implementation of government schemes like the Pradhan Mantri Jan Dhan Yojana (PMJDY) and Direct Benefit Transfer (DBT).

- **Research and Training:** NABARD conducts research and provides training to improve the productivity and effectiveness of rural financial institutions. It collaborates with academic institutions, research organizations, and non-governmental organizations (NGOs) to develop novel solutions for rural development challenges.

NABARD's contributions have been instrumental in transforming India's rural environment. It has helped with increasing agricultural productivity, boosting rural incomes, and improving the standard of living in rural areas. Through its initiatives, NABARD has also promoted gender equality and empowered marginalized communities.

### *SIDBI*

The Small Industries Development Bank of India (SIDBI) was established in 1990 as the principal financial institution for the promotion, financing, and development of micro, small, and medium enterprises (MSMEs) in India.

SIDBI's mission is to help and strengthen MSMEs' growth, which are necessary for economic development, employment generation, and equitable wealth distribution.

SIDBI's functions include:

- **Direct and Indirect Financing:** SIDBI provides direct finance to MSMEs through term loans, working capital loans, and equity financing. It also offers indirect finance by refinancing loans extended by commercial banks, regional rural banks, and other financial institutions to MSMEs. This two-pronged approach helps in addressing the diverse financial needs of MSMEs across many sectors.

- **Development and Promotional Activities:** SIDBI undertakes several development and promotional activities to support the growth and competitiveness of MSMEs. It provides advisory services, capacity-building programs, and technology upgradation support. SIDBI also promotes entrepreneurship by organizing workshops, training programs, and business development services.

- **Venture Capital and Equity Support:** Recognizing the importance of advance and start-ups, SIDBI offers venture capital and equity support to high-growth potential MSMEs. Through its venture capital arm, SIDBI Venture Capital Limited (SVCL), the bank invests in start-ups and early-stage companies in technology, manufacturing, and other sectors.
- **Microfinance and Financial Inclusion:** SIDBI is a player in promoting microfinance and financial inclusion in India. It supports microfinance institutions (MFIs) and self-help groups (SHGs) by providing financial assistance and capacity-building support. SIDBI also implements a number of government schemes aimed at providing affordable credit to underserved and unbanked populations.
- **Policy Advocacy and Research:** SIDBI factors into policy advocacy and research related to MSMEs. It collaborates with government agencies, industry associations, and academic institutions to identify challenges and opportunities in the MSME sector. SIDBI's research and policy recommendations contribute to the formulation of supportive policies and regulatory frameworks for MSMEs.

SIDBI's initiatives have markedly contributed to the growth and development of the MSME sector in India. By providing financial and non-financial support, SIDBI has enabled MSMEs to expand their businesses, adopt new technologies, and improve their competitiveness. The bank's efforts have also helped in creating employment opportunities and promoting inclusive economic growth.

### *NHB*

The National Housing Bank (NHB) was established in 1988 under the National Housing Bank Act, 1987, as a wholly owned Government of India institution following the transfer of the RBI's entire shareholding in 2019. NHB's objective is to promote housing finance institutions and support housing finance activities in India. The bank contributes to safeguarding the availability of affordable housing finance and encouraging the growth of a sound and effective housing finance system. Following the Finance Act, 2019, the regulation of Housing Finance Companies (HFCs) was transferred to the RBI, while NHB continues its developmental, supervisory, and refinancing functions. NHB's functions include:

- **Securitisation and Market Development:** NHB promotes the development of secondary mortgage markets in India. It supports the creation of residential mortgage-backed securities to enhance liquidity in the housing finance system. NHB also works towards standardisation of housing finance instruments and strengthening housing finance institutions across the country.

- **Refinancing and Financial Assistance:** NHB provides refinance support to banks and HFCs for their housing finance activities. This support helps increase the flow of credit to the housing sector, particularly for affordable housing. NHB also undertakes financial assistance and financing activities permitted under the National Housing Bank Act.

- **Developmental Activities:** NHB undertakes developmental activities to promote housing finance and support the housing sector. It collaborates with state governments, urban local bodies, and other stakeholders to implement housing-related initiatives. NHB also promotes research, development, and capacity-building in housing finance and urban development.

- **Promoting Affordable Housing:** One of NHB's objectives is to promote affordable housing and improve access to housing finance for low- and middle-income households. NHB supports government schemes such as the Pradhan Mantri Awas Yojana (PMAY). The bank also promotes housing development for economically weaker sections (EWS) and low-income groups (LIG).

- **Housing Market Development:** NHB is involved in developing the housing finance market in India. It supports the creation of a strong housing finance ecosystem by promoting transparency, standardisation, and effectiveness in the housing market. NHB also works towards the development of housing finance infrastructure, including mortgage-backed securities and housing finance institutions.

By providing refinance support, developmental initiatives, supervision, and market development, NHB has contributed to the growth of the housing sector and the achievement of the nation's housing goals.

### *EXIM Bank*

The Export-Import Bank of India (EXIM Bank) was established in 1982 as a statutory corporation under the Export-Import Bank of India Act, 1981. EXIM Bank is the principal financial institution in India for coordinating the financing of international trade and investment.

The bank's objective is to support and promote India's exports and imports, as well as to support the country's international economic activities. EXIM Bank's functions include:

- **Export Financing:** EXIM Bank provides many export financing solutions, including pre-shipment and post-shipment credit, export bills rediscounting, and export credit insurance. These financing options help Indian exporters manage their working capital needs and mitigate the risks associated with international trade. EXIM Bank also offers export guarantees and letters of credit to enable cross-border transactions.

- **Import Financing:** In addition to export financing, EXIM Bank provides import financing to support the import of capital goods, raw materials, and other needed inputs. The bank offers financing products, such as buyer's credit, supplier's credit, and import loans, to enable Indian businesses to acquire the necessary resources for their operations.

- **Project and Infrastructure Financing:** EXIM Bank contributes to financing overseas projects and infrastructure development. The bank provides long-term project finance, including loans and guarantees, to Indian companies executing projects abroad. EXIM Bank also supports Indian investments in foreign countries, including joint ventures and wholly-owned subsidiaries.

- **Advisory and Consultancy Services:** EXIM Bank offers advisory and consultancy services to Indian businesses looking to expand their international footprint. The bank provides market research, feasibility studies, and project consultancy to help companies identify opportunities and handle the complexities of international trade and investment.

- **Overseas Investment Support:** EXIM Bank supports Indian companies' overseas investments by providing equity finance, joint venture finance, and direct investment loans. The bank supports Indian businesses' entry into new markets and helps them establish a presence in foreign countries.

- **Promoting South-South Cooperation:** EXIM Bank actively promotes South-South cooperation by enabling trade and investment between India and other developing countries. The bank supports regional integration initiatives and collaborates with multilateral institutions, such as the Asian Development Bank (ADB) and the African Development Bank (AfDB), to promote trade and economic cooperation.

EXIM Bank has been instrumental in promoting India's international trade and investment activities. The bank's financing and support services have helped Indian businesses explore new markets, expand their global presence, and strengthen their competitiveness. EXIM Bank's contributions have also strengthened India's economic ties with other countries and promoted the country's integration into the global economy.

### 1.2.6 Small Finance Banks

Small Finance Banks (SFBs) are a specialized category of banks in India, established to further the cause of financial inclusion. They are designed to provide necessary banking services to segments of the population that have been traditionally underserved or entirely excluded from the formal banking sector. These banks aim to offer a wide array of basic banking services, including savings and current accounts, as well as loan products specifically tailored for small businesses, farmers, micro-enterprises, and other low-income groups. The establishment and functioning of SFBs are governed by specific regulations and guidelines set by the Reserve Bank of India (RBI), which secures that these banks operate within a structured and safe framework. The following sections explore into the licensing requirements and operational guidelines for SFBs, outlining the fundamental principles and regulatory frameworks that guide their operations.

*Licensing Requirements*

The creation and operation of Small Finance Banks are subject to strict licensing requirements set by the RBI. These requirements are designed to safeguard that SFBs have a clear focus on financial inclusion, possess the necessary financial stability, and are managed by capable and experienced individuals. The following are the components of the licensing requirements for SFBs:

*Objective and Focus:* The objective of establishing SFBs is to promote financial inclusion by providing financial services to underserved segments, such as small businesses, micro-enterprises, and rural populations. The emphasis is on reaching customers in areas where traditional banks may have limited presence, thus bridging the gap between the unbanked and the formal financial system.

*Eligibility Criteria:* The RBI has set forth specific eligibility criteria for entities applying for a SFB license. Eligible applicants include microfinance institutions (MFIs), local area banks (LABs), and other entities with a proven track record in financial services, especially those focused on financial inclusion. The RBI also encourages experienced professionals and groups with a background in banking, finance, or related fields to apply, provided they demonstrate a strong commitment to the objectives of SFBs.

***Promoter's Contribution:*** A marked requirement is that promoters must hold a minimum of 40% of the paid-up voting equity capital at the time of starting operations. This stake must be locked in for a minimum of five years from the date of commencement. The intent behind this requirement is to make certain that promoters have a vested interest in the long-term success and stability of the bank. Over time, promoters' stake can be gradually reduced, provided it remains in compliance with RBI regulations.

***Minimum Capital Requirements:*** The minimum paid-up voting equity capital for a SFB is ₹200 crore. This capital base is necessary to guarantee that the bank can sustain initial operational costs, absorb potential financial shocks, and support future expansion. The capital adequacy ratio, as per the Basel norms, must also be maintained, guaranteeing that the bank has enough capital to cover its risk-weighted assets.

***Fit and Proper Criteria:*** The RBI assesses the 'fit and proper' status of the promoters and directors, which includes evaluating their integrity, competence, financial soundness, and track record. This assessment helps prevent individuals with questionable backgrounds from being part of the banking system, thus safeguarding the interests of depositors and maintaining the integrity of the financial system.

***Business Plan and Viability:*** Applicants are required to submit a full business plan, detailing their strategy for achieving financial inclusion, their proposed product and service offerings, target customer segments, and financial projections. The business plan must demonstrate a clear understanding of the market, sound financial planning, and a viable path to profitability. The RBI scrutinizes these plans to secure that they align with the broader goals of financial inclusion and economic development.

***Application Process and Approval:*** The application process for a SFB license involves a detailed submission to the RBI, followed by a rigorous evaluation. The RBI assesses the financial and managerial resources of the applicants, their business plan, and their commitment to financial inclusion. If the application meets all the criteria, the RBI grants an in-principle approval, which is valid for 18 months. During this period, the applicants must fulfil all specified conditions to receive the final license and commence operations.

### Operational Guidelines

Once licensed, Small Finance Banks must adhere to a set of operational guidelines outlined by the RBI. These guidelines safeguard that SFBs operate prudently, focus on their core mission of financial inclusion, and comply with regulatory norms. The following are the main operational guidelines for SFBs:

***Permitted Activities:*** SFBs are permitted to engage in all basic banking activities, including accepting deposits, extending loans, and offering payment and remittance services. They can offer a variety of deposit products such as savings accounts, current accounts, fixed deposits, and recurring deposits. On the lending side, they can provide loans for many purposes, including agriculture, small businesses, housing, and personal needs. However, SFBs are not allowed to engage in sophisticated trading or high-risk investment activities that could jeopardize their financial stability.

***Credit Allocation and Priority Sector Lending:*** AN aspect of SFBs' operations is their obligation to allocate a substantial portion of their lending to priority sectors. According to the RBI guidelines, at least 75% of their Adjusted Net Bank Credit (ANBC) or Credit Equivalent Amount of Off-Balance Sheet Exposure, whichever is higher, must be directed towards priority sector advances. At least 50% of their loan portfolio should consist of loans and advances up to ₹25 lakhs. This focus safeguards that SFBs support sectors that are necessary for economic development and financial inclusion.

***Capital Adequacy and Risk Management:*** SFBs are required to maintain a minimum Capital to Risk (Weighted) Assets Ratio (CRAR) of 15% on a continuous basis, in line with the Basel III norms. This requirement guarantees that the banks have adequate capital to absorb losses and protect depositors' funds. Also, SFBs must implement complete risk management frameworks that address credit risk, market risk, operational risk, and liquidity risk. These frameworks should include policies and procedures for identifying, measuring, monitoring, and controlling risks.

***Branch and Infrastructure Requirements:*** To further their mission of financial inclusion, SFBs are required to open at least 25% of their branches in unbanked rural areas. This requirement secures that banking services reach remote and underserved regions, contributing to the overall development of these areas. SFBs must also invest in necessary infrastructure, including physical branches, automated teller machines (ATMs), and digital platforms, to provide accessible and convenient banking services.

***Technology and Digital Banking:*** The RBI encourages SFBs to use technology to boost their operational speed and customer service. This includes offering internet banking, mobile banking, and other digital payment solutions. The adoption of technology not only expands the reach of SFBs but also provides customers with convenient and secure access to banking services. The RBI also emphasizes the importance of cybersecurity measures to protect customer data and transactions from fraud and cyber threats.

***Customer Service and Consumer Protection:*** SFBs must adhere to high standards of customer service and make certain the protection of consumers' interests. They are required to establish reliable grievance redressal mechanisms to address customer complaints effectively. SFBs must comply with the RBI's fair practices code, securing transparency in their dealings with customers, including clear communication of terms and conditions for all banking products and services.

***Regulatory Compliance and Reporting:*** As regulated entities, SFBs must comply with all regulatory norms set by the RBI, including those related to income recognition, asset classification, provisioning, and capital adequacy. They are also required to submit regular reports to the RBI, covering several aspects of their operations, financial position, and compliance status. The RBI conducts regular inspections and audits to guarantee that SFBs adhere to these norms and operate in a safe and sound manner.

***Corporate Governance:*** A strong corporate governance framework is central for maintaining the trust and confidence of stakeholders. SFBs are required to have a well-defined governance structure, including a board of directors with adequate representation from independent directors. The governance framework should include a number of committees, such as the Audit Committee, Risk Management Committee, and Nomination and Remuneration Committee, to oversee the bank's operations and secure adherence to regulatory requirements.

***Transition and Conversion:*** SFBs have the option to transition into universal banks after completing a certain number of years of operation and meeting the RBI's specified criteria. This option allows SFBs to expand their service offerings and customer base, subject to additional regulatory requirements and approvals. The transition to a universal bank involves meeting higher capital requirements and broader operational standards, safeguarding that the bank can handle a more diverse range of banking activities.

## 1.2.7 Payments Banks

Payments Banks are a unique and fresh category of banks in India, created with the objective of furthering financial inclusion by providing important banking services to the underbanked and unbanked sections of society. Unlike traditional banks, Payments Banks are designed to operate on a smaller scale without engaging in credit risk or offering loans. Instead, they focus on providing a secure platform for transactions, deposits, and payment services. The concept of Payments Banks was introduced by the Reserve Bank of India (RBI) to draw on technology and new business models, thereby extending the reach of the formal banking system.

### Concept and Objectives

*Concept:* Payments Banks are a novel financial institution in India, bridging the gap between traditional banking and non-banking financial entities. The concept emerged from the need to provide accessible banking solutions to a vast population that remains outside the formal banking sector. Payments Banks operate on a low-cost model, using digital platforms and mobile technology to reach customers, especially in rural and remote areas. They are primarily intended to offer basic banking services such as accepting deposits, easing remittances, and providing payment and transaction services. However, they are restricted from engaging in lending activities or issuing credit cards, which differentiates them from other types of banks.

*Objectives:* The objectives of Payments Banks include:

*Financial Inclusion:* One of the objectives of Payments Banks is to promote financial inclusion by providing banking services to the unbanked and underbanked populations. By offering simple, secure, and accessible banking solutions, Payments Banks aim to integrate these segments into the formal financial system.

*Low-Cost Banking Services:* Payments Banks operate on a low-cost model, using technology to provide cost-effective banking services. This model enables them to offer services such as deposits, fund transfers, and payments at minimal or no charges, making banking more affordable for low-income individuals.

***Digital and Mobile Banking:*** Payments Banks are designed to be digital-first, with a strong focus on mobile banking. They use mobile phones and internet connectivity to offer banking services, allowing customers to conduct transactions, check balances, and pay bills without visiting a physical branch. This emphasis on digital channels aligns with India's growing digital economy and the government's push towards a cashless society.

***Secure and Quick Payments:*** Payments Banks ease secure and smooth payment transactions, including person-to-person (P2P) transfers, bill payments, and merchant transactions. By offering a secure platform for digital payments, they contribute to reducing the reliance on cash and promoting digital transactions.

***Government Payments and Subsidies:*** Payments Banks contribute to disbursing government payments and subsidies directly to beneficiaries' accounts. This function helps speed up the delivery of welfare benefits and reduces leakages, guaranteeing that the intended recipients receive the funds.

***Remittance Services:*** Payments Banks are authorized to provide domestic and cross-border remittance services. This capability is particularly beneficial for migrant workers and their families, enabling them to send and receive money smoothly and securely.

### Regulatory Framework

The regulatory framework for Payments Banks is outlined by the RBI, securing that these entities operate within a structured and safe environment. The framework includes specific guidelines on capital requirements, permissible activities, risk management, and corporate governance. The following are the components of the regulatory framework for Payments Banks:

***Licensing and Capital Requirements:*** Payments Banks are required to obtain a license from the RBI to commence operations. The minimum paid-up equity capital for Payments Banks is set at ₹100 crore. The promoter's contribution must be at least 40% of the paid-up equity capital for the first five years from the commencement of operations. The promoter's stake can be gradually reduced over time, subject to regulatory norms.

***Permissible Activities:*** Payments Banks are permitted to undertake a range of activities, including:

- **Acceptance of Demand Deposits:** Payments Banks can accept demand deposits, including savings and current accounts, from individuals and small businesses. However, the maximum balance per customer is capped at ₹2 lakh.

- **Issuance of Debit Cards and Prepaid Payment Instruments (PPIs):** Payments Banks can issue debit cards and PPIs, including mobile wallets, which can be used for transactions and withdrawals.
- **Payments and Remittance Services:** They can provide payment and remittance services, including P2P transfers, bill payments, and merchant transactions.
- **Cross-Border Remittances:** Payments Banks are authorized to help cross-border remittance transactions, subject to compliance with relevant regulations.
- **Distribution of Third-Party Financial Products:** Payments Banks can distribute third-party financial products such as insurance, mutual funds, and pension products, acting as business correspondents for other financial institutions.

Payments Banks are prohibited from engaging in lending activities, including issuing credit cards. This restriction safeguards that they operate with minimal credit risk and maintain a stable financial position.

***Prudential Norms and Risk Management:*** Payments Banks are subject to prudential norms set by the RBI, including maintaining a minimum Capital to Risk (Weighted) Assets Ratio (CRAR) of 15%. They must invest a specified percentage of their demand deposit balances in government securities or other approved securities to safeguard liquidity and safety. Payments Banks are also required to implement solid risk management frameworks to manage operational, market, and liquidity risks. These frameworks should include policies and procedures for identifying, measuring, monitoring, and controlling risks.

***Corporate Governance:*** The regulatory framework emphasizes strong corporate governance practices for Payments Banks. The RBI mandates a well-structured board of directors, including independent directors, to make certain objective decision-making. The governance framework should include committees, such as the Audit Committee, Risk Management Committee, and Nomination and Remuneration Committee, to oversee different aspects of the bank's operations. The RBI also requires Payments Banks to maintain transparency in their operations, including regular disclosures of financial performance, risk exposures, and compliance with regulatory norms.

***Consumer Protection and Grievance Redressal:*** Payments Banks must adhere to high standards of customer service and consumer protection. They are required to establish effective grievance redressal mechanisms to address customer complaints promptly. The RBI has also issued guidelines on the fair treatment of customers, including transparency in pricing, clear communication of terms and conditions, and protection against fraud and unauthorized transactions.

***Technology and Security Standards:*** Given their focus on digital and mobile banking, Payments Banks must comply with stringent technology and security standards. The RBI mandates the use of secure technology platforms, including multi-factor authentication, encryption, and secure coding practices, to protect customer data and transactions. Payments Banks are also required to conduct regular security audits and implement measures to prevent cyber-attacks and data breaches.

***Regulatory Reporting and Compliance:*** Payments Banks are subject to regular regulatory reporting and compliance requirements. They must submit periodic reports to the RBI, covering many aspects of their operations, financial position, and compliance status. The RBI conducts inspections and audits to guarantee that Payments Banks adhere to regulatory norms and operate in a safe and sound manner.

***Partnerships and Collaborations:*** Payments Banks are encouraged to collaborate with other financial institutions, technology companies, and service providers to increase their service offerings. These partnerships can include tie-ups with traditional banks for cash management services, collaborations with fintech companies for digital payment solutions, and alliances with insurance and investment firms for cross-selling financial products.

The Indian banking sector is diverse and includes several types of banks. As of 2024, there are 12 public sector banks (PSBs) and 21 private banks, 46 Foreign Banks operating in the country. Also, there are 12 small finance banks (SFBs) and 5 payment banks providing specialized services. The cooperative banking sector consists of 33 state cooperative banks (SCBs), 328 district/central cooperative banks (DCCBs), and 1,469 urban cooperative banks. There are 43 Regional Rural Banks (RRBs) that cater to the rural areas of India. These numbers reflect the current system of the banking sector in

India, showcasing a mix of public, private, and cooperative institutions serving a number of financial needs across the country.

## 1.3 Role of the Reserve Bank of India (RBI)

The Reserve Bank of India (RBI) is the central banking institution of India, entrusted with the regulation and supervision of the financial system. Established in 1935 under the Reserve Bank of India Act, the RBI helps with maintaining monetary stability, promoting economic growth, and safeguarding the smooth functioning of the financial markets. The RBI's responsibilities encompass functions, including the formulation and implementation of monetary policy, regulation and supervision of banks, management of foreign exchange, issuance of currency, and serving as the banker to the government. This section covers RBI's monetary policy functions, detailing its formulation and implementation tools.

### 1.3.1 Monetary Policy Functions

Monetary policy is one of the functions of the RBI, aimed at controlling the supply of money, maintaining price stability, and achieving sustainable economic growth. The RBI's monetary policy framework involves setting interest rates, regulating the availability of credit, and influencing the overall economic environment. The components of the RBI's monetary policy functions include the formulation of monetary policy and the implementation of tools to achieve the desired economic outcomes.

***Formulation of Monetary Policy***

The formulation of monetary policy involves setting the objectives, targets, and strategies to achieve macroeconomic stability. The RBI's monetary policy is designed to balance multiple objectives, such as controlling inflation, supporting economic growth, and maintaining financial stability. The RBI formulates its monetary policy in consultation with the Government of India, taking into account the prevailing economic conditions, global economic trends, and domestic financial developments. Now, coming bank to RBI again after briefly introducing earlier, to truly understand the intricate workings of the Reserve Bank of India (RBI), it helps to start at the beginning of its journey and how it came to be such a central figure in India's economic story. The RBI wasn't always the powerful institution it is today. Its creation was a response to the needs of an evolving economy during a time when India was still under British rule.

The idea of establishing a central bank in India was born out of the chaos of the early 20th century, when the country was grappling with economic instability, frequent currency crises, and the lack of a unified banking authority. The British government set up the Hilton Young Commission in the 1920s to study the economic conditions of the country and recommend a solution. The commission realized that India needed a central bank that could manage the currency, oversee banking operations, and act as a lender of last resort. This led to the establishment of the Reserve Bank of India on April 1, 1935, under the Reserve Bank of India Act of 1934.

In its early days, the RBI was privately owned, which was typical for central banks of that era. However, post-independence, the Indian government recognized the need to bring the central bank under its control to align it more closely with the country's developmental goals. Thus, in 1949, the RBI was nationalized, marking the beginning of its role as a public institution tasked with steering the nation's economy.

The RBI's primary mission is to secure monetary stability, essentially, making sure that prices don't rise too quickly (which we know as inflation) and that the economy grows at a healthy pace. But what does this really mean? How does the RBI go about achieving these goals?

One of the most tools the RBI has at its disposal is the power to influence interest rates, which are essentially the cost of borrowing money. When the economy is growing too fast and prices are rising, the RBI might increase interest rates to make borrowing more expensive. This tends to cool down spending and investment, helping to bring prices back under control. On the other hand, when the economy is sluggish and not enough money is circulating, the RBI can lower interest rates to make borrowing cheaper, encouraging businesses and consumers to spend more.

Let me take you on a journey through the corridors of the Reserve Bank of India, where the tools of monetary policy are not just dry mechanisms but living, breathing elements that keep the economy balanced. Imagine these tools as characters in a grand narrative, each contributing to shaping the financial field of the nation. In the heart of the RBI, there is a grand gate known as the Repo Rate. This gate is not like any ordinary gate, it's where the flow of money begins. Picture it as a massive, intricately designed gate, gleaming under the watchful eyes of the RBI's guardians. When this gate opens, it allows banks to borrow money from the RBI for short periods.

Now, imagine a scenario where the air is thick with concern because inflation is on the rise, prices are climbing too fast, and the economy is overheating. The RBI, with its deep understanding of the economic winds, decides that the time has come to raise the gate slightly higher. So, they adjust the Repo Rate from 5% to 5.5%. This small but major change means that banks now have to pay a little more to borrow money. As this cost is passed down the line, borrowing becomes more expensive for businesses and individuals alike. The effect is like a cooling breeze that slows down the overheating economy, curbing spending and bringing the inflationary flames under control. Next to the Lending Gate stands a formidable vault, the Reverse Repo Rate. This vault is where banks deposit their excess funds, a place of safety and profit. Imagine the vault's thick, impenetrable walls, safeguarding the nation's wealth. When the RBI notices that too much money is swirling around in the economy, threatening to fuel inflation, they might decide to make this vault even more attractive. By increasing the Reverse Repo Rate from 3.35% to 3.75%, the RBI encourages banks to store more of their excess money in this secure vault. The result? Money is effectively pulled out of circulation, cooling down the economy and helping to maintain price stability.

Every day at the RBI, a special window opens, known as the Liquidity Adjustment Facility. This window is like a daily balance check for the entire banking system, a moment where everything comes into alignment. Banks that find themselves short on funds can borrow what they need, while those with extra cash can lend it out. This delicate dance guarantees that the system remains in harmony, with just the right amount of money flowing through the veins of the economy.

But what happens when a bank finds itself in dire straits, with no other options left? This is where the RBI's Emergency Fund, the Marginal Standing Facility, comes into play. Imagine this as a sturdy lifeline, thrown to banks in their darkest hour. The cost of accessing this lifeline is higher, typically 0.25% above the Repo Rate, but it's a necessary safety net. By providing this last resort option, the RBI secures that no bank collapses under unexpected pressure, maintaining the stability of the entire financial system.

In the distance, a beacon shines brightly, the Bank Rate. This beacon is the RBI's way of signalling its long-term intentions for interest rates. When the RBI adjusts this rate, it's like a message sent across the financial seas. For instance, lowering the Bank Rate from 5.65% to 5.40% is a clear signal that the RBI expects interest rates to remain low for some time, encouraging long-term investments and boosting economic confidence.

At the foundation of the banking system lies a mandatory reserve, known as the Cash Reserve Ratio. Imagine this as a well-stocked reserve that every bank must maintain. The RBI carefully monitors the growth of credit and, if needed, might decide to increase this reserve from 4% to 4.5%. By doing so, banks are required to hold more money with the RBI, leaving them with less to lend out. This helps to control the money supply, guaranteeing that the economy doesn't grow too fast too quickly.

Alongside this reserve is another safeguard, the Statutory Liquidity Ratio. Picture it as a safety net of liquid assets, cash, gold, or government securities, that banks must always have on hand. If the RBI senses the need to strengthen the banking system, they might raise this ratio from 18% to 19%. This safeguards that banks have a solid cushion of safe, liquid assets, ready to withstand any financial shocks that might come their way.

Next, we move to a bustling marketplace where the RBI plays the role of a careful trader. This is the domain of Open Market Operations (OMO). Here, the RBI buys and sells government securities, subtly tweaking the money supply in the economy. Imagine the RBI sensing that the economy is running short on cash, businesses are struggling to find credit, and growth is stalling. The RBI steps into the market, purchasing securities and injecting liquidity into the system. On the other hand, if there's too much money sloshing around, fueling inflation, the RBI sells securities, drawing excess funds out of circulation. It's a delicate balancing act, one that requires constant vigilance and a deep understanding of the market's needs.

Each of these tools, from the beacon-like Bank Rate to the sturdy CRR pillar, factors into the RBI's mission to maintain economic stability and growth. They are the hidden gears of India's financial machinery, constantly turning to safeguard that the economy runs smoothly, that crises are averted, and that the path to prosperity remains clear. Together, they form a complex but beautifully orchestrated system, where every move, every adjustment, is made with precision and purpose to guide the nation towards a stable and thriving future. The RBI's role is not just about managing money supply and interest rates; it's also about maintaining confidence in the financial system. By regulating the banking sector and securing that banks operate in a safe and sound manner, the RBI helps protect depositors' money and maintains public confidence in the financial system.

To put it simply, the RBI is like the conductor of an orchestra, safeguarding that all the different instruments, whether it's the banks, the currency, or the broader financial system, play in harmony to keep the economy running smoothly. It's a delicate balancing act, and one that requires constant vigilance and a deep understanding of both the domestic and global economic landscapes.

## 1.3.2 Regulatory and Supervisory Roles

The Reserve Bank of India (RBI) contributes to regulating and supervising the Indian banking system. This responsibility guarantees the stability, productivity, and soundness of the financial sector, which is important for economic growth and maintaining public confidence. The RBI's regulatory and supervisory framework encompasses a range of activities, including the licensing of banks, the establishment of prudential norms, and the conduct of both on-site and off-site supervision. These functions are designed to safeguard the financial system from risks, make certain compliance with regulations, and promote good governance practices among financial institutions.

### *Licensing of Banks*

Licensing is the first step in the regulatory oversight of the banking sector. The RBI is the sole authority responsible for granting licenses to new banks in India. The licensing process is a rigorous procedure that secures only credible and capable entities enter the banking sector. It involves the assessment of several criteria, including the financial soundness of the applicants, the quality of their management, their business model, and their commitment to serving the public interest.

The RBI grants licenses for different types of banks, including commercial banks, small finance banks, payments banks, and cooperative banks. Each category has specific requirements and regulatory frameworks tailored to their functions and target markets. For instance, small finance banks and payments banks are subject to conditions that encourage financial inclusion and digital payment services, respectively. The RBI's licensing policy also includes provisions for the establishment of foreign banks in India. Foreign banks can either operate as branches or set up wholly-owned subsidiaries. The RBI evaluates applications based on the foreign bank's global reputation, financial strength, and adherence to international regulatory standards. The licensing process safeguards that foreign banks contribute positively to the Indian financial system while maintaining a level playing field with domestic banks. In recent years, the RBI has adopted a more open and transparent approach to licensing, with the introduction of new guidelines for differentiated banks like small finance banks and payments banks. This move aims to promote competition, breakthrough, and financial inclusion in the banking sector. The RBI periodically reviews and updates its licensing policies to align with the evolving economic and technological sector.

### Prudential Norms

Prudential norms are a set of regulations and guidelines established by the RBI to guarantee the financial stability and soundness of banks. These norms cover many aspects of banking operations, including capital adequacy, asset quality, risk management, and corporate governance. The objective of prudential norms is to mitigate risks and protect the interests of depositors and other stakeholders.

***Capital Adequacy:*** One of the prudential norms is the requirement for banks to maintain adequate capital levels to absorb potential losses. The RBI mandates that banks maintain a minimum Capital Adequacy Ratio (CAR) based on their risk-weighted assets. The CAR includes Tier 1 capital (core capital) and Tier 2 capital (supplementary capital). The RBI's capital adequacy requirements are aligned with international standards, such as the Basel Accords, to secure that Indian banks are resilient and can withstand financial shocks.

***Asset Quality:*** The RBI sets guidelines for the classification and provisioning of assets based on their quality and risk profile. Banks are required to classify their assets into categories such as standard, substandard, doubtful, and loss assets. For each category, the RBI prescribes specific provisioning norms to cover potential losses. This practice guarantees that banks maintain a healthy asset portfolio and are prepared for any deterioration in asset quality.

***Risk Management:*** The RBI emphasizes the importance of sturdy risk management practices in banks. It requires banks to establish thorough risk management frameworks that cover credit risk, market risk, operational risk, and liquidity risk. The RBI issues guidelines on risk management policies, processes, and internal controls to help banks identify, measure, monitor, and mitigate risks. Banks are also required to conduct regular stress testing and scenario analysis to assess their resilience to adverse conditions.

***Corporate Governance:*** The RBI sets standards for corporate governance in banks to promote transparency, accountability, and ethical conduct. The guidelines cover several aspects of governance, including the composition and functioning of the board of directors, the role of independent directors, the responsibilities of the audit committee, and the disclosure of financial and non-financial information. The RBI's corporate governance framework aims to safeguard that banks are managed in a sound and prudent manner, with a focus on protecting the interests of all stakeholders.

### On-site and Off-site Supervision

The RBI employs a dual approach to the supervision of banks, combining both on-site and off-site supervision to make certain broad oversight of the banking system. This approach enables the RBI to monitor the financial health and compliance of banks, identify potential risks, and take timely corrective actions.

***On-site Supervision:*** On-site supervision involves the physical inspection of banks' operations, records, and facilities by RBI examiners. These inspections are conducted periodically and cover a number of aspects of the bank's activities, including asset quality, risk management, internal controls, and compliance with regulatory norms. On-site examinations provide the RBI with an in-depth understanding of a bank's financial condition, governance practices, and operational risks. During on-site inspections, the RBI examiners review the bank's loan portfolio, investment activities, liquidity position, and capital adequacy. They also assess the effectiveness of the bank's internal control systems, risk management framework, and corporate governance practices. The findings of the on-site inspections are documented in a report, which includes recommendations for corrective actions and improvements.

***Off-site Supervision:*** Off-site supervision involves the continuous monitoring of banks' financial performance and compliance through the analysis of periodic reports and data submitted by banks. Banks are required to submit reports to the RBI, including financial statements, regulatory returns, risk assessment reports, and other disclosures. The RBI analyzes this data to assess the bank's financial condition, risk profile, and compliance with prudential norms. Off-site supervision allows the RBI to detect early warning signs of financial distress, such as a decline in asset quality, deteriorating liquidity position, or insufficient capital levels. The RBI uses advanced analytical tools and techniques to monitor trends and developments in the banking sector. This proactive approach enables the RBI to identify potential risks and take preventive measures before they escalate into systemic issues.

The combination of on-site and off-site supervision secures that the RBI maintains a full and real-time view of the banking system's health. It enables the RBI to detect and address emerging risks, enforce regulatory compliance, and protect the stability of the financial system. The RBI's supervisory framework is continuously evolving, incorporating new technologies, methodologies, and best practices to improve the effectiveness and effectiveness of bank supervision.

***Prompt Corrective Action (PCA)*** is a supervisory framework implemented by the Reserve Bank of India (RBI) to monitor and regulate banks facing financial stress. The framework is designed to intervene early when a bank shows signs of financial distress, aiming to restore the bank's financial health and prevent it from further deterioration. RBI introduced PCA in 2002 and revised it in 2017 to make it more effective.

The PCA framework uses three main indicators to assess a bank's financial health: Capital-to-risk weighted assets ratio (CRAR), Net non-performing assets (NPA) ratio, and Return on assets (ROA). PCA has three risk threshold levels, with each level triggering different corrective actions:

**Threshold 1** for early warning signs,

**Threshold 2** for heightened risk, and

**Threshold 3** for greatly high risk.

Depending on the threshold breached, the RBI may impose restrictions and require corrective actions. These can include restricting dividend distribution, limiting branch expansion, curbing management compensation and directors' fees, requiring recapitalization, prohibiting access to costly deposits or borrowings, and restricting lending to risky sectors. While PCA aims to safeguard the banking system, it has faced criticism for potentially limiting a bank's ability to grow out of its problems. However, proponents argue that it's necessary for maintaining the overall stability of the financial system. The RBI periodically reviews and updates the PCA framework to guarantee its effectiveness in addressing emerging challenges in the banking sector. PCA remains a tool in the RBI's supervisory arsenal, helping to maintain the health and stability of India's banking system by identifying and addressing potential issues before they escalate into more severe problems. Its implementation reflects the RBI's proactive approach to banking supervision and its commitment to maintaining a strong financial system in India.

## 1.3.3 Currency Management

Currency management is one of the functions of the Reserve Bank of India (RBI), encompassing the issuance, distribution, and monitoring of currency notes and coins in the country. As the sole authority responsible for the issuance of legal tender in India, the RBI is involved in guaranteeing an adequate and secure supply of currency, maintaining the integrity of the currency system, and instilling public confidence in the nation's monetary unit. This responsibility involves meticulous planning, effective logistics, and rigorous security measures to prevent counterfeiting and secure the smooth functioning of the economy. The RBI's currency management functions are carried out through its departments and a network of offices across the country, in collaboration with the Government of India and other stakeholders.

### *Note Issue Function*

The note issue function is a fundamental aspect of the RBI's currency management role. The RBI has the exclusive authority to issue and manage banknotes in India, a power vested in it by the Reserve Bank of India Act, 1934. This function includes the design, production, issuance, and withdrawal of banknotes, securing that the currency in circulation meets the public's demand and maintains its value.

***Design and Production:*** The RBI oversees the design of banknotes, which involves incorporating many security features to prevent counterfeiting. These features include watermarks, security threads, microprinting, intaglio printing, latent images, and optically variable ink. The design process also considers aesthetic elements and national symbols, reflecting India's heritage and culture. The production of banknotes is carried out at printing presses owned by the Government of India, such as the Bharatiya Reserve Bank Note Mudran Private Limited (BRBNMPL) and the Security Printing and Minting Corporation of India Limited (SPMCIL). The RBI coordinates with these entities to safeguard the timely production of notes in several denominations based on the country's currency needs.

***Issuance and Distribution:*** The RBI manages the issuance of banknotes through its Issue Department, which is responsible for maintaining the currency chest system. Currency chests are storage locations held by select branches of commercial banks and the RBI offices, where notes are stocked to meet the currency requirements of the economy. These chests support the quick distribution of banknotes across the country, safeguarding that banks and ATMs are adequately supplied. The RBI closely monitors the demand for currency in circulation and adjusts the supply accordingly. This involves forecasting cash demand based on factors such as economic growth, inflation, seasonal variations, and public expenditure patterns. The RBI also oversees the withdrawal and disposal of soiled and mutilated notes, guaranteeing that only clean and usable notes remain in circulation.

***Counterfeit Prevention:*** AN aspect of the note issue function is the prevention of counterfeit currency. The RBI continuously updates the security features of banknotes to stay ahead of counterfeiters. It also conducts public awareness campaigns to educate the public about identifying genuine banknotes. The RBI collaborates with law enforcement agencies to detect and curb the circulation of counterfeit notes, securing the integrity and trustworthiness of the currency system.

### Coin Management

Coin management is another needed component of the RBI's currency management responsibilities. While the RBI has the sole authority to issue banknotes, the Government of India is responsible for minting coins. However, the RBI helps with the distribution and management of coins, safeguarding their availability and smooth circulation throughout the economy.

***Minting and Design:*** The design and minting of coins are undertaken by the Government of India's mints, located in Mumbai, Hyderabad, Kolkata, and Noida. The design of coins is influenced by factors such as ease of recognition, durability, and cost-effectiveness. Coins are produced in a number of denominations, and their design often includes symbols and motifs reflecting India's cultural heritage and historical figures.

***Distribution and Circulation:*** The RBI acts as the agent of the Government of India for distributing coins. It procures coins from the mints and supplies them to the public through its network of Issue Offices and currency chests. Commercial banks also are involved in the distribution process, guaranteeing that coins are available to the public across the country. The RBI monitors the demand for coins and coordinates with the mints to make certain an adequate supply. This involves assessing the needs of different regions and sectors, such as retail businesses and public transportation, which rely heavily on coins for transactions. The RBI also enables the exchange of damaged and withdrawn coins, securing that only fit coins remain in circulation.

***Public Awareness and Education:*** The RBI undertakes initiatives to promote the proper use and handling of coins. It conducts public awareness campaigns to educate people about the different denominations and features of coins. These campaigns also address issues related to the shortage of coins and encourage the use of small denominations in transactions.

***Quality Control and Counterfeit Prevention:*** Safeguarding the quality of coins is an aspect of coin management. The RBI and the mints adhere to strict quality control measures during the minting process to produce durable and reliable coins. The RBI works with law enforcement agencies to prevent the circulation of counterfeit coins, protecting the public and maintaining the trustworthiness of the currency.

***Challenges in Coin Management:*** Coin management involves several challenges, including the rising cost of coin production due to fluctuations in metal prices, the logistical complexities of distribution, and the public's preference for banknotes and digital payments over coins. The RBI continually explores novel solutions to address these challenges, such as promoting the use of digital payments, improving the speed of coin distribution, and exploring alternative materials for coin minting.

## 1.3.4 Banker to the Government

As the central bank of India, the Reserve Bank of India (RBI) plays a role as the banker to the government. This function involves managing the government's banking needs, including the management of public debt and the execution of financial transactions on behalf of both the central and state governments. By acting as the government's banker, the RBI safeguards the smooth management of public finances, supports the implementation of fiscal policy, and contributes to the overall economic stability of the country. The following sections explore the central responsibilities of the RBI in its role as the banker to the government, focusing on the management of public debt and the handling of government banking transactions.

*Management of Public Debt*

One of the functions of the RBI as the banker to the government is the management of public debt. Public debt refers to the total amount of money that the government owes to external and internal creditors. This debt can arise from many sources, including the issuance of government securities, loans from international financial institutions, and other forms of borrowing. Effective management of public debt is necessary for maintaining fiscal discipline, guaranteeing adequate funding for government activities, and managing the cost of borrowing.

***Issuance of Government Securities:*** The RBI is responsible for issuing government securities on behalf of the central and state governments. These securities, which include Treasury Bills, dated securities, and bonds, are issued to raise funds for financing government expenditures and managing liquidity in the economy. The RBI conducts auctions for these securities, inviting bids from institutional and individual investors. The auction process guarantees transparency and competitive pricing, enabling the government to borrow at the best possible rates.

***Debt Management Strategy:*** The RBI, in consultation with the government, formulates and implements a debt management strategy. This strategy aims to guarantee a stable and predictable supply of government securities, minimize the cost of borrowing, and manage the risks associated with public debt. The RBI considers factors such as market conditions, investor demand, and the government's financing needs when determining the timing, size, and composition of debt issuances.

***Debt Servicing and Repayment:*** The RBI is responsible for servicing the government's debt, which includes paying interest and repaying principal on maturing securities. This involves maintaining accurate records of outstanding debt, calculating interest payments, and securing timely disbursement of funds to investors. The RBI also manages the redemption of maturing securities, either by repaying the principal or by rolling over the debt through the issuance of new securities.

***Debt Monitoring and Reporting:*** The RBI continuously monitors the government's debt levels and provides regular reports on the status of public debt. These reports include information on the composition, maturity profile, and interest costs of the government's debt portfolio. The RBI also provides analytical insights on the implications of public debt for the economy, including its impact on inflation, interest rates, and financial stability.

***Advisory Role:*** The RBI serves as an advisor to the government on matters related to public debt management. It provides expert advice on the formulation of debt policies, the design of debt instruments, and the development of the domestic debt market. The RBI's advisory role is critical in safeguarding that public debt is managed prudently and sustainably, contributing to the overall economic stability of the country.

### Government's Banking Transactions

In addition to managing public debt, the RBI handles the banking transactions of the government. This involves providing a range of banking services to the central and state governments, including the maintenance of government accounts, the management of receipts and payments, and the execution of financial transactions. The RBI's role in managing government banking transactions is important for the effective operation of government finances and the smooth implementation of fiscal policy.

***Maintenance of Government Accounts:*** The RBI maintains the principal accounts of the central and state governments. These accounts include the Consolidated Fund, the Contingency Fund, and the Public Account of India, as well as similar accounts for the state governments. The Consolidated Fund is the primary account through which all government revenues are deposited and expenditures are made. The Contingency Fund is used for emergency expenditures, while the Public Account includes funds such as provident funds, small savings, and other liabilities.

The RBI secures that all government transactions are accurately recorded in these accounts and provides periodic statements and reports to the government. The maintenance of these accounts involves reconciling the government's cash balances, guaranteeing the availability of funds for government expenditures, and managing the flow of funds between the central and state governments.

***Management of Receipts and Payments:*** The RBI is responsible for the collection and disbursement of government funds. It collects several types of government revenue, including taxes, fees, and other receipts, and credits them to the appropriate government accounts. The RBI also handles the disbursement of government payments, including salaries, pensions, subsidies, and other expenditures.

To enable these transactions, the RBI operates a network of government banking offices and collaborates with designated commercial banks, known as "agency banks." These agency banks act on behalf of the RBI to collect revenue and make payments in regions where the RBI does not have a direct presence. The RBI coordinates with these banks to secure the quick and timely execution of government transactions.

***Management of Expenditure Programs:*** The RBI factors into managing the implementation of government expenditure programs. It safeguards that funds are disbursed in accordance with the government's budgetary allocations and expenditure priorities. The RBI also monitors the use of funds to safeguard that they are used for their intended purposes. This involves verifying expenditure claims, authorizing payments, and providing financial reports to the government.

***Financial Advisory Services:*** The RBI provides financial advisory services to the government, offering expert guidance on a number of aspects of public finance. This includes advice on budget formulation, cash flow management, investment of surplus funds, and the management of government liabilities. The RBI's advisory role is particularly important in times of economic uncertainty, when the government may need to make critical fiscal policy decisions.

***Facilitation of Government Transactions:*** The RBI eases a broad set of government transactions, including the issuance of government cheques, the transfer of funds between government departments, and the management of foreign exchange transactions related to government activities. The RBI also provides support for the implementation of government schemes and programs, including direct benefit transfers (DBT) and other welfare initiatives.

***Securing Transparency and Accountability:*** The RBI contributes to safeguarding transparency and accountability in government financial transactions. It maintains detailed records of all government receipts and payments and provides regular financial statements and reports to the government. The RBI also collaborates with the Comptroller and Auditor General (CAG) of India to ease the audit of government accounts, guaranteeing that public funds are used effectively and quickly.

The RBI's role as the banker to the government encompasses all sorts of functions, from managing public debt to handling the government's banking transactions. Through these functions, the RBI supports the smooth management of public finances, contributes to the implementation of fiscal policy, and guarantees the smooth operation of the government's financial system. The RBI's expertise and oversight are critical in maintaining the stability and integrity of India's public finance system, building confidence in the country's economic governance.

## 1.3.5 Banker's Bank

The Reserve Bank of India (RBI) serves as the central bank of the country, acting as the banker's bank. This role involves providing important services to other banks within the Indian financial system, securing the stability and productivity of the overall banking environment. As the banker's bank, the RBI offers a range of services, including acting as the lender of last resort and managing clearing and settlement functions. These responsibilities are necessary for maintaining liquidity, supporting smooth interbank transactions, and safeguarding the stability of the financial system.

## 1.3.6 Lender of Last Resort

As the lender of last resort, the RBI provides emergency funding to banks facing liquidity shortages. This function is critical in preventing systemic crises and maintaining confidence in the financial system. The RBI steps in to provide liquidity support to banks that are unable to meet their short-term obligations due to sudden withdrawals or other financial pressures. This support is typically extended through short-term loans or advances against eligible collateral.

*Purpose and Importance:* The primary purpose of the lender of last resort function is to prevent a liquidity crisis from escalating into a solvency crisis. By providing timely assistance, the RBI secures that solvent but illiquid banks can continue to operate, thus preventing disruptions in the banking system. This role is particularly important during periods of financial stress or market volatility when banks may face unexpected liquidity demands.

*Mechanisms of Support:* The RBI provides liquidity support through mechanisms, including repurchase agreements (repos), reverse repos, and marginal standing facility (MSF). Under the repo mechanism, banks can borrow funds from the RBI by pledging eligible securities, such as government bonds, as collateral. The MSF allows banks to borrow overnight funds from the RBI at a rate higher than the repo rate, providing an additional source of liquidity.

***Conditions and Requirements:*** The RBI extends lender-of-last-resort facilities under strict conditions to prevent moral hazard and make certain that banks use the support responsibly. Banks are required to provide adequate collateral, and the RBI may impose certain conditions on the use of funds. The central bank closely monitors the borrowing bank's financial condition and may require the implementation of corrective measures to restore financial stability.

***Impact on Financial Stability:*** The lender of last resort function is involved in maintaining financial stability by preventing bank failures and guaranteeing the smooth functioning of the payment system. It helps to restore market confidence during crises, reduces the risk of bank runs, and mitigates the impact of financial shocks on the broader economy.

### 1.3.7 Clearing and Settlement Functions

The RBI's role as the banker's bank also includes managing the clearing and settlement functions within the Indian banking system. Clearing and settlement processes are critical for the smooth execution of payment transactions, including interbank transfers, securities transactions, and retail payments. The RBI operates and oversees clearing and settlement systems to guarantee the effective and secure processing of transactions.

***Clearing House Operations:*** The RBI operates a network of clearinghouses that help the clearing and settlement of cheques, demand drafts, and other paper-based instruments. These clearinghouses act as intermediaries, processing and reconciling transactions between participating banks. The clearing process involves the exchange of payment instructions, the calculation of net obligations, and the final settlement of funds. The RBI safeguards that the clearing process is conducted effectively, accurately, and securely.

***Electronic Payment Systems:*** In addition to paper-based clearing, the RBI manages several electronic payment systems that enable real-time and batch processing of transactions. Principal systems include the Real-Time Gross Settlement (RTGS) system, the National Electronic Funds Transfer (NEFT) system, and the Immediate Payment Service (IMPS). The RTGS system allows for the immediate and final settlement of high-value transactions on a real-time basis. The NEFT system processes retail transactions in batches, providing a cost-effective and quick way to transfer funds.

***Securities Settlement:*** The RBI also is involved in the settlement of securities transactions. It operates the Central Securities Depository (CSD) and the Securities Settlement System (SSS), which support the electronic settlement of government securities and other financial instruments. The CSD holds securities in dematerialized form, while the SSS guarantees the delivery of securities against payment. These systems are needed for the smooth functioning of the capital markets and the smooth execution of monetary policy.

## 1.3.8 Risk Management and Oversight

The RBI is responsible for managing the risks associated with clearing and settlement activities. It sets regulatory standards and operational guidelines to secure the safety and effectiveness of these systems. The RBI monitors the credit and liquidity risks faced by participating banks and implements measures to mitigate these risks. It also conducts regular audits and assessments of the systems to safeguard compliance with international standards and best practices.

***Advances and Upgrades:*** The RBI continuously works to strengthen the speed and security of clearing and settlement systems through technological developments and upgrades. This includes the adoption of new technologies, such as blockchain and distributed ledger technology, to simplify processes and reduce settlement times. The RBI also collaborates with other central banks and international organizations to develop and implement global standards for payment systems.

***Interbank Settlement:*** The RBI supports interbank settlement by maintaining settlement accounts for participating banks. These accounts are used to settle net obligations arising from clearinghouse operations and electronic payment systems. The RBI secures the finality and irrevocability of settlements, providing a stable foundation for the banking system. It also acts as the ultimate settlement agent, providing liquidity support to banks as needed.

***Role in Monetary Policy Implementation:*** The clearing and settlement functions of the RBI are closely linked to the implementation of monetary policy. By managing the payment systems and securing the smooth flow of funds, the RBI can influence liquidity conditions in the banking system. This, in turn, affects interest rates, credit availability, and overall economic activity.

The RBI's ability to manage the payment systems effectively is critical for the successful implementation of monetary policy.

## 1.4 Regulatory Framework and Policies

India's banking sector operates under a reliable regulatory framework designed to make certain stability, protect the interests of depositors, and promote effective functioning. The regulatory environment has evolved over the years, shaped by many laws, policies, and amendments. One of the basis legislations in this framework is the Banking Regulation Act, 1949. This Act, along with its subsequent amendments, lays down the fundamental rules and guidelines governing the operation, supervision, and regulation of banks in India. This section covers provisions of the Banking Regulation Act, 1949, and highlights considerable amendments that have been made over time to adapt to the changing financial environment.

### 1.4.1 Banking Regulation Act, 1949

The Banking Regulation Act, 1949, is a complete piece of legislation that provides the legal foundation for the regulation and supervision of banking companies in India. Enacted on March 16, 1949, the Act aimed to consolidate and amend the law relating to banking. It serves as the primary legal instrument guiding the Reserve Bank of India (RBI) in regulating the activities of commercial banks, both public and private. The Act's provisions cover several aspects of banking, including licensing, management, operations, and mergers and acquisitions.

**Provisions**

The Banking Regulation Act, 1949, encompasses a span of provisions that are important for maintaining the soundness and stability of the banking sector. Some of the main provisions include:

***Licensing of Banks:*** One of the primary provisions of the Act is the requirement for all banking companies to obtain a license from the RBI before commencing business. The RBI has the authority to grant licenses based on specific criteria, including the capital adequacy of the applicant, the need for banking services in the proposed location, and the public interest. The licensing provision safeguards that only financially sound and competent entities are allowed to operate as banks.

*Capital Requirements:* The Act specifies the minimum paid-up capital and reserves that a banking company must maintain to be eligible for a license. These requirements vary based on the category of the bank, such as scheduled and non-scheduled banks. The capital requirements are designed to guarantee that banks have sufficient financial resources to absorb losses and protect depositors' interests.

*Management and Governance:* The Act outlines the rules for the appointment, qualifications, and responsibilities of the management and directors of banking companies. It mandates that the board of directors should have a certain number of independent directors with relevant expertise. The RBI has the power to remove any director or management personnel deemed unfit for the role. These provisions aim to secure good governance and accountability in the management of banks.

*Reserve Fund and Profit Allocation:* The Act requires banks to create a reserve fund and transfer a specified percentage of their net profits to this fund each year. This provision helps banks build a buffer against potential losses. The Act lays down guidelines for the declaration and distribution of dividends to shareholders, safeguarding that profits are distributed prudently without compromising the bank's financial health.

*Restriction on Loans and Advances:* To prevent conflicts of interest and promote prudent lending practices, the Act imposes restrictions on loans and advances to directors, their relatives, and companies in which they have a substantial interest. It also limits the amount of unsecured loans and advances a bank can grant. These measures are aimed at mitigating credit risk and guaranteeing that lending decisions are made objectively.

*Audit and Inspection:* The Act mandates that every banking company must have its accounts audited annually by a qualified auditor. The RBI has the authority to appoint auditors, inspect the books of accounts, and conduct special audits if necessary. The audit and inspection provisions are central for maintaining transparency and accountability in the financial reporting of banks.

*Amalgamation and Reconstruction:* The Act provides a legal framework for the amalgamation and reconstruction of banking companies. The RBI has the power to approve or reject proposals for mergers and acquisitions based on factors such as the financial position of the banks involved, public interest, and the potential impact on competition. This provision guarantees that consolidation in the banking sector occurs in an orderly and regulated manner.

***Regulation of Banking Operations:*** The Act grants the RBI the authority to regulate a number of aspects of banking operations, including the maintenance of cash reserves, the percentage of liquid assets to be maintained, and the forms of investments banks can make. It also enables the RBI to issue directives to banks to safeguard the smooth functioning of the banking system.

***Winding Up and Liquidation:*** The Act outlines the procedures for the voluntary winding up and liquidation of banking companies. The RBI helps with overseeing the winding-up process, securing that the interests of depositors and other stakeholders are protected. The Act also provides for the appointment of a liquidator to manage the distribution of assets during liquidation.

***Consumer Protection:*** While the primary focus of the Act is on regulating banking companies, it also includes provisions aimed at protecting consumers' interests. For example, the Act requires banks to disclose interest rates, charges, and other terms and conditions associated with their products and services. It also mandates the maintenance of a grievance redressal mechanism to address customer complaints.

### Amendments Over Time

Since its enactment, the Banking Regulation Act, 1949, has undergone several amendments to address emerging challenges and align with global best practices.

## 1.4.2 Priority Sector Lending

Priority sector lending (PSL) is a central policy initiative that mandates banks to allocate a certain percentage of their total credit to specific sectors considered necessary for the economic and social development of the country.The objective of PSL is to make certain adequate credit flow to underserved and vulnerable sectors of the economy, thereby promoting inclusive growth and reducing regional disparities.

***Categories and Targets:*** The priority sectors identified by the RBI include agriculture, micro, small and medium enterprises (MSMEs), export credit, education, housing, social infrastructure, and renewable energy. Each of these sectors has specific sub-targets and credit limits to guarantee focused attention. For instance, within the agriculture sector, there are sub-targets for small and marginal farmers. The overall PSL target for domestic scheduled commercial banks and foreign banks with more than 20 branches is set at 40% of adjusted net bank credit (ANBC) or credit equivalent amount of off-balance sheet exposure, whichever is higher.

***Implementation and Monitoring:*** Banks are required to achieve the PSL targets on an annual basis. The RBI closely monitors the performance of banks in meeting these targets and issues guidelines to secure compliance. Non-compliance can lead to penalties, including the requirement to deposit the shortfall amount in funds like the Rural Infrastructure Development Fund (RIDF), managed by NABARD. Also, banks are encouraged to adopt fresh approaches, such as lending through self-help groups (SHGs), joint liability groups (JLGs), and producer organizations, to meet their PSL targets.

***Impact and Challenges:*** The PSL policy has had a notable impact on expanding access to credit for sectors that are necessary for socio-economic development. It has facilitated the growth of agriculture, MSMEs, and other priority areas by providing much-needed financial support. However, the policy also poses challenges, such as the potential for increased non-performing assets (NPAs) in the priority sectors, particularly in agriculture, which is subject to weather and market risks. To address these challenges, the RBI periodically reviews and updates the PSL guidelines, safeguarding that they remain relevant and effective in achieving their objectives.

## 1.4.3 Foreign Investment in the Banking Sector

Foreign investment in India's banking sector has been a factor in improving the sector's growth, productivity, and global integration. The Indian government and the RBI have formulated policies to regulate and promote foreign investment in both public and private sector banks. The objectives of these policies are to attract capital, introduce global best practices, and encourage competition in the banking industry.

***Foreign Direct Investment (FDI) Limits:*** The FDI policy sets out the maximum permissible limits for foreign investment in Indian banks. For private sector banks, the aggregate foreign investment, including FDI, foreign institutional investors (FIIs), foreign portfolio investors (FPIs), and non-resident Indians (NRIs), is allowed up to 74% of the paid-up capital. This includes both the automatic route (up to 49%) and the government approval route (beyond 49% and up to 74%). For public sector banks, FDI is allowed up to 20% under the government approval route. These limits are subject to periodic review and adjustment by the government and the RBI.

***Entry of Foreign Banks:*** The entry of foreign banks into India is governed by specific guidelines issued by the RBI. Foreign banks can establish a presence in India through three main modes: branch operations, wholly-owned subsidiaries (WOS), and representative offices. Branch operations and WOS are subject to RBI approval and must comply with regulatory requirements, including capital adequacy norms, asset classification, and exposure limits. Representative offices, on the other hand, are limited to liaison activities and cannot undertake banking transactions.

***Regulatory Framework and Compliance:*** Foreign banks operating in India are subject to the same regulatory framework as domestic banks, including compliance with prudential norms, anti-money laundering (AML) regulations, and know-your-customer (KYC) guidelines. The RBI also monitors the governance and management of foreign banks to safeguard that they operate in a safe and sound manner. Foreign banks are required to maintain a certain level of local capital and liquidity, guaranteeing that they can meet their obligations in India.

***Benefits and Challenges:*** The presence of foreign banks and foreign investment in the Indian banking sector has brought several benefits. It has introduced advanced technology, new financial products, and global best practices, strengthening the overall effectiveness and competitiveness of the sector. Foreign banks have also contributed to the development of India's financial markets, particularly in areas such as derivatives, foreign exchange, and trade finance.

However, the integration of foreign banks into the Indian banking system also presents challenges. There are concerns about the potential for capital flight in times of financial instability, as foreign banks may repatriate profits to their home countries. The dominance of foreign banks in certain segments, such as corporate banking and investment banking, can create competitive pressures for domestic banks. The RBI and the government continue to monitor these challenges, securing that the regulatory framework remains solid and that the benefits of foreign investment are maximized.

## 1.4.4 Basel Norms Implementation in India

India's banking sector, like many others worldwide, has been shaped by international regulatory frameworks that aim to boost the stability and resilience of financial institutions. Among these frameworks, the Basel Accords have been particularly influential. Developed by the Basel Committee on Banking Supervision (BCBS), these accords set global standards for bank capital adequacy, stress testing, and market liquidity risk. The Reserve Bank of India (RBI), as the nation's central bank and financial regulator, has been instrumental in implementing these norms in the Indian banking system. The Basel norms have evolved over time, starting from Basel I, advancing through Basel II, and currently being in the process of implementing Basel III. Each phase brought marked changes to the regulatory system, focusing on different aspects of risk management and capital adequacy.

### Basel I

Introduced in 1988, Basel I was the first accord established by the BCBS to provide a uniform framework for bank capital adequacy. The objective of Basel I was to make certain that banks maintain enough capital to cover the risks associated with their assets, thus boosting the stability and soundness of the international banking system. The accord introduced a risk-weighted approach to capital adequacy, where different asset classes were assigned specific risk weights based on their perceived riskiness.

***Implementation in India:*** India adopted Basel I norms in 1992, marking a substantial shift in the country's approach to bank regulation. The RBI mandated that all scheduled commercial banks in India adhere to a minimum capital adequacy ratio (CAR) of 8% of their risk-weighted assets, which was later increased to 9% to provide a cushion against potential losses. The CAR was calculated by dividing a bank's capital by its risk-weighted assets, with capital consisting of Tier 1 and Tier 2 components.

Tier 1 capital, also known as core capital, included equity capital and disclosed reserves, which provided the primary buffer against losses. Tier 2 capital comprised subordinate debt and undisclosed reserves, offering an additional layer of protection. The distinction between Tier 1 and Tier 2 capital was important, as Tier 1 capital was considered more reliable and stable, given its ability to absorb losses on a going concern basis.

***Impact and Challenges:*** The implementation of Basel I norms had a profound impact on the Indian banking sector. It introduced a more structured and standardized approach to risk management, compelling banks to maintain adequate capital reserves relative to their risk exposure. This requirement led to a major improvement in the capital adequacy ratios of Indian banks, improving their resilience to financial shocks.

However, Basel I also had its limitations. The accord's risk-weighting system was relatively simplistic, as it did not adequately differentiate between different types of credit risk within asset classes. For instance, all corporate loans were assigned the same risk weight, regardless of the borrower's creditworthiness. This lack of granularity led to potential distortions in the allocation of capital and risk management practices. Basel I focused primarily on credit risk, without adequately addressing other types of risk, such as market risk and operational risk.

### Basel II

***Introduction Features:*** In response to the limitations of Basel I, the BCBS introduced Basel II in 2004. Basel II aimed to provide a more thorough and risk-sensitive framework for bank regulation, addressing the deficiencies of its predecessor. The accord introduced the concept of three pillars: Minimum Capital Requirements, Supervisory Review Process, and Market Discipline. These pillars collectively aimed to increase the stability and transparency of the banking system.

**Pillar 1: Minimum Capital Requirements** focused on improving the risk sensitivity of capital adequacy. Basel II introduced more sophisticated risk-weighting mechanisms for credit risk, including the Internal Ratings-Based (IRB) approach, which allowed banks to use their internal risk assessment models to determine capital requirements. The accord also introduced capital charges for market risk and operational risk, safeguarding a more broad coverage of risks faced by banks.

**Pillar 2: Supervisory Review Process** emphasized the role of regulators in assessing the adequacy of banks' capital beyond the minimum requirements. It encouraged regulators to evaluate the quality of banks' risk management practices, internal control systems, and governance structures. This pillar also allowed for the imposition of additional capital requirements based on the overall risk profile of individual banks.

**Pillar 3: Market Discipline** aimed to improve transparency and accountability in the banking sector. It required banks to disclose detailed information about their risk exposures, capital structure, and risk management practices. This increased transparency was intended to enable market participants to make more informed decisions, thereby promoting market discipline.

***Implementation in India:*** India began implementing Basel II norms in a phased manner, with the full adoption completed by 2009. The RBI issued full guidelines for Indian banks, outlining the requirements for each of the three pillars. Under Pillar 1, Indian banks were required to maintain a minimum CAR of 9%, with capital charges for credit, market, and operational risks. The RBI also provided guidelines for the adoption of the Standardized Approach and the IRB approach for credit risk, as well as the Basic Indicator Approach and the Standardized Approach for operational risk. Pillar 2 was implemented through the Supervisory Review and Evaluation Process (SREP), which involved regular assessments of banks' risk management systems and capital adequacy by the RBI. The RBI also encouraged banks to develop their internal capital adequacy assessment process (ICAAP), enabling them to evaluate their capital needs based on their specific risk profile. Under Pillar 3, the RBI mandated detailed disclosures on banks' risk exposures, capital structure, and risk management practices. These disclosures were intended to improve market transparency and enable stakeholders to assess the financial health and risk profile of banks.

***Challenges and Outcomes:*** The implementation of Basel II in India brought about several benefits, including a more risk-sensitive approach to capital adequacy and an improved focus on complete risk management. However, the transition also posed challenges. The complexity of the new risk-weighting mechanisms required banks to invest in advanced risk assessment models and data management systems. Also, the increased transparency requirements under Pillar 3 necessitated considerable improvements in banks' internal reporting and disclosure processes.

Despite these challenges, Basel II contributed to a more resilient and stable banking system in India. The framework's emphasis on thorough risk management and supervisory oversight helped Indian banks better manage the global financial crisis of 2008, with the country's banking sector remaining relatively insulated from the turmoil experienced in other parts of the world.

### Basel III

***Introduction and Rationale:*** The global financial crisis of 2008 exposed notable weaknesses in the international financial system, particularly in areas such as capital adequacy, tap, and liquidity management. In response, the

BCBS introduced Basel III, a broad set of reforms aimed at strengthening the regulation, supervision, and risk management of banks. Basel III sought to address the shortcomings of Basel II and strengthen the resilience of banks to economic and financial shocks.

***Capital Requirements:*** One of the elements of Basel III is the introduction of more stringent capital requirements. Basel III raised the minimum common equity Tier 1 (CET1) capital ratio from 2% to 4.5% of risk-weighted assets. Banks were required to hold a capital conservation buffer of 2.5% of risk-weighted assets, composed entirely of CET1 capital, bringing the total minimum CET1 requirement to 7%.

Basel III also introduced a countercyclical capital buffer, ranging from 0% to 2.5% of risk-weighted assets, to be maintained during periods of excessive credit growth. This buffer aimed to protect the banking sector from systemic risks arising from cyclical economic conditions. Basel III introduced an employ ratio, defined as Tier 1 capital divided by the bank's average total consolidated assets, with a minimum requirement of 3%. The use ratio aimed to constrain excessive draw on and provide a simple, non-risk-based measure to supplement the risk-weighted capital requirements.

***Liquidity Standards:*** In addition to strengthening capital adequacy, Basel III introduced new global liquidity standards to address the issue of liquidity risk, which had been a marked factor in the financial crisis. The two liquidity standards introduced under Basel III are the Liquidity Coverage Ratio (LCR) and the Net Stable Funding Ratio (NSFR).

***Liquidity Coverage Ratio (LCR):*** The LCR requires banks to hold a sufficient high-quality liquid assets (HQLA) to cover their total net cash outflows over a 30-day stress period. The purpose of the LCR is to guarantee that banks have an adequate liquidity buffer to withstand short-term liquidity disruptions. The LCR is calculated as the ratio of HQLA to total net cash outflows, with a minimum requirement of 100%.

***Net Stable Funding Ratio (NSFR):*** The NSFR requires banks to maintain a stable funding profile in relation to the composition of their assets and off-balance-sheet activities. The NSFR is designed to promote resilience over a longer time horizon by requiring banks to fund their activities with stable sources of funding, such as equity and long-term debt. The NSFR is calculated as the ratio of available stable funding (ASF) to required stable funding (RSF), with a minimum requirement of 100%.

***Implementation in India:*** India started adopting Basel III norms in 2013, with a phased implementation timeline extending to 2019. The RBI issued full guidelines for Indian banks, specifying the capital and liquidity requirements, as well as the timelines for compliance. Indian banks were required to maintain a minimum CET1 ratio of 5.5% and a total CAR of 11.5%, including the capital conservation buffer. The implementation of the LCR and NSFR posed challenges for Indian banks, particularly in terms of managing liquidity and funding profiles. The RBI provided guidance and support to banks in meeting the new liquidity standards, including the recognition of government securities as HQLA for LCR purposes.

***Challenges and Considerations:*** The implementation of Basel III in India has had several implications for the banking sector. The higher capital requirements and stringent liquidity standards have strengthened the resilience of Indian banks, guaranteeing that they are better equipped to withstand financial shocks. However, these requirements have also increased the cost of capital for banks, potentially impacting their profitability and lending capacity.

The RBI has taken a balanced approach to the implementation of Basel III, considering the characteristics of the Indian banking sector and the broader economic environment. The phased implementation timeline has provided banks with sufficient time to build up their capital and liquidity buffers, while also securing a smooth transition to the new regulatory framework.

## 1.4.5 Non-performing Assets (NPAs) and Resolution Mechanisms

Non-performing assets (NPAs) have been a persistent challenge for the Indian banking sector. NPAs are loans and advances that are in default or in arrears on scheduled payments of principal or interest. The rise in NPAs not only affects the profitability of banks but also poses substantial risks to the stability of the financial system. In response to this challenge, mechanisms have been established to manage, resolve, and recover these distressed assets. This section provides a complete overview of NPAs, including their definition and classification, provisioning norms, and the recovery mechanisms available under Indian law.

## Definition and Classification of NPAs

***Definition of NPAs:*** Non-performing assets are loans or advances for which the principal or interest payment remains overdue for a period of 90 days or more. This definition is in line with the norms set by the Reserve Bank of India (RBI), which provides a standardized framework for the classification and management of NPAs. When a borrower fails to make payments as per the loan agreement, the asset is classified as "non-performing." NPAs are a critical indicator of the asset quality of banks and are used to assess the financial health of the banking sector.

***Classification of NPAs:*** The RBI mandates that banks classify NPAs into three categories based on the duration of the non-payment and the likelihood of recovery. These categories are:

***Substandard Assets:*** An asset is classified as substandard if it has remained non-performing for a period less than or equal to 12 months. These assets are considered to be in a state of incipient weakness, with the possibility of some loss if deficiencies are not corrected. Substandard assets require close monitoring and prompt action to prevent further deterioration.

***Doubtful Assets:*** An asset is classified as doubtful if it has remained in the substandard category for more than 12 months. Doubtful assets exhibit major weaknesses that make collection or liquidation highly questionable. The degree of loss is difficult to estimate, and these assets pose a high risk of default. Banks are required to assess the potential loss associated with doubtful assets and make appropriate provisions.

***Loss Assets:*** An asset is classified as a loss asset when it is identified by the bank, internal or external auditors, or the RBI as uncollectible and of such little value that its continuance as a bankable asset is not warranted. Although there may be some salvage or recovery value, the entire asset is considered a loss. Banks must write off loss assets and make full provisions for the amount.

The classification of NPAs helps banks and regulators understand the extent of problem assets and the potential impact on the financial system. It also enables banks to take timely corrective actions and implement recovery strategies to mitigate losses.

## Provisioning Norms

Provisioning norms refer to the rules set by the RBI for banks to set aside a portion of their earnings to cover potential losses from NPAs. These norms are designed to secure that banks have adequate financial buffers to absorb losses arising from bad loans. The level of provisioning required depends on the classification of the asset and the likelihood of recovery

**Provisioning Requirements:**

***Substandard Assets:*** For substandard assets, banks are required to make a general provision of 15% of the outstanding loan amount. If the asset is unsecured, an additional provision of 10% is required, bringing the total provisioning to 25%. For loans classified as restructured under the guidelines for restructuring, a higher provisioning requirement of 20% is applicable.

***Doubtful Assets:*** The provisioning for doubtful assets depends on the period for which the asset has remained in the doubtful category. The provisioning requirements are as follows:

- Up to one year: 25% of the outstanding amount.
- One to three years: 40% of the outstanding amount.
- More than three years: 100% of the outstanding amount.

***Loss Assets:*** For loss assets, banks must make a full provision of 100% of the outstanding loan amount, as these assets are considered irrecoverable.

***Dynamic Provisioning Framework:*** In addition to the standard provisioning norms, the RBI has introduced a dynamic provisioning framework to account for cyclical fluctuations in asset quality. This framework requires banks to build up a buffer of provisions during good times, which can be used to cover losses during economic downturns. The dynamic provisioning buffer is based on the expected losses in the loan portfolio and is calculated using a forward-looking approach.

***Impact of Provisioning on Bank Profitability:*** Provisioning for NPAs directly affects the profitability of banks, as it requires them to set aside a portion of their earnings to cover potential losses. Higher provisioning reduces the net income available to shareholders and can impact the capital adequacy ratios of banks. However, adequate provisioning is necessary for maintaining the financial stability and resilience of the banking sector. It secures that banks have sufficient capital to absorb losses and continue their operations without compromising financial stability.

**Recovery Mechanisms**

Recovery mechanisms are processes and tools used by banks and financial institutions to recover dues from defaulting borrowers. In India, several legal and institutional frameworks have been established to enable the recovery of

NPAs. These mechanisms include the Securitization and Reconstruction of Financial Assets and Enforcement of Security Interest (SARFAESI) Act, Debt Recovery Tribunals (DRTs), and the Insolvency and Bankruptcy Code (IBC). These frameworks provide banks with legal avenues to enforce their claims, recover dues, and resolve distressed assets.

## Recent Mergers and Acquisitions in Indian Banks

The Indian banking sector has experienced a considerable wave of mergers and acquisitions (M&A) in recent years. These consolidations are part of a broader strategy by the government to create stronger banks that can effectively reduce non-performing assets (NPAs), boost speed, and compete on both domestic and international fronts. By merging smaller banks into larger entities, the government aims to fortify the banking system and contribute to the country's economic growth.

In 2019, Bank of Baroda merged with Vijaya Bank and Dena Bank, creating one of the largest public sector banks in India. This merger expanded the bank's branch network and operational capacity. Similarly, in 2017, State Bank of India (SBI) merged with its associate banks and Bharatiya Mahila Bank, a move that solidified SBI's position as one of the largest banks in the country.

The year 2020 saw multiple major mergers. Punjab National Bank (PNB) combined with Oriental Bank of Commerce (OBC) and United Bank of India (UBI), creating one of the largest public sector banks in terms of branch network. Canara Bank's merger with Syndicate Bank, also effective in 2020, increased its scale and reach. Union Bank of India merged with Andhra Bank and Corporation Bank, further boosting its competitive position. Finally, Indian Bank's merger with Allahabad Bank in 2020 considerably expanded its customer base and operational productivity.

These mergers have led to several positive outcomes for the Indian banking sector. The creation of larger banks has improved their ability to compete with both domestic and international financial institutions, leading to a more sturdy banking environment. The consolidation has facilitated better management of NPAs, improving the sector's overall financial health. The mergers have also resulted in operational efficiencies, reduced costs, and improved customer service, thanks to a wider network of branches and ATMs.

However, the rapid pace of M&AN activity has also raised concerns about market concentration and the potential for anti-competitive practices. To address these issues, the government and regulatory bodies are closely monitoring the situation to safeguard that the banking environment remains balanced and competitive.

## 1.4.6 SARFAESI Act

The SARFAESI Act, enacted in 2002, is a landmark legislation that provides a framework for the securitization and reconstruction of financial assets and the enforcement of security interests. The Act equips banks and financial institutions to take possession of collateral, sell the assets, and recover dues without the intervention of courts. It aims to ease faster recovery of NPAs and improve the effectiveness of the credit system. It will be discussed in more detail in the following chapters.

## 1.4.7 Debt Recovery Tribunals

Debt Recovery Tribunals (DRTs) were established under the Recovery of Debts Due to Banks and Financial Institutions Act, 1993 (RDDBFI Act), to provide a specialized and expeditious forum for the recovery of debts. DRTs have the jurisdiction to adjudicate disputes related to the recovery of debts above a specified threshold, involving banks and financial institutions. The establishment of DRTs aimed to reduce the burden on civil courts and expedite the recovery process.

***Structure and Functioning:*** DRTs are quasi-judicial bodies with the power to adjudicate and pass orders on matters related to debt recovery. Each DRT is headed by a Presiding Officer, who is typically a judicial officer with experience in banking and finance. The orders passed by DRTs can be appealed to the Debt Recovery Appellate Tribunal (DRAT). The process of debt recovery through DRTs involves filing an application by the creditor, followed by the issuance of notices to the borrower. The DRT conducts hearings and examines the evidence presented by both parties. Based on the merits of the case, the tribunal can pass orders for the recovery of the debt, including the sale of the secured assets. DRTs have the authority to issue recovery certificates, which are enforceable like a decree of a civil court.

**Features:**

- **Exclusive Jurisdiction:** DRTs have exclusive jurisdiction over cases involving the recovery of debts by banks and financial institutions. This specialization safeguards that cases are handled by experts familiar with banking laws and practices.

- **Speedy Disposal:** The RDDBFI Act mandates the time-bound disposal of cases, with a focus on expediting the recovery process. DRTs are required to decide cases within 180 days of filing, although delays can occur due to many reasons.

- **Wide Powers:** DRTs have wide-ranging powers, including the power to attach and sell secured assets, appoint receivers, and issue warrants for the arrest of defaulters. The tribunals can also grant interim relief, such as injunctions and stay orders.

***Challenges and Effectiveness:*** While DRTs have contributed to the recovery of NPAs, their effectiveness has been limited by several challenges. The backlog of cases and shortage of presiding officers have led to delays in the adjudication process. The enforcement of orders and recovery of dues have also been hindered by legal challenges and non-cooperation from borrowers.

## 1.4.8 Insolvency and Bankruptcy Code

The Insolvency and Bankruptcy Code (IBC), enacted in 2016, is a thorough legislation that consolidates and amends the laws relating to insolvency and bankruptcy in India. The IBC provides a time-bound process for the resolution of insolvency, both for corporates and individuals. It aims to promote entrepreneurship, availability of credit, and balance the interests of all stakeholders, including creditors and debtors.

***Features:***

- **Corporate Insolvency Resolution Process (CIRP):** The IBC outlines a corporate insolvency resolution process for companies facing financial distress. The process can be initiated by financial creditors, operational creditors, or the debtor company itself. Upon initiation, the National Company Law Tribunal (NCLT) appoints an Interim Resolution Professional (IRP) to take control of the company's assets and operations. The IRP, in consultation with the Committee of Creditors (CoC), develops a resolution plan to revive the company or sell its assets.

- **Time-bound Resolution:** The IBC mandates a time-bound resolution process, with a maximum period of 330 days for the completion of CIRP, including any extensions and litigation. This provision aims to prevent protracted insolvency proceedings and make certain swift resolution.

- **Moratorium:** Upon initiation of CIRP, a moratorium is imposed on the debtor company's assets, preventing creditors from taking legal action or enforcing claims. The moratorium provides a breathing space for the company to restructure its debts and operations.

- **Liquidation:** If the resolution plan is not approved by the CoC or if the company fails to achieve a resolution within the stipulated time frame, the company proceeds to liquidation. The assets of the company are sold, and the proceeds are distributed among the creditors in accordance with the priority established under the IBC.
- **Individual Insolvency:** The IBC also provides a framework for the resolution of individual insolvency. It offers mechanisms for fresh start, insolvency resolution, and bankruptcy for individuals, including personal guarantors to corporate debtors.

*Impact and Challenges:* The IBC has been a game-changer in the Indian insolvency field, providing a strong and quick mechanism for the resolution of distressed assets. It has empowered creditors by providing them with control over the insolvency resolution process and has facilitated the timely recovery of dues. The IBC has also promoted the development of a vibrant market for stressed assets, with investors showing increased interest in acquiring distressed companies. However, the implementation of the IBC has faced challenges, including delays in the resolution process, high litigation costs, and a lack of adequate infrastructure. The capacity of the NCLT and the availability of qualified professionals have also been areas of concern. Despite these challenges, the IBC has made marked strides in improving the insolvency resolution process in India. The management and resolution of NPAs are critical for the stability and growth of the Indian banking sector. The regulatory framework and policies established by the RBI, along with the legal mechanisms provided by the SARFAESI Act, DRTs, and the IBC, have created a broad system for addressing the issue of bad loans. While challenges remain, the continued refinement and strengthening of these mechanisms will be central in safeguarding the health and resilience of India's financial system. As the economy evolves and new challenges emerge, the regulatory and legal frameworks must adapt to maintain the effectiveness of NPA resolution strategies and support the overall stability of the banking sector.

## 1.4.9 Lead Bank Scheme

It was introduced by the Reserve Bank of India (RBI) in 1969 to address regional disparities in banking and promote financial inclusion, particularly in rural and semi-urban areas. Based on the recommendations of the Gadgil

Study Group, the scheme became fully operational across India by 1970. The central idea was to designate a single bank, known as the Lead Bank, in each district to coordinate the efforts of all banks operating in that area. This coordination aimed to guarantee a more smooth distribution of financial resources and a focused approach to regional development.

The scheme was designed with objectives: promoting financial inclusion by guaranteeing banking services reached every district, especially underserved ones; supervising and coordinating the activities of all banks in the district; enabling development planning through the creation of a District Credit Plan (DCP), which set targets for lending to critical sectors like agriculture and small industries; and implementing government-sponsored initiatives such as poverty alleviation and rural development projects. The DCP, prepared by the Lead Bank, served as a roadmap for lending activities, while regular meetings with other banks and district officials ensured alignment with development goals. A strong emphasis was placed on lending to weaker sections of society, including small farmers and entrepreneurs.

Despite its successes, the Lead Bank Scheme faced challenges, such as difficulties in coordination among banks, resource constraints, and the need to adapt to the evolving banking sector with the rise of digital banking and non-banking financial companies (NBFCs).

# Chapter 2
# Payment and Settlement Systems in India

According to the Bank for International Settlements (BIS), Payment and Settlement Systems (PSS) are the mechanisms, arrangements, and infrastructures that help the transfer of funds and financial instruments between participants in financial markets. These systems secure that transactions are processed, cleared, and settled in a secure and effective manner, being involved in maintaining financial stability and reducing systemic risk.

**Payment** refers to the process of transferring money from one party (the payer) to another (the payee) to settle a financial obligation. This can involve a number of instruments such as cash, checks, electronic transfers, or digital payment methods like credit cards, mobile payments, or cryptocurrencies. The payment process typically begins when the payer initiates the transaction and ends when the payee receives the funds or confirmation of the payment.

**Settlement** is the final step in the payment process, where the transfer of funds or securities is completed, and the obligations between the parties involved are fulfilled. Settlement guarantees that the payment or transfer is finalized, and that the payee receives the agreed-upon funds or assets. In financial markets, settlement may also involve the transfer of securities or other financial instruments in exchange for payment. Settlement can occur in real-time or on a deferred basis, depending on the system used.

## 2.1 Evolution of Payment Systems in India

The evolution of payment systems in India has been a fascinating journey, reflecting the country's socio-economic changes and technological advancements. From traditional methods rooted in cultural practices to modern digital platforms, India's payment environment has undergone substantial transformations. This narrative explores the primary phases in the evolution of payment systems in India, focusing on traditional payment methods and the modernization initiatives that have reshaped the way transactions are conducted in the country.

## 2.1.1 Traditional Payment Methods

In the early stages of India's economic history, the payment systems were largely based on barter and commodity money. As trade and commerce developed, more structured forms of payment emerged, including the use of precious metals, cowry shells, and indigenous instruments like the "hundi." These traditional payment methods laid the foundation for the more sophisticated systems that followed.

***Barter System:*** The barter system was one of the earliest forms of payment in India, prevalent in ancient and medieval times. People exchanged goods and services directly without a standardized medium of exchange. For example, a farmer might trade a portion of his grain for tools from a blacksmith. While this system facilitated local trade, it was limited by the need for a double coincidence of wants, making it inefficient for larger-scale transactions.

***Commodity Money:*** As trade expanded, commodities like grain, livestock, and metal objects began to serve as money. In particular, precious metals such as gold and silver became popular due to their intrinsic value, divisibility, and durability. These metals were often weighed and used as a medium of exchange in marketplaces. The use of commodity money marked a major advancement from the barter system, as it provided a more standardized measure of value.

***Cowry Shells:*** Cowry shells were another form of money used in ancient India, particularly in regions like Bengal. These shells were collected from the ocean and were valued for their rarity and beauty. They were used for small transactions and were an early form of currency that could be easily transported and counted. The use of cowry shells highlights the diversity of payment methods across different regions of India.

***The Hundi System:*** Though it was introduced in the first chapter, It is indeed needed to reiterate it, to create an all-round view of present evolution discussion. The hundi system was a highly sophisticated traditional financial instrument used extensively in medieval India. A hundi is a bill of exchange, similar to a modern-day cheque or promissory note, that facilitated the transfer of money and goods over long distances. Hundis were widely used by merchants and traders for both domestic and international trade.

There were types of hundis, each serving a specific purpose. For instance, a "darshani hundi" was payable on demand, while a "muddati hundi" had a specified maturity date. Hundis could be transferred by endorsement, making them a flexible tool for business transactions. The issuer of a hundi, known as the "drawer," promised to pay a certain amount to the "payee" or "bearer" upon presentation.

The hundi system provided several advantages. It reduced the need to carry large sums of money, thus minimizing the risk of theft. It also facilitated trade by providing credit, allowing merchants to purchase goods without immediate cash payment. The system operated on trust and was supported by a network of brokers and agents who helped in the negotiation and settlement of hundis. These brokers charged a commission for their services, which was an additional source of income in the trade and financial ecosystem.

The hundi system was not only a financial instrument but also a reflection of the strong social and business networks that existed in India at the time. It relied heavily on trust and reputation, as the drawer's credibility was necessary for the acceptance of a hundi. This traditional system laid the groundwork for more formal banking practices that developed in the subsequent eras.

## 2.1.2 Modernization Initiatives

The modernization of payment systems in India has been driven by technological advancements, regulatory reforms, and the growing demand for quick and secure payment methods. The transition from paper-based to electronic systems has been marked by several principal initiatives that have transformed the system of payments in India.

***Introduction of Paper Money:*** The introduction of paper money by the British colonial administration was a considerable milestone in the modernization of India's payment systems. The first paper currency notes were issued by the Bank of Hindostan in the late 18th century. Later, the Presidency Banks issued banknotes, followed by the Reserve Bank of India (RBI) after its establishment in 1935. The introduction of paper money facilitated larger and more secure transactions, replacing the cumbersome and risky use of metal coins.

***Negotiable instruments***, governed by the Negotiable Instruments Act of 1881 in India, are standardized documents major in commercial transactions and banking. These instruments, primarily cheques, bills of exchange, and promissory notes, represent promises to pay specific sums of money either on demand or at fixed future dates. The Act defines their characteristics, usage, and legal implications, providing a framework for issuance, acceptance, negotiation, and payment.

features of negotiable instruments include transferability, negotiability, presumption of consideration, and the requirement for writing and signature. The Act outlines rules for making, accepting, and negotiating these instruments, as well as regulations on presentment, payment, and dishonor. It also delineates the rights and liabilities of involved parties and procedures for noting and protesting in cases of non-acceptance or non-payment. While electronic payment systems have reduced the use of traditional negotiable instruments, they remain relevant in certain business contexts. The Act has undergone several amendments to address evolving commercial needs and technological advancements, including provisions for dealing with cheque dishonor and electronic image-based clearing systems. It continues to help with easing commercial transactions and providing legal recourse in cases of default or fraud, maintaining its significance in modern banking and commerce.

***Establishment of the Reserve Bank of India:*** The establishment of the RBI was an important moment in the evolution of India's payment systems. As the central bank, the RBI assumed the role of regulating the issue of currency and managing the country's monetary policy. The RBI's role extended to overseeing the banking sector, including the regulation of payment systems. The centralization of currency issuance and the regulation of banks laid the foundation for a more organized and reliable payment infrastructure.

***Nationalization of Banks:*** The nationalization of banks in 1969 and 1980 was another step in the modernization of India's payment systems. The nationalization aimed to safeguard that banking services reached all segments of society, including rural and underserved areas. It led to a notable expansion of the banking network, making formal financial services more accessible. The increased reach of banks facilitated the adoption of modern payment methods, such as cheques and demand drafts.

***Development of Electronic Payment Systems:*** The advent of electronic payment systems marked a new era in India's financial field. The RBI and other stakeholders undertook several initiatives to develop and promote electronic payments. These systems offered greater speed, security, and convenience compared to traditional methods. The evolution of electronic payment systems in India began with the introduction of Electronic Clearing Services (ECS), which enabled bulk payments like salary disbursements, dividends, and utility bills through automated fund transfers, minimizing the need for physical cheques. The Real-Time Gross Settlement (RTGS) system, launched in 2004, further advanced the sector by allowing real-time, high-value transactions between banks, offering a secure and smooth way to transfer funds instantly, beneficial for businesses and financial institutions. Following this, the National Electronic Funds Transfer (NEFT) system was introduced in 2005, providing a cost-effective solution for electronic fund transfers across bank accounts, processing transactions in batches. In 2010, the Immediate Payment Service (IMPS) revolutionized the payment ecosystem by enabling instant, 24/7 money transfers through mobile and electronic channels, catering to the need for real-time transactions. The Unified Payments Interface (UPI), launched in 2016 by the National Payments Corporation of India (NPCI), transformed digital payments by offering an interoperable platform for frictionless peer-to-peer and person-to-merchant transactions. UPI's novel system allowed users to link multiple bank accounts to a single mobile app and make payments using a unique Virtual Payment Address (VPA), encouraging an environment of advance and competition in the digital payment space.

***Digital Wallets and Mobile Payments:*** The rise of digital wallets and mobile payment solutions further accelerated the adoption of electronic payments in India. Companies like Paytm, PhonePe, and Google Pay offered user-friendly mobile applications that allowed customers to store money, pay bills, and make purchases. These wallets gained popularity, especially after the demonetization of high-value currency notes in 2016, which led to a surge in digital transactions.

***Aadhaar and Financial Inclusion:*** The Aadhaar program, launched in 2009, factored into improving financial inclusion and modernizing payment systems. Aadhaar is a unique identification number issued to residents of India, linked to their biometric and demographic information. The Aadhaar Enabled Payment System (AePS) allowed individuals to perform basic banking transactions using their Aadhaar number and biometric authentication. AePS facilitated cash withdrawals, balance inquiries, and fund transfers, particularly in rural and remote areas with limited banking infrastructure.

***Regulatory and Policy Reforms:*** The RBI and the Indian government have implemented regulatory and policy reforms to support the modernization of payment systems. The Payment and Settlement Systems Act, 2007, provided a legal framework for the regulation and oversight of payment systems in India.

It empowered the RBI to regulate payment system operators, securing their safety, security, and productivity.

The RBI also introduced guidelines for the issuance and operation of prepaid payment instruments (PPIs), such as digital wallets and prepaid cards. These guidelines set standards for KYC (Know Your Customer) compliance, transaction limits, and consumer protection. The RBI's proactive approach to regulation fostered a secure and trustworthy environment for digital payments.

The evolution of payment systems in India has been a remarkable journey, shaped by historical practices, technological advancements, and regulatory initiatives. From traditional methods like barter and hundi to modern electronic systems like UPI and digital wallets, India's payment environment has undergone a profound transformation. The modernization initiatives have not only strengthened the effectiveness and security of payments but also promoted financial inclusion and economic growth.

As India continues to embrace digital payments, the future holds exciting possibilities, including the integration of emerging technologies like blockchain, artificial intelligence, and the Internet of Things (IoT). The ongoing efforts to strengthen the regulatory framework, increase cybersecurity, and promote digital literacy will be central in realizing the full potential of India's payment systems. The journey ahead promises to be as dynamic and major as the past, making India's payment systems a model for development and inclusivity in the global financial system.

### 2.1.3  Role of Technology in Payment System Development

The role of technology in the development of payment systems in India has been far-reaching, enabling marked advancements in speed, security, and accessibility. Technology has facilitated the shift from traditional, paper-based transactions to electronic and digital methods, transforming the way payments are made and received.

*Automation and Productivity*: The introduction of technologies such as the Electronic Clearing Service (ECS) enabled automated bulk payments, reducing the manual effort involved in processing transactions like salary disbursements and utility bills. This automation simplified processes, minimized errors, and sped up transaction times.

*Real-Time Transactions*: The implementation of Real-Time Gross Settlement (RTGS) allowed for immediate high-value fund transfers, providing a secure platform for settling large transactions between banks in real-time. This breakthrough eliminated the risk of transaction delays and ensured the finality of payments, which was necessary for businesses and financial institutions.

***Batch Processing Systems***: The National Electronic Funds Transfer (NEFT) system introduced batch processing for electronic funds transfers, making it possible to handle a large volume of transactions smoothly. This system democratized access to electronic payments, making them more affordable and accessible to a broader audience, including small businesses and individuals.

***Mobile and Digital Payments***: The emergence of mobile technologies and services like the Immediate Payment Service (IMPS) enabled instant money transfers via mobile phones, even outside regular banking hours. IMPS provided a flexible, real-time payment solution that was particularly useful for urgent transactions.

***Effortless and Interoperable Platforms***: The Unified Payments Interface (UPI) created an interoperable and user-friendly platform for digital payments. By allowing multiple bank accounts to be linked to a single mobile application, UPI simplified the payment process and encouraged widespread adoption. Its open API architecture facilitated integration with many financial services, promoting advance and competition in the digital payment space.

***Security and Trust***: Technological advancements have also was involved in strengthening the security of payment systems. The use of encryption, two-factor authentication, and other security protocols has helped protect users' data and transactions, building trust in digital payment methods.

***Financial Inclusion***: Technology has been a driver in promoting financial inclusion. Digital payment systems have made banking services more accessible to underserved and rural populations, bridging the gap between traditional banking infrastructure and the needs of the unbanked. Advances like mobile banking and digital wallets have provided convenient financial services to millions of people, supporting economic participation.

***Regulatory Framework and Compliance***: The integration of technology in payment systems has been complemented by a reliable regulatory framework that secures compliance, security, and customer protection. The Reserve Bank of India (RBI) and other regulatory bodies have established guidelines and standards for electronic transactions, safeguarding the integrity of the payment systems.

***The Indian Financial System Code (IFSC)*** is a component of India's banking infrastructure, enabling electronic fund transfers and boosting the effectiveness of financial transactions. This unique 11-character alphanumeric code serves as a precise identifier for bank branches participating in electronic funds transfer systems across the country.

IFSC codes are structured in a specific format to make certain clarity and accuracy in identifying banks and their branches. The code is composed as follows:

AAAA0BBBBBB

Where:

AAAA represents the first four characters, which are alphabetic and identify the bank

0 is always the fifth character

BBBBBB represents the last six characters, which are alphanumeric and identify the specific branch

The Reserve Bank of India (RBI) is responsible for assigning and regulating IFSC codes. Each bank branch in India that participates in the NEFT/RTGS system is issued a unique IFSC. This standardization safeguards that every transaction can be routed accurately to its intended destination. IFSC codes are involved in several banking operations, including online fund transfers, direct deposits, check clearance, and automated teller transactions. When initiating an online fund transfer, the sender must provide the recipient's IFSC along with their account number. This dual identification system minimizes errors and improves the security of electronic transactions. For customers, IFSC codes can typically be found on cheque books, bank statements, and often on banks' official websites. The RBI also maintains a centralized database of IFSC codes, accessible to the public, further easing easy access to this important information. As digital banking continues to evolve, the importance of IFSC codes in India's financial ecosystem remains central. They contribute notably to reducing errors in fund transfers, speeding up electronic transactions, and improving the overall speed and security of the banking system. With the rise of mobile banking apps, many now include IFSC code lookup features, further simplifying the process for users and reinforcing the code's role in modern Indian banking.

## 2.2 Types of Payment Systems

Payment systems in India have evolved to meet the diverse needs of a growing economy, offering a range of services for a number of transaction sizes and purposes. The systems can broadly be categorized into large value systems and retail payment systems. Large value systems are central for settling substantial transactions between financial institutions and corporations, safeguarding smooth operation of the financial markets.

### 2.2.1 Large Value Systems

Large value payment systems are designed to handle high-value and high-priority transactions. These systems are critical for the stability of the financial markets, as they support the transfer of funds and securities between banks and financial institutions. In India, the most prominent large value system is the Real Time Gross Settlement (RTGS) system.

*Real Time Gross Settlement (RTGS)*

The RTGS system is a specialized payment system that enables the instantaneous transfer of funds and securities. It is used primarily for high-value transactions that require immediate and irrevocable settlement. RTGS is a real-time and gross settlement system, meaning that transactions are processed individually and settled as soon as they are initiated, without netting debits with credits across participants.

*Features and Participants*

RTGS in India is managed and operated by the Reserve Bank of India (RBI). The system's primary participants include all scheduled commercial banks, major financial institutions, and clearing corporations. Features of the RTGS system include:

**Real-Time Processing**: Transactions are settled instantly, providing immediate finality and reducing the settlement risk for high-value payments.

**Gross Settlement**: Transactions are settled individually, rather than netted against each other. This guarantees that each payment is processed as a standalone transaction, further strengthening security and reliability.

**High Security**: The RTGS system employs solid security protocols, including encryption and secure messaging standards, to protect transaction data and guarantee the confidentiality of information.

**Centralized Oversight**: As the central bank, the RBI oversees the RTGS system, guaranteeing its smooth operation and compliance with regulatory standards.

***Settlement Process:*** The settlement process in the RTGS system involves several steps:

**Initiation**: A participant initiates a payment instruction through the RTGS platform, specifying the amount and the recipient's account details.

**Verification**: The system verifies the availability of sufficient funds in the initiating bank's RTGS account. If funds are available, the transaction proceeds; otherwise, it is queued until funds become available.

**Processing**: Once verified, the transaction is processed in real-time. The system debits the initiating bank's account and credits the receiving bank's account immediately.

**Confirmation**: Both the initiating and receiving banks receive confirmation messages, indicating the completion of the transaction. The finality of settlement is assured, meaning that the payment is irrevocable and unconditional.

**Notification**: Customers of the participating banks are notified of the successful transaction, completing the payment process.

The RTGS system operates during specific business hours, typically aligned with banking hours. However, in recent years, the RBI has extended RTGS availability to 24/7, reflecting the growing demand for round-the-clock financial services.

### *Intraday Liquidity Management*

Intraday liquidity management is a necessary aspect of the RTGS system. It refers to the management of a bank's funds within a single business day to secure smooth settlement of payments without delay or disruption. The RTGS system provides several tools and mechanisms to enable intraday liquidity management:

**Intraday Liquidity Facility (ILF)**: The RBI provides an ILF to banks participating in the RTGS system. This facility allows banks to access short-term credit from the central bank to meet their immediate liquidity needs. The ILF is collateralized, typically by government securities, securing that the central bank is protected against potential defaults.

**Collateralized Borrowing and Lending Obligation (CBLO)**: Banks can use the CBLO market to borrow and lend funds on an intraday basis. This market enables banks to manage their liquidity quickly, borrowing funds when needed and lending excess funds to earn interest.

**Standing Facilities**: The RBI offers standing facilities, such as the Marginal Standing Facility (MSF) and the Liquidity Adjustment Facility (LAF), which provide additional avenues for banks to manage their liquidity. These facilities are available at the discretion of the central bank and are typically used to manage short-term liquidity mismatches.

The effective management of intraday liquidity is necessary for the smooth operation of the RTGS system. It secures that banks have sufficient funds to settle their transactions promptly, minimizing the risk of gridlock or delays in the payment system. Also, effective intraday liquidity management helps maintain overall financial stability by preventing systemic risks associated with payment failures.

## 2.2.2 Retail Payment Systems

Retail payment systems in India have undergone major transformation over the years, evolving from traditional methods to highly sophisticated digital platforms. These systems are designed to ease smaller, everyday transactions for consumers and businesses alike. They are major for promoting financial inclusion, boosting customer convenience, and supporting the overall productivity of the economy. The primary retail payment systems in India include the National Electronic Funds Transfer (NEFT), Immediate Payment Service (IMPS), and Unified Payments Interface (UPI). Each of these systems offers features and functionalities that cater to the diverse needs of the Indian populace.

### National Electronic Funds Transfer (NEFT)

The National Electronic Funds Transfer (NEFT) system is one of the earliest and most widely used electronic payment systems in India. Introduced by the Reserve Bank of India (RBI), NEFT allows individuals and businesses to transfer funds from one bank account to another across the country. It is a reliable and quick system that has contributed markedly to the growth of digital payments in India.

### Operating Procedure

The NEFT system operates on a deferred net settlement basis, which means that transactions are processed and settled in batches at specific intervals. The operating procedure of NEFT is straightforward, making it accessible to many users. To initiate a NEFT transaction, the remitter must provide needed details such as the beneficiary's name, bank branch, account number, and the Indian Financial System Code (IFSC) of the beneficiary's bank branch. The IFSC is a unique alphanumeric code that identifies each bank branch participating in the NEFT system.

Once the remitter submits the transaction request, the originating bank verifies the details and debits the remitter's account. The transaction is then sent to the NEFT clearing center, operated by the RBI, which processes the transaction in the next available settlement batch. The clearing center consolidates all the transactions received from banks and sorts them according to the destination bank branches.

The sorted transactions are then transmitted to the respective banks, which credit the funds to the beneficiary accounts. The entire process, from initiation to settlement, typically takes a few hours, depending on the timing of the transaction and the settlement cycle. NEFT transactions can be initiated through channels, including online banking, mobile banking, ATMs, and bank branches, offering flexibility to users.

## Settlement Cycles

- Initially, NEFT operated with a limited number of settlement cycles during the day, which meant that transactions could only be processed at specific times. However, recognizing the growing demand for more frequent transactions, the RBI has progressively increased the number of settlement cycles. As of now, NEFT operates on a 24x7 basis, with half-hourly settlement cycles throughout the day. This continuous settlement framework has greatly boosted the convenience and utility of the NEFT system, allowing for faster fund transfers and reduced transaction turnaround times.

- The settlement process involves the netting of transactions, where the clearing center calculates the net position of each bank. This means that the sum of the debits and credits for each bank is calculated, and only the net amounts are settled between banks. This method of settlement reduces the overall liquidity requirements for the banking system and safeguards smooth use of funds.

- The 24x7 availability of NEFT has made it an indispensable tool for businesses and individuals, enabling smooth and timely payments. It supports a broad set of transactions, including salary payments, bill payments, tax payments, and more. The elimination of time constraints and the ease of use have contributed to the widespread adoption of NEFT across India.

## Immediate Payment Service (IMPS)

The Immediate Payment Service (IMPS) is a real-time payment system that has revolutionized the field of retail payments in India. Launched by the National Payments Corporation of India (NPCI) in 2010, IMPS allows instant interbank fund transfers through many channels, including mobile phones, internet banking, ATMs, and more. IMPS is designed to provide round-the-clock availability, making it a highly convenient option for users who require immediate payment solutions.

- **24x7 Availability**

One of the standout features of IMPS is its 24x7 availability. Unlike traditional banking systems, which operate only during business hours, IMPS allows users to initiate and receive payments at any time of the day, including weekends and holidays. This round-the-clock availability is particularly beneficial for emergencies, last-minute payments, and situations where immediate fund transfer is necessary.

The 24x7 nature of IMPS is made possible by the system's sturdy infrastructure, which guarantees that transactions are processed and settled in real time. When a user initiates a transaction, the IMPS system immediately verifies the availability of funds in the sender's account. Once verified, the system debits the sender's account and credits the beneficiary's account instantaneously. The entire process is completed within seconds, providing users with immediate confirmation of the transaction.

This real-time processing capability has made IMPS a preferred choice for several use cases, including person-to-person (P2P) payments, person-to-merchant (P2M) payments, utility bill payments, and more. The system's ability to provide instant fund transfers has also made it a tool for e-commerce transactions, where quick payment settlement is often required.

- **Transaction Limits**

IMPS supports all sorts of transaction amounts, catering to the needs of different users. While there is no minimum limit for transactions, the maximum limit is typically set by individual banks and may vary based on the channel used (e.g., mobile banking, internet banking). Generally, the maximum limit for IMPS transactions ranges from Rs. 1 lakh to Rs. 5 lakhs per day per account, depending on the bank's policies.

These transaction limits are designed to balance convenience and security. For small-value transactions, IMPS offers a quick and effective payment solution without the need for extensive verification processes. For higher-value transactions, banks may implement additional security measures, such as multi-factor authentication, to safeguard the safety of the funds being transferred.

IMPS also supports multiple modes of transaction initiation, including the use of a Mobile Money Identifier (MMID) and mobile number, Account Number and IFSC, and Aadhaar number. The MMID is a unique identifier provided by banks to their customers, enabling secure transactions without disclosing the full account number. This feature strengthens the privacy and security of the transaction, making IMPS a versatile and user-friendly payment system.

## Unified Payments Interface (UPI)

The Unified Payments Interface (UPI) is a groundbreaking payment system that has transformed the way digital payments are conducted in India. Developed by the NPCI and launched in 2016, UPI provides a frictionless and interoperable platform for instant fund transfers and a span of payment services. It has gained immense popularity due to its simplicity, flexibility, and extensive functionality, making it a bedrock of India's digital payments ecosystem.

### 2.2.3 Card Payment Systems

Card payment systems have become a fundamental component of India's financial ecosystem, providing a convenient and secure means for consumers to transact without the need for cash. The widespread adoption of credit cards, debit cards, and prepaid payment instruments has facilitated the growth of digital transactions, promoting a shift towards a cashless economy. Each type of card offers features and benefits, catering to the diverse needs of consumers and businesses.

### Credit Cards

Credit cards are a popular payment method that allows consumers to borrow funds from a credit issuer to make purchases, which they can repay later. These cards offer a revolving line of credit with a predetermined limit, enabling cardholders to manage their expenses flexibly. Credit cards are widely used for online shopping, travel bookings, and everyday purchases, offering a range of rewards, cashback, and other benefits.

## Features and Benefits

Credit cards provide several advantages, including convenience, security, and the ability to manage cash flow. Cardholders can make purchases without immediate payment, which can be particularly useful for managing large or unexpected expenses. Many credit cards offer rewards programs, where users earn points or cashback on their spending. These rewards can be redeemed for a number of products, services, or discounts, providing added value to cardholders.Credit cards also come with additional features such as travel insurance, purchase protection, and extended warranties on purchased items. Some cards offer exclusive access to airport lounges, concierge services, and other premium benefits, catering to affluent consumers. The widespread acceptance of credit cards, both domestically and internationally, makes them a versatile payment option for travelers.

## Security and Fraud Protection

Credit cards incorporate several security features to protect against fraud and unauthorized use. These include EMV chip technology, which provides improved security for in-person transactions by generating a unique code for each transaction. Many credit cards offer zero-liability protection, safeguarding that cardholders are not held responsible for fraudulent charges.

Online transactions are secured through measures such as two-factor authentication, where users must provide an additional piece of information (e.g., a one-time password) to complete a transaction. Card networks and issuers continuously monitor transactions for suspicious activity and may block transactions that appear unusual, adding an extra layer of security.

## Credit Card Usage and Challenges in India

In India, credit card usage has been on the rise, driven by increasing consumer spending, e-commerce growth, and digitalization. However, credit cards also present certain challenges. One of the primary concerns is the risk of overspending and accumulating debt. High-interest rates on unpaid balances can lead to considerable financial burdens for cardholders who do not manage their spending responsibly.

Despite the growing popularity of credit cards, their penetration remains relatively low compared to debit cards. This is due in part to stringent eligibility criteria, such as credit history and income requirements, which limit access for a large segment of the population. Financial literacy and awareness about responsible credit card usage are necessary to mitigate the risks associated with credit cards and make certain that consumers can benefit from their advantages.

## *Debit Cards*

Debit cards are another widely used payment method in India, directly linked to the cardholder's bank account. Unlike credit cards, debit cards do not provide a line of credit; instead, they allow users to access the funds in their account to make purchases or withdraw cash. Debit cards are a component of India's digital payment infrastructure, offering a simple and quick way to manage everyday expenses.

### Features and Benefits

One of the advantages of debit cards is that they enable cardholders to control their spending, as transactions are limited to the available balance in the linked bank account. This feature helps prevent overspending and promotes financial discipline. Debit cards are widely accepted at retail outlets, online stores, and ATMs, making them a versatile payment tool.

Debit cards also offer convenience and security. They eliminate the need to carry cash, reducing the risk of theft or loss. Transactions can be completed quickly and securely, whether in-store, online, or at ATMs. Many banks offer additional benefits with debit cards, such as discounts on purchases, cashback offers, and reward points, improving the value proposition for cardholders.

### Security Features and Consumer Protection

Like credit cards, debit cards incorporate security measures to protect against fraud. EMV chip technology, personal identification numbers (PINs), and two-factor authentication are standard features that improve the security of transactions. Many banks also offer fraud monitoring services, alerting cardholders to suspicious activity and enabling quick response to potential threats.

Debit cards typically have lower liability for fraudulent transactions compared to credit cards, as they do not involve borrowed funds. However, since debit card transactions directly impact the cardholder's bank account, timely reporting of lost or stolen cards and unauthorized transactions is important to prevent financial loss.

## Growth and Challenges in India

The use of debit cards in India has seen substantial growth, supported by government initiatives to promote digital payments and financial inclusion. The introduction of the Pradhan Mantri Jan Dhan Yojana (PMJDY) scheme, which aimed to provide banking facilities to the unbanked population, considerably boosted debit card issuance. The rise of e-commerce and the availability of POS terminals have further fueled debit card usage.

Despite the widespread adoption of debit cards, challenges remain. The primary issue is the limited penetration of electronic payment infrastructure in rural and semi-urban areas, where cash remains the predominant payment method. Also, the preference for cash-on-delivery (COD) in e-commerce transactions poses a challenge for increasing digital payments through debit cards. Efforts to expand the acceptance network and educate consumers about the benefits of digital transactions are important to overcome these challenges.

## 2.2.4 Prepaid Payment Instruments

Prepaid payment instruments (PPIs) are a versatile and convenient payment option that allows users to load a specific amount of money onto a card or digital wallet, which can then be used for transactions. PPIs encompass many products, including prepaid cards, digital wallets, and mobile wallets. They offer a flexible alternative to traditional bank accounts and are widely used for many purposes, such as gift cards, travel cards, and employee benefit cards.

### *Types and Usage*

**Prepaid Cards**: Prepaid cards function similarly to debit cards but are not linked to a bank account. Users can load funds onto the card and use it for purchases or cash withdrawals. Prepaid cards are available in different formats, including reloadable cards and single-use gift cards. They are commonly used for gifting, travel, and expense management.

**Digital Wallets**: Digital wallets, also known as e-wallets, are mobile or online platforms that store digital versions of payment instruments, such as debit or credit cards. Users can load money into the wallet and use it for online shopping, bill payments, and peer-to-peer transfers. Popular digital wallets in India include Paytm, PhonePe, and Google Pay. These wallets offer several features, such as QR code payments, loyalty programs, and integration with other financial services.

**Mobile Wallets**: Mobile wallets are a subset of digital wallets designed specifically for mobile devices. They offer additional features, such as contactless payments using Near Field Communication (NFC) technology and in-app purchases. Mobile wallets provide a convenient and secure way to make payments, drawing on the widespread use of smartphones.

## Benefits and Advantages

Prepaid payment instruments offer several benefits, including convenience, security, and accessibility. They provide a secure way to carry funds without the need for cash or a traditional bank account. PPIs are especially useful for individuals who may not have access to formal banking services, offering an alternative means to participate in the digital economy.

PPIs also provide flexibility in managing expenses, as users can load a specific amount and use it as needed. This feature is particularly beneficial for budgeting and controlling spending. For businesses, prepaid cards can be used to manage employee benefits, incentives, and reimbursements, providing a smooth and smooth solution.

## Regulatory Framework and Consumer Protection

In India, the issuance and operation of prepaid payment instruments are regulated by the Reserve Bank of India (RBI). The RBI has established guidelines to guarantee the safety and security of PPIs, including requirements for Know Your Customer (KYC) compliance, anti-money laundering (AML) measures, and consumer protection.

PPIs are categorized into different types based on the level of KYC compliance, transaction limits, and usage restrictions. These categories include closed system PPIs (usable only at specific merchants), semi-closed system PPIs (usable at a group of merchants), and open system PPIs (usable at all merchants and ATMs). The regulatory framework secures that PPIs are used responsibly and transparently, protecting consumers from fraud and misuse.

## Challenges and Future Outlook

While PPIs have gained popularity in India, they face certain challenges. One of the primary issues is the limited acceptance network, especially in rural and semi-urban areas. Expanding the infrastructure for PPI acceptance and educating consumers and merchants about their benefits is central for increasing adoption.

Another challenge is the competition from other digital payment methods, such as UPI and mobile banking, which offer similar convenience and security features. To remain competitive, PPI providers must innovate and offer additional value-added services, such as loyalty programs, cashback offers, and integration with other financial products.

Despite these challenges, the future outlook for PPIs in India remains positive. The growing trend towards digitalization, the increasing penetration of smartphones, and the government's push for a cashless economy provide notable growth opportunities for PPIs. As the digital payment sector continues to evolve, PPIs are expected to help with providing inclusive and accessible financial services to a diverse population.

## 2.2.5 ATM Networks

Automated Teller Machines (ATMs) have been a necessary component of the banking infrastructure, providing customers with easy access to cash and other banking services. The ATM network in India has evolved notably, with advancements in technology and changes in regulatory policies strengthening its reach and effectiveness. Two aspects of the ATM network in India are the National Financial Switch (NFS) and the introduction of White Label ATMs.

### *National Financial Switch (NFS)*

The National Financial Switch (NFS) is a centralized switching system that enables the interconnectivity of ATMs across different banks in India. Launched by the Institute for Development and Research in Banking Technology (IDRBT) in 2004 and later taken over by the National Payments Corporation of India (NPCI), the NFS has helped with expanding the reach of ATM services.

### Role and Functionality

NFS acts as a backbone for the interoperability of ATMs, enabling customers of participating banks to access their accounts and perform transactions from any ATM, regardless of the bank. This interoperability has markedly increased convenience for customers, as they are not restricted to using only their bank's ATMs. NFS handles a broad set of transactions, including cash withdrawals, balance inquiries, mini-statements, and fund transfers.

### Impact on ATM Usage

The introduction of NFS has greatly strengthened the usability of ATMs in India. It has reduced the cost and complexity for banks to operate their own ATM networks, as they can tap the shared infrastructure. This shared network has also encouraged the deployment of ATMs in remote and underserved areas, improving financial inclusion by providing basic banking services to a broader population.

## Transaction Fees and Charges

To manage the costs associated with operating the shared network, NFS implements an interchange fee structure. This fee is charged by the acquiring bank (the bank that owns the ATM) to the issuing bank (the bank that issued the card) for each transaction. While banks typically absorb these fees for a limited number of transactions per month, they may charge customers for transactions beyond this limit.

## Security and Governance

NFS safeguards the security of transactions through strong encryption and monitoring systems. NPCI, as the governing body, oversees the network's operations, guaranteeing compliance with regulatory standards and implementing measures to prevent fraud and unauthorized access. The network's governance structure also includes representatives from member banks, providing a collaborative approach to managing the network.

## 2.2.6 White Label ATMs

White Label ATMs (WLAs) are ATMs operated by non-bank entities, authorized by the Reserve Bank of India (RBI) to offer ATM services to the public. Unlike traditional ATMs, which are owned and operated by banks, WLAs are owned by private companies that specialize in providing ATM services. The introduction of WLAs aimed to expand the ATM network, particularly in rural and semi-urban areas, where bank-operated ATMs were scarce.

## Concept and Objectives

The concept of WLAs was introduced in India to address the challenges of ATM availability in less populated regions. Banks often find it financially unviable to set up and maintain ATMs in rural areas due to lower transaction volumes. WLAs, operated by specialized entities, focus on providing ATM services without offering other banking services like loans or deposits. This separation allows for a focused business model that can effectively manage costs and scale operations.

## Operating Model

WLAs operate on a revenue model primarily based on interchange fees and transaction charges. The WLA operator earns revenue from the fees paid by the issuing banks for transactions conducted at their ATMs. They may charge customers a fee for services such as balance inquiries or cash withdrawals beyond a certain number of free transactions.

WLAs must be connected to the NFS to secure interoperability with bank-issued cards. This connectivity allows WLA operators to offer services to customers of all participating banks, providing an effortless experience similar to that of bank-operated ATMs.

## Deployment and Reach

WLAs have factored into increasing the penetration of ATMs in remote and underserved areas. The RBI has mandated that a certain percentage of WLAs must be deployed in rural and semi-urban locations to strengthen financial inclusion. This mandate has led to a more equitable distribution of ATM services, securing that people in less accessible areas have the same access to cash and basic banking services as those in urban centers.

## Challenges and Considerations

While WLAs have expanded ATM access, they also face several challenges. One of the primary challenges is the lower transaction volume in rural areas, which can affect the profitability of WLA operations. The cost of maintaining ATMs, including security and cash management, can be higher in remote areas due to logistical challenges.

Another consideration is the customer experience. Since WLAs are not operated by banks, they may lack certain features and services that bank customers are accustomed to, such as depositing cash or checks. Customers may be less familiar with WLA brands, which could affect their willingness to use these ATMs.

The future of WLAs in India looks promising, given the increasing emphasis on digital and financial inclusion. The government's push towards a cashless economy and the growing adoption of digital payments are likely to complement the role of WLAs in providing cash access. Technological advancements, such as biometric authentication and mobile app integrations, may also boost the functionality and security of WLAs, making them a part of the banking infrastructure.

## 2.2.7 Cheque Clearing Systems

The cheque clearing systems in India have undergone substantial transformation over the years, transitioning from manual processes to sophisticated digital systems. These systems are major for the settlement of cheque transactions between banks, safeguarding the effective and secure transfer of funds. The two components of the cheque clearing system in India are the Cheque Truncation System (CTS) and Magnetic Ink Character Recognition (MICR) Clearing.

### *Cheque Truncation System (CTS)*

The Cheque Truncation System (CTS) was introduced in India to speed up the cheque clearing process and increase the speed of the banking system. Launched by the Reserve Bank of India (RBI) in 2010, CTS is an image-based clearing system that eliminates the physical movement of cheques between banks, replacing it with the electronic exchange of images and data. This system has been instrumental in speeding up the clearing process, reducing costs, and improving accuracy.

### Process and Workflow

Under CTS, when a customer deposits a cheque, the bank captures the cheque's image along with relevant data (such as the MICR code, date, and amount) using a scanner. These images and data are then securely transmitted to the clearing house and the drawee bank. The clearing house processes these images and data, and the drawee bank verifies the authenticity and validity of the cheque before processing the payment.

The advantage of CTS is the elimination of the need to physically transfer cheques across bank branches and cities, which greatly reduces the time taken for clearing. The electronic exchange of images also minimizes the risk of cheque fraud and loss during transit. Also, CTS eases quicker settlement cycles, enabling faster credit to customers' accounts.

### Implementation and Impact

The implementation of CTS was carried out in phases across the country. Initially, it was introduced in the National Capital Region (NCR) and Chennai, and subsequently extended to other regions. The RBI mandated the use of CTS-compliant cheques, which have specific security features and standardized formats, to safeguard smooth processing.

CTS has had a profound impact on the productivity and security of cheque transactions in India. The reduction in the clearing cycle time from several days to just one or two days has improved the liquidity position of businesses and individuals. The system has also brought about a reduction in operational costs for banks, as it minimizes the need for physical infrastructure and manual processing.

Also, CTS has boosted the accuracy of cheque clearing, as the digital images allow for better scrutiny and verification. The system also supports the generation of electronic records, which can be used for audit and reconciliation purposes. CTS has modernized the cheque clearing process in India, making it faster, safer, and more reliable.

## MICR Clearing

Magnetic Ink Character Recognition (MICR) is a technology used to verify the legitimacy and authenticity of paper documents, particularly cheques. Introduced in India in the 1980s, MICR technology uses a special ink containing magnetic material to print unique codes on cheques. These codes, known as MICR codes, include information about the bank branch, cheque number, and account details.

The MICR code is typically printed at the bottom of the cheque and is read by MICR readers during the clearing process. The magnetic properties of the ink allow for automated reading and processing, considerably reducing the chances of errors and boosting the speed of cheque clearing.

### *Process and Functioning*

The MICR clearing process involves several steps. When a cheque is presented for clearing, it is encoded with the MICR code. The cheque is then processed through a MICR reader, which captures the code and transmits the data to the clearing house. The clearing house sorts the cheques based on the MICR code and forwards them to the respective drawee banks for payment.

The use of MICR technology allows for the automatic sorting and processing of cheques, which accelerates the clearing cycle. The technology also boosts the security of cheque transactions, as the MICR code is difficult to alter or forge. MICR codes provide a standardized way of identifying banks and branches, guaranteeing consistency and accuracy in cheque clearing.

### *Role in the Banking System*

MICR clearing has contributed to the evolution of India's banking system. Before the advent of MICR technology, cheque clearing was a manual and time-consuming process, often leading to delays and errors. MICR technology brought about a revolution in the processing of cheques, enabling banks to handle large volumes of cheques quickly and accurately.

The adoption of MICR technology also facilitated the expansion of banking services in India. By standardizing cheque processing, MICR made it easier for banks to offer cheque-based services across a wide geographical area. This standardization was particularly important in a diverse and vast country like India, where regional variations in cheque formats and banking practices could pose challenges.

As the banking sector continues to evolve, the role of cheque clearing systems may diminish with the increasing adoption of digital payment methods. However, the legacy of MICR and CTS technologies will continue to influence the development of secure and quick payment systems. The lessons learned from these systems will inform the future of financial development and the pursuit of smooth and secure payment solutions in India.

## 2.3 Players and Stakeholders

The environment of payment systems in India is shaped by a diverse set of players and stakeholders, each being involved in securing the smooth functioning of transactions and financial services. These stakeholders include banks, financial institutions, non-bank payment service providers, payment system operators, technology service providers, merchants, and consumers. Together, they create a complex ecosystem that enables the transfer of funds, supports economic activity, and encourages breakthrough in the financial sector.

### 2.3.1 Banks and Financial Institutions

Banks and financial institutions are the backbone of India's payment systems, providing the necessary infrastructure, regulatory oversight, and financial products to enable transactions. They serve multiple roles, including the provision of accounts, transaction processing, and compliance with regulatory requirements. Their involvement is critical for maintaining the integrity, security, and effectiveness of payment systems.

### Role in Payment Systems

Banks and financial institutions factor into the functioning of payment systems. They are responsible for issuing accounts to individuals and businesses, which are needed for conducting transactions. These institutions provide a range of payment instruments, such as debit cards, credit cards, prepaid cards, and digital wallets, enabling customers to make payments for goods and services.

One of the functions of banks in payment systems is to help the transfer of funds. They do this by processing payments through a number of channels, such as ATMs, internet banking, mobile banking, and point-of-sale (POS) terminals. Banks are also involved in the clearing and settlement of transactions, safeguarding that funds are transferred accurately and smoothly between accounts.

In addition to these functions, banks contribute to guaranteeing the security and compliance of payment systems. They implement reliable risk management practices, including fraud detection, anti-money laundering (AML) measures, and cybersecurity protocols. Banks also adhere to regulatory guidelines set by the Reserve Bank of India (RBI) and other regulatory bodies, securing that payment systems operate within the legal and regulatory framework.

Banks act as intermediaries between consumers and businesses, supporting transactions and providing support for payment methods. They work closely with payment system operators and technology providers to develop and maintain the infrastructure needed for payment processing. This collaboration is central for the continuous improvement of payment systems and the introduction of new technologies and services.

### *Issuer and Acquirer Functions*

In the payment systems ecosystem, banks and financial institutions often perform the roles of issuers and acquirers. These functions are necessary for the operation of card-based payment systems, such as credit cards and debit cards, as well as for digital wallets and other electronic payment methods.

### Issuer Functions:

As issuers, banks provide payment instruments, such as cards and digital wallets, to consumers. They are responsible for issuing these instruments, managing accounts, and enabling transactions. When a customer uses a payment instrument issued by a bank, the bank verifies the transaction and authorizes the payment. The issuer is also responsible for billing and collecting payments from customers, as well as managing customer accounts and providing customer service.

Issuers are involved in managing the risk associated with payment instruments. They assess the creditworthiness of customers, set credit limits, and monitor transactions for potential fraud or suspicious activity. Issuers also work with payment networks, such as Visa, Mastercard, and RuPay, to process transactions and make certain the smooth functioning of the payment system.

**Acquirer Functions:**

As acquirers, banks and financial institutions work with merchants to support the acceptance of payment instruments. Acquirers provide merchants with the necessary equipment, such as POS terminals, and software to accept card payments. They also handle the processing of transactions, safeguarding that funds are transferred from the customer's account to the merchant's account.

Acquirers help with enabling merchants to accept all sorts of payment methods, including cards, digital wallets, and contactless payments. They provide support for transaction processing, including authorization, clearing, and settlement. Acquirers also manage the relationship between merchants and payment networks, guaranteeing compliance with network rules and regulations.

In addition to these functions, acquirers offer value-added services to merchants, such as data analytics, loyalty programs, and fraud prevention tools. These services help merchants improve their operations, improve the customer experience, and increase sales.

*Collaboration and Advance:*

The roles of issuers and acquirers are interconnected, requiring close collaboration between banks, payment networks, and technology providers. This collaboration is important for the development and deployment of new payment technologies, such as contactless payments, mobile payments, and biometric authentication.

Banks and financial institutions are also players in the development of payment systems. They invest in research and development to create new products and services that meet the evolving needs of consumers and businesses. This includes the development of secure and user-friendly payment solutions, such as tokenization, biometric verification, and blockchain-based systems.

The involvement of banks and financial institutions in payment systems extends beyond traditional banking services. They are actively engaged in initiatives to promote financial inclusion, digital literacy, and cashless transactions. These efforts contribute to the broader goal of creating a more inclusive and smooth financial ecosystem in India.

### *Non-bank Payment Service Providers*

The system of payment systems in India has evolved notably over the past few decades, with non-bank payment service providers helping with this transformation. These entities, including e-wallet companies and payment aggregators, have introduced fresh solutions that have improved the convenience, accessibility, and speed of payments for consumers and businesses alike.

Let us visit and clarify the principal concepts we come across the payments field, which often create confusion here before proceeding further into chapters:

1. **Payment Gateway**: A payment gateway is a technology infrastructure that securely transmits payment data between an online merchant, the customer, and the acquiring bank or payment processor. It acts as a bridge to guarantee the secure transmission of payment information, easing the authorization and processing of transactions.

2. **Payment Aggregator**: A payment aggregator, also known as a payment facilitator or payment service provider, acts as an intermediary between merchants and financial institutions to enable electronic payment processing. It provides a unified platform or API integration that simplifies payment acceptance, handles tasks such as onboarding merchants, integrating payment methods, processing transactions, and settling funds.

3. **Payment Processor**: A payment processor is a company that handles the transaction between the merchant and the financial institution. It acts as a liaison between the merchant and the bank, securing that the payment is processed securely and quickly. Payment processors manage the exchange of payment information between the merchant and the bank, supporting the authorization and settlement of transactions.

**Critical Differences**: The primary difference between a payment gateway, payment aggregator, and payment processor lies in their roles within the payment ecosystem. A payment gateway securely transmits payment data, a payment aggregator simplifies payment acceptance by consolidating multiple merchant accounts, and a payment processor manages the transaction flow between banks. While a payment gateway is a subset of a payment aggregator, a payment processor is needed for the actual transfer of funds. Understanding these distinctions is important for businesses to choose the appropriate payment solutions that meet their needs and secure secure, effective transactions.

## 2.3.2 Payment System Operators

In the vast and complex sector of India's payment systems, Payment System Operators (PSOs) factor into enabling and managing the infrastructure that supports payment methods. These operators are responsible for safeguarding the frictionless and secure functioning of the systems that enable transactions across multiple channels, including electronic fund transfers, card payments, and mobile payments. Among the many entities operating in this domain, the National Payments Corporation of India (NPCI) stands out as a player. This section looks at establishment, objectives, and the wide array of products and services offered by NPCI, highlighting its considerable impact on India's payment ecosystem.

### National Payments Corporation of India (NPCI)

The National Payments Corporation of India (NPCI) is a central organization in India's payment environment. Established with a vision to create a solid, inclusive, and quick payment infrastructure, NPCI has was involved in digitizing the country's financial transactions. As a not-for-profit entity, NPCI operates under the guidance of the Reserve Bank of India (RBI) and the Indian Banks' Association (IBA), guaranteeing that its initiatives align with the broader goals of financial inclusion and breakthrough in the payment space.

### Establishment and Objectives

NPCI was founded in 2008 as an initiative to consolidate and integrate many retail payment systems in India. Before its establishment, the payment systems in the country were fragmented, with multiple clearing houses and settlement systems operating independently. This fragmentation led to inefficiencies, higher costs, and limited accessibility, particularly in rural and semi-urban areas. Recognizing the need for a unified payment infrastructure, the RBI and IBA collaborated to create NPCI, with the mandate to simplify and strengthen the productivity of India's payment systems.

One of the objectives of NPCI is to promote digital payments and reduce the dependency on cash. This objective aligns with the Indian government's broader vision of a cashless economy, which aims to boost transparency, reduce the costs associated with cash handling, and improve the effectiveness of transactions. NPCI's role is to develop and operate payment systems that are accessible, secure, and cost-effective, catering to the diverse needs of consumers, businesses, and financial institutions.

Another objective of NPCI is to safeguard the interoperability of payment systems. Interoperability allows different payment systems and channels to work smoothly together, enabling users to transfer funds across different platforms without friction. This feature is necessary for promoting competition, advance, and consumer choice in the payment system. By providing a common platform for several payment services, NPCI has helped eliminate the silos that previously existed, making it easier for users to access and use digital payment solutions.

NPCI also focuses on financial inclusion, aiming to bring the unbanked and underbanked segments of the population into the formal financial system. Through initiatives like the Aadhaar-enabled Payment System (AePS) and the Unified Payments Interface (UPI), NPCI has provided low-cost, accessible payment solutions that cater to the needs of rural and underserved communities. These initiatives have not only expanded the reach of digital payments but also contributed to the overall goal of inclusive economic growth.

**Products and Services**

NPCI has developed a full suite of products and services that cater to a number of aspects of the payment ecosystem. These offerings are designed to provide secure, smooth, and convenient payment options for consumers, businesses, and financial institutions. Some of the most notable systems introduced earlier can also be seen in this section as services/products introduced by NPCI include:

***Unified Payments Interface (UPI):***

UPI is one of the most new and popular payment systems developed by NPCI. Launched in 2016, UPI allows users to transfer money between bank accounts instantly using a mobile device. Unlike traditional payment methods that require account details, UPI transactions can be initiated using a Virtual Payment Address (VPA), which simplifies the payment process. UPI supports transaction types, including peer-to-peer (P2P) transfers, bill payments, and merchant payments. Its effortless interoperability across banks and financial institutions has made it a foundation of India's digital payment ecosystem.

***Bharat Interface for Money (BHIM):***

BHIM is a mobile application that uses the UPI infrastructure to provide a user-friendly interface for digital payments. Launched by NPCI with the support of the Indian government, BHIM aims to promote UPI adoption among the general public. The app allows users to send and receive money, check account balances, and pay for goods and services using UPI. BHIM's simplicity and ease of use have made it a popular choice among users, particularly those new to digital payments.

***Immediate Payment Service (IMPS):***

IMPS is another critical payment service offered by NPCI, enabling real-time fund transfers across bank accounts. Unlike traditional methods like NEFT, which operate in batches, IMPS processes transactions instantly, 24/7. This service is particularly useful for urgent transactions and has been widely adopted by both individuals and businesses. IMPS also supports channels, including mobile banking, internet banking, and ATMs, providing users with multiple options for initiating transactions.

***National Automated Clearing House (NACH):***

NACH is an electronic payment system designed for bulk transactions, such as salary disbursements, dividend payments, and utility bill collections. NACH provides a secure and effective platform for automating recurring payments, reducing the reliance on paper-based instruments like cheques. It supports both credit and debit transactions, making it a versatile solution for businesses and government agencies. NACH has simplified the process of handling large volumes of transactions, improving speed and accuracy.

***Aadhaar-enabled Payment System (AePS):***

AePS is a payment system that draws on the Aadhaar biometric identification system to enable banking transactions. It allows users to perform basic banking activities, such as cash withdrawals, balance inquiries, and fund transfers, using their Aadhaar number and biometric authentication. AePS is particularly beneficial for rural and remote areas where access to traditional banking infrastructure is limited. By providing a secure and straightforward way to access banking services, AePS has helped with advancing financial inclusion in India.

***Bharat Bill Payment System (BBPS):***

BBPS is an integrated bill payment system that offers a unified platform for customers to pay their utility bills, such as electricity, water, gas, and telecom.

It provides a convenient and secure way for consumers to manage their bill payments, with options for both online and offline transactions. BBPS also supports recurring payments, securing that customers can set up automatic payments for their regular bills. This system has simplified the bill payment process and increased transparency and productivity.

### *National Electronic Toll Collection (NETC):*

NETC is a system designed to ease electronic toll payments across India's highway network. It uses RFID technology and a unified payment interface to enable cashless toll payments, reducing congestion and improving effectiveness at toll plazas. NETC is linked to the FASTag system, which allows vehicles to pass through toll gates without stopping for cash payments. This initiative has not only improved the convenience of toll payments but also contributed to the smooth flow of traffic on India's highways.

### *National Financial Switch (NFS):*

NFS is a network that connects ATMs across India, allowing customers of different banks to withdraw cash, check balances, and perform other transactions at any participating ATM. NFS has markedly expanded the reach of ATM services, providing greater convenience and accessibility for bank customers. It has also reduced the operational costs for banks by sharing the infrastructure and resources.

### *Cheque Truncation System (CTS):*

CTS is a digital system for processing cheques, which replaces the physical movement of cheques with electronic images and data. This system has smooth the cheque clearing process, reducing the time required for cheque processing and settlement. CTS has also strengthened the security and speed of the cheque clearing process, minimizing the risks of fraud and errors.

### *RuPay:*

RuPay is India's indigenous card payment network, developed by NPCI to provide a cost-effective alternative to international card networks like Visa and Mastercard. Launched in 2012, RuPay has gained widespread acceptance and is now used for many types of transactions, including ATM withdrawals, point-of-sale (POS) payments, and online shopping. RuPay cards are available in debit, credit, and prepaid variants, catering to the diverse needs of Indian consumers. The introduction of RuPay has not only reduced the cost of card transactions but also fostered competition in the card payment space.

### 2.3.3 Technology Service Providers

In the digital age, technology service providers factor into the functioning and development of payment systems. These providers supply the necessary technological infrastructure, software, hardware, and cloud services that enable smooth, secure, and quick digital transactions. The synergy between these technology providers and financial institutions has transformed the payment field, making digital payments more accessible and reliable. Here we examine the players in this domain, including software providers, hardware providers, and cloud service providers, highlighting their contributions to the evolution of payment systems.

***Software Providers***

Software providers are important in developing the applications and platforms that underpin modern payment systems. These companies create the software solutions that help transactions, make certain security, and provide user-friendly interfaces for customers and businesses. Their offerings range from point-of-sale (POS) software, mobile payment applications, and payment gateways to fraud detection systems and customer relationship management (CRM) tools.

### Role and Contributions:

Software providers develop and maintain the core applications that enable payment processing. For instance, they create the software that powers POS systems, allowing merchants to accept payments via credit and debit cards. These systems are important for processing transactions, recording sales data, and managing inventory. The integration of payment software with other business systems, such as accounting and inventory management, simplifies operations and improves productivity.

In addition to POS systems, software providers offer mobile payment applications that support transactions via smartphones and tablets. These apps enable users to make payments, transfer funds, and manage their accounts on the go. They often include features like QR code scanning, near-field communication (NFC) technology, and biometric authentication, improving the convenience and security of mobile payments.

Payment gateways are another critical offering from software providers. These gateways serve as intermediaries between merchants and financial institutions, authorizing and processing online transactions. They encrypt sensitive data, such as credit card numbers, safeguarding that payment information is transmitted securely. Payment gateways also support multiple payment methods, including cards, e-wallets, and bank transfers, providing customers with a range of options.

Software providers also contribute to guaranteeing the security of payment systems. They develop fraud detection and prevention solutions that monitor transactions for suspicious activity. These systems use advanced technologies like artificial intelligence (AI) and machine learning (ML) to analyze transaction patterns and identify potential threats. By quickly detecting and mitigating fraud, software providers help protect both consumers and businesses from financial losses.

**Players:**

Some of the prominent software providers in the payment industry include companies like Oracle, SAP, ACI Worldwide, FIS, and Fiserv. These companies offer complete payment solutions that cater to the diverse needs of financial institutions, merchants, and consumers. Their products are used worldwide, supporting millions of transactions daily and securing the smooth operation of global payment systems.

### *Hardware Providers*

Hardware providers are responsible for supplying the physical devices and infrastructure that support payment systems. These include POS terminals, ATMs, card readers, and other needed equipment used in processing transactions. Hardware providers also offer the underlying technology that powers these devices, including chips, sensors, and communication modules.

**Role and Contributions:**

POS terminals are a basis of in-store payment systems. Hardware providers design and manufacture these devices, which enable merchants to accept payments via credit and debit cards. Modern POS terminals are equipped with several features, such as EMV chip readers, NFC for contactless payments, and touchscreen interfaces. These terminals are often integrated with other business systems, allowing for smooth transaction processing and inventory management.

ATMs are another component of the payment infrastructure. Hardware providers supply the machines that dispense cash, accept deposits, and provide account information to customers. ATMs have evolved greatly over the years, incorporating advanced features like biometric authentication, video banking, and multi-currency capabilities. They are involved in extending banking services to remote areas, providing customers with convenient access to cash and banking services.

Card readers are necessary for enabling payments via cards, whether in-store or online. Hardware providers develop a number of types of card readers, including magnetic stripe readers, chip readers, and contactless readers. These devices are integrated into POS terminals, ATMs, and mobile payment solutions, allowing for secure and smooth transaction processing.

In addition to these devices, hardware providers also supply the technology that powers them. This includes microprocessors, security chips, communication modules, and other components that guarantee the reliability and security of payment systems. The development of secure elements, such as hardware security modules (HSMs) and trusted platform modules (TPMs), has been central in protecting sensitive payment data and preventing fraud.

**Players:**

Leading hardware providers in the payment industry include companies like Ingenico, Verifone, NCR Corporation, Diebold Nixdorf, and PAX Technology. These companies offer a span of hardware solutions, catering to the needs of merchants, banks, and consumers worldwide. Their products are known for their durability, security, and ease of use, making them components of the global payment infrastructure.

**Cloud Service Providers**

Cloud service providers (CSPs) have become increasingly important in the payment industry, offering scalable and flexible solutions for data storage, processing, and security. Cloud services enable financial institutions and payment providers to manage their operations more effectively, reduce costs, and increase their capabilities. CSPs offer services, including infrastructure as a service (IaaS), platform as a service (PaaS), and software as a service (SaaS), which are critical for modern payment systems.

**Role and Contributions:**

Cloud service providers offer scalable infrastructure solutions that allow payment providers to manage large volumes of transactions and data. By tapping cloud infrastructure, payment providers can scale their operations up or down based on demand, safeguarding that they can handle peak transaction volumes without investing in expensive hardware. This flexibility is particularly valuable for handling seasonal spikes in transactions, such as during holidays or sales events.

In addition to infrastructure, CSPs provide platforms and software solutions that speed up payment processing and management. PaaS offerings allow payment providers to develop, test, and deploy applications in a secure and scalable environment. These platforms often include tools for application development, database management, and analytics, enabling payment providers to build and customize their solutions.

SaaS offerings from CSPs provide ready-to-use software solutions for payment processing, fraud detection, customer relationship management, and more. These solutions are hosted in the cloud, eliminating the need for on-premises installations and maintenance. SaaS solutions are often subscription-based, providing payment providers with access to the latest features and updates without the need for substantial capital investment.

Security is a critical concern for payment systems, and CSPs offer sturdy security measures to protect sensitive data. Cloud services typically include encryption, firewalls, identity and access management (IAM), and threat detection capabilities. CSPs also adhere to industry standards and regulations, such as the Payment Card Industry Data Security Standard (PCI DSS), guaranteeing compliance and data protection.

**Players:**

Prominent cloud service providers in the payment industry include Amazon Web Services (AWS), Microsoft Azure, Google Cloud Platform (GCP), IBM Cloud, and Oracle Cloud. These companies offer thorough cloud solutions that support the entire payment ecosystem, from transaction processing and data storage to security and compliance. Their global presence and extensive infrastructure make them ideal partners for payment providers looking to expand their services and improve their capabilities.

## 2.3.4 Merchants and Consumers

In the evolving sector of India's payment systems, merchants and consumers are the two primary stakeholders driving the adoption and success of digital payment solutions. The interplay between merchants' willingness to accept digital payments and consumers' readiness to use them shapes the trajectory of India's journey toward a cashless economy. We now turn to the adoption trends among these groups, the factors influencing their choices, and their user experience and preferences, providing a broad understanding of the dynamics at play.

## Adoption Trends

### Merchants:

The adoption of digital payment systems among merchants in India has seen a major upsurge over the past decade. This trend has been driven by a combination of government initiatives, technological advancements, and changing consumer behavior. The Indian government's push for a digital economy, particularly through demonetization in 2016 and subsequent policies like Digital India, has factored into encouraging merchants to embrace digital payment methods.

Small and medium-sized enterprises (SMEs), which form the backbone of the Indian economy, have increasingly adopted digital payment solutions. The convenience of receiving payments directly into bank accounts, reducing the need for cash handling, has been a major incentive. The availability of affordable digital payment solutions, such as UPI, QR codes, and mobile wallets, has lowered the entry barriers for these businesses. Even street vendors and small shop owners are now equipped with QR code-based payment systems, reflecting a considerable shift from traditional cash transactions.

Large retailers and e-commerce platforms have also contributed to the widespread adoption of digital payments. Companies like Amazon, Flipkart, and Reliance Retail have integrated multiple payment options, including credit and debit cards, net banking, UPI, and e-wallets, providing consumers with a range of choices. The pandemic further accelerated this trend, as businesses sought contactless payment methods to secure safety and comply with social distancing norms.

### Consumers:

On the consumer side, the adoption of digital payments has been equally far-reaching. A growing segment of the population, especially in urban areas, now prefers digital payments over cash for their convenience, speed, and security. The proliferation of smartphones and affordable internet access has been a catalyst in this shift, enabling a broader demographic to access digital payment services.

The younger generation, in particular, has been quick to adopt new payment technologies. Digital natives are comfortable using mobile wallets, UPI, and other app-based payment systems for a variety of transactions, from shopping and dining to utility bill payments and money transfers. The rise of digital payment platforms like Paytm, Google Pay, and PhonePe has made transactions easier, often incentivized by cashback offers, discounts, and rewards.

Rural areas, traditionally dominated by cash transactions, have also seen a gradual shift toward digital payments. Initiatives like Jan Dhan Yojana, which aims to increase financial inclusion, have brought millions of unbanked individuals into the formal banking system. The use of Aadhaar-enabled payment systems and mobile banking has further facilitated this transition, providing rural consumers with secure and straightforward ways to conduct transactions.

## User Experience and Preferences

### Merchants:

For merchants, the user experience with digital payment systems revolves around ease of use, cost-effectiveness, and security. One of the considerations is the integration process. Merchants prefer systems that are easy to set up and integrate with their existing infrastructure, whether it's a physical store or an online platform. This ease of integration reduces the learning curve and operational disruptions.

The cost of transactions is another factor. Merchants are sensitive to transaction fees, often referred to as the Merchant Discount Rate (MDR). Lower MDRs make digital payment systems more attractive, especially for small businesses with tight profit margins. The Indian government's efforts to cap MDR for certain transactions have encouraged more merchants to adopt digital payments. The availability of zero-cost solutions like UPI, which often come with no MDR for certain types of transactions, has been a driver of adoption.

Security is a critical concern for merchants. The risk of fraud and chargebacks can be a deterrent to adopting digital payments. Thus, merchants favor systems with strong security features, including encryption, secure authentication, and fraud detection mechanisms. The introduction of two-factor authentication for card payments and biometric verification for Aadhaar-linked payments has boosted the security of digital transactions, providing merchants with greater confidence.

The ability to track and manage transactions digitally is a marked advantage. Digital payments come with the benefit of detailed transaction records, which can be integrated into accounting systems for better financial management. This feature is particularly useful for merchants during tax filing and audits, offering a level of transparency and accountability that is difficult to achieve with cash transactions.

**Consumers:**

Consumers, on the other hand, prioritize convenience, speed, and incentives when choosing digital payment methods. The convenience of being able to pay with a smartphone, without the need for cash or cards, is an advantage. Mobile payment apps offer a frictionless experience, allowing users to pay bills, transfer money, and make purchases with just a few taps. The ability to link multiple bank accounts and manage transactions from a single platform further increases this convenience.

Speed is another factor influencing consumer preferences. Digital payments are typically faster than traditional methods, such as cash or cheque transactions. Systems like UPI enable instant transfers, making it an ideal choice for urgent payments. The real-time nature of these transactions also provides immediate confirmation, adding to the user experience.

Incentives help with consumer adoption of digital payments. Cashback offers, discounts, and reward points are common strategies used by payment providers to attract and retain users. These incentives not only provide immediate value to consumers but also encourage repeat usage. For example, many mobile wallets and UPI apps offer cashback on specific transactions, making them more appealing compared to cash payments.

Security and privacy are also considerations for consumers. With the increasing awareness of cybersecurity threats, consumers prefer payment systems that offer reliable security features. This includes secure authentication methods, such as biometric verification and one-time passwords (OTPs), and encryption of sensitive data. The assurance of secure transactions improves consumer trust and willingness to use digital payments.

However, challenges remain in achieving universal adoption across different demographics and regions. While urban and younger consumers are more inclined toward digital payments, older generations and rural populations may still prefer cash due to familiarity and trust issues. Also, the digital divide, characterized by limited internet access and smartphone penetration in certain areas, poses a challenge to the widespread adoption of digital payment systems.

### 2.3.5 Regulatory Environment

The regulatory environment in India factors into securing the secure, effective, and reliable functioning of payment systems. As the digital payment environment evolves, there is a need for a full legal and regulatory framework. The Payment and Settlement Systems Act, 2007 (PSS Act), forms the bedrock of this framework, alongside regulations such as the Board for Regulation and Supervision of Payment and Settlement Systems (BPSS) regulations established in 2008.

**Payment and Settlement Systems Act, 2007**

The Payment and Settlement Systems Act, 2007, provides the legal foundation for the regulation and oversight of payment systems in India. The Act designates the Reserve Bank of India (RBI) as the central authority responsible for regulating and supervising payment systems, safeguarding their safety and effectiveness.

**Provisions**

The PSS Act encompasses several main provisions needed for the governance of payment systems in India:

***Regulation and Supervision:*** The Act grants the RBI authority to regulate and supervise payment systems, guaranteeing their secure and quick operation. It enables the RBI to issue guidelines, set standards, and oversee the functioning of all payment system providers in India.

***Authorization Requirement:*** All entities intending to operate a payment system in India must obtain prior authorization from the RBI under the PSS Act. This requirement helps safeguard that only credible and capable entities manage payment systems, thus protecting consumer interests and maintaining systemic integrity.

***Legal Recognition:*** The Act provides legal recognition to payment systems, including electronic fund transfers and card networks. This recognition is important for the enforceability and reliability of electronic transactions.

***Consumer Protection:*** The PSS Act mandates that all payment systems adhere to principles of transparency and fairness. It includes provisions for addressing consumer grievances and disputes related to payment transactions, securing that consumer interests are safeguarded.

***Data and Information Security:*** The Act emphasizes the importance of data security and confidentiality. Payment system operators are required to implement solid security measures to protect sensitive information, complying with prescribed standards and protocols.

***Finality of Settlement:*** The Act stipulates the finality of payment settlements, safeguarding that once a transaction is completed, it cannot be reversed. This provision is central for maintaining confidence in electronic payments and minimizing systemic risk.

***Penalties and Enforcement:*** The Act outlines penalties for non-compliance with its provisions. The RBI is authorized to impose fines, suspend operations, or revoke the authorization of payment system operators found in violation of the regulations.

## 2.3.6 RBI's Role in Payment System Regulation

The Reserve Bank of India (RBI) contributes to regulating and overseeing payment systems in India, guaranteeing their safe and smooth operation. As the central bank of the country, the RBI's mandate includes maintaining monetary stability, promoting financial stability, and securing the robustness of the payment infrastructure. The RBI's role in payment system regulation encompasses many aspects, including licensing and authorization of payment system operators and the implementation of complete oversight mechanisms. These functions are critical in building a secure, transparent, and inclusive payment ecosystem.

### *Licensing and Authorization*

One of the core responsibilities of the RBI in regulating payment systems is the licensing and authorization of entities that wish to operate in this space. This function is governed by the Payment and Settlement Systems Act, 2007 (PSS Act), which grants the RBI the authority to regulate and supervise payment systems. The licensing and authorization process is a step in safeguarding that only competent and financially sound entities are allowed to provide payment services, thus safeguarding consumer interests and maintaining the integrity of the financial system.

***Criteria for Authorization:*** The RBI has established stringent criteria that entities must meet to obtain a license to operate a payment system. These criteria include the financial soundness of the applicant, the technical and managerial competence, and the infrastructure capabilities. Applicants must demonstrate their ability to comply with regulatory requirements, including data security, customer protection, and operational resilience. The RBI assesses these factors to make certain that the applicant can provide secure, effective, and reliable payment services.

***Types of Payment System Operators:*** The RBI grants licenses to several types of payment system operators, including payment aggregators, prepaid payment instrument (PPI) issuers, card networks, and payment gateways. Each category of operator has specific regulatory requirements tailored to the nature of the services provided. For example, PPI issuers must comply with guidelines related to customer KYC (Know Your Customer), transaction limits, and fund safety, while payment gateways must adhere to standards for data security and transaction processing.

***Application Process:*** The process of obtaining a license involves submitting a detailed application to the RBI, outlining the proposed business model, technical infrastructure, risk management framework, and compliance measures. The RBI conducts a thorough review of the application, including an assessment of the applicant's financial position, corporate governance, and track record. The application process may also involve on-site inspections and meetings with the applicant's management team to assess their capability and commitment to regulatory compliance.

***Approval and Compliance:*** Once the RBI grants a license, the payment system operator must adhere to ongoing compliance requirements. These include periodic reporting of financial and operational metrics, maintaining adequate capital, and adhering to prescribed transaction limits. The RBI monitors compliance through regular audits and inspections, guaranteeing that the operators maintain high standards of operation. Non-compliance with regulatory requirements can result in penalties, suspension, or revocation of the license.

### Oversight Mechanisms

In addition to licensing and authorization, the RBI implements a thorough set of oversight mechanisms to guarantee the safety, speed, and stability of payment systems. These mechanisms are designed to monitor the functioning of payment systems, identify potential risks, and implement measures to mitigate these risks. The RBI's oversight framework encompasses several areas, including risk management, operational resilience, and consumer protection.

***Risk Management:*** The RBI places major emphasis on the risk management practices of payment system operators. This includes the management of credit risk, liquidity risk, operational risk, and cybersecurity risk. Payment system operators are required to implement sturdy risk management frameworks, including the establishment of risk committees, internal controls, and audit functions. The RBI conducts regular assessments of these frameworks, securing that operators are prepared to handle a number of risk scenarios and maintain the stability of the payment system.

***Operational Resilience:*** Operational resilience is an aspect of the RBI's oversight framework. The central bank guarantees that payment system operators have strong business continuity and disaster recovery plans in place. These plans must address potential disruptions, such as cyber-attacks, technical failures, or natural disasters, and outline procedures for maintaining critical operations during such events. The RBI also mandates regular testing of these plans to secure their effectiveness.

***Cybersecurity and Data Protection:*** Given the increasing reliance on digital payment systems, cybersecurity and data protection have become central concerns for the RBI. The central bank requires payment system operators to implement stringent cybersecurity measures, including encryption, multi-factor authentication, and secure coding practices. Operators must also comply with data protection regulations, such as the localization of payment data and the protection of customer information. The RBI conducts regular audits and assessments to safeguard compliance with these requirements and to identify potential vulnerabilities.

***Consumer Protection:*** The RBI's oversight mechanisms include a strong focus on consumer protection. Payment system operators are required to provide transparent and fair services, including clear disclosure of fees, charges, and terms of service. The RBI also mandates the establishment of reliable grievance redressal mechanisms, safeguarding that consumers have access to effective channels for resolving disputes and complaints. The central bank monitors the handling of consumer complaints and takes action against operators that fail to address grievances adequately.

***Monitoring and Supervision:*** The RBI employs a combination of on-site and off-site monitoring to supervise payment system operators. On-site inspections involve visits to the operator's premises to assess compliance with regulatory requirements, review operational processes, and evaluate risk management practices. Off-site monitoring includes the analysis of periodic reports submitted by operators, such as financial statements, transaction data, and incident reports. The RBI uses these reports to identify trends, assess the overall health of the payment system, and detect early warning signs of potential issues.

***Collaboration and Coordination:*** The RBI collaborates with other regulatory and supervisory bodies, both domestically and internationally, to strengthen the oversight of payment systems. This includes coordination with entities such as the Securities and Exchange Board of India (SEBI), the Insurance Regulatory and Development Authority (IRDA), and international organizations like the Financial Stability Board (FSB) and the Basel Committee on Banking Supervision (BCBS). These collaborations help make certain a consistent and broad regulatory approach, address cross-border risks, and promote the adoption of international best practices.

***Regulatory Updates and Guidelines:*** The RBI continuously updates its regulatory framework to keep pace with technological advancements and evolving market dynamics. This includes issuing guidelines on emerging technologies, such as blockchain and distributed ledger technology (DLT), and new payment methods, such as contactless payments and tokenization. The RBI also provides guidance on the adoption of international standards, such as the ISO 20022 messaging standard for payment systems, to boost interoperability and productivity.

## 2.3.7 Licensing and Authorization Processes

The licensing and authorization processes for payment systems in India are components of the regulatory framework established by the Reserve Bank of India (RBI). These processes guarantee that entities operating in the payment ecosystem meet stringent standards for safety, security, and financial integrity. The RBI's oversight helps maintain the stability and reliability of payment systems, protecting the interests of consumers and other stakeholders. This section outlines the requirements for different payment systems and the compliance and reporting obligations they must adhere to.

### Requirements for Different Payment Systems

The RBI classifies payment systems into categories, each with specific requirements for licensing and authorization. These categories include payment gateways, prepaid payment instruments (PPIs), payment aggregators, card networks, and other specialized payment services. The requirements for each type of payment system are designed to address the unique risks and operational challenges associated with their activities.

***Payment Gateways and Payment Aggregators:*** Payment gateways and aggregators enable online transactions by providing a secure platform for the transfer of payment information between merchants and financial institutions. To operate as a payment gateway or aggregator, entities must obtain authorization from the RBI. The requirements include:

***Capital Adequacy:*** Entities must have a minimum net worth, guaranteeing they have sufficient financial resources to support their operations and manage risks.

***Security Standards:*** Compliance with data security standards, such as the Payment Card Industry Data Security Standard (PCI-DSS), is mandatory. This secures the protection of sensitive customer data during transactions.

***Technology Infrastructure:*** Entities must have solid technological infrastructure, including secure servers, encryption protocols, and fraud detection systems.

***Operational Capabilities:*** Adequate systems for transaction monitoring, dispute resolution, and customer support are required to handle the volume and complexity of transactions.

***Prepaid Payment Instruments (PPIs):*** PPIs include digital wallets, prepaid cards, and other instruments that ease the purchase of goods and services. Entities issuing PPIs must adhere to specific guidelines:

***KYC Requirements:*** Entities must implement Know Your Customer (KYC) procedures to verify the identity of customers and prevent money laundering and other illicit activities.

***Fund Security:*** Adequate measures must be in place to safeguard customer funds, including the maintenance of an escrow account where the funds are held separately from the entity's operating funds.

***Transaction Limits:*** The RBI sets limits on the maximum value of transactions that can be conducted using PPIs, depending on the level of KYC compliance achieved by the customer.

***Customer Protection:*** Clear terms and conditions, refund policies, and dispute resolution mechanisms must be provided to secure customer protection.

***Card Networks:*** Card networks, such as Visa, Mastercard, and RuPay, help card-based transactions and manage the settlement process between issuing and acquiring banks. The requirements for card networks include:

*Network Security:* Compliance with PCI-DSS and other security standards to protect cardholder data and safeguard secure transaction processing.

*Interoperability:* Card networks must make certain interoperability with other networks and payment systems to support effortless transactions across different platforms.

*Clearing and Settlement:* Sturdy systems for the clearing and settlement of transactions, securing timely and accurate processing of payments between banks.

*Specialized Payment Services:* This category includes entities providing niche payment services, such as bill payment systems, cross-border remittance services, and peer-to-peer (P2P) lending platforms. The requirements for these services vary based on their specific nature and risks. Common requirements include:

*Licensing:* Authorization from the RBI or relevant regulatory authority, depending on the scope and nature of the services offered.

*Risk Management:* Implementation of full risk management frameworks to address operational, credit, and market risks associated with the services.

*Compliance:* Adherence to applicable laws and regulations, including those related to anti-money laundering (AML) and counter-terrorism financing (CTF).

### Compliance and Reporting Obligations

Once authorized, payment system operators must comply with a range of regulatory obligations to maintain their license and operate within the legal framework. The RBI sets out these obligations to guarantee transparency, accountability, and the smooth functioning of payment systems.

*Periodic Reporting:* Authorized payment system operators are required to submit periodic reports to the RBI. These reports include financial statements, transaction volumes, and details of operational incidents. The frequency and content of these reports vary based on the type of payment system and its risk profile. The RBI uses this information to monitor the financial health of the entities and assess the stability of the payment system as a whole.

*Compliance Audits:* The RBI mandates regular compliance audits to secure that payment system operators adhere to regulatory requirements. These audits may be conducted by internal or external auditors and cover aspects of the entity's operations, including financial controls, security measures, and adherence to KYC norms. The findings of these audits must be reported to the RBI, along with any corrective actions taken by the operator.

***Data Security and Privacy:*** Data security and privacy are aspects of compliance for payment system operators. The RBI mandates the implementation of strong data protection measures, including encryption, access controls, and regular security assessments. Operators must also comply with data localization requirements, safeguarding that sensitive customer data is stored within India. Any data breaches or security incidents must be reported to the RBI immediately, along with details of the measures taken to mitigate the impact.

***Anti-Money Laundering (AML) and Counter-Terrorism Financing (CTF):*** Payment system operators must comply with AML and CTF regulations, implementing effective KYC procedures, transaction monitoring, and reporting of suspicious transactions. The RBI requires operators to have a designated compliance officer responsible for overseeing AML/CTF compliance and guaranteeing that all employees are trained on these regulations.

***Operational Resilience:*** Operators must maintain operational resilience, including business continuity and disaster recovery plans. These plans should outline procedures for maintaining critical operations during disruptions and safeguard the rapid recovery of services. The RBI may require operators to conduct regular testing of these plans and report the results.

***Changes in Ownership or Structure:*** Any considerable changes in the ownership, management, or structure of a payment system operator must be reported to the RBI. This includes mergers, acquisitions, changes in the board of directors, and alterations in the business model. The RBI assesses these changes to make certain that they do not adversely affect the operator's ability to comply with regulatory requirements or maintain financial stability.

### 2.3.8 Consumer Protection Measures

Consumer protection is a necessary aspect of the regulatory environment governing payment systems in India. The Reserve Bank of India (RBI) has implemented a complete framework to safeguard consumers' interests, securing that they receive fair treatment and that their rights are protected. The framework includes grievance redressal mechanisms and a liability framework for unauthorized transactions, among other measures. These provisions are designed to increase consumer confidence in digital payment systems and guarantee the security and reliability of transactions.

### Grievance Redressal Mechanisms

Grievance redressal mechanisms are necessary for addressing consumer complaints and resolving disputes in a timely and quick manner. The RBI mandates that all payment system operators, including banks, non-bank payment service providers, and payment aggregators, establish a strong grievance redressal system. This system is major for maintaining consumer trust and safeguarding a positive user experience.

***Establishment of Dedicated Channels:*** Operators must provide dedicated channels for consumers to lodge complaints. These channels can include customer service helplines, email support, online portals, and physical complaint boxes at bank branches. The availability of multiple channels safeguards that consumers can easily access support regardless of their preferred mode of communication.

***Designated Grievance Redressal Officers:*** Each payment system operator is required to appoint a Grievance Redressal Officer (GRO) responsible for handling consumer complaints. The GRO is tasked with overseeing the resolution process, guaranteeing that complaints are addressed promptly and fairly. The contact details of the GRO, along with the procedure for escalating unresolved complaints, must be prominently displayed on the operator's website and other communication channels.

***Timelines for Resolution:*** The RBI sets specific timelines for resolving consumer complaints. For most cases, the complaint should be resolved within a maximum of 30 days from the date of receipt. If a complaint requires more time, the consumer must be informed of the delay and provided with an expected resolution date. These timelines secure that consumers receive timely responses and that issues are not left unresolved indefinitely.

***Escalation Process:*** If a consumer is not satisfied with the resolution provided by the payment system operator, they have the right to escalate the complaint. The RBI has established an ombudsman scheme for digital transactions, providing an independent forum for resolving disputes between consumers and payment service providers. The ombudsman can issue binding decisions, securing fair and impartial resolution of complaints.

***Tracking and Monitoring:*** Payment system operators must implement systems for tracking and monitoring the status of consumer complaints. This includes maintaining a log of all complaints received, the actions taken, and the final resolution provided. The data collected from these logs is used for internal reviews and audits, helping operators identify and address systemic issues that may be causing consumer dissatisfaction.

***Public Awareness and Education:*** To improve consumer awareness, payment system operators must provide clear and concise information about the grievance redressal process. This includes educating consumers about their rights, the types of complaints that can be lodged, and the steps to follow in case of disputes. Public awareness campaigns, workshops, and informational materials are often used to educate consumers about their options for redressal.

### Liability Framework for Unauthorized Transactions

The liability framework for unauthorized transactions is a component of consumer protection in digital payment systems. It defines the responsibilities and liabilities of consumers and payment service providers in cases of unauthorized transactions. The RBI's guidelines on this matter aim to protect consumers from financial losses due to fraud, errors, or system failures, while also promoting accountability among service providers.

***Consumer Liability:*** The RBI has established clear guidelines regarding consumer liability in cases of unauthorized transactions. The liability of a consumer depends on the time taken to report the unauthorized transaction and the circumstances under which it occurred. The RBI's guidelines categorize these cases into three scenarios:

***Zero Liability:*** Consumers have zero liability if the unauthorized transaction occurs due to negligence or fraud on the part of the payment system operator or its employees, or if the transaction happens without the consumer's knowledge (e.g., due to hacking). In such cases, the consumer is not required to bear any financial loss.

***Limited Liability:*** Consumers may have limited liability if they report the unauthorized transaction within three working days of receiving the transaction alert. The extent of liability is determined based on the amount involved and the circumstances of the transaction. The RBI has set specific limits for different types of accounts (e.g., basic savings accounts, other savings accounts, prepaid payment instruments).

***Full Liability:*** Consumers may be fully liable if they fail to report the unauthorized transaction within the specified time frame or if the transaction occurs due to the consumer's negligence (e.g., sharing sensitive information like PINs or passwords). In such cases, the consumer bears the entire loss resulting from the transaction.

***Refund Process:*** In cases of unauthorized transactions, payment service providers must initiate a refund process promptly. Once the unauthorized transaction is reported, the provider is required to credit the consumer's account with the disputed amount within ten working days, pending investigation. This provisional credit guarantees that consumers are not deprived of their funds while the investigation is ongoing.

***Investigation and Resolution:*** Payment service providers must conduct a thorough investigation into the reported unauthorized transaction. The investigation involves reviewing transaction logs, security protocols, and any other relevant evidence. The provider must communicate the outcome of the investigation to the consumer within a specified time frame. If the investigation determines that the consumer is not liable, the provisional credit becomes permanent.

***Consumer Education on Safe Practices:*** To minimize the risk of unauthorized transactions, payment service providers must educate consumers on safe practices for using digital payment systems. This includes advising consumers to keep their personal information secure, use strong passwords, and avoid sharing sensitive information with unknown parties. Regular awareness campaigns, educational materials, and alerts are used to reinforce these messages.

***Technology and Security Measures:*** Payment service providers must implement advanced security measures to prevent unauthorized transactions. This includes multi-factor authentication, encryption, transaction monitoring, and fraud detection systems. Providers are also required to conduct regular security audits and assessments to identify and address vulnerabilities in their systems.

***Role of the RBI:*** The RBI helps with overseeing the implementation of the liability framework for unauthorized transactions. It monitors compliance with the guidelines, conducts audits, and takes enforcement actions against non-compliant entities. The RBI also updates the guidelines periodically to address emerging risks and technological advancements in the payment ecosystem.

## 2.4 Recent Developments

The system of digital payments in India has experienced a rapid transformation over the past decade. The country's payment systems have evolved from traditional methods to highly sophisticated and novel platforms, driven by technological advancements, regulatory support, and changing consumer behaviors. Among these developments, the introduction of the Unified Payments Interface (UPI) stands out as a game-changer, reshaping the way transactions are conducted in India. This section covers recent developments and advances in the payment systems, focusing on the introduction of UPI, its features, and the impact it has had on the Indian economy.

### 2.4.1 UPI and its Impact

The Unified Payments Interface (UPI), launched by the National Payments Corporation of India (NPCI) in 2016, represents a notable leap in the evolution of digital payment systems in India. UPI is a real-time payment system that eases instant money transfers between bank accounts through a mobile platform. It has become a foundation of India's digital payment ecosystem, offering a smooth and interoperable interface for users to transact effortlessly.

**Features of UPI:**

***Instant Money Transfer:*** UPI allows for the immediate transfer of funds between bank accounts, providing a convenient and smooth alternative to traditional banking methods.

***Interoperability:*** UPI's open architecture enables interoperability across different banks and payment service providers, making it a versatile and inclusive platform.

***Virtual Payment Address (VPA):*** Users can create a unique VPA, such as 'name@bank', eliminating the need to share sensitive information like bank account numbers or IFSC codes.

***24/7 Availability:*** UPI services are available 24/7, including weekends and holidays, safeguarding continuous access to banking services.

***Multiple Accounts and Apps:*** Users can link multiple bank accounts to a single UPI ID and use different UPI apps, providing flexibility and convenience.

The introduction of UPI marked a paradigm shift in the Indian payment field. It provided a unified platform that simplified the payment process, reduced dependency on cash, and brought millions of unbanked and underbanked individuals into the formal financial system. UPI's ease of use, security features, and widespread acceptance have made it the preferred choice for many transactions, from peer-to-peer transfers to merchant payments.

## UPI 2.0 Features

In August 2018, NPCI introduced UPI 2.0, an upgraded version of the original platform, with several improved features aimed at further improving the user experience and expanding the scope of UPI transactions. The features of UPI 2.0 include:

***Mandates and Pre-Authorized Transactions:*** UPI 2.0 introduced the concept of mandates, allowing users to pre-authorize transactions for recurring payments, such as utility bills, subscriptions, and loans. This feature enables automatic debits from the user's account on a specified date, reducing the hassle of manual payments.

***Overdraft Account Linking:*** Users can now link their overdraft accounts to UPI, providing them with the flexibility to access funds beyond their savings or current account balances. This feature is particularly beneficial for small businesses and individuals who need short-term credit.

***Invoice in the Inbox:*** UPI 2.0 allows users to view and verify invoices before making a payment, guaranteeing greater transparency and accuracy. This feature helps users confirm the transaction details and avoid errors.

***Signed Intent and QR Codes:*** UPI 2.0 introduced signed intent and QR codes, which strengthen the security of QR code-based payments. Merchants can digitally sign their QR codes, providing assurance to customers about the authenticity of the transaction.

***Single Click Two-Factor Authentication:*** To boost security and simplify the payment process, UPI 2.0 implemented single-click two-factor authentication. This feature allows users to authenticate transactions with a single click, combining security with ease of use.

***Foreign Merchant Integration:*** UPI 2.0 opened the door for foreign merchants to integrate with the UPI ecosystem, enabling cross-border transactions. This feature supports international payments, making it easier for Indian users to transact with global merchants.

***AutoPay:*** UPI 2.0 introduced the AutoPay feature, which allows users to set up recurring payments for services such as OTT subscriptions, insurance premiums, and other recurring expenses. This feature simplifies payment management and secures timely payments.

These improvements in UPI 2.0 have considerably broadened the use cases of UPI, making it a thorough platform for a broad set of financial transactions. The introduction of features like mandates, invoice verification, and overdraft account linking has made UPI more appealing to both individual users and businesses, encouraging greater adoption and usage.

## 2.4.2 Growth and Adoption Statistics

Since its inception, UPI has witnessed exponential growth, becoming one of the most widely used payment systems in India. The growth trajectory of UPI can be attributed to several factors, including its user-friendly interface, interoperability, and strong support from the government and regulatory bodies. The following statistics highlight the remarkable growth and adoption of UPI in India:

***Transaction Volume and Value:*** UPI has consistently recorded impressive transaction volumes and values. From a modest start in 2016, UPI transactions have surged, reaching billions of transactions per month. For instance, in October 2021, UPI crossed the milestone of 4 billion transactions in a single month, with a total transaction value exceeding ₹7 lakh crore. This growth demonstrates the widespread acceptance of UPI as a preferred mode of payment.

***User Base:*** The UPI platform has attracted a vast user base, with millions of individuals and businesses adopting the platform for their payment needs. The number of UPI users has grown rapidly, thanks to the proliferation of smartphones, increased internet penetration, and the availability of affordable data plans. The user-friendly nature of UPI has made it accessible to a diverse demographic, including the tech-savvy youth and older generations.

***Merchant Acceptance:*** UPI has gained marked traction among merchants, from small kirana stores to large e-commerce platforms. The low-cost and easy integration process has made UPI an attractive option for merchants, enabling them to accept digital payments without friction. The use of UPI for merchant payments has been further boosted by the government's push for digital transactions and the introduction of incentives and subsidies for merchants.

***Diverse Use Cases:*** UPI's versatility has led to its adoption across many sectors and use cases. It is widely used for peer-to-peer transfers, utility bill payments, online shopping, and even government services. The platform's ability to enable quick and secure payments has made it a popular choice for a range of transactions, from daily expenses to high-value purchases.

***Collaborations and Partnerships:*** The growth of UPI has been supported by collaborations and partnerships with several stakeholders in the financial ecosystem. Banks, fintech companies, and technology providers have partnered with NPCI to offer UPI services, contributing to the platform's widespread reach. The involvement of international players has expanded UPI's footprint, making it a global payment solution.

***Government Initiatives:*** The Indian government's initiatives to promote digital payments have was involved in the growth of UPI. The government's push for a cashless economy, demonetization, and the launch of schemes like Digital India and Jan Dhan Yojana have created a conducive environment for the adoption of digital payments. The government has also incentivized the use of UPI through cashback schemes and discounts on digital transactions.

***Security and Trust:*** UPI's reliable security features, including two-factor authentication, end-to-end encryption, and real-time transaction monitoring, have instilled trust among users. The platform's commitment to security has mitigated concerns about fraud and data breaches, encouraging more users to adopt UPI for their payment needs.

***Development and Future Prospects:*** The UPI ecosystem continues to evolve with new developments and features. The introduction of UPI 2.0 and the development of UPI Lite and UPI Lite X, which aimed to ease offline payments and through NFC, are examples of NPCI's efforts to increase the platform. Prospects for UPI include international expansion, integration with emerging technologies like blockchain, and the development of new products and services.

### 2.4.3 Contactless Payments

The advent of contactless payments has been a substantial breakthrough in digital transactions, offering a quick, convenient, and secure way to make payments. This payment method has gained traction globally, including in India, where it has been increasingly adopted across a number of sectors. Contactless payments allow users to complete transactions without physically swiping or inserting their cards, reducing the need for direct contact with payment terminals. This technology has become particularly relevant in the wake of the COVID-19 pandemic, as it minimizes physical interaction and strengthens hygiene. The following sections examine into the technologies underpinning contactless payments: Near Field Communication (NFC) and Tokenization.

## NFC Technology

Near Field Communication (NFC) technology is the basis of contactless payments. NFC is a short-range wireless communication technology that enables the exchange of data between devices over a distance of a few centimeters. It operates on radio-frequency identification (RFID) principles, allowing devices like smartphones, smartwatches, and contactless cards to communicate with payment terminals.

**Features and Benefits of NFC Technology:**

- **Convenience and Speed:** NFC technology offers unparalleled convenience and speed for making payments. Users can simply tap their NFC-enabled device or card on a compatible payment terminal to complete a transaction, eliminating the need to enter a PIN or sign a receipt for small-value payments. This tap-and-go functionality notably reduces transaction time, making it ideal for high-traffic environments like retail stores, public transportation, and food outlets.

- **Strengthened Security:** NFC payments are inherently secure due to their proximity-based nature, which reduces the risk of interception by unauthorized parties. The short-range communication safeguards that transactions can only be initiated within a few centimeters of the payment terminal. Also, NFC technology often employs additional security measures, such as secure elements (SE) in the device or SIM card, to store sensitive information securely.

- **Wide Compatibility:** NFC technology is widely compatible with devices and payment systems. Many modern smartphones and wearables come equipped with NFC capabilities, allowing users to link their bank accounts, credit/debit cards, or digital wallets for frictionless payments. NFC-enabled cards, such as contactless debit and credit cards, are increasingly issued by banks, providing consumers with multiple payment options.

- **Multi-Purpose Functionality:** Beyond payments, NFC technology supports a range of functionalities, including access control, ticketing, and data exchange. For instance, NFC can be used for contactless entry to secure buildings or events, as well as for public transportation ticketing, making it a versatile technology with broad applications.

- **Adoption in India:** In India, the adoption of NFC technology has been steadily growing, driven by the proliferation of NFC-enabled devices and the expansion of contactless payment infrastructure. Major financial institutions and payment service providers have embraced NFC, offering contactless cards and integrating the technology into their mobile banking apps. The Reserve Bank of India (RBI) has also played a supportive role by increasing the transaction limit for contactless payments, further encouraging their use.

- **COVID-19 Pandemic Impact:** The COVID-19 pandemic has accelerated the adoption of contactless payments in India. With a heightened focus on hygiene and social distancing, consumers and businesses have turned to contactless options to minimize physical contact. This shift has led to an increase in the deployment of NFC-enabled point-of-sale (POS) terminals across the country, making contactless payments more accessible.

## 2.4.4 Tokenization

Tokenization is a critical technology that boosts the security of contactless payments. It involves replacing sensitive payment information, such as a card number, with a unique identifier known as a "token." This token is used to process transactions, while the actual payment details are securely stored and protected. Tokenization reduces the risk of fraud and data breaches, as the token itself is useless to hackers without the original payment information.

**Features and Benefits of Tokenization:**

***Boosted Security:*** Tokenization markedly increases the security of digital transactions by masking the actual payment details. Even if a token is intercepted during a transaction, it cannot be used to access the cardholder's information. This makes tokenized transactions less vulnerable to fraud and data breaches.

***Dynamic Token Generation:*** Tokens are typically generated dynamically for each transaction, meaning that the same token cannot be reused for another transaction. This dynamic nature further strengthens security, as it prevents the reuse of tokens in fraudulent activities.

***Ease of Use:*** Tokenization smoothly integrates into the payment process, providing a frictionless experience for users. Consumers can continue to use their devices or cards as usual, with the tokenization process occurring behind the scenes. This guarantees that security measures do not compromise the convenience of contactless payments.

***Broad Application:*** Tokenization is used across payment methods, including NFC-based contactless payments, in-app purchases, and online transactions. It is compatible with digital wallets, mobile banking apps, and payment platforms, making it a versatile security solution.

***Compliance and Standards:*** Tokenization helps businesses comply with regulatory standards, such as the Payment Card Industry Data Security Standard (PCI DSS), which mandates the protection of cardholder data. By implementing tokenization, businesses can reduce their PCI DSS scope and minimize the risks associated with storing sensitive payment information.

***Adoption in India:*** In India, tokenization has been widely adopted by financial institutions, payment processors, and technology providers. Major digital wallets and payment platforms, such as Google Pay, PhonePe, and Paytm, use tokenization to secure transactions. The RBI has also supported tokenization initiatives, issuing guidelines that promote the adoption of secure payment technologies.

***Future Prospects:*** The future of tokenization in India looks promising, with ongoing developments in digital payments and increasing awareness of data security. As contactless payments continue to gain traction, tokenization will factor into securing the safety and security of transactions. The expansion of tokenization to new payment methods and technologies, such as Internet of Things (IoT) devices and wearables, is expected to further improve its adoption.

### 2.4.5 QR Code-based Payments

QR code-based payments have emerged as a popular and convenient method for conducting digital transactions in India. Quick Response (QR) codes are two-dimensional barcodes that store information in a matrix of black and white squares. They can be scanned using a smartphone camera, allowing for quick access to information or, in the case of payments, easing the transfer of funds. QR code-based payments have gained major traction in India due to their simplicity, cost-effectiveness, and widespread adoption across many sectors, from small street vendors to large retail chains. This payment method eliminates the need for physical cards or cash, enabling effortless and secure transactions with minimal infrastructure requirements. In this section, we explore the role of Bharat QR and interoperable QR codes in India's digital payment sector.

### *Bharat QR*

Bharat QR is an interoperable QR code payment system launched by the National Payments Corporation of India (NPCI) in collaboration with major card networks such as Visa, Mastercard, and RuPay. It was introduced as a unified QR code solution to standardize the diverse QR code payment ecosystem in India. Prior to Bharat QR, different payment providers had their proprietary QR codes, causing fragmentation and confusion among merchants and consumers. Bharat QR addresses this issue by providing a single QR code that can be used by all participating banks and payment networks.

### *Interoperable QR Codes*

Interoperable QR codes are a component of India's digital payment infrastructure, designed to strengthen the convenience and accessibility of QR code-based payments. Unlike proprietary QR codes that are limited to specific payment providers, interoperable QR codes can be scanned and used by multiple payment apps and platforms, regardless of the issuer. This interoperability promotes a more inclusive payment ecosystem, where consumers and merchants can transact without friction across different payment networks.

**Features and Benefits of Interoperable QR Codes:**

- **Universal Acceptance:** Interoperable QR codes are universally accepted across several payment platforms, including UPI-based apps, mobile wallets, and banking apps. This means that consumers can use their preferred payment app to scan the same QR code and make payments, regardless of the app or platform used by the merchant. This universal acceptance simplifies the payment process and eliminates the need for multiple QR codes.

- **Improved Convenience:** For consumers, interoperable QR codes offer strengthened convenience, as they can make payments without worrying about compatibility issues. They can simply scan the QR code with their chosen app and complete the transaction. This convenience is particularly beneficial in a country like India, where all sorts of payment apps and platforms are available.

- **Improved Merchant Experience:** Merchants benefit greatly from interoperable QR codes, as they only need to display one QR code to accept payments from a number of payment apps. This reduces the complexity and clutter at the point of sale and speeds up the payment process. Merchants also have the flexibility to choose the payment provider or bank that offers the best terms and services, without being tied to a specific QR code issuer.

- **Increased Payment Options:** Interoperable QR codes support a variety of payment methods, including bank transfers, mobile wallets, and card payments. This versatility allows consumers to use different funding sources, depending on their preferences and the availability of funds. For instance, a consumer can use a UPI app to pay directly from their bank account or use a mobile wallet linked to a credit card.

- **Security and Compliance:** Interoperable QR codes adhere to stringent security standards set by regulatory authorities and payment networks. They incorporate security features such as encryption, tokenization, and two-factor authentication to safeguard transactions. Also, these QR codes comply with the regulatory guidelines issued by the Reserve Bank of India (RBI) and the NPCI, safeguarding a secure and reliable payment experience.

- **Facilitation of Digital Payments:** The widespread adoption of interoperable QR codes has facilitated the growth of digital payments in India. By providing a simple and accessible payment solution, interoperable QR codes have encouraged more consumers and businesses to embrace digital transactions. This shift has been instrumental in advancing the country's digital economy and promoting financial inclusion.

- **Support for Government Initiatives:** Interoperable QR codes align with the Indian government's initiatives to promote digital payments and reduce the reliance on cash. Programs such as the Digital India campaign and the BHIM (Bharat Interface for Money) app have emphasized the importance of interoperable solutions in achieving a cashless economy. By supporting these initiatives, interoperable QR codes contribute to the broader goal of financial inclusion and economic growth.

## 2.4.6 Developments in Cross-border Payments

In the context of an increasingly interconnected global economy, cross-border payments contribute to supporting international trade, investment, and remittances. India's engagement with the global financial system has led to considerable advancements in cross-border payment mechanisms. This section looks at development and adoption of principal technologies and systems, focusing on the introduction of SWIFT gpi and bilateral arrangements with other countries.

### *SWIFT*

The Society for Worldwide Interbank Financial Telecommunication, commonly known as SWIFT, is a global cooperative network that enables secure and standardized communication between financial institutions. Established in 1973, SWIFT provides a reliable messaging system that enables banks and other financial entities to exchange information regarding financial transactions. The network is headquartered in Belgium and connects over 11,000 institutions across more than 200 countries and territories.

SWIFT does not move money itself but transmits payment instructions between banks using standardized codes, such as the SWIFT code or BIC (Bank Identifier Code). These codes safeguard the accuracy and effectiveness of international transactions, making SWIFT a bedrock of global banking infrastructure. The messages sent through the SWIFT network include details of the sender, receiver, and the nature of the transaction, guaranteeing secure and accurate communication.

The SWIFT code format is a standardized alphanumeric code used to identify banks and financial institutions worldwide. It consists of 8 to 11 characters, structured as follows:

1. **Bank Code**: The first four characters, usually letters, represent the bank itself.

2. **Country Code**: The next two characters, also letters, represent the country in which the bank is located.

3. **Location Code**: The following two characters, which can be letters or numbers, indicate the location of the bank's head office.

4. **Branch Code**: The last three characters, optional, specify a particular branch of the bank. If not used, it is often replaced with "XXX".

For example, the SWIFT code UNCRITMMXXX breaks down as follows:

- UNCR is the bank code for UniCredit.
- IT is the country code for Italy.
- MM is the location code for Milan.
- XXX indicates that no specific branch code is used, so the transfer will go to the bank's main office in Milan

**SWIFT GPI (Global Payments Advance):**

In response to the growing demand for faster, more transparent, and traceable cross-border payments, SWIFT introduced the Global Payments Development (gpi) service. Launched in 2017, SWIFT gpi is designed to address the limitations of traditional cross-border payment systems, which often involve delays, lack of transparency, and complex fee structures.

**Features and Benefits of SWIFT gpi:**

- **Faster Transaction Speeds:** One of the advantages of SWIFT gpi is its ability to expedite cross-border payments. Traditional SWIFT transactions could take several days to settle due to the involvement of multiple correspondent banks. In contrast, SWIFT gpi enables near real-time processing, with most transactions being completed within minutes or a few hours. This rapid settlement is particularly beneficial for businesses engaged in international trade, as it improves liquidity and reduces the uncertainty associated with payment delays.

- **Transparency and Traceability:** SWIFT gpi introduces unprecedented transparency into the cross-border payment process. Each transaction is assigned a unique end-to-end transaction reference (UETR), allowing both the sender and recipient to track the payment's progress in real time. This transparency extends to fees and charges, enabling the sender to know the exact amount that will be received by the beneficiary. The ability to trace payments at every stage improves customer confidence and reduces the risk of disputes.

- **Full Fee Transparency:** Unlike traditional payment methods, where fees can be opaque and unpredictable, SWIFT gpi provides full transparency regarding the costs associated with a transaction. All charges, including those levied by intermediary banks, are disclosed upfront. This clarity helps businesses and individuals plan their finances more effectively, avoiding unexpected deductions and securing that the intended amount reaches the recipient.

- **Improved Customer Experience:** The improvements brought by SWIFT gpi considerably improve the customer experience. By offering faster transactions, greater transparency, and the ability to track payments in real time, SWIFT gpi addresses many of the pain points associated with traditional cross-border payments. Financial institutions using SWIFT gpi can offer their clients a superior service, thereby strengthening customer satisfaction and loyalty.

- **Compliance and Security:** SWIFT gpi adheres to stringent compliance and security standards, safeguarding that all transactions are conducted securely and in accordance with regulatory requirements. The network's solid security infrastructure protects against fraud and cyber threats, making it a trusted platform for international payments. The ability to trace transactions helps in complying with anti-money laundering (AML) and counter-terrorism financing (CTF) regulations.

- **Adoption and Integration:** SWIFT gpi has seen widespread adoption among banks and financial institutions globally. In India, several major banks have integrated SWIFT gpi into their systems, offering boosted cross-border payment services to their customers. This adoption is driven by India's growing international trade and investment activities and the increasing demand for effective and transparent payment solutions. The adoption of SWIFT gpi in India has simplified the cross-border payment process, making it more quick and customer-friendly.

### *Bilateral Arrangements with Other Countries*

In addition to using global platforms like SWIFT gpi, India has pursued bilateral arrangements with other countries to help cross-border payments. These arrangements aim to simplify payment processes, reduce costs, and boost the speed of international transactions. Bilateral arrangements often involve agreements between central banks or financial regulators to establish frameworks for the smooth transfer of funds and to address regulatory challenges.

### Aspects of Bilateral Arrangements:

- **Smooth Payment Channels:** Bilateral arrangements often include the establishment of direct payment channels between countries, bypassing the need for multiple intermediaries. This speeding up can reduce the time and cost associated with cross-border payments. For instance, India has explored direct payment mechanisms with countries in the Middle East and Southeast Asia, regions with notable trade and diaspora connections.

- **Local Currency Settlements:** Another aspect of bilateral arrangements is the promotion of local currency settlements. By allowing transactions to be settled in the local currencies of the participating countries, these arrangements reduce the reliance on third-party currencies, such as the US dollar. This not only mitigates exchange rate risk but also reduces transaction costs. India has pursued such arrangements with countries like Russia and Iran, enabling trade despite international sanctions and currency fluctuations.

- **Regulatory Cooperation:** Bilateral arrangements often involve cooperation between the regulatory authorities of the participating countries. This cooperation can include harmonizing regulatory standards, sharing information, and collaborating on anti-money laundering (AML) and counter-terrorism financing (CTF) measures. Such regulatory cooperation secures the smooth functioning of cross-border payment systems and strengthens the security and integrity of transactions.

- **Technological Integration:** Technological integration is a component of bilateral arrangements. Countries may agree on the use of specific payment technologies or platforms to support cross-border transactions. For example, India has explored integrating its Unified Payments Interface (UPI) with payment systems in neighboring countries to enable frictionless cross-border payments. Such integrations can promote interoperability and expand the reach of digital payment solutions.

- **Trade Facilitation:** Bilateral payment arrangements are often linked to broader trade facilitation initiatives. By simplifying payment processes, these arrangements can increase the ease of doing business and promote trade between the participating countries. For instance, India's bilateral payment arrangements with countries in Africa and Latin America aim to boost exports of goods and services, particularly in sectors like pharmaceuticals, information technology, and textiles.

- **Remittance Flows:** Bilateral arrangements also are involved in easing remittance flows. India, being one of the largest recipients of remittances globally, has a vested interest in guaranteeing the smooth and cost-effective transfer of funds from its diaspora.

## Chapter 3
# Traditional Banking Services

## 3.1 Deposits and Accounts

The foundation of banking is built upon the deposit and account services offered by financial institutions. These services not only provide customers with a secure place to store their money but also offer a range of financial products that cater to different savings and transaction needs. In the Indian context, banks have developed a wide array of deposit accounts, each designed with specific features and benefits to meet the diverse requirements of individuals, businesses, and institutions. This section looks at types of deposit accounts available in India, exploring their characteristics, eligibility criteria, and other pertinent details.

### 3.1.1 Types of Deposit Accounts

Deposit accounts are broadly categorized under demand deposits as savings accounts, current accounts, and term deposits as fixed deposits, and recurring deposits. Each of these accounts serves a distinct purpose, catering to different financial needs and preferences.

***Savings Accounts***

Savings accounts are one of the most popular and widely used types of deposit accounts in India. They are designed to encourage individuals to save money while providing easy access to funds when needed. Savings accounts are typically opened by individuals for personal use, and they offer a safe place to keep money with the added benefit of earning interest.

**Features and Eligibility**

Savings accounts are characterized by several features. They offer liquidity, allowing account holders to deposit and withdraw funds at their convenience. Most savings accounts come with a passbook or a digital statement, which helps customers keep track of their transactions. Many banks provide an ATM/debit card linked to the savings account, enabling cash withdrawals, point-of-sale transactions, and online payments.

Eligibility for opening a savings account varies slightly among banks, but the general criteria include being a resident of India, having valid identification, and meeting the minimum age requirement (typically 18 years). Minors can also open savings accounts, usually with a parent or guardian as a joint account holder, which helps inculcate saving habits from a young age.

**Interest Calculation Methods**

The interest on savings accounts is calculated on a daily basis and credited quarterly or half-yearly, depending on the bank's policy. The interest rate on savings accounts can vary across banks and may also differ based on the balance maintained. Some banks offer higher interest rates for larger balances or for specific account categories. The interest earned on savings accounts is subject to tax under the Income Tax Act, but individuals can claim deductions under Section 80TTA for interest earned up to ₹10,000 per financial year.

**Minimum Balance Requirements**

Minimum balance requirements for savings accounts vary depending on the bank and the type of savings account. Some banks offer zero-balance accounts, especially for basic savings accounts or salary accounts, while others may require a minimum balance ranging from a few hundred to several thousand rupees. Failure to maintain the required minimum balance often results in penalty charges, which can vary based on the shortfall amount and the bank's policy.

*Current Accounts*

Current accounts are designed primarily for business transactions and are best suited for individuals and entities that require frequent access to funds. Unlike savings accounts, current accounts do not offer interest on the deposited amount. Instead, they focus on providing liquidity and supporting high-volume transactions.

**Target Customers**

Current accounts are typically targeted at businesses, companies, partnerships, sole proprietorships, public and private sector organizations, and other entities involved in commercial activities. These accounts are important for managing day-to-day business operations, as they allow for an unlimited number of transactions without restrictions on withdrawals or deposits.

**Overdraft Facilities**

One of the features of current accounts is the availability of overdraft facilities. An overdraft allows account holders to withdraw more money than is currently available in their account, up to a pre-approved limit. This facility provides businesses with the flexibility to manage cash flow issues, cover short-term expenses, or take advantage of investment opportunities. The overdraft limit and interest rates are determined by the bank based on the account holder's creditworthiness and the nature of their business.

## Transaction Limits

While current accounts do not have a limit on the number of transactions, some banks may impose limits on the transaction amount per day, particularly for cash withdrawals. These limits are typically higher than those for savings accounts, reflecting the account's intended use for business purposes. Also, banks may charge fees for certain services, such as cash handling, cheque book issuance, and account maintenance.

### *Fixed Deposits*

Fixed deposits (FDs) are a popular investment option offered by banks, providing a safe and stable way to grow savings. FDs involve depositing a lump sum amount with the bank for a fixed period, during which the deposited amount earns interest at a predetermined rate. The interest rate on FDs is generally higher than that offered on savings accounts, making them an attractive option for individuals looking to earn a stable return on their savings.

## Tenure Options

Fixed deposits offer a range of tenure options, typically ranging from 7 days to 10 years. The depositor can choose the tenure based on their financial goals and liquidity requirements. The interest rate on FDs varies depending on the tenure, with longer tenures generally offering higher interest rates. Banks also provide the option to reinvest the interest earned, compounding it over the investment period, or to receive it at regular intervals.

## Interest Rate Structures

The interest rate on fixed deposits is determined by the bank and may vary based on factors such as the deposit amount, tenure, and the prevailing market conditions. Banks may offer special interest rates for senior citizens, usually 0.25% to 0.50% higher than the standard rates. The interest earned on FDs is taxable, and tax is deducted at source (TDS) if the interest income exceeds a certain threshold in a financial year. However, individuals can submit Form 15G/15H to the bank to avoid TDS if their total income is below the taxable limit.

## Premature Withdrawal Penalties

Fixed deposits are meant to be held until maturity, but banks do provide the option for premature withdrawal. However, this comes with certain penalties. The penalty for premature withdrawal typically involves a reduction in the interest rate, usually by 0.5% to 1%, depending on the bank's policy. The effective interest rate for the period the deposit was actually held may also be lower than the original rate promised. Some banks may waive the penalty for certain customers or account types, but it's generally advisable to hold the FD until maturity to maximize returns.

## *Recurring Deposits*

Recurring deposits (RDs) are another popular form of investment offered by banks, allowing individuals to deposit a fixed amount regularly over a specified period. RDs are ideal for individuals who wish to build a corpus through small, regular savings. The account holder deposits a predetermined amount every month, which earns interest at a fixed rate.

## Monthly Installment Options

Recurring deposits require the account holder to deposit a fixed amount on a monthly basis. The minimum and maximum deposit amounts vary across banks, but they generally start from as low as ₹100. The tenure for RDs ranges from 6 months to 10 years, allowing customers to choose a period that aligns with their financial goals. The interest rate on RDs is similar to that of fixed deposits for the same tenure.

## Maturity Calculations

At the end of the chosen tenure, the total amount deposited, along with the interest earned, is paid out to the account holder. The maturity amount of a RD is calculated based on the principal deposited and the interest accrued over the investment period. The interest is compounded quarterly, adding to the overall returns. Similar to FDs, the interest earned on RDs is taxable, and TDS is applicable if the interest income exceeds the specified threshold.

While discussing about international remittances we also come across these typical accounts:

## Nostro and Vostro Accounts

A **Nostro account** is an account that a bank holds in a foreign country in the currency of that country. The term "Nostro" is derived from the Latin word for "ours," indicating that it is "our account with you." It is used by a domestic bank to enable transactions in the foreign currency of the country where the account is held.

Example: An Indian bank holds a USD account with a bank in the United States to manage its dollar-denominated transactions.

A **Vostro account,** on the other hand, is the opposite. It is an account that a foreign bank holds with a domestic bank in the domestic currency. The term "Vostro" means "yours" in Latin, indicating that it is "your account with us."

Example: A US bank holds a rupee account with an Indian bank to manage its transactions in Indian Rupees.

## 3.1.2 Account Opening Procedures

The account opening process in Indian banks involves several steps, with an emphasis on compliance, security, and customer convenience. The procedures are designed to make certain that banks can establish the identity of their customers, verify their addresses, and maintain accurate records, all while adhering to regulatory standards. This section outlines the needed components of the account opening process, including Know Your Customer (KYC) norms, documentation requirements, and the evolving environment of electronic and video KYC methods.

### KYC Norms

Know Your Customer (KYC) norms are a set of guidelines implemented by banks to verify the identity and address of their customers. These norms are mandated by the Reserve Bank of India (RBI) and aim to prevent money laundering, terrorist financing, and other illegal activities. KYC compliance is an aspect of the account opening process, as it helps maintain the integrity and security of the banking system.

*Acceptable Identity Proofs*

To comply with KYC norms, customers are required to provide valid identity proofs during the account opening process. The RBI has specified a list of acceptable identity documents, which typically include:

*Aadhaar Card:* A unique identification number issued by the Unique Identification Authority of India (UIDAI).

*Passport:* An official travel document issued by the government, serving as proof of identity and citizenship.

*Voter ID Card:* A photo identity card issued by the Election Commission of India.

**PAN Card:** A Permanent Account Number card issued by the Income Tax Department.

**Driving License:** An official document permitting the holder to operate a vehicle.

These documents must be current and valid at the time of submission. In cases where the customer's photograph is not available on the document, a recent passport-sized photograph may also be required.

### Address Verification Process

In addition to identity proof, customers must provide proof of address to comply with KYC norms. Acceptable address proofs may include:

**Utility Bills:** Recent bills for electricity, water, gas, or telephone services, typically not older than three months.

**Bank Statement:** A recent bank account statement showing the customer's address.

**Rent Agreement:** A registered lease or rental agreement for the customer's residence.

**Aadhaar Card:** If the Aadhaar card contains the customer's current address, it can serve as both identity and address proof.

**Passport:** If it includes the current address, it can also serve as address proof.

Banks may conduct additional verification through physical visits or contacting the customer at the provided address. This safeguards the accuracy of the address information and helps in maintaining updated records.

### Documentation Requirements

Apart from identity and address proofs, customers may need to submit additional documents depending on the type of account and the bank's policies. These documents typically include:

**Account Opening Form:** A standard form provided by the bank, requiring thecustomer's personal and financial details, such as name, date of birth, contact information, occupation, and income.

**Photographs:** Passport-sized photographs as per the bank's requirement.

**PAN Card:** A mandatory requirement for most account types, as it helps in tax reporting and compliance.

**Introduction or Reference:** In some cases, banks may require an introduction from an existing account holder or a reference letter from a recognized individual or organization.

***Signature Specimen:*** A sample of the customer's signature for verification purposes.

For joint accounts, all account holders must provide the required documents. For accounts opened by minors, guardians must provide their documents along with the minor's birth certificate.

### e-KYC and Video KYC

In recent years, banks have increasingly adopted electronic methods for KYC compliance, making the account opening process more smooth and convenient. The introduction of e-KYC and video KYC has revolutionized the traditional account opening procedures, allowing for faster and paperless verification.

***e-KYC:*** Electronic KYC (e-KYC) is a process where a customer's identity and address are verified electronically using their Aadhaar number. With the customer's consent, banks can access their Aadhaar details, including demographic information and photograph, from the UIDAI database. e-KYC offers an effortless and instant verification process, reducing the need for physical documents and in-person visits. This method is widely used for opening types of accounts, including savings, current, and digital wallets.

***Video KYC:*** Video KYC is a breakthrough in the customer onboarding process, especially useful during the COVID-19 pandemic when physical interactions were restricted. In video KYC, customers can complete the KYC process through a live video call with a bank representative. During the call, the representative verifies the customer's identity and address proofs, captures their photograph, and obtains their signature specimen. The entire process is recorded and stored as part of the bank's records.

Video KYC offers several benefits, including convenience, security, and compliance with social distancing norms. It also reduces the time and cost associated with traditional KYC methods. The RBI has provided guidelines to guarantee that video KYC is conducted securely, with proper encryption and data protection measures.

The account opening procedures in Indian banks have evolved notably, with a strong focus on compliance, security, and customer convenience. KYC norms help with securing that banks have accurate and up-to-date information about their customers, thereby preventing fraudulent activities and maintaining the integrity of the financial system. The adoption of e-KYC and video KYC has further simplified the process, offering a quick and effective way to verify customer identities and open accounts.

### 3.1.3 Interest Rates and Calculations

Interest rates and their calculations are fundamental aspects of banking, directly impacting the returns customers receive on their deposits and the cost of borrowing. Banks offer many types of accounts and deposit products, each with distinct interest rate structures and calculation methods. This section explores how interest is computed on savings accounts and term deposits, highlighting the factors that influence these rates and the methodologies employed by banks.

*Savings Account Interest Computation*

Savings accounts are one of the most common types of deposit accounts offered by banks. They provide a safe place for customers to store their money while earning a modest return in the form of interest. The interest rate on savings accounts is generally lower compared to other deposit products, as these accounts are highly liquid, allowing customers to withdraw funds at any time.

**Interest Rate Structure:**

*Variable Rates:* Savings account interest rates are typically variable, meaning they can change based on the bank's policy, market conditions, and regulatory directives. In India, the Reserve Bank of India (RBI) deregulated savings account interest rates in 2011, allowing banks to set their own rates. As a result, rates can vary markedly between banks.

*Daily Balance Method:* The interest on savings accounts is usually calculated using the daily balance method. Under this method, interest is computed on the closing balance of the account for each day.

*Quarterly or Half-Yearly Payouts:* Although interest is calculated daily, it is typically credited to the account on a quarterly or half-yearly basis. This means that the total interest accrued over the period is added to the account balance at the end of each quarter or half-year.

*Term Deposit Interest Calculations*

Term deposits, also known as fixed deposits (FDs), are a popular investment option offered by banks. Customers deposit a lump sum amount for a fixed tenure, earning a higher interest rate compared to savings accounts.

The interest rate on term deposits depends on several factors, including the tenure of the deposit, the deposit amount, and the bank's policies.

**Interest Rate Structure:**

*Fixed Rates:* Unlike savings accounts, term deposits generally offer fixed interest rates for the entire tenure. This provides customers with the certainty of returns, as the interest rate agreed upon at the time of opening the FD remains unchanged, regardless of market fluctuations.

*Cumulative vs. Non-Cumulative:* Term deposits can be cumulative or non-cumulative, affecting how interest is paid:

- **Cumulative:** In cumulative FDs, interest is compounded periodically (quarterly, half-yearly, or annually) and paid along with the principal at maturity. This option allows for the reinvestment of interest, leading to a higher effective yield due to compounding.
- **Non-Cumulative:** In non-cumulative FDs, interest is paid out periodically (monthly, quarterly, half-yearly, or annually) to the customer. This option is suitable for those seeking regular income rather than capital appreciation.

**Interest Calculation:**

- **Simple Interest:** For non-cumulative term deposits with simple interest.
- **Compound Interest:** For cumulative term deposits, interest is compounded periodically.

*Factors Influencing Interest Rates:*

*Economic Conditions:* Inflation, economic growth, and RBI's monetary policy decisions greatly impact the interest rates offered by banks.

*Market Competition:* Banks may adjust interest rates to attract more customers or match the rates offered by competitors.

*Deposit Amount and Tenure:* Generally, higher deposit amounts and longer tenures attract higher interest rates, providing better returns to customers.

*Customer Category:* Special interest rates may be offered to specific customer categories, such as senior citizens, who often receive higher rates on term deposits.

Understanding the intricacies of interest rates and their calculations is necessary for customers when choosing between different deposit products. Savings accounts offer flexibility and liquidity, while term deposits provide higher returns through fixed and predictable interest payments. The choice between simple and compound interest, cumulative and non-cumulative options, and the tenure of deposits can considerably affect the returns. As banks continue to innovate and offer varied deposit products, customers must stay informed and select options that align with their financial goals and risk tolerance.

### 3.1.4 Deposit Insurance

Deposit insurance is an aspect of the banking system, providing a safety net for depositors in the event of a bank failure. It aims to maintain public confidence in the banking system and protect small depositors from losing their savings. In India, the Deposit Insurance and Credit Guarantee Corporation (DICGC) factors into this domain. This section turns to role of the DICGC, the coverage limits of deposit insurance, and the types of deposits covered under this scheme.

**Role of Deposit Insurance and Credit Guarantee Corporation (DICGC)**

The DICGC, a wholly-owned subsidiary of the Reserve Bank of India (RBI), was established in 1978 under the Deposit Insurance and Credit Guarantee Corporation Act, 1961. The objective of the DICGC is to provide insurance protection to depositors' funds in banks, safeguarding that even in the event of a bank failure, depositors receive a portion of their savings back. This mechanism is critical in promoting stability and trust in the banking sector.

The DICGC's role extends beyond merely insuring deposits. It also aims to promote the orderly growth of the banking system, safeguard the interests of small depositors, and contribute to the financial stability of the country. The corporation insures deposits held in all commercial banks, including branches of foreign banks operating in India, regional rural banks (RRBs), and cooperative banks. The process of deposit insurance is relatively straightforward. Banks are required to pay a premium to the DICGC, which is calculated as a percentage of their assessable deposits. In return, the DICGC provides insurance coverage for deposits up to a specified limit. In the event of a bank failure, the DICGC reimburses the insured amount to the depositors, guaranteeing they do not lose their hard-earned savings entirely.

The DICGC operates under a well-defined framework that includes the identification of insured banks, assessment of insurance premiums, and settlement of claims. The corporation regularly reviews and updates its policies to align with the evolving needs of the banking sector and depositors. This proactive approach guarantees that the deposit insurance system remains sturdy and responsive to changes in the financial system.

## Coverage Limits

One of the aspects of deposit insurance is the coverage limit, which determines the maximum amount insured per depositor per bank. The coverage limit is a factor as it directly impacts the extent of protection offered to depositors. In India, the DICGC has periodically revised the coverage limits to keep pace with economic changes and the rising income levels of the population.

As of the most recent revision, the coverage limit for deposit insurance in India is INR 5 lakh per depositor per bank. This limit applies to the total of all deposits held by a depositor in a bank, including savings accounts, fixed deposits, recurring deposits, and other types of deposits. The increase in the coverage limit, from INR 1 lakh to INR 5 lakh, was implemented in February 2020, marking a substantial improvement in depositor protection. The decision to raise the coverage limit was driven by several factors. Firstly, it aimed to provide better security to depositors, especially in the wake of banking sector challenges and the failure of a few cooperative banks. Secondly, the increased limit was intended to encourage more people to deposit their savings in banks, thereby promoting financial inclusion. Lastly, it aligned with international standards, where many countries offer deposit insurance coverage at similar or higher levels.

The coverage limit is central for small depositors, as it provides them with a safety net and secures that they receive a substantial portion of their funds back in case of a bank failure. For larger depositors, the limit serves as a reminder to diversify their deposits across multiple banks to maximize their insurance coverage.

### *Types of Deposits Covered*

The DICGC provides insurance coverage for a span of deposit accounts, securing that a number of types of deposits are protected under the scheme. This broad coverage is necessary to safeguard the interests of all categories of depositors, from individual savers to businesses and institutions.

- **Savings Accounts:** Savings accounts are one of the most common types of deposit accounts, offering liquidity and moderate interest rates. The DICGC insures the balances held in these accounts, providing depositors with the assurance that their money is safe even if the bank fails.

- ○ **Fixed Deposits:** Fixed deposits, also known as term deposits, are popular investment options that offer higher interest rates than savings accounts. These deposits are held for a fixed tenure and can be cumulative or non-cumulative. The DICGC insures the principal and interest accrued on fixed deposits up to the coverage limit.

- ○ **Recurring Deposits:** Recurring deposits allow depositors to save a fixed amount regularly over a specified period, earning interest similar to fixed deposits. These accounts are also covered under the DICGC insurance scheme, safeguarding that the total amount deposited, along with the interest earned, is protected.

- ○ **Current Accounts:** Current accounts are primarily used by businesses and professionals for day-to-day transactions. These accounts typically do not earn interest but offer high liquidity. The DICGC insures the balances held in current accounts, providing businesses with the confidence to maintain operational funds in banks.

- ○ **Other Deposits:** The DICGC insurance scheme also covers other types of deposits, such as call deposits, recurring deposits, and time liabilities. This broad coverage safeguards that all forms of deposits, regardless of their nature or purpose, are protected under the insurance scheme.

the DICGC insurance coverage is applicable on a per depositor per bank basis. This means that if a depositor holds accounts in multiple branches of the same bank, the insurance coverage limit applies to the total amount held across all branches. However, if the depositor holds accounts in different banks, each account is insured separately up to the coverage limit.

## 3.2 Loans and Advances

Within banking, loans and advances are fundamental financial services provided to individuals, businesses, and organizations to meet their financial needs. These form assets for the banks whereas deposits indicate liabilities. These facilities allow borrowers to access funds for a range of purposes, including personal expenses, business investments, and other financial commitments. The banking sector offers a diverse array of loan products tailored to meet the specific needs of borrowers. We now examine the types of loans, focusing on personal loans, and covers eligibility criteria, documentation requirements, and interest rate structures.

## 3.2.1 Types of Loans

Loans can be broadly categorized into several types based on their purpose, tenure, and security. The categories include personal loans, home loans, vehicle loans, education loans, business loans, and secured loans. Each type of loan serves a distinct purpose and comes with specific features, benefits, and terms. For the purpose of this discussion, we will focus on personal loans, which are among the most commonly availed loan products in the banking sector.

### *Personal Loans*

Personal loans are unsecured loans offered by banks and financial institutions to individuals for personal expenses. These loans do not require collateral, which is an asset or property pledged by a borrower to secure a loan, which can be seized by the lender if the borrower defaults., making them accessible to a broad range of customers. Personal loans are versatile and can be used for a variety of purposes, including medical expenses, home renovations, travel, weddings, and debt consolidation. Given their unsecured nature, personal loans typically come with higher interest rates compared to secured loans.

### Eligibility Criteria

Eligibility criteria for personal loans vary across banks and financial institutions. However, there are some common factors that lenders consider when evaluating loan applications. These include:

*Income Level:* Lenders assess the applicant's income level to determine their repayment capacity. A steady and sufficient income is necessary for loan approval. Employed individuals, self-employed professionals, and business owners may have different income thresholds and documentation requirements.

*Credit Score:* A good credit score is a factor in determining loan eligibility. It reflects the applicant's creditworthiness and repayment history. A higher credit score increases the chances of loan approval and may also result in favorable interest rates.

***Employment Status:*** Lenders prefer applicants with stable employment. For salaried individuals, a minimum period of employment with the current employer may be required. Self-employed individuals may need to demonstrate a steady income stream over a specific period.

***Age:*** The applicant's age is another important criterion. Most banks have a minimum and maximum age limit for personal loan applicants, typically ranging from 21 to 60 years.

***Debt-to-Income Ratio:*** Lenders assess the applicant's existing debt obligations relative to their income. A lower debt-to-income ratio indicates a better capacity to repay the loan.

***Residency Status:*** Applicants must provide proof of residence. Some banks may require the applicant to have resided at the current address for a minimum period.

## Documentation Requirements

When applying for a personal loan, borrowers must submit specific documents to support their application. These documents help the lender verify the applicant's identity, income, and creditworthiness. The required documents typically include:

***Identity Proof:*** Valid identity proof documents include a passport, Aadhaar card, PAN card, voter ID, or driving license.

***Address Proof:*** Acceptable address proof documents include utility bills (electricity, water, gas), rental agreement, passport, Aadhaar card, or driving license.

***Income Proof:*** For salaried individuals, income proof may include recent salary slips, Form 16, and bank statements. For self-employed individuals, income tax returns, bank statements, and audited financial statements may be required.

***Employment Proof:*** A letter from the employer, employment contract, or business registration certificate may serve as proof of employment.

***Photographs:*** Recent passport-sized photographs may be required.

***Loan Application Form:*** A duly filled and signed loan application form is mandatory.

Lenders may request additional documents based on the applicant's profile and loan amount. It's needed for borrowers to secure that all provided information and documents are accurate and up-to-date to avoid delays in the loan approval process.

**Interest Rate Structures**

Interest rates on personal loans vary depending on several factors, including the applicant's creditworthiness, loan amount, tenure, and prevailing market conditions. Personal loan interest rates can be fixed or floating.

- **Fixed Interest Rates:** Under a fixed interest rate structure, the interest rate remains constant throughout the loan tenure. This offers predictability and stability in monthly repayments, making it easier for borrowers to plan their finances. Fixed interest rates are ideal for borrowers who prefer a consistent repayment schedule.

- **Floating Interest Rates:** Floating interest rates are subject to change based on fluctuations in market interest rates. These rates are typically linked to a benchmark rate, such as the bank's base rate or the RBI's repo rate. While floating rates can result in lower initial interest rates, they carry the risk of increasing over time, which can affect the total cost of the loan.

- **Annual Percentage Rate (APR):** The APR represents the total cost of borrowing, including the interest rate and any additional fees or charges. It's a useful measure for comparing different loan offers, as it provides a full view of the loan's cost.

- **Interest Calculation Methods:** Interest on personal loans can be calculated using different methods, including the flat rate method and the reducing balance method. Under the flat rate method, interest is calculated on the entire loan amount throughout the tenure, resulting in higher total interest payments. The reducing balance method calculates interest on the outstanding loan amount, leading to lower interest payments over time as the principal reduces.

Personal loans offer flexible repayment options, typically ranging from one to five years. Borrowers can choose a tenure based on their repayment capacity and financial goals. However, longer tenures may result in higher total interest payments, even if the monthly instalments are lower.

*Home Loans*

Home loans are financial products offered by banks and financial institutions to individuals for purchasing, constructing, or renovating a residential property. These loans are secured by the property being financed, meaning the property serves as collateral for the loan. Home loans are one of the most major financial commitments for most individuals, given the substantial amounts involved and the long repayment periods. This section explores aspects of home loans, including Loan-to-Value (LTV) ratios, repayment tenures, and the choice between fixed and floating interest rates.

## Loan-to-Value (LTV) Ratios

The Loan-to-Value (LTV) ratio is a factor in home loans, representing the percentage of the property's value that a lender is willing to finance through a loan. The LTV ratio is calculated by dividing the loan amount by the appraised value or purchase price of the property, whichever is lower. For example, if a property is valued at ₹50 lakh and the loan amount is ₹40 lakh, the LTV ratio is 80%.

LTV ratios are important because they determine the amount of down payment a borrower must make and the loan amount they can avail themselves of. In India, the Reserve Bank of India (RBI) and other regulatory bodies set guidelines for maximum LTV ratios based on the loan amount. Typically, the LTV ratio can go up to 90% for loan amounts up to ₹30 lakh, 80% for loans between ₹30 lakh and ₹75 lakh, and 75% for loans above ₹75 lakh. These ratios are subject to periodic revisions based on market conditions and regulatory considerations.

A lower LTV ratio generally implies a higher down payment from the borrower, reducing the lender's risk. Conversely, a higher LTV ratio indicates a lower down payment, potentially increasing the lender's risk. Lenders may adjust interest rates based on the LTV ratio, with higher LTV ratios possibly attracting higher interest rates due to the increased risk.

## Repayment Tenures

Repayment tenure refers to the period over which the borrower repays the home loan. The tenure can notably affect the monthly installment amount (EMI) and the total interest paid over the life of the loan. Home loan tenures in India typically range from 5 to 30 years, depending on the borrower's age, financial stability, and lender policies.

A longer repayment tenure generally results in lower EMIs, making it easier for borrowers to manage their monthly expenses. However, it also means paying more interest over the loan term, increasing the overall cost of the loan. On the other hand, a shorter tenure results in higher EMIs but reduces the total interest outgo, making the loan cheaper in the long run.

Borrowers often have the flexibility to choose the repayment tenure based on their financial situation and future income prospects. Some lenders also offer the option of prepayment, allowing borrowers to pay off their loan before the end of the tenure. While prepayment can reduce the interest burden, lenders may charge a prepayment penalty, particularly for loans with fixed interest rates.

### Fixed vs. Floating Interest Rates

When taking a home loan, borrowers can choose between fixed and floating interest rates. The choice of interest rate type can markedly impact the cost of the loan and the borrower's financial planning.

**Fixed Interest Rates**: Under a fixed interest rate home loan, the interest rate remains constant throughout the loan tenure. This provides stability and predictability in EMI payments, as borrowers know exactly how much they will pay each month. Fixed rates are ideal for borrowers who prefer a consistent repayment schedule and want to avoid the uncertainty of fluctuating interest rates. However, fixed-rate loans often come with slightly higher interest rates compared to floating rates and may include a reset clause, allowing the lender to revise the rate after a certain period.

**Floating Interest Rates**: Floating or variable interest rates fluctuate based on changes in market interest rates. These rates are typically linked to a benchmark rate, such as the RBI's repo rate or the lender's base rate. When market rates rise, the interest rate on the loan increases, leading to higher EMIs. Conversely, when market rates fall, the interest rate and EMIs decrease. Floating rates can be beneficial when interest rates are expected to decline, as borrowers can take advantage of lower rates. However, they come with the risk of rising rates, which can increase the financial burden on borrowers.

**Hybrid Interest Rates**: Some lenders offer hybrid home loan products that combine fixed and floating interest rate features. These loans start with a fixed rate for an initial period, typically 2 to 5 years, and then switch to a floating rate for the remaining tenure. Hybrid loans provide a balance between stability and flexibility, offering the benefits of both fixed and floating rates.

### *Vehicle Loans*

Vehicle loans are financial products offered by banks and non-banking financial companies (NBFCs) to help individuals purchase automobiles, including cars, motorcycles, and commercial vehicles. These loans are secured by the vehicle itself, serving as collateral until the loan is fully repaid. Vehicle loans are a popular financing option due to their accessibility, competitive interest rates, and flexible repayment options. Here we examine the aspects of vehicle loans, focusing on new versus used vehicle financing and down payment requirements.

**New vs. Used Vehicle Financing**

When considering a vehicle loan, borrowers can choose between financing a new vehicle or a used (pre-owned) vehicle. The decision between these options depends on factors such as budget, vehicle preference, and the availability of financing options.

**New Vehicle Financing:**

New vehicle financing refers to loans provided for the purchase of brand-new vehicles. These loans typically offer several advantages, including:

**Lower Interest Rates**: New vehicle loans often come with lower interest rates compared to used vehicle loans. This is because new vehicles have a higher value and less risk of depreciation in the short term, making them more attractive to lenders.

**Longer Loan Tenure**: Lenders may offer longer loan tenures for new vehicles, making monthly installments more affordable. This can be particularly beneficial for borrowers looking to spread the cost over a more extended period.

**Warranty and Insurance Benefits**: New vehicles typically come with manufacturer warranties and insurance coverage, providing additional peace of mind to borrowers.

**Used Vehicle Financing:**

Used vehicle financing refers to loans provided for the purchase of pre-owned vehicles. These loans have become increasingly popular due to the affordability of used cars and the growing demand for budget-friendly transportation options. considerations for used vehicle financing include:

- **Higher Interest Rates**: Used vehicle loans generally have higher interest rates compared to new vehicle loans. This is due to the increased risk associated with the potential depreciation and maintenance issues of used vehicles.

- **Shorter Loan Tenure**: Lenders may offer shorter loan tenures for used vehicles, as these vehicles have a lower residual value over time. Borrowers may need to make higher monthly payments to repay the loan within a shorter period.

- **Vehicle Condition and Age**: The condition and age of the used vehicle contribute to loan approval. Lenders may have specific criteria regarding the maximum age and mileage of the vehicle. A thorough inspection and valuation of the vehicle are often required to determine its worth and loan eligibility.

## Down Payment Requirements

Down payment refers to the initial amount a borrower pays out of pocket when purchasing a vehicle or any other bank financed product. It represents a percentage of the vehicle's total cost in the case of a vehicle loan and is paid upfront at the time of purchase. The down payment amount can vary based on the lender's policies, the borrower's credit profile, and the type of vehicle being financed.

**Importance of Down Payment**:

- **Reduced Loan Amount**: A higher down payment reduces the total loan amount, resulting in lower monthly installments and interest costs. It also decreases the lender's risk by lowering the loan-to-value (LTV) ratio, making the loan more secure.

- **Better Loan Terms**: Borrowers who make a substantial down payment may qualify for better loan terms, such as lower interest rates and longer repayment tenures. This is because a considerable down payment demonstrates the borrower's financial commitment and reduces the lender's risk.

- **Increased Approval Chances**: Making a higher down payment can improve the chances of loan approval, especially for borrowers with less-than-perfect credit scores. It shows financial stability and a lower reliance on borrowed funds.

**Down Payment Amount**:

The down payment amount typically ranges from 10% to 30% of the vehicle's purchase price, depending on the lender's requirements and the borrower's creditworthiness. Some lenders may offer zero down payment options for qualified borrowers, allowing them to finance the entire cost of the vehicle. However, such options often come with higher interest rates and stricter eligibility criteria.

**Down Payment for New vs. Used Vehicles**:

- **New Vehicles**: Lenders may require a lower down payment for new vehicles, as these vehicles have a higher market value and lower risk of depreciation. The down payment for new vehicles can range from 10% to 20% of the purchase price.

- **Used Vehicles**: Used vehicle loans may require a higher down payment, typically ranging from 20% to 30% of the vehicle's value. The increased down payment is due to the higher risk associated with the potential depreciation and maintenance costs of used vehicles.

### *Education Loans*

Education loans are financial instruments designed to support students in pursuing higher education, both domestically and internationally. These loans cover many educational expenses, including tuition fees, books, accommodation, and other related costs. The objective of education loans is to make quality education accessible to students, regardless of their financial background. We now turn to the many aspects of education loans, including the types of courses covered, the moratorium period, and collateral requirements.

### Courses Covered

Education loans are available for a diverse range of courses and academic programs. These include:

**Undergraduate Courses**: Loans are provided for pursuing undergraduate degrees in several fields, including arts, science, commerce, engineering, medicine, law, and more. These courses typically span three to five years, depending on the discipline.

**Postgraduate Courses**: Students seeking advanced education through postgraduate programs, such as master's degrees, MBA, M.Tech, or specialized diplomas, can also avail themselves of education loans. These courses usually last one to two years.

**Professional Courses**: Professional programs like Chartered Accountancy (CA), Company Secretary (CS), Cost and Management Accountancy (CMA), and others are eligible for education loans. These courses often involve a combination of academic study and practical training.

**Technical and Vocational Courses**: Loans are available for technical and vocational training programs that provide skills and certifications in specific trades or industries, such as IT, hospitality, aviation, and healthcare.

**Doctoral and Research Programs**: Students pursuing doctoral (Ph.D.) and research-oriented programs can also obtain education loans. These loans cover expenses related to research materials, fieldwork, and other academic necessities.

**Study Abroad Programs**: Education loans can be availed for pursuing education abroad, covering courses offered by foreign universities and institutions. This includes undergraduate, postgraduate, and doctoral programs, as well as short-term certificate courses.

The availability of education loans for specific courses depends on the policies of the lending institution and the recognized status of the educational institution. Banks and financial institutions generally have a list of approved courses and institutions eligible for loan financing.

## Moratorium Period

The moratorium period, also known as the repayment holiday which accompanies almost all types of loan depending on conditions, becomes a feature of education loans. It refers to the period during which the borrower is not required to make any principal or interest payments on the loan. The moratorium period typically extends from the time the loan is disbursed until a specified duration after the completion of the course.

- **Duration of Moratorium**: The standard moratorium period includes the duration of the course plus an additional 6 to 12 months, known as the grace period. This grace period allows students to secure employment and establish a stable income before beginning repayment. The length of the moratorium may vary depending on the lender's policies and the nature of the course.

- **Interest Accrual**: During the moratorium period, interest on the loan amount may continue to accrue. Some lenders offer the option to pay simple interest during the moratorium, reducing the overall interest burden. Alternatively, the accrued interest may be capitalized, meaning it is added to the principal amount, which increases the total repayment obligation.

- **Repayment After Moratorium**: Once the moratorium period ends, the borrower is required to start repaying the loan through Equated Monthly Installments (EMIs). The repayment tenure typically ranges from 5 to 15 years, depending on the loan amount and the borrower's repayment capacity. Early repayment options are often available, allowing borrowers to pay off the loan ahead of schedule without incurring prepayment penalties.

The moratorium period provides notable relief to students, as it allows them to focus on their studies without the immediate pressure of loan repayments. It also eases a smoother transition from academic life to professional life, enabling graduates to manage their finances effectively once they begin earning.

**Collateral Requirements**

Collateral requirements for education loans vary based on the loan amount, the lender's policies, and the borrower's financial profile. Collateral serves as security for the lender, guaranteeing the recovery of the loan amount in case of default. The aspects of collateral requirements are as follows:

- **Loan Amount and Collateral**: For education loans up to a certain limit (typically around INR 4 lakhs in India), collateral is generally not required. These loans are often sanctioned based on the student's academic performance and the co-borrower's financial status. For loan amounts exceeding this threshold, lenders may require collateral to mitigate the risk.

- **Types of Collateral**: Acceptable forms of collateral include immovable property (such as residential or commercial real estate), fixed deposits, government securities, and insurance policies. The value of the collateral should be sufficient to cover the loan amount. The lender assesses the market value and legal validity of the collateral before sanctioning the loan.

- **Third-Party Guarantee**: In some cases, instead of physical collateral, a third-party guarantee may be accepted. This involves a guarantor, usually a family member or a financially stable individual, who agrees to repay the loan if the borrower defaults. The guarantor's financial stability and creditworthiness are assessed by the lender.

- **Hypothecation of Future Income**: For loans without collateral, the borrower's future income potential may serve as an implicit form of security. This is particularly relevant for students pursuing high-demand professional courses with strong employment prospects. Lenders may assess the anticipated earning capacity of the borrower based on the chosen field of study and the institution's reputation.

- **Documentation and Legal Formalities**: The process of pledging collateral involves thorough documentation and legal formalities. The borrower must provide property ownership documents, proof of insurance, and other relevant paperwork. The lender may also conduct a legal and technical verification of the collateral to safeguard its validity and adequacy.

### *Business Loans*

Business loans are financial products designed to meet the diverse funding needs of businesses. These loans are necessary for maintaining daily operations, expanding business activities, purchasing equipment, and other business-related expenditures. They are necessary for building entrepreneurship, driving economic growth, and supporting job creation. Business loans can be categorized into a number of types, depending on their purpose and structure. This section focuses on the types of business loans: working capital loans, term loans, and financing schemes specifically tailored for Micro, Small, and Medium Enterprises (MSMEs).

### Working Capital Loans

Working capital loans are designed to help businesses manage their short-term financial needs and maintain smooth operations. They are typically used to cover day-to-day expenses, such as purchasing inventory, paying salaries, and managing overhead costs. These loans are major for businesses that experience seasonal fluctuations in cash flow or need immediate funds to bridge the gap between receivables and payables.

**Purpose and Usage**: Working capital loans are intended to finance the operational needs of a business rather than long-term investments. They are commonly used to purchase raw materials, stock up on inventory, pay suppliers, and meet other short-term obligations. These loans help businesses maintain liquidity and make certain that they can continue operations without interruptions.

**Loan Structure**: Working capital loans can be structured as revolving credit facilities, overdrafts, or short-term loans. Revolving credit facilities and overdrafts provide businesses with a flexible credit line that can be drawn upon as needed and repaid within a specified period. This allows businesses to manage cash flow fluctuations more effectively. Short-term loans, on the other hand, provide a lump sum amount that must be repaid within a short period, usually less than a year.

**Eligibility and Criteria**: The eligibility for working capital loans depends on factors, including the business's credit history, financial statements, cash flow projections, and the nature of the business. Lenders may require collateral, such as inventory, receivables, or other assets, to secure the loan.

However, unsecured working capital loans are also available, especially for businesses with strong credit profiles.

**Repayment and Interest Rates**: The repayment terms for working capital loans vary depending on the loan structure and the lender's policies. Revolving credit facilities and overdrafts usually require businesses to pay interest only on the amount used, while short-term loans may have fixed or variable interest rates. The interest rates for working capital loans can be higher than other types of loans due to the short-term nature and higher risk associated with them.

## Term Loans

Term loans are long-term financing options provided to businesses for specific purposes, such as purchasing equipment, expanding operations, or investing in real estate. These loans have a fixed repayment schedule and are usually repaid over a period of several years. Term loans are a tool for businesses looking to make marked investments that require substantial capital outlay.

**Purpose and Usage**: Term loans are used for purposes, including capital expenditures, business expansion, infrastructure development, and purchasing fixed assets like machinery and property. They are suitable for businesses that require substantial funding for long-term projects and can repay the loan over an extended period.

**Loan Structure**: Term loans can be structured as short-term, medium-term, or long-term loans, depending on the repayment period. Short-term term loans typically have a tenure of one to three years, medium-term loans range from three to five years, and long-term loans extend beyond five years. The repayment schedule can include monthly, quarterly, or annual installments, depending on the loan agreement.

**Eligibility and Criteria**: Eligibility for term loans depends on the business's financial health, creditworthiness, business plan, and the purpose of the loan. Lenders assess the business's ability to generate sufficient cash flow to meet the loan's repayment obligations. Collateral may be required to secure the loan, and the value of the collateral often determines the loan amount. Businesses with strong financials and a solid business plan may qualify for unsecured term loans.

**Repayment and Interest Rates**: The repayment terms for term loans are typically fixed, with the principal and interest spread over the loan tenure. Interest rates can be fixed or variable, depending on the lender's policies and the prevailing market conditions. Fixed interest rates provide stability in repayments, while variable rates may fluctuate based on market trends. The interest rates for term loans are generally lower than those for short-term loans, reflecting the lower risk associated with longer-term investments.

**MSME Financing Schemes**

Micro, Small, and Medium Enterprises (MSMEs) are a component of the Indian economy, contributing greatly to employment, exports, and GDP. Recognizing the importance of MSMEs, the government and financial institutions have developed many financing schemes to support their growth and development. These schemes provide MSMEs with access to affordable credit, helping them overcome financial constraints and capitalize on business opportunities.

**Purpose and Objectives**: MSME financing schemes are designed to provide financial assistance to small businesses for several purposes, including working capital needs, technology upgrades, business expansion, and market diversification. The objective of these schemes is to promote entrepreneurship, promote advance, and strengthen the competitiveness of MSMEs in the domestic and international markets.

**Central MSME Financing Schemes**: Several MSME financing schemes are available in India, each with specific features and benefits. Some of the prominent schemes include:

- **Pradhan Mantri Mudra Yojana (PMMY)**: This scheme offers loans up to INR 10 lakhs to non-corporate, non-farm small and micro-enterprises. It is categorized into three products: Shishu (loans up to INR 50,000), Kishor (loans from INR 50,001 to INR 5 lakhs), and Tarun (loans from INR 5,00,001 to INR 10 lakhs). The scheme aims to promote entrepreneurship and financial inclusion.

- **Credit Guarantee Fund Trust for Micro and Small Enterprises (CGTMSE)**: This scheme provides collateral-free credit to MSMEs. It offers a credit guarantee cover to banks and financial institutions for loans extended to MSMEs, reducing the risk associated with lending to small businesses. The scheme encourages lenders to provide credit to new and existing enterprises without requiring collateral.

- **Stand-Up India Scheme**: This scheme supports bank loans between INR 10 lakhs and INR 1 crore to at least one Scheduled Caste (SC) or Scheduled Tribe (ST) borrower and at least one woman borrower per bank branch for setting up a greenfield enterprise. The scheme aims to promote entrepreneurship among underrepresented groups.

- **Interest Subvention Scheme for MSMEs**: This scheme provides an interest subsidy of 2% on incremental loans up to INR 1 crore to MSMEs. It aims to reduce the cost of borrowing for MSMEs and support their growth and expansion.

- **Eligibility and Application Process**: The eligibility criteria for MSME financing schemes vary depending on the specific scheme and the lender's policies. Generally, businesses must be classified as micro, small, or medium enterprises based on their investment in plant and machinery or equipment. The application process typically involves submitting a detailed business plan, financial statements, and other relevant documents. The government and financial institutions have also introduced online platforms and portals to simplify the application and approval process for MSME loans.

- **Benefits and Impact**: MSME financing schemes provide several benefits, including easy access to credit, lower interest rates, flexible repayment terms, and collateral-free loans. These schemes enable MSMEs to invest in new technologies, expand their operations, and enter new markets. They also help in creating employment opportunities, encouraging development, and contributing to the overall economic development of the country.

Banks also are involved in enabling large-scale financing through a variety of loan arrangements, each designed to meet the complex and diverse needs of borrowers requiring substantial capital:

## Consortium Lending

Consortium lending involves multiple banks coming together to jointly finance a large loan to a single borrower. This arrangement is typically used when the loan amount is too substantial for a single bank to handle independently. In a consortium, each participating bank contributes a portion of the total loan amount, and the risk is shared among all members. The consortium is usually led by one or more lead banks that coordinate the loan process, manage documentation, and act as the point of contact for the borrower. Consortium lending is common in large infrastructure projects, real estate developments, and other capital-intensive ventures.

## Syndicated Loan

A syndicated loan is another method where multiple banks or financial institutions collaborate to provide a large loan to a single borrower. Unlike consortium lending, syndicated loans are typically arranged and managed by a lead bank, known as the syndicate agent or lead arranger. This lead bank structures the loan, negotiates terms with the borrower, and handles the distribution of funds and repayments among the participating lenders. Syndicated loans are often used for major corporate financing needs, such as mergers and acquisitions, large-scale infrastructure projects, and international trade financing.

## Club Deal

A club deal is a type of syndicated loan but involves a smaller group of banks or financial institutions, usually with equal participation from each lender. In a club deal, there is typically no lead arranger; instead, all participating banks share equal responsibility for structuring the loan and managing the relationship with the borrower. Club deals are often used for medium-sized financing needs, where the borrower prefers to deal with a smaller group of lenders and the loan size is not as large as in a typical syndicated loan.

## Bilateral Loan

A bilateral loan is a straightforward loan agreement between a single lender and a single borrower. However, when the loan amount is large, and the lender wants to spread its risk, it may bring in another bank to share the loan under a bilateral arrangement. While not as common as consortium or syndicated loans for very large amounts, bilateral loans can be structured to involve multiple lenders without forming a full consortium or syndicate, making them a flexible option for large borrowers.

## Project Finance

Project finance is a method of financing large infrastructure and industrial projects through a combination of equity and debt. In project finance, the loan is secured by the project's assets and revenue streams rather than the overall balance sheet of the borrower. Multiple lenders, including banks and other financial institutions, typically participate in providing the necessary funding. The lenders are repaid from the cash flow generated by the project, making this a highly structured and complex form of loan arrangement, often used for energy projects, transportation infrastructure, and large-scale real estate developments.

## Mezzanine Financing

Mezzanine financing is a hybrid form of debt that combines elements of both debt and equity financing. It is often used in large transactions where the borrower needs to raise additional capital beyond what can be secured through traditional senior loans. In a mezzanine loan arrangement, the lender receives the right to convert the debt into equity in the event of a default, making it a higher-risk, higher-reward option for lenders. This type of financing is frequently used in leveraged buyouts, expansions, and recapitalizations, where the borrower seeks to maximize their access to capital while minimizing equity dilution.

### 3.2.2 Credit Appraisal Process

The credit appraisal process is a step in the lending cycle, where financial institutions assess the creditworthiness of potential borrowers. This process helps lenders determine the likelihood of a borrower repaying a loan and is central for minimizing the risk of default. The evaluation involves a detailed analysis of a number of aspects of the borrower's financial profile, business plan, and market conditions. The core of this process often revolves around the "5 Cs of Credit," which provide a structured framework for assessing the different dimensions of credit risk.

### 5 Cs of Credit

The 5 Cs of Credit are a set of criteria used by lenders to evaluate the creditworthiness of a borrower. They include Character, Capacity, Capital, Collateral, and Conditions. Each "C" represents an aspect of the borrower's profile, providing a complete view of their ability and willingness to repay the loan.

### Character

Character refers to the borrower's reputation and track record in managing financial obligations. It is a qualitative assessment that considers the borrower's honesty, integrity, and reliability. Lenders evaluate character by examining the borrower's credit history, past interactions with financial institutions, and references from previous lenders or business partners.

- **Credit History**: A borrower's credit history is a record of their past borrowing and repayment behavior. It includes information about previous loans, credit card usage, and any instances of late payments or defaults. A strong credit history with timely repayments indicates good character, while a poor history may raise concerns about the borrower's reliability.

- **Reputation**: Beyond credit history, lenders may also consider the borrower's reputation in the industry or community. This can be assessed through personal interviews, feedback from peers, and public records. A borrower with a good reputation is perceived as more trustworthy and likely to honor their commitments.

- **Integrity**: Lenders assess the integrity of a borrower by considering their ethical behavior and compliance with laws and regulations. Borrowers with a history of legal issues, fraudulent activities, or unethical business practices are viewed as high-risk.

## Capacity

Capacity refers to the borrower's ability to repay the loan based on their current and projected income and cash flow. It is a quantitative assessment that involves analyzing financial statements, income sources, and debt-to-income ratios.

- **Income and Cash Flow Analysis**: Lenders review the borrower's income sources, including salary, business revenues, and investments. For businesses, this involves analyzing financial statements such as profit and loss accounts, balance sheets, and cash flow statements. The goal is to determine if the borrower generates sufficient income to cover the loan repayments.

- **Debt-to-Income Ratio**: This ratio measures the borrower's total monthly debt payments relative to their gross monthly income. A lower debt-to-income ratio indicates that the borrower has a manageable level of debt, making them more likely to repay the loan. Lenders prefer borrowers with a ratio below a certain threshold, typically around 35-40%.

- **Employment Stability**: For individual borrowers, employment stability is a necessary factor. Lenders assess the borrower's job stability, industry, and length of employment. A stable job history in a steady industry suggests reliable income, reducing the risk of default.

## Capital

Capital refers to the borrower's financial assets and net worth, which indicate their financial strength and stability. It includes personal or business savings, investments, and other assets that can be used to repay the loan in case of financial difficulties.

- **Net Worth**: Lenders calculate the borrower's net worth by subtracting total liabilities from total assets. A higher net worth indicates greater financial stability and a lower risk of default. It also suggests that the borrower has a financial cushion to fall back on in challenging times.
- **Investment Portfolio**: The borrower's investments in stocks, bonds, real estate, and other assets provide an additional layer of security. Lenders consider the liquidity and market value of these investments, as they can be liquidated to meet loan obligations if necessary.
- **Equity Contribution**: For business loans, lenders assess the amount of equity the borrower has invested in their business. A considerable equity contribution demonstrates the borrower's commitment and confidence in their business, making them a more attractive candidate for a loan.

## Collateral

Collateral refers to the assets or property pledged by the borrower to secure the loan. It acts as a safety net for the lender, providing a way to recover the loan amount in case of default. The value and quality of the collateral are factors in the credit appraisal process.

- **Type of Collateral**: Common types of collateral include real estate, vehicles, equipment, inventory, and receivables. The choice of collateral depends on the loan type and the borrower's available assets. Real estate is often preferred due to its stable value and ease of liquidation.
- **Valuation and Appraisal**: Lenders require an independent appraisal of the collateral to determine its current market value. The appraisal considers factors such as the condition, location, and market demand for the asset. The loan-to-value (LTV) ratio, which compares the loan amount to the appraised value of the collateral, helps assess the adequacy of the security.
- **Legal Considerations**: Lenders guarantee that the collateral is free from legal encumbrances, such as existing loans, liens, or disputes. A clear title and proper documentation are needed to avoid complications in the event of default. Lenders may also require insurance coverage for the collateral to protect against potential losses.

The concept of collateral, types and valuation are explained in more detail in the coming sections.

## Conditions

Conditions refer to the external factors that may affect the borrower's ability to repay the loan. These include economic conditions, industry trends, and the purpose of the loan. Lenders consider these factors to assess the overall risk associated with the loan.

- **Economic Environment**: Lenders analyze the current economic conditions, including inflation rates, interest rates, and market stability. A stable and growing economy reduces the risk of default, while economic downturns can increase the likelihood of financial difficulties for borrowers.
- **Industry Analysis**: The borrower's industry is involved in the credit appraisal process. Lenders assess the industry's growth prospects, competitive field, and potential risks. Borrowers in stable and growing industries are considered less risky compared to those in volatile or declining sectors.
- **Purpose of the Loan**: The intended use of the loan funds is a consideration. Lenders prefer loans for productive purposes, such as business expansion, capital investment, or education. Loans for speculative activities or non-necessary expenses may be viewed with caution.
- **Loan Structure**: The terms and conditions of the loan, including the interest rate, repayment schedule, and covenants, are tailored to the borrower's risk profile and financial needs. Lenders may include specific conditions, such as maintaining a certain debt-to-equity ratio or providing regular financial updates, to mitigate risk.

## Credit Scoring Models

Credit scoring models are tools used by lenders to assess the creditworthiness of potential borrowers. These models use statistical techniques to evaluate a borrower's credit risk based on financial and non-financial factors. By assigning a numerical score, credit scoring models provide a standardized and objective measure of a borrower's likelihood to repay a loan. This process helps lenders make informed decisions, minimize defaults, and speed up the lending process. There are two types of credit scoring models: internal scoring systems developed by individual financial institutions and external credit bureaus that provide thorough credit reports and scores.

## Internal Scoring Systems

Internal scoring systems are proprietary credit evaluation models developed and used by individual financial institutions. These systems are tailored to the specific lending criteria and risk appetite of the institution. Internal scoring systems employ a combination of historical data, borrower-specific information, and proprietary algorithms to generate a credit score for each applicant. The components of internal scoring systems include:

- **Customizable Criteria**: Financial institutions have the flexibility to define and adjust the criteria used in their internal scoring systems. These criteria may include income, employment history, existing debt, past banking relationships, and other relevant factors. The customization allows institutions to align their lending practices with their strategic goals and risk management policies.

- **Proprietary Algorithms**: Internal scoring models rely on proprietary algorithms that weigh different factors according to their perceived impact on credit risk. The algorithms are often based on statistical analysis of historical data, including past defaults, repayment patterns, and economic conditions. The resulting credit score reflects the borrower's overall risk profile as determined by the institution.

- **Dynamic Adjustments**: Internal scoring systems can be updated and refined over time to incorporate new data, changes in economic conditions, and shifts in the institution's risk tolerance. This dynamic nature allows lenders to respond to evolving market conditions and maintain the accuracy and relevance of their credit assessments.

- **Confidentiality and Competitive Advantage**: The proprietary nature of internal scoring systems provides financial institutions with a competitive advantage. The specific criteria and algorithms used are closely guarded secrets, giving institutions a unique approach to credit evaluation. This confidentiality also helps prevent manipulation or gaming of the system by potential borrowers.

- **Integration with Decision-Making Processes**: Internal credit scores are integrated into the broader decision-making processes of financial institutions. Along with other factors, such as loan amount and collateral, the internal credit score influences loan approval, interest rates, and terms and conditions. This integration guarantees a consistent and quick approach to lending.

## External Credit Bureaus

External credit bureaus are independent organizations that collect and maintain broad credit information on individuals and businesses. They aggregate data from financial institutions, utilities, and other credit providers to compile detailed credit reports and generate standardized credit scores. External credit bureaus help with the credit evaluation process by providing a consistent and objective assessment of a borrower's credit history and risk. The features and functions of external credit bureaus include:

- **Data Collection and Aggregation**: Credit bureaus collect data from a broad set of sources, including banks, credit card companies, mortgage lenders, utility providers, and public records. This data encompasses payment history, outstanding debts, credit inquiries, and any derogatory marks, such as bankruptcies or late payments. By aggregating this information, credit bureaus create a full profile of a borrower's credit behavior.

- **Credit Reports**: A credit report is a detailed summary of an individual's or business's credit history as maintained by a credit bureau. It includes personal information, account details, payment history, credit inquiries, and public records. Credit reports are used by lenders to assess the creditworthiness of applicants and to monitor existing borrowers' credit behavior. Consumers can also access their credit reports to review their credit history and identify any discrepancies or inaccuracies.

- **Credit Scores**: Credit bureaus use proprietary scoring models to generate credit scores, which provide a numerical representation of a borrower's credit risk. The most commonly used scoring model is the FICO score, which ranges from 300 to 850, with higher scores indicating lower credit risk. Other popular scoring models include VantageScore and CIBIL Score (in India). Credit scores are calculated based on factors such as payment history, credit use, length of credit history, types of credit, and recent credit inquiries.

- **Standardization and Objectivity**: One of the advantages of external credit bureaus is the standardization and objectivity they bring to the credit evaluation process. Since credit bureaus collect data from multiple sources and apply consistent scoring methodologies, their credit scores provide a uniform measure of credit risk. This standardization helps lenders compare applicants and make unbiased lending decisions.

- **Regulatory Oversight and Compliance**: Credit bureaus operate under strict regulatory frameworks to secure the accuracy, privacy, and security of credit information. In many countries, credit bureaus are subject to regulations such as the Fair Credit Reporting Act (FCRA) in the United States or the Credit Information Companies (Regulation) Act in India. These regulations protect consumers' rights and establish guidelines for the collection, use, and disclosure of credit information.

- **Consumer Services**: In addition to providing credit reports and scores to lenders, credit bureaus offer many services to consumers. These services include credit monitoring, identity theft protection, and credit score improvement tools. Consumers can also dispute inaccuracies in their credit reports and request corrections, securing that their credit profiles accurately reflect their financial behavior.

## Credit Rating Agencies and Their Rating Mechanisms

Credit rating agencies (CRAs) factor into the financial markets by providing independent assessments of the creditworthiness of borrowers, including corporations, governments, and financial instruments. These agencies evaluate the ability and willingness of a borrower to repay debt, and they assign ratings that reflect the risk associated with the entity or security. Credit ratings are necessary for investors, as they help in assessing the risk and making informed investment decisions. Below, we provide an overview of the major credit rating agencies and their rating mechanisms for long term.

**CIBIL (Credit Information Bureau India Limited)**, established in August 2000, is India's first credit information company. It was formed as a joint venture between State Bank of India, other major banks, and TransUnion International Inc. In 2010, CIBIL received its Certificate of Registration from the Reserve Bank of India under the Credit Information Companies (Regulation) Act, 2005. CIBIL collects and maintains credit records of individuals and companies, generating credit reports and scores that range from 300 to 900. This scoring system, developed by CIBIL based on statistical analysis and industry standards, is widely used in India's financial sector. Scores are generally interpreted as: 300-549 (Poor), 550-649 (Fair), 650-749 (Good), and 750-900 (Excellent). CIBIL's reports and scores serve multiple purposes: they are central for credit risk assessment, loan approval processes, and interest rate determination by banks and financial institutions. They also promote responsible borrowing, contribute to financial inclusion by helping assess credit risk for those without extensive credit histories, aid in fraud prevention, and provide insights into the overall health of India's credit market. While other credit information companies like Experian and Equifax have entered the Indian market with their own scoring models, CIBIL's system remains the most recognized. Through these functions, CIBIL helps with creating a more smooth, transparent, and stable credit system in India, benefiting both lenders and borrowers in the financial ecosystem.

### Standard & Poor's (S&P) Global Ratings

S&P Global Ratings is one of the world's leading credit rating agencies, providing ratings for all sorts of entities, including corporations, governments, and financial instruments.

**Rating Scale**: S&P uses a letter-based rating scale, ranging from AAA to D.

- **AAA**: Extremely strong capacity to meet financial commitments. Lowest risk.
- **AA**: Very strong capacity to meet financial commitments. Low risk.
- **A**: Strong capacity to meet financial commitments but somewhat susceptible to adverse economic conditions.
- **BBB**: Adequate capacity to meet financial commitments. More susceptible to economic changes.
- **BB**: Less vulnerable in the near term but faces major ongoing uncertainties.
- **B**: More vulnerable to adverse business, financial, and economic conditions.
- **CCC**: Currently vulnerable and dependent on favorable conditions to meet commitments.
- **CC**: Highly vulnerable. Speculative.
- **C**: Currently highly vulnerable.
- **D**: Payment default on financial commitments.

**Rating Mechanism**: S&P's rating process involves analyzing an issuer's financial statements, business model, industry position, and economic environment. The agency also considers qualitative factors such as management effectiveness and strategy.

## Moody's Investors Service

Moody's is another prominent credit rating agency that provides credit ratings, research, and risk analysis.

**Rating Scale**: Moody's uses a letter-based system with numeric modifiers, ranging from Aaa to C.

- **Aaa**: Highest quality with minimal credit risk.
- **Aa1, Aa2, Aa3**: High quality with very low credit risk.
- **A1, A2, A3**: Upper-medium grade, low credit risk.
- **Baa1, Baa2, Baa3**: Medium grade, moderate credit risk.
- **Ba1, Ba2, Ba3**: Speculative, substantial credit risk.
- **B1, B2, B3**: Highly speculative, high credit risk.
- **Caa1, Caa2, Caa3**: Poor quality, very high credit risk.
- **Ca**: Highly speculative, likely in or very near default.
- **C**: Lowest rated, typically in default.

**Rating Mechanism**: Moody's assesses factors such as economic and financial trends, the issuer's ability to meet debt obligations, and the legal structure of debt. The agency also evaluates industry risk, management quality, and the competitive environment.

## Fitch Ratings

Fitch Ratings provides credit ratings, commentary, and research for global financial markets. Fitch's ratings cover sovereigns, financial institutions, corporates, and structured finance.

**Rating Scale**: Fitch's rating scale is similar to S&P's, ranging from AAA to D.

- **AAA**: Highest credit quality. Lowest expectation of default risk.
- **AA**: Very high credit quality. Very low default risk.
- **A**: High credit quality. Low default risk.
- **BBB**: Good credit quality. Low default risk.
- **BB**: Speculative. Elevated vulnerability to default.
- **B**: Highly speculative. Material risk of default.
- **CCC**: Substantial credit risk. Default is a real possibility.
- **CC**: Very high levels of credit risk. Default is probable.
- **C**: Exceptionally high levels of credit risk. Near default.
- **RD**: Restricted Default

- **D**: Default.

**Rating Mechanism**: Fitch evaluates quantitative factors such as financial ratios, cash flow analysis, and capital structure. Qualitative factors include corporate governance, regulatory environment, and industry dynamics. The agency also considers macroeconomic trends and sector-specific risks.

## CRISIL (Credit Rating Information Services of India Limited)

CRISIL is a leading credit rating agency in India, providing ratings, research, and risk analysis for several entities and instruments.

**Rating Scale**: CRISIL's rating scale ranges from AAA to D for long-term ratings, and A1 to D for short-term ratings.

- **AAA**: Highest degree of safety. Lowest credit risk.
- **AA**: High degree of safety. Very low credit risk.
- **A**: Adequate safety. Low credit risk.
- **BBB**: Moderate safety. Moderate credit risk.
- **BB**: Moderate risk of default.
- **B**: High risk of default.
- **C**: Very high risk of default.
- **D**: Default.

**Rating Mechanism**: CRISIL evaluates an issuer's business and financial risk profile, including market position, management quality, and financial metrics. The agency also considers economic and regulatory factors that could impact the issuer's creditworthiness.

## ICRA (Investment Information and Credit Rating Agency)

ICRA is another major credit rating agency in India, offering ratings, research, and advisory services.

**Rating Scale**: ICRA's long-term rating scale ranges from AAA to D, similar to other agencies.

- **AAA**: Highest credit quality. Least credit risk.
- **AA**: High credit quality. Very low credit risk.
- **A**: Adequate credit quality. Low credit risk.
- **BBB**: Moderate credit quality. Moderate credit risk.
- **BB**: Moderate risk of default.
- **B**: High risk of default.
- **C**: Very high risk of default.

- **D**: Default.

**Rating Mechanism**: ICRA assesses factors such as financial performance, industry position, management capabilities, and regulatory environment. The agency also considers the economic outlook and market conditions that may affect the issuer's credit profile.

## CARE Ratings (Credit Analysis and Research Limited)

CARE Ratings is a leading credit rating agency in India, providing a span of ratings and assessments for a number of financial instruments and entities.

**Rating Scale**: CARE Ratings' scale ranges from AAA to D.

- **AAA**: Highest safety. Lowest credit risk.
- **AA**: High safety. Very low credit risk.
- **A**: Adequate safety. Low credit risk.
- **BBB**: Moderate safety. Moderate credit risk.
- **BB**: Moderate risk of default.
- **B**: High risk of default.
- **C**: Very high risk of default.
- **D**: Default.

**Rating Mechanism**: CARE Ratings evaluates the financial strength, business profile, and management quality of the issuer. The agency also considers macroeconomic factors, industry trends, and regulatory changes that could impact the issuer's ability to meet its financial obligations.

## 3.2.3 Loan Pricing and Interest Rate Determination

The process of determining loan pricing and interest rates is an aspect of banking that directly impacts borrowers and the financial institution's profitability. factors influence how banks price loans, including the cost of funds, risk assessment, competition, and regulatory requirements. In India, the Reserve Bank of India (RBI) has introduced several frameworks to safeguard transparency and fairness in interest rate determination. The principal systems include the Base Rate system, the Marginal Cost of Funds based Lending Rate (MCLR), and the External Benchmark Linked Lending Rate (EBLR). These systems aim to standardize lending rates across banks and make loan pricing more responsive to changes in the broader economic environment.

*Base Rate System*

The Base Rate system was introduced by the RBI in July 2010, replacing the Benchmark Prime Lending Rate (BPLR) system. The Base Rate is the minimum rate at which a bank can lend to its most creditworthy customers and serves as the floor for all lending rates. It was designed to make certain greater transparency in the credit pricing framework and to pass on the benefits of low rates to customers.

**Components of the Base Rate System:**

**Cost of Funds**: The Base Rate is calculated by considering the average cost of deposits and other funds raised by the bank.

**Operational Costs**: It includes the bank's operating expenses, which are needed for conducting its lending activities.

**Profit Margin**: A certain profit margin is added to cover the risk premium and guarantee the bank's profitability.

**Regulatory Requirements**: The cost of maintaining the statutory reserve requirements, such as the Cash Reserve Ratio (CRR) and Statutory Liquidity Ratio (SLR), is factored in.

Under the Base Rate system, banks were required to review their rates at least once every quarter. The system aimed to secure that the rates were reflective of the actual cost of funds and operational productivity, promoting fair lending practices. However, the system faced criticism for its rigidity and lack of sensitivity to changes in market conditions.

*Marginal Cost of Funds based Lending Rate (MCLR)*

To address the limitations of the Base Rate system, the RBI introduced the Marginal Cost of Funds based Lending Rate (MCLR) on April 1, 2016. The MCLR aims to make the interest rate transmission more transparent and responsive to changes in the cost of funds. Unlike the Base Rate, which considered the average cost of funds, the MCLR is based on the marginal cost of funds, which includes the incremental cost of raising new deposits and borrowings.

**Components of the MCLR:**

**Marginal Cost of Funds**: The MCLR takes into account the marginal cost of deposits and other borrowings. This reflects the cost incurred by the bank in raising additional funds.

**Negative Carry on Account of CRR**: The cost of maintaining the CRR, which does not earn any interest, is considered in the MCLR.

**Operating Costs**: Similar to the Base Rate, the MCLR includes the bank's operating expenses.

**Tenor Premium**: The MCLR varies based on the tenure of the loan, with longer-term loans typically having a higher rate due to the increased risk and uncertainty.

Banks are required to publish their MCLR for different tenures, such as overnight, one month, three months, six months, and one year. The interest rate for a particular loan is determined by adding a spread to the applicable MCLR, which reflects the borrower's credit risk and other factors. The MCLR system requires banks to reset the interest rates at predetermined intervals, safeguarding that borrowers benefit from reductions in the cost of funds.

### External Benchmark Linked Lending Rate (EBLR)

In October 2019, the RBI mandated the adoption of the External Benchmark Linked Lending Rate (EBLR) for all new floating rate loans to retail and micro, small, and medium enterprises (MSME) sectors. The EBLR is designed to improve the transmission of monetary policy rates and safeguard that changes in policy rates are swiftly reflected in lending rates.

**Features of the EBLR:**

**External Benchmarks**: Banks can choose from a set of external benchmarks, including the RBI's policy repo rate, the three-month or six-month Treasury bill yield published by the Financial Benchmarks India Private Ltd (FBIL), or any other benchmark market interest rate published by FBIL. The chosen benchmark must be consistent for all similar loan products.

**Transparency**: The EBLR system is transparent as it directly links the lending rates to an external benchmark, guaranteeing that the rates are market-driven.

**Periodic Reset**: The EBLR must be reset at least once every three months, securing that the lending rates reflect the current market conditions.

The introduction of the EBLR was a marked step towards improving the monetary policy transmission mechanism. By linking loan rates to external benchmarks, the RBI aimed to make certain that reductions in policy rates were promptly passed on to borrowers, thereby boosting credit growth and economic activity.

***Comparison and Impact:*** The transition from the Base Rate to the MCLR and then to the EBLR represents a gradual shift towards more market-oriented and transparent loan pricing mechanisms. The Base Rate system, while improving upon the BPLR system, lacked responsiveness to market changes. The MCLR addressed some of these issues by considering the marginal cost of funds, but it still relied on internal calculations by banks. The EBLR, with its reliance on external benchmarks, represents a substantial departure, safeguarding that lending rates are more closely aligned with prevailing market rates.

The impact of these changes has been multifaceted. For borrowers, the shift to the MCLR and EBLR systems has generally led to a more predictable and transparent interest rate environment. Borrowers are now better positioned to benefit from reductions in the cost of funds, as banks are required to pass on the benefits of lower external benchmark rates. For banks, the move towards external benchmarks has necessitated adjustments in their risk management and pricing strategies, as they must now account for the increased volatility in interest rates.

### *Repo Rate-Based Bank Interest Rates*

In a repo rate-based system, the interest rates on loans and deposits offered by banks are directly influenced by the repo rate set by the central bank. This approach secures that changes in monetary policy are quickly reflected in the interest rates that banks charge on loans and offer on deposits.

When the central bank increases the repo rate, the cost of borrowing for banks rises. To maintain their profit margins, banks typically pass this increased cost on to their customers by raising the interest rates on loans. This makes loans more expensive for borrowers, which can lead to a reduction in borrowing and spending. The goal of this adjustment is often to curb inflation by slowing down economic activity. Conversely, when the central bank lowers the repo rate, the cost of funds for banks decreases. Banks can then reduce the interest rates on loans, making borrowing cheaper. This encourages consumers and businesses to take more loans, which can stimulate economic growth by increasing spending and investment.

## 3.2.4 Collateral and Securities

In the area of banking and finance, collateral factors into securing loans and mitigating the risks associated with lending. Collateral as earlier stated in previous sections refers to assets pledged by a borrower to secure a loan, providing a lender with a safety net in case of default. It acts as a secondary source of repayment, allowing the lender to recover the loan amount by liquidating the collateral if necessary. The importance of collateral is especially pronounced in secured loans, where it is a fundamental aspect of the credit appraisal process. This section covers types of collateral, valuation methods, and relevant legal provisions under the SARFAESI Act, which govern the handling and recovery of secured assets in India and is detailed in the coming sections.

Primary securities are the assets directly financed by a loan and serve as the main collateral for the lender. For example, in a mortgage loan, the property being purchased with the loan funds acts as the primary security. Similarly, in an auto loan, the vehicle being financed is the primary security. These assets are the first line of defense for the lender in case of a default, as they are directly tied to the purpose of the loan. On the other hand, secondary securities are additional assets or collateral provided by the borrower to offer further assurance to the lender. These may include other forms of collateral such as fixed deposits, shares, or additional properties, etc. For instance, if a borrower pledges their fixed deposit or an additional piece of real estate along with their primary property for a mortgage, these would be considered secondary securities. Secondary securities provide an extra layer of protection, helping to mitigate the lender's risk if the primary security does not fully cover the outstanding loan amount in the event of a default.

### Types of Collateral

Collateral can take many forms, depending on the nature of the loan, the borrower's profile, and the lender's requirements. The types of collateral used in banking include immovable property, movable assets, and financial securities. Each type of collateral has characteristics and implications for both the borrower and the lender.

### Immovable Property

Immovable property, such as real estate, is one of the most commonly used forms of collateral in lending. This category includes residential properties, commercial buildings, land, and agricultural properties. Immovable property is favored by lenders due to its relatively stable value and the difficulty of concealing or disposing of it without proper documentation.

The use of immovable property as collateral involves the creation of a mortgage. There are several types of mortgages, including:

**Equitable Mortgage**: Also known as a mortgage by deposit of title deeds, this type of mortgage involves the borrower depositing the property title deeds with the lender as security for the loan. It does not require registration, making it a cost-effective and quick process.

**Legal Mortgage**: This type involves a formal transfer of legal ownership of the property to the lender until the loan is repaid. The mortgage deed is registered with the relevant authority, providing a higher level of security for the lender.

**Reverse Mortgage**: A reverse mortgage is a unique product designed for senior citizens. It allows them to pledge their residential property to a lender in exchange for periodic payments, providing a source of income without losing ownership.

Immovable property as collateral offers several advantages, including a relatively low risk of value depreciation and a well-established legal framework for recovery. However, it also involves challenges such as the potential for legal disputes over property ownership and the time-consuming process of property liquidation in case of default.

## Movable Assets

Movable assets encompass many tangible and intangible items that can be pledged as collateral. These include vehicles, machinery, inventory, receivables, and other personal property. Movable assets are particularly relevant in business and industrial loans, where companies may use machinery, stock, or accounts receivable as security.

Aspects of using movable assets as collateral include:

**Hypothecation**: This involves pledging movable assets as security for a loan while retaining possession and usage. The lender has a legal claim over the assets but does not take physical custody unless there is a default.

**Pledge**: In a pledge, the borrower transfers possession of the movable assets to the lender as security. The lender has the right to sell the assets in case of default to recover the loan amount.

**Lien**: A lien gives the lender a legal right to retain possession of an asset until the debt is repaid. Unlike a pledge, a lien does not involve the transfer of possession.

Movable assets as collateral are often preferred for their liquidity and ease of valuation. However, they may also pose risks such as depreciation, theft, and obsolescence. Lenders must carefully assess the value and condition of the movable assets to guarantee adequate security coverage.

**Financial Securities**

Financial securities, including stocks, bonds, mutual funds, and other investment instruments, are another common form of collateral. These assets are highly liquid and can be quickly converted into cash, making them an attractive option for lenders.

Considerations when using financial securities as collateral include:

**Margin Requirements**: Lenders typically apply a margin or haircut to the value of the securities, reflecting the potential volatility and risk associated with the assets. For example, if a borrower pledges stocks worth INR 1,000,000, the lender may only consider INR 800,000 as collateral value, applying a 20% margin.

**Market Risks**: The value of financial securities can fluctuate based on market conditions, interest rates, and other factors. Lenders must monitor the value of the pledged securities and may require additional collateral if the value falls below a certain threshold.

**Custody and Control**: The lender may hold the securities in a designated account, guaranteeing control over the assets in case of default. This provides a straightforward mechanism for liquidation if necessary.

The use of financial securities as collateral is particularly prevalent in margin trading, loans against shares, and securities-backed lending. It offers a flexible and effective way to secure loans, but it also requires careful management of market risks and valuation.

### 3.2.5 Valuation Methods

Accurate valuation of collateral is necessary for determining the loan amount and assessing the risk involved. Valuation methods vary depending on the type of collateral and the context of the loan. The primary valuation methods include market value, book value, liquidation value, and appraised value.

**Market Value**: Market value refers to the estimated price at which an asset can be sold in the open market. For immovable property, market value is determined based on recent sales of similar properties, location, condition, and other factors. For financial securities, market value is based on the current trading price.

**Book Value**: Book value represents the asset's value on the company's balance sheet, calculated as the cost of acquisition minus depreciation. It is commonly used for movable assets and provides a conservative estimate of the asset's worth.

**Liquidation Value**: Liquidation value is the estimated amount that can be recovered from selling the asset in a distressed sale. It is typically lower than market value and is used in scenarios where quick disposal of assets is necessary, such as bankruptcy or default.

**Appraised Value**: Appraised value is determined by a professional appraiser who assesses the asset's condition, market trends, and other relevant factors. This method is commonly used for specialized assets, such as machinery, artwork, or antiques.

Lenders often rely on third-party valuation agencies or internal experts to conduct thorough assessments and secure accurate valuation. Regular revaluation of collateral may also be required, especially for assets with volatile market values.

## 3.2.6 SARFAESI Act Provisions

The Securitisation and Reconstruction of Financial Assets and Enforcement of Security Interest (SARFAESI) Act, 2002, is a major legislative framework in India that governs the recovery of loans and management of secured assets. The Act provides a legal mechanism for banks and financial institutions to recover their dues without resorting to the lengthy judicial process. It applies to secured loans where collateral has been provided by the borrower.

**Principal Provisions of the SARFAESI Act:**

- **Enforcement of Security Interest**: The Act allows lenders to take possession of the secured assets and sell them to recover the outstanding loan amount. This can be done without the intervention of the court, provided the loan is classified as a non-performing asset (NPA) and the borrower has been notified.

- **Asset Reconstruction Companies (ARCs)**: The SARFAESI Act enables the establishment of ARCs, which specialize in acquiring distressed assets from banks and financial institutions. ARCs manage and recover these assets through a number of strategies, including restructuring, securitization, and asset sales.

- **Securitization**: The Act provides a framework for securitization, allowing financial institutions to convert loans into tradable securities. This enables the transfer of credit risk and liquidity management.

- **Appeal and Redressal**: Borrowers have the right to appeal against the actions taken by the lender under the SARFAESI Act. The Debt Recovery Tribunal (DRT) and the Appellate Tribunal are designated authorities for handling disputes and appeals related to the enforcement of security interests.

***Impact and Significance of the SARFAESI Act:*** The SARFAESI Act has been a game-changer in the Indian banking sector, considerably boosting the effectiveness and effectiveness of loan recovery processes. By allowing lenders to bypass the traditional judicial route, the Act has reduced the time and cost associated with debt recovery. It has also strengthened the position of lenders in negotiations with defaulting borrowers, providing a credible threat of asset seizure and sale.

The Act has facilitated the growth of a market for distressed assets, with ARCs contributing to managing and resolving bad loans. This has contributed to the overall stability and health of the banking sector, enabling banks to clean up their balance sheets and focus on fresh lending.

However, the SARFAESI Act has also faced criticism and challenges. Concerns have been raised about the protection of borrower rights and the potential misuse of the Act by lenders. There have been instances where borrowers have alleged harassment and coercion by recovery agents. The judicial system has also helped with balancing the interests of lenders and borrowers, securing fair and just enforcement of the Act's provisions.

## 3.3 Investment Services

Investment services factor into helping individuals and institutions manage and grow their wealth. These services encompass a broad set of financial products and solutions designed to meet the diverse needs of investors. Among the investment options available, mutual funds have gained immense popularity due to their simplicity, diversification, and professional management. This section provides an in-depth exploration of mutual funds, including their types, net asset value (NAV) calculation, and distribution channels.

### 3.3.1 Mutual Funds

A mutual fund is an investment vehicle that pools money from multiple investors to purchase a diversified portfolio of securities, such as stocks, bonds, and other assets. The fund is managed by professional portfolio managers who make investment decisions on behalf of the investors. Mutual funds offer several benefits, including diversification, liquidity, and access to professional management. They are regulated by the Securities and Exchange Board of India (SEBI) in India, safeguarding transparency and investor protection.

*Types of Mutual Funds*

Mutual funds can be categorized based on factors, such as the asset class they invest in, the investment objective, and the structure of the fund. Understanding the different types of mutual funds is necessary for investors to align their investments with their financial goals and risk tolerance.

## Equity Funds

Equity funds, also known as stock funds, primarily invest in equity shares of companies. These funds aim to provide capital appreciation over the long term by investing in a diversified portfolio of stocks. Equity funds are further categorized based on market capitalization, investment style, and sector focus:

**Large-Cap Funds**: These funds invest in large-cap companies with a considerable market share and stable performance. They offer relatively lower risk and steady returns compared to mid-cap and small-cap funds.

**Mid-Cap Funds**: Mid-cap funds invest in medium-sized companies with growth potential. While they offer higher growth opportunities, they also come with increased volatility and risk.

**Small-Cap Funds**: These funds focus on small-cap companies, which are often in the early stages of growth. Small-cap funds can provide substantial returns but are also associated with higher risk due to market fluctuations.

**Sectoral and Thematic Funds**: These funds invest in specific sectors or themes, such as technology, healthcare, or energy. They allow investors to capitalize on industry trends but come with concentration risk.

**Multi-Cap Funds**: Multi-cap funds invest across companies of different market capitalizations, offering a balanced exposure to large-cap, mid-cap, and small-cap stocks.

## Debt Funds

Debt funds invest in fixed-income securities, such as bonds, government securities, corporate debt, and money market instruments. These funds are designed to provide regular income and preserve capital, making them suitable for conservative investors. Debt funds can be categorized based on the duration of the securities they invest in and the credit quality:

**Liquid Funds**: Liquid funds invest in short-term money market instruments with maturities of up to 91 days. They offer high liquidity and are ideal for parking surplus cash.

**Short-Term Funds**: These funds invest in debt instruments with a maturity of one to three years. They offer a balance between yield and interest rate risk.

**Income Funds**: Income funds invest in a mix of short, medium, and long-term debt securities. They aim to provide regular income through interest payments.

**Credit Risk Funds**: These funds invest in lower-rated corporate bonds, offering higher yields but with increased credit risk.

**Gilt Funds**: Gilt funds invest in government securities, which are considered low-risk as they are backed by the government. They are suitable for risk-averse investors seeking safety and stability.

## Hybrid Funds

Hybrid funds, also known as balanced funds, invest in a mix of equity and debt instruments. They aim to provide a balance between capital appreciation and income generation. The allocation between equity and debt can vary based on the fund's investment objective and market conditions. Hybrid funds can be categorized into the following types:

**Aggressive Hybrid Funds**: These funds have a higher allocation to equities (typically 65-80%) and a smaller portion in debt. They are suitable for investors with a moderate to high-risk appetite.

**Conservative Hybrid Funds**: Conservative hybrid funds have a larger allocation to debt instruments (typically 70-75%) and a smaller portion in equities. They offer relatively lower risk and are ideal for conservative investors.

**Balanced Advantage Funds**: These funds dynamically adjust their allocation between equity and debt based on market conditions. They aim to provide stable returns with reduced volatility.

**Arbitrage Funds**: Arbitrage funds seek to exploit price differences between the cash and derivatives markets. They invest in both equity and debt instruments to provide relatively stable returns with low risk.

### *NAV Calculation*

The Net Asset Value (NAV) of a mutual fund represents the per-unit value of the fund's assets, minus its liabilities. NAV is a critical metric used by investors to assess the performance and value of a mutual fund. It is calculated at the end of each trading day, reflecting the closing market prices of the securities in the fund's portfolio. It comprises of

- **Total Assets**: This includes the market value of all the securities held in the fund's portfolio, along with any cash or cash equivalents.
- **Total Liabilities**: This includes expenses such as management fees, administrative costs, and any other liabilities incurred by the fund.
- **Number of Outstanding Units**: This represents the total number of units issued to investors.

NAV is a tool for investors to determine the value of their investment in a mutual fund. It also serves as a basis for calculating entry and exit prices when buying or selling mutual fund units. However, NAV alone does not indicate the performance of a fund, as it does not account for factors like dividend distribution, market conditions, and fund expenses.

### *Distribution Channels*

Mutual funds are distributed through many channels, providing investors with multiple options to access these investment products. The distribution channels include direct plans, distributors, online platforms, and financial advisors. Each channel has its advantages and disadvantages, depending on the investor's preferences and requirements.

- **Direct Plans**: Direct plans are offered directly by the mutual fund houses without any intermediaries. They have lower expense ratios compared to regular plans, as they do not involve distributor commissions. Investors can invest in direct plans through the fund house's website, customer service centers, or online portals. Direct plans are suitable for experienced investors who can make informed decisions without the need for advisory services.

- **Distributors**: Distributors include banks, non-banking financial companies (NBFCs), and individual agents who sell mutual funds on behalf of fund houses. They earn commissions from the fund houses for their services. Distributors provide personalized services, helping investors choose the right funds based on their financial goals and risk appetite. However, the presence of commissions may lead to a conflict of interest, as distributors might prioritize funds that offer higher commissions.

- **Online Platforms**: Online platforms, including fintech companies and investment portals, have gained popularity as convenient and cost-effective channels for investing in mutual funds. These platforms offer all sorts of funds from different fund houses, along with tools for research, comparison, and portfolio management. Online platforms often provide both direct and regular plans, allowing investors to choose based on their preferences. The ease of access and digital interface make online platforms attractive to tech-savvy investors.

- **Financial Advisors**: Financial advisors provide complete investment advisory services, including mutual fund recommendations, financial planning, and portfolio management. They assess the investor's financial situation, risk tolerance, and investment goals to create a customized investment strategy. Financial advisors may charge a fee for their services, which can be based on assets under management, a fixed fee, or a commission. The personalized guidance and expertise offered by financial advisors make them valuable for investors seeking professional support.

## 3.3.2 Insurance Products

Insurance products contribute to financial planning and risk management, offering individuals and businesses a way to protect against unforeseen events. In India, the insurance industry has evolved notably over the years, providing a span of products to cater to the diverse needs of the population. This section looks at several types of insurance products, with a focus on life insurance and its subcategories, including term insurance, endowment plans, and unit-linked insurance plans (ULIPs).

a. **Life Insurance**

Life insurance is a contract between an individual and an insurance company, wherein the insurer agrees to pay a specified sum of money to the designated beneficiaries upon the insured person's death. The primary purpose of life insurance is to provide financial security to the policyholder's family in the event of their demise. Life insurance can also serve as a tool for savings and investment, depending on the type of policy chosen.

Life insurance products can be broadly classified into three categories: term insurance, endowment plans, and unit-linked insurance plans (ULIPs). Each of these products has features and benefits, catering to different financial goals and risk profiles.

**Term Insurance**

Term insurance is the most basic and affordable form of life insurance. It provides pure risk coverage for a specified period, known as the policy term. If the policyholder dies during the term, the insurer pays the death benefit to the beneficiaries. However, if the policyholder survives the term, no payout is made, and the policy lapses without any maturity benefit.

**Features of Term Insurance:**

**Coverage**: Term insurance offers high coverage at relatively low premiums, making it an attractive option for individuals seeking substantial financial protection for their families.

**Policy Term**: The policy term can range from a few years to several decades, depending on the policyholder's requirements. Common terms include 10, 20, and 30 years, with some policies extending up to the policyholder's 99th year.

**Premiums**: Premiums for term insurance are typically lower than those for other life insurance products because it only provides death benefits without any savings or investment component. Premiums can be fixed for the entire term or may increase at specified intervals.

**Death Benefit**: The death benefit is the sum assured, which is paid to the beneficiaries upon the policyholder's death. The benefit amount can be chosen by the policyholder based on their financial needs and goals.

**Riders and Add-ons**: Term insurance policies can be improved with riders and add-ons, such as accidental death benefit, critical illness cover, waiver of premium, and disability cover. These additional covers provide extra protection against specific risks.

**Benefits of Term Insurance:**

**Financial Security**: Term insurance provides financial protection to the policyholder's family, guaranteeing that they can maintain their standard of living and meet financial obligations in the event of the policyholder's death.

**Affordability**: The low premiums make term insurance an affordable option for individuals seeking substantial coverage.

**Flexibility**: Policyholders can choose the coverage amount and policy term based on their financial situation and goals.

**Tax Benefits**: Premiums paid for term insurance are eligible for tax deductions under Section 80C of the Income Tax Act, 1961. The death benefit received by the beneficiaries is also tax-exempt under Section 10(10D), subject to certain conditions.

**Limitations of Term Insurance:**

- **No Maturity Benefit**: Unlike other life insurance products, term insurance does not offer a maturity benefit. If the policyholder survives the policy term, no payout is made.

- **Premium Increases with Age**: Premiums for new term insurance policies may increase with age, making it more expensive to purchase coverage later in life.

## Endowment Plans

Endowment plans are a type of life insurance that combines risk coverage with a savings component. These plans provide a death benefit to the beneficiaries in case of the policyholder's demise during the policy term and a maturity benefit if the policyholder survives the term. The maturity benefit includes the sum assured and, in many cases, bonuses declared by the insurer.

**Features of Endowment Plans:**

**Coverage and Savings**: Endowment plans offer life coverage along with a savings component, making them a suitable option for individuals looking to build a corpus for future financial goals, such as education, marriage, or retirement.

**Policy Term**: The policy term for endowment plans can range from 10 to 30 years, depending on the policyholder's financial goals and needs.

**Premiums**: Premiums for endowment plans are higher than those for term insurance due to the savings component. Premiums can be paid as a lump sum or in regular installments (monthly, quarterly, semi-annually, or annually).

**Death Benefit**: The death benefit includes the sum assured and any bonuses declared by the insurer. It is paid to the beneficiaries upon the policyholder's death during the policy term.

**Maturity Benefit**: The maturity benefit is paid to the policyholder if they survive the policy term. It includes the sum assured and accrued bonuses.

**Bonuses**: Endowment plans may offer bonuses, which are a share of the insurer's profits distributed to policyholders. Bonuses can be reversionary (added to the sum assured and paid at maturity) or terminal (paid at the end of the policy term).

**Benefits of Endowment Plans:**

**Dual Benefit**: Endowment plans provide both life coverage and savings, offering a lump sum payout at maturity, in addition to the death benefit.

**Financial Discipline**: The regular premium payments encourage financial discipline and systematic savings.

**Guaranteed Returns**: The maturity benefit provides guaranteed returns, making endowment plans a relatively low-risk investment option.

**Tax Benefits**: Premiums paid for endowment plans are eligible for tax deductions under Section 80C of the Income Tax Act, 1961. The maturity proceeds are also tax-exempt under Section 10(10D), subject to certain conditions.

## Limitations of Endowment Plans:

- **Lower Returns**: The returns on endowment plans are generally lower than those of other investment options, such as mutual funds or equities.
- **High Premiums**: The premiums for endowment plans are higher compared to term insurance, as they include a savings component.

## Unit-Linked Insurance Plans (ULIPs)

Unit-Linked Insurance Plans (ULIPs) are a hybrid insurance-cum-investment product that provides life coverage along with the opportunity to invest in a number of market-linked instruments. ULIPs allow policyholders to allocate their premiums across different investment options, such as equity, debt, or balanced funds, based on their risk appetite and financial goals.

## Features of ULIPs:

**Investment and Insurance**: ULIPs offer both investment and insurance benefits. A portion of the premium is allocated towards life coverage, while the rest is invested in chosen funds.

**Fund Options**: ULIPs provide a range of fund options, including equity, debt, and balanced funds. Policyholders can switch between funds based on their investment preferences and market conditions.

**Flexibility**: ULIPs offer flexibility in premium payments (single, regular, or limited) and the choice of funds. Policyholders can adjust their investment strategy through fund switches and premium redirections.

**Lock-in Period**: ULIPs have a minimum lock-in period of five years, during which partial withdrawals are not allowed. This lock-in period encourages long-term investment and wealth accumulation.

**Charges**: ULIPs have charges, such as premium allocation charges, fund management charges, policy administration charges, and mortality charges. These charges can impact the overall returns on the investment.

**Death Benefit**: The death benefit in ULIPs is the higher of the sum assured or the fund value at the time of the policyholder's death. This safeguards a minimum payout to the beneficiaries.

**Benefits of ULIPs:**

**Wealth Creation**: ULIPs offer the potential for wealth creation through market-linked investments. The returns on ULIPs depend on the performance of the underlying funds.

**Flexibility and Control**: Policyholders have the flexibility to choose and switch funds, allowing them to align their investments with their financial goals and risk tolerance.

**Tax Benefits**: Premiums paid for ULIPs are eligible for tax deductions under Section 80C of the Income Tax Act, 1961. The maturity proceeds are also tax-exempt under Section 10(10D), subject to certain conditions.

**Limitations of ULIPs:**

- **Market Risk**: ULIPs are subject to market risks, and the returns are not guaranteed. The fund value can fluctuate based on market conditions.

- **High Charges**: ULIPs have several charges that can impact the overall returns. Policyholders should carefully consider these charges before investing.

- Insurance products, including life insurance, endowment plans, and ULIPs, contribute to financial planning by providing financial protection and investment opportunities. Each product type offers features and benefits, catering to different financial goals and risk appetites. Term insurance provides pure risk coverage at an affordable cost, making it an ideal choice for individuals seeking substantial financial protection. Endowment plans offer a combination of savings and life coverage, providing guaranteed returns and financial security. ULIPs, with their investment and insurance components, offer the potential for wealth creation through market-linked investments.

- Understanding the nuances of these insurance products is needed for making informed decisions. Policyholders should carefully evaluate their financial goals, risk tolerance, and investment preferences before choosing an insurance product. The tax benefits associated with insurance products can provide notable savings, improving the overall value of the investment.

b. **General Insurance**

General insurance, also known as non-life insurance, provides financial protection against specific risks and losses that may not necessarily involve life or death. Unlike life insurance, general insurance policies offer coverage for a fixed term and compensate the policyholder for the actual financial loss incurred due to the occurrence of an insured event. The scope of general insurance in India is vast, covering many products such as health insurance, motor insurance, property insurance, and more. This section explores these central general insurance products, along with the bancassurance model, which is a distribution channel for insurance products through banks.

## Health Insurance

Health insurance is a component of financial planning, offering protection against the financial burden of medical expenses. It covers hospitalization costs, medical treatments, surgeries, and other healthcare-related expenses. Health insurance policies in India can be broadly categorized into individual health plans, family floater plans, critical illness plans, and top-up or super top-up plans.

## Features of Health Insurance:

**Coverage**: Health insurance policies typically cover hospitalization expenses, including room charges, doctor's fees, surgery costs, diagnostic tests, and medication. Some plans also offer coverage for outpatient treatments, preventive health check-ups, and alternative therapies like Ayurveda and Homeopathy.

**Cashless and Reimbursement Claims**: Most health insurance providers have tie-ups with a network of hospitals, offering cashless treatment to policyholders. In the case of non-network hospitals, the policyholder can file for reimbursement after settling the bills.

**Pre-existing Conditions**: Health insurance policies may cover pre-existing conditions after a specified waiting period, typically ranging from two to four years.

**No-claim Bonus**: Insurers often reward policyholders with a no-claim bonus for every claim-free year, which can either increase the sum insured or reduce the premium for the next year.

**Tax Benefits**: Premiums paid for health insurance are eligible for tax deductions under Section 80D of the Income Tax Act, 1961.

**Types of Health Insurance Plans:**

- **Individual Health Plans**: These plans cover a single individual against medical expenses. The premium and sum insured are based on the insured's age, medical history, and other factors.

- **Family Floater Plans**: These plans offer coverage to the entire family under a single policy. The sum insured is shared among the family members, making it a cost-effective option.

- **Critical Illness Plans**: These plans provide a lump sum payout upon the diagnosis of specified critical illnesses like cancer, heart attack, stroke, etc. The payout can be used for treatment or any other financial need.

- **Top-up and Super Top-up Plans**: These plans offer additional coverage above a certain threshold, known as the deductible. They are useful for strengthening existing coverage without incurring high premiums.

**Benefits and Importance:**

- **Financial Protection**: Health insurance shields individuals and families from the high costs of medical treatments, reducing the financial burden during medical emergencies.

- **Access to Quality Healthcare**: With cashless facilities and a wide network of hospitals, health insurance guarantees access to quality healthcare services.

- **Peace of Mind**: Health insurance provides peace of mind by mitigating the financial risks associated with unexpected medical expenses.

## Motor Insurance

Motor insurance is a mandatory form of general insurance in India, required by law for all motor vehicles. It provides financial protection against damages to the vehicle and third-party liabilities arising from accidents. Motor insurance can be broadly classified into two types: third-party liability insurance and thorough insurance.

**Features of Motor Insurance:**

**Third-Party Liability Insurance**: This is the minimum legal requirement for all vehicles in India. It covers damages caused to third-party property or injuries/death of third-party individuals due to an accident involving the insured vehicle. It does not cover damages to the insured vehicle.

**Broad Insurance**: This type of insurance offers broader coverage, including third-party liabilities, as well as damages to the insured vehicle due to accidents, theft, fire, natural calamities, and vandalism. It also covers personal accident benefits for the owner-driver.

**Add-on Covers**: Policyholders can boost their full insurance with add-on covers such as zero depreciation, engine protection, roadside assistance, and consumables cover, among others.

**No-claim Bonus (NCB)**: Insurers offer a discount on the premium for each claim-free year, known as the no-claim bonus. NCB can markedly reduce the cost of motor insurance over time.

## Importance of Motor Insurance:

- **Legal Compliance**: Motor insurance is mandatory in India, and driving without valid insurance can result in fines and legal consequences.

- **Financial Protection**: It provides financial protection against the cost of repairs or replacement of the vehicle and covers third-party liabilities, thereby reducing the financial impact of accidents.

- **Peace of Mind**: Motor insurance offers peace of mind by securing that the policyholder is protected against unexpected expenses related to vehicle damages and legal liabilities.

## Property Insurance

Property insurance provides coverage against risks associated with physical assets, such as homes, commercial buildings, and other properties. It protects the insured property from damages caused by natural disasters, fire, theft, vandalism, and other perils. Property insurance can be categorized into types, including home insurance, shop insurance, and commercial property insurance.

## Features of Property Insurance:

**Coverage**: Property insurance policies typically cover the structure of the insured property and its contents. The coverage includes damages caused by fire, lightning, explosion, earthquake, storm, flood, and other natural and man-made perils.

**Home Insurance**: Home insurance provides coverage for residential properties, including the building structure and personal belongings. It may also cover additional living expenses if the home becomes uninhabitable due to a covered event.

**Commercial Property Insurance**: This type of insurance covers commercial establishments, such as offices, shops, factories, and warehouses.

It protects against damages to the building and business assets, including machinery, inventory, and equipment.

**Shop Insurance**: Shop insurance is tailored for retail businesses and provides coverage for the shop's contents, including merchandise, furniture, fixtures, and fittings. It may also cover loss of income due to business interruption caused by insured events.

**Benefits of Property Insurance:**

- **Financial Security**: Property insurance provides financial security by covering the cost of repairs or replacement of the insured property and its contents.

- **Protection Against Natural Disasters**: It offers protection against damages caused by natural disasters, such as earthquakes, floods, and storms, which can cause marked financial losses.

- **Peace of Mind**: Property insurance offers peace of mind to property owners by safeguarding that they are financially protected against unforeseen events.

c. **Bancassurance Model**

The bancassurance model is a distribution channel for insurance products through banks. In this model, banks and insurance companies collaborate to offer insurance products to the bank's customers. Bancassurance has gained popularity in India due to its convenience and wide reach, allowing insurance companies to tap into the bank's customer base and use the bank's distribution network.

**Features of the Bancassurance Model:**

**Partnership Between Banks and Insurers**: Bancassurance involves a partnership between banks and insurance companies, where the bank acts as a corporate agent or broker to sell insurance products to its customers.

**Product Offerings**: Banks offer a range of insurance products, including life insurance, health insurance, motor insurance, and property insurance. These products are often integrated with the bank's existing financial services, such as loans and investment accounts.

**Distribution Channel**: The bancassurance model taps the bank's branch network, online platforms, and customer service channels to distribute insurance products. This provides customers with easy access to insurance services through familiar and trusted banking channels.

**Customer Convenience**: Bancassurance offers convenience to customers by providing a one-stop solution for banking and insurance needs. Customers can purchase insurance products while conducting their regular banking transactions, making it a hassle-free experience.

**Benefits of Bancassurance:**

- **Increased Reach**: Bancassurance enables insurance companies to reach a larger customer base through the bank's extensive network of branches and digital channels.

- **Cross-Selling Opportunities**: Banks can cross-sell insurance products to their existing customers, drawing on their knowledge of the customer's financial needs and preferences.

- **Strengthened Customer Experience**: The integration of banking and insurance services boosts the customer experience by providing a smooth and convenient platform for purchasing insurance products.

- **Revenue Generation**: Bancassurance provides an additional revenue stream for banks through commissions and fees earned from the sale of insurance products.

**Challenges of Bancassurance:**

- **Regulatory Compliance**: The bancassurance model requires compliance with regulations set by both banking and insurance regulatory authorities. Guaranteeing adherence to these regulations can be complex and challenging.

- **Conflict of Interest**: There is a potential for conflicts of interest, as banks may prioritize their own products or services over those of the insurance partner. Securing fair and unbiased product offerings is necessary.

- **Training and Expertise**: Bank staff need to be adequately trained and knowledgeable about insurance products to effectively sell and service them. This requires investment in training and development.

### 3.3.3 Government Securities

Government securities (G-secs) are debt instruments issued by the government to raise funds for public expenditure. They are considered one of the safest investment options as they are backed by the government, offering a low-risk avenue for investors. G-secs can be broadly classified into two categories: Treasury Bills (T-Bills) and Dated Securities.

This section explores these instruments in detail and highlights the growing trend of retail participation in G-secs.

### *Treasury Bills*

Treasury Bills, commonly known as T-Bills, are short-term debt instruments issued by the government to meet temporary funding needs. They are issued at a discount and redeemed at face value upon maturity, with the difference between the purchase price and the face value representing the interest earned by the investor. T-Bills are highly liquid and are a tool for managing short-term liquidity in the financial system.

**Features of Treasury Bills:**

**Short-Term Maturity**: T-Bills have maturities of up to one year, typically issued with tenors of 91 days, 182 days, and 364 days. They are suitable for investors looking for short-term investment opportunities.

**Issued at a Discount**: T-Bills are issued at a discount to their face value. For example, a T-Bill with a face value of ₹100 may be issued at ₹98, and the investor earns the difference as interest upon maturity.

**No Coupon Payments**: Unlike other debt instruments, T-Bills do not pay periodic interest (coupons). The return to the investor is the difference between the issue price and the redemption value.

**High Liquidity**: T-Bills are highly liquid instruments, easily tradable in the secondary market. This liquidity makes them an attractive option for institutional investors and short-term investors.

**Safe Investment**: T-Bills are considered one of the safest investments as they are backed by the full faith and credit of the government. They carry minimal credit risk.

**Types of Treasury Bills:**

- **91-Day T-Bills**: These are the most common T-Bills with a maturity of 91 days. They are frequently issued and are a popular choice for short-term investment.

- **182-Day T-Bills**: These T-Bills have a maturity of 182 days and are issued less frequently than 91-day T-Bills.

- **364-Day T-Bills**: With a maturity of 364 days, these T-Bills provide a slightly longer investment horizon for investors looking for short-term government securities.

**Uses of Treasury Bills:**

- **Government Funding**: T-Bills are primarily used by the government to raise short-term funds to meet temporary funding requirements.

- **Monetary Policy Tool**: The Reserve Bank of India (RBI) uses T-Bills as a monetary policy tool to manage liquidity in the financial system. By issuing or redeeming T-Bills, the RBI can influence short-term interest rates and money supply.

- **Investment and Risk Management**: T-Bills are a popular investment option for institutional investors, including banks, mutual funds, and insurance companies, for managing liquidity and as a safe investment vehicle.

### Dated Securities

Dated securities are long-term debt instruments issued by the government to finance its long-term expenditure. These securities have fixed or floating interest rates, known as coupons, and are issued with tenures ranging from 5 to 40 years. Dated securities are a component of the government's borrowing program and are involved in the bond market.

**Features of Dated Securities:**

**Long-Term Maturity**: Dated securities have maturities ranging from 5 years to 40 years, providing a long-term investment option for investors.

**Coupon Payments**: Unlike T-Bills, dated securities pay periodic interest (coupons) to investors, typically on a semi-annual basis. The coupon rate is determined at the time of issuance and remains fixed for the life of the security.

**Principal Repayment**: The principal amount is repaid to the investor at the end of the maturity period. Investors receive regular coupon payments and the principal at maturity.

**Tradability**: Dated securities are tradable in the secondary market, allowing investors to buy and sell these instruments before maturity. The market value of dated securities can fluctuate based on interest rate movements, making them subject to interest rate risk.

**Risk and Return**: Dated securities are considered low-risk investments, given their government backing. However, they are subject to interest rate risk and inflation risk, which can affect their market value and real return

**Types of Dated Securities:**

- **Fixed Rate Bonds**: These securities pay a fixed coupon rate for the life of the bond. They provide a predictable stream of income to investors.

- **Floating Rate Bonds**: The coupon rate on these bonds is linked to a benchmark rate, such as the Mumbai Interbank Offer Rate (MIBOR), and can vary over time. They offer protection against interest rate volatility.

- **Inflation-Indexed Bonds**: These bonds are designed to protect investors from inflation. The principal and interest payments are adjusted for inflation, safeguarding that the real value of the investment is maintained.

- **Zero Coupon Bonds**: These bonds do not pay periodic interest but are issued at a deep discount to their face value. The investor receives the face value at maturity, with the difference representing the return.

**Uses of Dated Securities:**

- **Government Borrowing**: Dated securities are a primary source of long-term funding for the government. They finance infrastructure projects, social welfare programs, and other long-term expenditure.

- **Investment and Portfolio Diversification**: Dated securities are a popular choice for investors seeking stable income and portfolio diversification. They are widely held by institutional investors, including pension funds, mutual funds, and insurance companies.

- **Benchmarking**: Dated securities serve as a benchmark for pricing corporate bonds and other debt instruments in the market. They provide a reference rate for interest rate swaps and other financial derivatives.

### 3.3.4 Retail Participation in G-secs

Historically, the government securities market in India has been dominated by institutional investors, such as banks, mutual funds, insurance companies, and foreign institutional investors. However, in recent years, there has been a concerted effort to encourage retail participation in the G-sec market. This initiative aims to diversify the investor base, deepen the market, and provide retail investors with a safe and accessible investment option.

**Drivers of Retail Participation:**

- **Safe Investment**: G-secs are considered one of the safest investment options due to their government backing. This safety appeals to retail investors seeking to preserve capital while earning a steady income.

- **Attractive Returns**: G-secs offer relatively higher returns compared to other low-risk investment options, such as fixed deposits and savings accounts. The regular coupon payments provide a stable income stream for retail investors.

- **Tax Benefits**: In certain cases, interest earned on G-secs may be exempt from income tax, providing an additional incentive for retail investors.

- **Diversification**: G-secs offer retail investors an opportunity to diversify their investment portfolio, reducing overall risk and boosting returns.

**Initiatives to Promote Retail Participation:**

- **RBI Retail Direct Scheme**: Launched by the Reserve Bank of India (RBI) in 2021, the RBI Retail Direct Scheme provides a dedicated platform for retail investors to invest in government securities. The platform allows retail investors to open an account directly with the RBI and trade in G-secs without intermediaries. The scheme offers a user-friendly interface, real-time access to the market, and transparent pricing.

- **Non-Competitive Bidding**: Retail investors can participate in the primary issuance of G-secs through the non-competitive bidding process. This allows retail investors to bid for G-secs without specifying the price, guaranteeing allotment at the weighted average yield of competitive bids. This process simplifies the investment process for retail investors.

- **Dematerialization and Trading**: G-secs can be held in dematerialized form in investor demat accounts, making them easy to trade and transfer. The dematerialization of G-secs has improved liquidity and ease of access for retail investors.

- **Financial Literacy and Awareness**: The RBI and other financial institutions have undertaken many initiatives to educate retail investors about G-secs and their benefits. Financial literacy programs, workshops, and seminars have been conducted to raise awareness and encourage participation.

**Challenges and Opportunities:**

- **Liquidity and Accessibility**: While G-secs are highly liquid in the institutional market, retail investors may face challenges in accessing liquidity, especially for long-term securities. Efforts are being made to increase market-making and trading infrastructure to improve liquidity for retail investors.

- **Complexity and Understanding**: The G-sec market can be complex, with several types of securities and pricing mechanisms. Retail investors may require additional support and education to understand the nuances of investing in G-secs.

- **Regulatory Support**: The continued support and initiatives from the RBI and government are major to promoting retail participation in the G-sec market. Policies aimed at simplifying the investment process, improving transparency, and securing investor protection are necessary.

## 3.4 Other Financial Services

In addition to traditional banking products and investment services, banks and financial institutions offer a range of other financial services that cater to a number of customer needs. These services improve the overall financial ecosystem by providing additional avenues for fund transfers, secure storage, and financial management. This section covers diverse array of other financial services, with a particular focus on remittance services, which ease the transfer of money domestically and internationally.

### 3.4.1 Remittance Services

Remittance services are a component of the financial sector and also the main theme of this book, enabling individuals to transfer money across different locations. These services are especially necessary for individuals working away from their families, as they provide a convenient and quick means to send money back home. In India, remittance services have evolved greatly with the advent of digital banking and electronic payment systems. Every aspect of remittances is intricately tied to the payment and settlement systems, and this relationship will be revisited in the payment system chapters from a different perspective, further emphasizing the cohesive and interdependent nature of banks and payment systems. Here we examine the different types of remittance services available, focusing on domestic remittances facilitated by NEFT, RTGS, and IMPS.

### *Domestic Remittances*

Domestic remittances refer to the transfer of funds within a country from one individual or entity to another. In India, domestic remittances are facilitated by electronic payment systems, each offering distinct features and benefits. The three primary systems used for domestic remittances are the

National Electronic Funds Transfer (NEFT), Real-Time Gross Settlement (RTGS), and Immediate Payment Service (IMPS).

### *International Remittances*

International remittances refer to the transfer of funds from individuals residing in one country to beneficiaries in another. These transfers are important for many families and economies, particularly in countries like India, which is one of the largest recipients of remittances globally. The international remittance market has evolved considerably, with systems and services easing these transactions. We now turn to the mechanisms for international remittances, focusing on the Society for Worldwide Interbank Financial Telecommunication (SWIFT) and the Money Transfer Service Scheme (MTSS).

As discussed in earlier chapter, SWIFT acts as an intermediary and agent for international money transfers. It does not hold accounts or perform clearing or settlement functions. Instead, SWIFT provides a standardized and secure messaging system that banks and financial institutions use to communicate payment instructions and other financial information. When a bank in one country wants to send money to a bank in another country, it sends a SWIFT message containing the payment instructions. This message is then routed through the SWIFT network to the recipient bank.

## Usage in India:

In India, SWIFT is widely used by banks and financial institutions for international remittances, trade finance, and other cross-border transactions. Indian banks draw on SWIFT's secure messaging system to handle large volumes of international payments, safeguarding compliance with regulatory standards and minimizing the risk of errors. SWIFT's integration with Indian banks' core banking systems simplifies the process of sending and receiving international payments, making it a preferred choice for businesses and individuals alike.

## Impact on International Remittances:

SWIFT has revolutionized the international remittance market by providing a reliable and smooth means of transferring funds across borders. It has enabled faster and more transparent transactions, reducing the reliance on traditional methods like checks and drafts. SWIFT's role in standardizing financial messaging has also facilitated greater interoperability between banks, promoting global financial integration.

## Money Transfer Service Scheme (MTSS)

The Money Transfer Service Scheme (MTSS) is a remittance service framework established by the Reserve Bank of India (RBI) to help the inward remittance of funds from abroad to India. MTSS enables individuals in foreign countries to send money to beneficiaries in India through authorized money transfer operators (MTOs). It is a quick and effective way to receive small value cross-border remittances without the need for a bank account.

### Functionality:

MTSS involves a partnership between foreign MTOs and Indian agents, typically banks, non-banking financial companies (NBFCs), and other authorized entities. The foreign MTOs receive funds from senders abroad and transfer the equivalent amount, in Indian Rupees, to the Indian agent. The Indian agent then disburses the funds to the beneficiary, who can collect the remittance in cash or have it credited to their bank account.

### Features:

*Convenience:* MTSS allows beneficiaries to receive money without the need for a bank account, making it accessible to a broader population, including those in rural and remote areas.

*Speed:* The scheme enables rapid disbursement of funds, often within minutes, depending on the network and operational speed of the MTOs and agents.

*Limitations:* As per RBI regulations, the maximum amount that can be remitted through MTSS in a single transaction is USD 2,500, and a beneficiary can receive a maximum of 30 remittances in a calendar year.

*Security and Compliance:* MTSS transactions are subject to strict regulatory oversight to prevent money laundering and safeguard compliance with anti-money laundering (AML) and counter-terrorism financing (CTF) laws.

### Usage in India:

In India, MTSS is a popular channel for receiving remittances from expatriates and migrant workers, particularly from regions with large Indian diaspora populations, such as the Middle East, North America, and Europe. The scheme's accessibility and productivity make it an attractive option for individuals who do not have access to formal banking services. Indian agents help with guaranteeing the smooth operation of MTSS, providing disbursement services through a wide network of branches and outlets.

**Impact on International Remittances:**

MTSS has had a major impact on the international remittance environment in India. It has provided a formal and regulated channel for remittances, reducing the reliance on informal and potentially risky methods. The scheme has also contributed to financial inclusion by enabling individuals without bank accounts to receive money from abroad. MTSS has facilitated the flow of remittances into India, supporting household incomes, education, healthcare, and other important needs.

**Challenges and Considerations:**

Despite its advantages, MTSS faces challenges, including regulatory compliance and the risk of misuse for illicit activities. The RBI has implemented stringent KYC (Know Your Customer) and AML norms to mitigate these risks. Also, the relatively low transaction limit may be a constraint for beneficiaries who need to receive larger sums of money.

## 3.4.2 Safe Deposit Lockers

Safe deposit lockers are a secure and convenient service offered by banks and financial institutions, allowing customers to store valuable items such as jewellery, important documents, and other valuables in a secure environment. This service has been a needed feature of banking operations for many years, providing customers with peace of mind and protection against theft, loss, or damage. In this section, we explore the operational aspects and regulatory guidelines related to safe deposit lockers in India.

*Operational Aspects*

**Allocation and Access:**

Safe deposit lockers are typically available in many sizes to accommodate different storage needs, ranging from small lockers suitable for documents to larger ones for bulkier items. Customers can choose a locker size based on their requirements and availability at the bank.

To access a locker, customers are provided with an or a combination code, depending on the system used by the bank. The locker can only be opened when the customer and a bank official simultaneously use their respective keys. This dual control system secures that the locker cannot be accessed by the customer alone or by the bank staff without the customer, providing an additional layer of security.

## Rental Charges and Agreement:

The rental charges for safe deposit lockers vary based on the size of the locker, the location of the bank branch, and the bank's policies. Customers are required to pay an annual rental fee, which may also include a security deposit in some cases. The rental charges are typically higher in urban areas due to increased demand and the cost of real estate.

When a customer rents a locker, they enter into an agreement with the bank, outlining the terms and conditions of the service. This agreement includes details about the rental charges, duration, the rights and responsibilities of both parties, and the bank's liability in case of loss or damage to the contents. The agreement also specifies the procedures for accessing the locker and the steps to be followed in case the customer loses the or forgets the combination.

## Security and Surveillance:

Banks implement stringent security measures to protect the safe deposit locker area. This includes surveillance cameras, security personnel, and access control systems. The locker area is usually located in a secure section of the bank, with restricted access to authorized personnel and customers only.

In addition to physical security measures, banks may also employ electronic surveillance systems to monitor access and activities within the locker area. This helps in maintaining a record of all entries and exits, securing accountability and preventing unauthorized access.

## Usage and Maintenance:

Customers can access their lockers during the bank's operational hours, subject to the bank's policies and the availability of the locker area. The bank maintains a log of each visit, recording the date, time, and identity of the customer accessing the locker. This log helps in tracking usage and safeguarding security.

Regular maintenance of the locker area is conducted to make certain the proper functioning of the lockers and the security systems. In case of any issues, such as a malfunctioning lock or a lost main, the bank provides assistance to resolve the problem. However, customers are advised to keep their keys secure and to avoid sharing them with others to prevent unauthorized access.

## Regulatory Guidelines

### Know Your Customer (KYC) Compliance:

In line with the Reserve Bank of India's (RBI) guidelines, banks must comply with KYC norms when allotting safe deposit lockers. Customers are required to provide valid identity and address proofs, along with other necessary documents, to verify their identity. This is to prevent misuse of lockers for illegal activities, such as money laundering or storing contraband.

The KYC process includes periodic updates and re-verification of customer information to guarantee the accuracy and relevance of the data. Banks are also required to maintain records of the KYC documents and make them available for inspection by regulatory authorities.

### Locker Allotment and Operation:

The RBI has laid down guidelines for the allotment and operation of safe deposit lockers. Banks are required to maintain a waitlist for locker allotment and must inform customers of the availability of lockers based on a transparent and non-discriminatory process. The allotment should be done on a first-come, first-served basis, subject to the availability of lockers.

Banks are also required to formulate a complete locker agreement, detailing the terms and conditions of the service. This agreement should be clear and concise, guaranteeing that customers are fully aware of their rights and obligations. The bank must also provide a copy of the agreement to the customer for their records.

### Liability and Insurance:

The liability of banks concerning the contents of the locker is an aspect of the service. According to RBI guidelines, banks are not liable for the loss of contents due to theft, fire, natural calamities, or other unforeseen events. However, banks are expected to take reasonable care in maintaining the security and integrity of the locker area.

To mitigate the risks, customers are encouraged to take separate insurance for the valuables stored in the locker. While banks may offer insurance services in collaboration with insurance companies, it is the customer's responsibility to secure that the contents are adequately insured.

### Surrender and Termination:

Customers may choose to surrender their locker at any time by providing written notice to the bank. The surrender process includes clearing all dues, returning the central, and signing the necessary documents. In case of the customer's death, the legal heirs or nominees can access the locker following the bank's procedures for the settlement of claims.

Banks may also terminate the locker agreement if the customer fails to comply with the terms and conditions, such as non-payment of rental charges or misuse of the locker. In such cases, the bank must provide adequate notice to the customer before taking any action.

### Safety and Security Protocols:

The RBI has mandated that banks implement strong safety and security protocols for safe deposit lockers. This includes regular audits and inspections of the locker area, maintenance of security equipment, and training of staff in handling locker operations. Banks must also have contingency plans in place to address emergencies, such as fire or theft.

Banks are required to educate customers about the safe use of lockers and the importance of not storing hazardous materials or illegal items. Customers are also advised to keep a detailed inventory of the items stored in the locker, as this information may be required in case of any disputes or claims.

## 3.4.3 Foreign Exchange Services

Foreign exchange services factor into supporting international trade, travel, and investment. These services are necessary for converting one currency into another, enabling transactions across borders. Banks and financial institutions offer a range of foreign exchange services to meet the diverse needs of individuals and businesses. This section covers components of foreign exchange services, including forex cards, currency exchange, and trade finance products.

### *Forex Cards*

Forex cards, also known as travel cards or prepaid currency cards, are a convenient and secure way for travelers to carry foreign currency. These cards are preloaded with a specific amount of foreign currency and can be used for making payments or withdrawing cash while abroad. Forex cards are widely accepted at merchants, ATMs, and online platforms, providing a hassle-free alternative to carrying cash.

### Features:

***Multi-Currency Support:*** Many forex cards support multiple currencies, allowing travelers to load different currencies on a single card. This feature is particularly useful for those traveling to multiple countries, as it eliminates the need to carry separate cards or cash for each currency.

*Security:* Forex cards offer boosted security compared to carrying cash. They come with features like PIN protection, EMV chip technology, and the option to block the card in case of loss or theft. Transactions made using forex cards are often monitored for any suspicious activity, providing an added layer of protection.

*Reloadable:* Forex cards can be reloaded with additional funds, either online or through the issuing bank. This flexibility safeguards that travelers have access to sufficient funds throughout their trip.

*Competitive Exchange Rates:* Banks typically offer competitive exchange rates on forex cards, which can be more favorable than those available for cash exchange. This helps travelers get more value for their money.

## Usage and Benefits:

Forex cards can be used for several purposes, including shopping, dining, hotel bookings, and withdrawing cash from ATMs. They offer the convenience of not having to carry large amounts of cash, reducing the risk of theft or loss. Also, forex cards provide a clear record of all transactions, making it easier for travelers to manage their expenses.

## Application Process:

To obtain a forex card, customers need to approach a bank or authorized forex dealer. The application process involves submitting relevant documents, such as a passport, visa, travel itinerary, and proof of residence. Once the card is issued, it can be loaded with the desired currency, either at the time of issuance or later.

## Currency Exchange

Currency exchange services enable the conversion of one currency into another. This service is important for individuals traveling abroad, businesses engaged in international trade, and investors dealing in foreign assets. Banks, currency exchange counters, and authorized forex dealers offer currency exchange services at competitive rates.

## Process:

Currency exchange involves the buying and selling of currencies based on the prevailing exchange rates. These rates are determined by factors such as supply and demand, geopolitical events, economic indicators, and market sentiment.

Banks and forex dealers offer both cash and non-cash currency exchange services, including travelers' cheques and demand drafts.

## Factors Influencing Exchange Rates:

*Market Demand and Supply:* The demand for and supply of a currency in the forex market notably impact its exchange rate. For instance, a high demand for a currency relative to its supply can lead to an appreciation in its value.

*Economic Indicators:* Principal economic indicators, such as inflation, interest rates, and GDP growth, influence exchange rates. For example, a country with a strong economy and low inflation is likely to have a strong currency.

*Geopolitical Events:* Political stability, government policies, and international relations can affect exchange rates. For instance, political unrest or trade disputes can lead to currency depreciation.

*Speculation:* Traders and investors speculate on currency movements, which can lead to short-term fluctuations in exchange rates. Speculative activities are influenced by factors such as market sentiment and expectations of future economic conditions.

## Compliance and Documentation:

Currency exchange transactions are subject to regulatory compliance, including adherence to foreign exchange laws and anti-money laundering (AML) regulations. Customers are required to provide identification and relevant documentation, such as a passport, visa, and proof of travel, to complete the transaction. This guarantees transparency and prevents illegal activities, such as money laundering and terrorism financing.

## Trade Finance Products

Trade finance products are financial instruments and services that support international trade transactions. They provide liquidity, mitigate risks, and safeguard the smooth flow of goods and services across borders. Trade finance products are needed for exporters and importers, as they help manage the complexities of cross-border trade, such as currency fluctuations, payment risks, and regulatory compliance.

## Products:

- **Letters of Credit (LCs):** A LC is a financial document issued by a bank on behalf of an importer, guaranteeing payment to the exporter upon the fulfillment of specified terms and conditions. LCs provide assurance to both parties, securing that the exporter receives payment and the importer receives the goods as agreed.

- **Bills of Exchange:** A bill of exchange is a written order used in international trade to obligate the importer to pay a specified amount to the exporter at a future date. It serves as a negotiable instrument and can be discounted or sold in the financial markets to raise funds.
- **Bank Guarantees:** A bank guarantee is a financial commitment provided by a bank on behalf of a client, assuring the counterparty that the bank will fulfill the client's contractual obligations if the client fails to do so. Bank guarantees are commonly used in international trade to cover performance, payment, and bid bond guarantees.
- **Trade Credit Insurance:** Trade credit insurance protects exporters against the risk of non-payment by foreign buyers. It covers losses arising from commercial risks, such as insolvency or default, and political risks, such as currency inconvertibility or expropriation.

**Benefits:**

Trade finance products offer several benefits to exporters and importers, including:

- **Risk Mitigation:** Trade finance instruments, such as LCs and bank guarantees, reduce the risk of non-payment and make certain that transactions are completed as agreed.
- **Liquidity Management:** Trade finance products provide access to working capital and liquidity, allowing businesses to manage cash flow and fund their operations effectively.
- **Improved Cash Flow:** Exporters can receive immediate payment or access to funds through trade finance instruments, improving their cash flow and reducing the need for external financing.
- **Improved Credibility:** The involvement of reputable banks and financial institutions in trade finance transactions increases the credibility of the parties involved, enabling smoother negotiations and transactions.

**Application Process:**

To access trade finance products, businesses must approach banks or financial institutions that offer these services. The application process involves providing relevant documentation, such as the commercial contract, invoice, bill of lading, and other trade-related documents. Banks assess the creditworthiness of the parties involved and the risks associated with the transaction before issuing the trade finance product.

### 3.4.4 Advisory Services

Advisory services in banking encompass a broad set of professional guidance offered to individuals, businesses, and corporations to help them make informed financial decisions. These services are provided by financial experts who possess deep knowledge of market trends, investment strategies, financial regulations, and risk management. Advisory services are major for optimizing financial planning, investment portfolios, and corporate strategies. This section looks at three categories of advisory services: financial planning, investment advisory, and corporate advisory services.

*Financial Planning*

Financial planning is the process of setting, planning, achieving, and reviewing financial goals. It involves a thorough assessment of an individual's or family's current financial situation and future needs. The goal is to create a roadmap that secures financial security and meets life goals, such as buying a home, saving for education, retirement planning, and wealth accumulation.

**Components:**

***Budgeting and Cash Flow Management:*** Financial planning begins with understanding income and expenses. Advisors help clients create budgets, track spending, and manage cash flow to guarantee they live within their means and save for the future.

***Risk Management and Insurance:*** AN aspect of financial planning is identifying potential risks and implementing strategies to mitigate them. This includes assessing the need for a number of insurance policies, such as life, health, disability, and property insurance.

***Tax Planning:*** Effective tax planning minimizes tax liabilities and maximizes after-tax returns. Advisors guide clients on tax-quick investment strategies, retirement contributions, deductions, and credits.

***Retirement Planning:*** Advisors help clients determine the amount needed for retirement and develop strategies to accumulate and preserve wealth for post-retirement years. This includes selecting suitable retirement accounts, such as provident funds, pension plans, and individual retirement accounts (IRAs).

*Estate Planning:* Estate planning involves the preparation of wills, trusts, and other legal documents to manage and distribute an individual's assets upon death. Advisors secure that clients' estates are managed smoothly, minimizing taxes and safeguarding that beneficiaries receive their rightful inheritance.

**Process and Implementation:**

The financial planning process typically involves several steps, including:

*Data Gathering:* Collecting detailed information about the client's financial situation, goals, risk tolerance, and time horizon.

*Analysis:* Analyzing the collected data to identify strengths, weaknesses, opportunities, and threats in the client's financial situation.

*Plan Development:* Creating a tailored financial plan that outlines specific strategies to achieve the client's financial goals.

*Implementation:* Executing the recommended strategies, such as investing in selected assets, purchasing insurance, and setting up retirement accounts.

*Monitoring and Review:* Regularly reviewing and adjusting the financial plan to account for changes in the client's circumstances, market conditions, and financial goals.

**Investment Advisory**

Investment advisory services involve providing expert guidance on investment decisions to help clients achieve their financial objectives. These services are tailored to individual and institutional investors, offering personalized advice on portfolio management, asset allocation, and investment strategies. Investment advisors analyze market trends, economic indicators, and financial statements to recommend suitable investment options.

**Main Services:**

*Portfolio Management:* Advisors assist clients in constructing and managing diversified investment portfolios that align with their risk tolerance, financial goals, and investment horizon. They recommend asset allocation strategies, such as stocks, bonds, mutual funds, and alternative investments.

*Security Analysis:* Investment advisors conduct in-depth analysis of securities, including equities, fixed income, and derivatives. They evaluate factors such as company fundamentals, industry trends, and macroeconomic conditions to identify investment opportunities.

*__Market Research and Analysis:__* Advisors provide insights into market trends, economic developments, and geopolitical events that may impact investment returns. This includes analyzing market cycles, interest rates, inflation, and currency fluctuations.

*__Risk Assessment and Management:__* Advisors assess the risk profile of clients and recommend strategies to manage and mitigate investment risks. This includes diversification, hedging, and using financial instruments like options and futures.

*__Performance Monitoring:__* Investment advisors continuously monitor the performance of clients' portfolios, providing regular reports and updates. They assess the impact of market movements on portfolio returns and make adjustments as needed.

## Regulatory Compliance and Fiduciary Duty:

Investment advisors are subject to regulatory oversight and must adhere to ethical standards and fiduciary duties. They are required to act in the best interests of their clients, guaranteeing that investment recommendations are suitable and aligned with clients' financial goals. Advisors must disclose any potential conflicts of interest and maintain transparency in their fee structures.

## Corporate Advisory Services

Corporate advisory services provide specialized guidance to businesses and corporations on financial and strategic matters. These services are designed to help companies optimize their financial performance, work through complex transactions, and achieve their corporate objectives. Corporate advisors work closely with senior management, boards of directors, and shareholders to provide insights and solutions.

## Central Services:

*__Mergers and Acquisitions (M&A):__* Corporate advisors assist companies in identifying, evaluating, and executing mergers, acquisitions, and divestitures. They conduct due diligence, valuation, negotiation, and deal structuring, securing that transactions align with the company's strategic goals.

*__Capital Raising:__* Advisors help businesses raise capital through equity, debt, or hybrid instruments. This includes advising on initial public offerings (IPOs), private placements, bond issuances, and syndicated loans. Advisors also guide companies in determining the optimal capital structure.

***Corporate Restructuring:*** Corporate advisors provide expertise in restructuring initiatives, such as spin-offs, carve-outs, and recapitalizations. They help companies simplify operations, improve effectiveness, and strengthen shareholder value.

***Strategic Planning:*** Advisors assist companies in developing and implementing strategic plans to achieve long-term growth and competitiveness. This includes market analysis, business model evaluation, and identifying growth opportunities.

***Financial Analysis and Modeling:*** Corporate advisors conduct financial analysis and modeling to assess the viability and impact of business decisions. This includes forecasting financial performance, evaluating investment projects, and analyzing cost structures.

***Corporate Governance:*** Advisors provide guidance on corporate governance practices, including board composition, executive compensation, and shareholder relations. They help companies adhere to regulatory requirements and best practices.

## Confidentiality and Ethical Standards:

Corporate advisors adhere to strict confidentiality and ethical standards. They handle sensitive information with the utmost care and safeguard that their advice is unbiased and in the best interests of their clients. Advisors must maintain transparency in their recommendations and avoid conflicts of interest.

**Chapter 4**
# Digital Transformation in Banking

The advent of digital technologies has markedly transformed the banking sector, reshaping how financial services are delivered and consumed. This transformation has led to increased convenience, speed, and accessibility for customers while enabling banks to offer fresh products and services. One of the most aspects of this digital transformation is the rise of online banking, which encompasses internet banking platforms and mobile banking applications. This chapter focuses on the impact of internet banking platforms, including their features, functionalities, and specific offerings for corporate clients.

## 4.1 Online Banking

Online banking, also known as internet banking or e-banking, refers to the use of digital platforms by banks to provide financial services and products to customers over the internet. This service allows customers to perform all sorts of banking transactions from the comfort of their homes or offices, without the need to visit a physical branch. Online banking has revolutionized the banking industry, offering customers the convenience of 24/7 access to their accounts and the ability to manage their finances at any time.

### Internet Banking Platforms

Internet banking platforms are web-based interfaces provided by banks that allow customers to access and manage their accounts online. These platforms are designed to be user-friendly, secure, and broad, offering a span of services that cater to the needs of both retail and corporate customers.

### Features and Functionalities

The features and functionalities of internet banking platforms have evolved greatly over the years, driven by advancements in technology and changing customer expectations. Some of the features and functionalities offered by modern internet banking platforms include:

*Account Management:* Customers can view their account balances, transaction history, and statements online. They can also manage multiple accounts, including savings, checking, and investment accounts, from a single dashboard.

***Fund Transfers:*** Internet banking platforms enable customers to transfer funds between their own accounts, to other accounts within the same bank, or to accounts in other banks. This includes domestic and international transfers, facilitated by services like NEFT, RTGS, and IMPS.

***Bill Payments:*** Customers can pay utility bills, credit card bills, and other recurring payments online. Many platforms offer the option to set up automatic payments, safeguarding that bills are paid on time.

***Investment Services:*** Banks offer investment products such as mutual funds, fixed deposits, and bonds through their internet banking platforms. Customers can invest, redeem, and track their investments online.

***Loan Services:*** Customers can apply for loans, such as personal loans, home loans, and auto loans, through internet banking platforms. They can also check their loan eligibility, track loan status, and make EMI payments online.

***Credit and Debit Card Management:*** Internet banking platforms allow customers to manage their credit and debit cards, including viewing transactions, setting spending limits, and reporting lost or stolen cards.

***Security Features:*** Banks employ advanced security measures to protect customer information and transactions. These include two-factor authentication, encryption, secure login procedures, and transaction alerts.

***Customer Service:*** Many platforms offer customer support through chatbots, secure messaging, and live chat, allowing customers to resolve issues and seek assistance without visiting a branch.

***Mobile Integration:*** Internet banking platforms are often integrated with mobile banking apps, providing a frictionless experience across devices. Customers can access their accounts and perform transactions on both their computers and mobile devices.

### 4.1.1 Corporate Internet Banking

Corporate internet banking, also known as business or corporate banking, caters to the specific needs of businesses, ranging from small enterprises to large corporations. These platforms offer a range of services designed to speed up business banking operations, improve cash flow management, and boost financial decision-making.

**Cash Management Services:** Corporate internet banking platforms offer full cash management solutions, allowing businesses to manage their liquidity quickly. This includes services such as account sweeps, zero-balance accounts, and cash concentration.

**Payment Solutions:** Businesses can make bulk payments, such as payroll disbursements, vendor payments, and tax payments, through corporate internet banking platforms. These platforms support many payment modes, including NEFT, RTGS, IMPS, and electronic fund transfer (EFT).

**Trade Finance:** Corporate internet banking provides trade finance solutions, including letters of credit, bank guarantees, and trade loans. Businesses can apply for trade finance products, track their status, and manage trade transactions online.

**Treasury and Investment Services:** Businesses can manage their investments, including fixed deposits, mutual funds, and foreign exchange transactions, through corporate internet banking platforms. These platforms provide tools for treasury management, including forex hedging and interest rate risk management.

**Account and Transaction Reporting:** Corporate internet banking platforms offer detailed account and transaction reporting, providing businesses with real-time insights into their financial position. Businesses can generate customized reports, download statements, and reconcile accounts.

**Security and Authorization:** Corporate internet banking platforms incorporate reliable security features, including multi-level authorization, user access controls, and audit trails. Businesses can set up multiple user roles with specific access rights, guaranteeing secure and controlled access to banking services.

**Integrated Solutions:** Many corporate internet banking platforms offer integration with accounting and enterprise resource planning (ERP) systems. This enables effortless data exchange between the bank and the business's financial systems, reducing manual entry and errors.

**Global Banking Services:** For businesses with international operations, corporate internet banking platforms offer global banking services, including foreign currency accounts, cross-border payments, and international trade finance.

**Virtual Accounts:** Some corporate internet banking platforms offer virtual account services, allowing businesses to simplify collections by assigning unique virtual account numbers to different customers. This simplifies reconciliation and improves cash flow management.

***Customer Support:*** Corporate internet banking platforms provide dedicated customer support through relationship managers, help desks, and online support channels. Businesses can access expert advice and assistance to address their banking needs.

## 4.1.2 Fund Transfers

Fund transfers are one of the most fundamental and widely used features of internet banking. This service allows customers to transfer money smoothly between accounts, either within the same bank or across different banks. The convenience and speed of digital fund transfers have made them a necessary aspect of modern banking.

***Intra-bank Transfers:*** Customers can transfer funds between their accounts within the same bank. This is often used to manage savings and investments, pay off loans, or allocate funds for specific purposes.

***Inter-bank Transfers:*** Internet banking enables inter-bank transfers, allowing customers to send money to accounts held in other banks. This is commonly done through systems like the National Electronic Funds Transfer (NEFT), Real-Time Gross Settlement (RTGS), and Immediate Payment Service (IMPS). Each system has its own set of features regarding transaction limits, settlement times, and costs.

***International Transfers:*** Many internet banking platforms offer international fund transfer services, enabling customers to send money overseas. These transfers are typically executed through SWIFT (Society for Worldwide Interbank Financial Telecommunication) and involve foreign exchange conversions.

***Scheduled Transfers:*** Customers can schedule transfers to occur at a future date. This feature is particularly useful for setting up regular payments, such as rent or loan EMIs, securing that payments are made on time without manual intervention.

***Standing Instructions:*** For recurring transfers, such as monthly savings or investments, customers can set up standing instructions. This automates the transfer process, safeguarding consistency and helping in systematic financial planning.

***Fund Transfer Tracking:*** Most internet banking platforms provide tracking features that allow customers to monitor the status of their transfers. They can view the transaction history, check pending transfers, and confirm successful transactions.

***Security Features:*** To make certain the safety of transactions, banks employ multiple layers of security, including two-factor authentication (2FA), transaction limits, and secure encryption protocols. Customers are often required to enter a one-time password (OTP) sent to their registered mobile number to authorize transactions.

### 4.1.3 Bill Payments

Bill payments are another feature of internet banking, offering customers a convenient way to manage their recurring financial obligations. This service simplifies the process of paying utility bills, credit card bills, taxes, and other recurring expenses.

***Utility Bill Payments:*** Internet banking platforms allow customers to pay their electricity, water, gas, and telephone bills online. This eliminates the need to visit physical payment centers and offers the convenience of managing all bills from a single platform.

***Credit Card Bill Payments:*** Customers can easily pay their credit card bills through internet banking. They can either pay the full outstanding amount, the minimum due, or any amount of their choice. This feature helps in maintaining a good credit score by guaranteeing timely payments.

***Tax Payments:*** Many banks offer the facility to pay taxes online, including income tax, property tax, and GST. This feature is particularly useful for businesses and individuals who need to manage their tax liabilities effectively.

***Subscription Services:*** Internet banking can also be used to pay for subscription services such as insurance premiums, magazine subscriptions, or digital content services. Customers can set up automatic payments for these services, securing they do not miss any due dates.

***Bill Payment History:*** The platform maintains a record of all bill payments, allowing customers to track their expenses and view past transactions. This feature is helpful for budgeting and financial planning.

***Notifications and Alerts:*** Banks often provide notifications and alerts for due dates and successful payments. Customers receive these alerts via SMS or email, helping them stay on top of their financial commitments.

***Automatic Payments:*** Customers can set up automatic payments for their bills, safeguarding that they are paid on time every month. This feature is particularly useful for managing utilities and other recurring bills without manual intervention.

***Integration with Financial Management Tools:*** Some internet banking platforms integrate with personal financial management tools, allowing customers to categorize and analyze their bill payments. This helps in tracking expenses and managing budgets effectively.

### 4.1.4 Service Requests

Internet banking platforms offer a range of service request features, enabling customers to perform several banking-related tasks without visiting a branch. These services are designed to increase customer convenience and speed up banking operations.

***Cheque Book Request:*** Customers can request a new cheque book through their internet banking account. They can select the number of cheque leaves and the delivery address, with the cheque book usually dispatched within a few working days.

***Account Statement:*** Customers can request account statements for specific periods, either in electronic or physical format. This feature is useful for keeping track of transactions and for submission as proof of income or for loan applications.

***Stop Cheque Payment:*** If a customer needs to stop a cheque from being processed, they can place a stop payment request online. This feature provides a quick and smooth way to prevent unauthorized or incorrect transactions.

***Update Contact Information:*** Customers can update their personal information, such as address, phone number, and email, through internet banking. This safeguards that they receive timely communication and updates from the bank.

***Block/Unblock Cards:*** In case of a lost or stolen card, customers can quickly block their debit or credit card through internet banking. They can also request a new card or unblock a previously blocked card.

***Apply for Loans and Credit Cards:*** Internet banking platforms often allow customers to apply for a number of loan products and credit cards. Customers can fill out the application form, upload required documents, and track the status of their application online.

***Update Nominee Details:*** Customers can update or change nominee details for their accounts through internet banking. This is a feature for managing inheritance and estate planning.

***Request for Overdraft Facility:*** Customers can request an overdraft facility or increase their existing overdraft limit through internet banking. This provides additional funds for emergencies or unexpected expenses.

***Investment Services:*** Customers can also make service requests related to their investments, such as purchasing or redeeming mutual funds, subscribing to IPOs, or managing fixed deposits.

***Feedback and Complaints:*** Internet banking platforms often have sections where customers can submit feedback or register complaints. This feature helps banks improve their services and address customer concerns promptly.

### 4.1.5 Security Measures

As internet banking has become increasingly popular, guaranteeing the security of online transactions has become a foremost concern for banks and customers alike. To safeguard sensitive information and protect against unauthorized access, security measures have been implemented. This section turns to principal security measures employed in internet banking, including multi-factor authentication, SSL encryption, and virtual keyboards.

### Multi-factor Authentication

Multi-factor authentication (MFA) is a security process that requires users to provide two or more verification factors to gain access to their accounts. This method improves security by combining something the user knows (such as a password), something the user has (such as a mobile phone or security token), and sometimes something the user is (such as biometric verification).

***Password:*** The first layer of protection typically involves a strong password created by the user. It should be complex, containing a combination of letters, numbers, and special characters, and it should be changed regularly to prevent unauthorized access.

***One-Time Password (OTP):*** OTPs are dynamic, time-sensitive codes sent to the user's registered mobile number or email address. They are used as a second layer of verification, providing an additional security check during login or high-risk transactions, such as large fund transfers.

***Security Tokens:*** Some banks provide hardware tokens that generate OTPs for secure access. These tokens are not connected to the internet, making them immune to online hacking attempts. They add an extra layer of security, especially for business or high-value accounts.

***Biometric Authentication:*** Many banks offer biometric authentication methods, such as fingerprint or facial recognition, to verify the identity of the user. These methods provide a secure and convenient way to access accounts, as they rely on unique physical characteristics that are difficult to replicate.

***Security Questions:*** As an additional layer of security, users may be required to answer pre-set security questions. These questions typically relate to personal information that only the account holder would know, adding another hurdle for potential intruders.

Multi-factor authentication considerably reduces the risk of unauthorized access, even if a user's password is compromised. It guarantees that even if one security factor is breached, the additional layers provide adequate protection against fraud.

## 4.1.6 SSL Encryption

Secure Sockets Layer (SSL) encryption is a standard security technology for establishing an encrypted link between a web server and a browser. This link secures that all data transmitted between the web server and the browser remains private and essential. SSL encryption is a fundamental component of internet banking security, protecting sensitive information such as account details, personal data, and transaction records.

***Data Encryption:*** SSL encrypts data, converting it into a coded format that can only be deciphered by authorized parties. This prevents unauthorized individuals from intercepting and reading the data as it travels over the internet.

***SSL Certificates:*** Banks use SSL certificates to verify their identity and establish a secure connection with their customers. These certificates are issued by trusted certificate authorities (CAs) and contain information about the bank and the CA that issued the certificate. The presence of a SSL certificate can be verified by checking for the padlock icon in the browser's address bar and securing the website URL begins with "https://".

***Server Authentication:*** SSL certificates authenticate the bank's server, safeguarding that customers are communicating with the legitimate bank's website and not a fraudulent site. This protects against phishing attacks, where attackers create fake websites to steal sensitive information.

***Data Integrity:*** SSL encryption safeguards that the data transmitted between the bank's server and the customer's browser is not altered or tampered with during transmission. This guarantees the accuracy and reliability of the information exchanged.

***Secure Sessions:*** SSL provides a secure environment for online banking sessions, protecting the user's session from eavesdropping and man-in-the-middle attacks. This security measure is especially important when conducting sensitive transactions, such as transferring funds or accessing account details.

The use of SSL encryption is a necessary aspect of maintaining the confidentiality and security of online banking transactions. It provides customers with the confidence that their personal and financial information is safe from interception and tampering.

### 4.1.7 Virtual Keyboards

Virtual keyboards are software-based keyboards displayed on a computer or mobile screen. They are an important security feature in internet banking, designed to protect users from keylogging attacks, where malicious software records keystrokes to capture sensitive information like usernames and passwords.

***Protection Against Keyloggers:*** Virtual keyboards prevent keyloggers from recording the keystrokes entered on a physical keyboard. Since virtual keyboards require users to click on the keys with a mouse or tap on a touchscreen, there are no physical keystrokes for keyloggers to capture.

***Randomized Layout:*** Some virtual keyboards have a randomized layout that changes with each use. This further strengthens security by preventing screen loggers from capturing the sequence of mouse clicks or taps to decipher the entered information.

***Visibility and Accessibility:*** Virtual keyboards are prominently displayed during the login process and for entering sensitive information. They are easy to use and accessible to all users, including those who may not be tech-savvy. This feature guarantees that all customers can benefit from strengthened security measures.

***Use in Public Spaces:*** Virtual keyboards are particularly useful when accessing internet banking services from public computers or shared networks. In such environments, the risk of keylogging and other forms of malware is higher. Using a virtual keyboard adds an extra layer of protection, reducing the chances of sensitive information being compromised.

***Integration with Other Security Features:*** Virtual keyboards are often integrated with other security features, such as OTPs and biometric authentication. This multi-layered approach provides complete protection against cyber threats.

The implementation of virtual keyboards in internet banking platforms is a simple yet effective way to safeguard sensitive information. By preventing keylogging attacks and guaranteeing secure data entry, virtual keyboards contribute to the overall security and trustworthiness of online banking services.

## 4.2 Mobile Banking

Mobile banking has revolutionized the way people manage their finances, offering unprecedented convenience and accessibility. As smartphones have become ubiquitous, mobile banking apps have emerged as a primary channel for conducting financial transactions. We now examine the features and functionalities of mobile banking apps, with a particular focus on OS-specific features for iOS and Android platforms, as well as the security measures that guarantee the safety of users' financial data.

### 4.2.1 Mobile Banking Apps

Mobile banking apps are software applications designed to allow users to conduct financial transactions directly from their smartphones or tablets. These apps provide many banking services, including checking account balances, transferring funds, paying bills, and managing investments. The popularity of mobile banking apps has surged due to their ease of use, real-time access to banking services, and the ability to perform transactions on the go.

**OS-specific Features (iOS, Android)**

Mobile banking apps are designed to cater to the specific features and capabilities of different operating systems (OS), with iOS and Android being the most prominent platforms. Each OS offers unique functionalities that improve the user experience and provide additional security features.

**iOS-specific Features:**

***Touch ID and Face ID:*** One of the standout features of iOS devices is the integration of biometric authentication methods, such as Touch ID (fingerprint recognition) and Face ID (facial recognition). Mobile banking apps on iOS tap these features to provide secure and quick access to the app, securing that only authorized users can access sensitive financial information.

*Apple Pay Integration:* iOS apps often integrate with Apple Pay, allowing users to make secure payments using their Apple devices. This integration enables users to link their bank accounts or credit cards to Apple Pay and use their devices for contactless payments at supported merchants.

*iCloud Keychain:* iOS devices offer iCloud Keychain, a feature that securely stores and synchronizes passwords and credit card information across Apple devices. Mobile banking apps can use iCloud Keychain to simplify the login process and strengthen security by automatically filling in credentials.

*Push Notifications:* iOS apps can send push notifications to users, alerting them of important events such as transaction alerts, payment due dates, or promotional offers. This feature secures that users stay informed and can take timely action when needed.

**Android-specific Features:**

*Fingerprint Authentication:* Similar to iOS, Android devices support fingerprint authentication, allowing users to access mobile banking apps securely. Many Android devices come with fingerprint scanners, which mobile banking apps can use to authenticate users quickly and securely.

*Google Pay Integration:* Android users can link their bank accounts and cards to Google Pay, easing smooth payments within mobile banking apps. Google Pay's widespread acceptance makes it a popular choice for contactless payments and in-app purchases.

*App Shortcuts and Widgets:* Android allows apps to create shortcuts and widgets on the home screen, providing quick access to frequently used features. Mobile banking apps can use these shortcuts to enable users to check their balances, transfer funds, or view recent transactions without opening the app.

*Customizable User Interface:* Android's open nature allows for greater customization of the user interface. Mobile banking apps can take advantage of this flexibility to offer personalized themes, color schemes, and layouts, strengthening the overall user experience.

## Device Binding

Device binding is a security measure that links a user's bank account to a specific mobile device. This safeguards that transactions can only be initiated from the registered device, even if the user's credentials are compromised. Device binding involves the following steps:

- **Registration:** During the initial setup, the user registers their mobile device with the bank's system. The device's unique identifier (such as the IMEI number) is stored in the bank's database.

- **Verification:** When a transaction is initiated, the bank verifies the device's identifier to secure it matches the registered device. If there is a mismatch, the transaction is flagged, and the user is notified.

- **Multi-device Support:** Some banks offer multi-device support, allowing users to register multiple devices for their accounts. Each device undergoes the same registration and verification process.

## App Based Security Measures

Security is a central concern for mobile banking apps, as they handle sensitive financial information and enable transactions. To protect users' data and safeguard secure transactions, mobile banking apps implement a range of security measures:

*Encryption:* Mobile banking apps use encryption to protect data transmitted between the user's device and the bank's servers. End-to-end encryption guarantees that data is unreadable to unauthorized parties, safeguarding users' personal and financial information from interception.

*Secure Sockets Layer (SSL) and Transport Layer Security (TLS):* SSL and TLS protocols are used to establish a secure connection between the app and the bank's servers. These protocols authenticate the server and encrypt data in transit, preventing eavesdropping and tampering.

*Two-Factor Authentication (2FA):* Many mobile banking apps offer 2FA, adding an extra layer of security. In addition to a password, users must provide a second form of authentication, such as a one-time password (OTP) sent to their registered mobile number or email. This secures that even if a password is compromised, unauthorized access is still prevented.

*Biometric Authentication:* As mentioned earlier, biometric authentication methods like fingerprint and facial recognition provide a secure and convenient way to access mobile banking apps. These methods are difficult to replicate, making them more secure than traditional passwords.

***Secure Logins:*** Mobile banking apps often include features like automatic logout after a period of inactivity and limiting the number of failed login attempts. These measures prevent unauthorized access in case the device is lost or stolen.

***Session Management:*** Proper session management safeguards that users' sessions are securely established and terminated. Mobile banking apps maintain secure session tokens, which are invalidated upon logout or inactivity, preventing session hijacking.

***App Permissions and Data Access:*** Mobile banking apps request specific permissions to access device features, such as the camera for check deposits or the microphone for voice commands. Users are prompted to grant these permissions, and apps are designed to minimize data access to only what is necessary for functionality.

***Anti-Malware and Anti-Phishing Features:*** Some mobile banking apps include built-in protections against malware and phishing attacks. These features can detect and block suspicious links, warn users about potential scams, and provide tips for safe online banking practices.

***Secure Storage of Data:*** Sensitive data, such as account numbers and transaction history, is securely stored on the device using encryption and secure storage mechanisms. This guarantees that even if the device is compromised, the data remains protected.

***Regular Security Updates:*** Banks and app developers regularly release security updates to address vulnerabilities and improve the app's security posture. Users are encouraged to update their apps and operating systems to the latest versions to benefit from these improvements.

***Fraud Detection and Monitoring:*** Banks use advanced fraud detection systems to monitor transactions and identify suspicious activities. Mobile banking apps can alert users to potential fraud and provide mechanisms to report unauthorized transactions.

Mobile banking apps offer a convenient and secure way for users to manage their finances. The integration of OS-specific features boosts the user experience, while solid security measures protect users' data and transactions. As technology continues to evolve, mobile banking apps will likely incorporate new features and security protocols, further improving their functionality and security.

## 4.2.2 SMS and USSD-based Banking

SMS and USSD-based banking services have been instrumental in expanding financial inclusion, particularly in regions with limited internet access. These technologies enable users to perform a range of banking transactions using simple text messages (SMS) or Unstructured Supplementary Service Data (USSD) codes. They are especially popular in emerging markets where smartphone penetration may be low, but mobile phone usage is widespread. This section looks at aspects of SMS and USSD-based banking, focusing on the *99# USSD service and SMS banking commands.

### SMS Banking Commands

SMS banking allows users to perform banking transactions and access account information by sending predefined SMS commands to a designated number provided by their bank. This service is widely used for its simplicity and convenience, especially in areas with poor internet connectivity.

Both SMS and USSD-based banking offer a range of features that cater to the diverse needs of users. These features provide basic banking services and additional functionalities that boost the overall user experience.

### Account Management

Account management features allow users to access and manage their bank accounts easily. These features include:

*Balance Inquiry:* Users can check their account balance by sending a specific command or using the USSD menu. This is one of the most commonly used features, providing users with real-time information about their account status.

*Mini Statements:* Users can request a mini statement to view recent transactions. This feature helps users track their spending and identify any unauthorized transactions.

*Transaction History:* Some banks offer the option to view a detailed transaction history via SMS or USSD. This feature provides a thorough overview of all transactions made over a specified period.

*Account Alerts:* Users can set up alerts for many activities, such as low balance, large transactions, or failed payments. These alerts are sent via SMS and help users stay informed about their account activities.

## Payments and Transfers

SMS and USSD-based banking enable users to make payments and transfer funds securely and conveniently.

- **Fund Transfers:** Users can transfer funds between their accounts or to other bank accounts using SMS commands or the USSD interface. This includes interbank transfers through services like IMPS (Immediate Payment Service) or NEFT (National Electronic Funds Transfer).
- **Bill Payments:** Users can pay utility bills, such as electricity, water, and gas, directly from their bank accounts. They can also recharge mobile phones, pay for insurance premiums, and make other recurring payments.
- **Merchant Payments:** Some banks allow users to make payments to merchants using SMS or USSD. This feature is particularly useful for small businesses that do not have access to point-of-sale (POS) terminals.

## Value-added Services

In addition to basic banking services, SMS and USSD-based banking offer several value-added services that increase the customer experience.

- **Mobile Top-up:** Users can recharge their mobile phones by sending a SMS or using a USSD code. This service is quick and convenient, allowing users to stay connected at all times.
- **Cheque Book Requests:** Users can request a new cheque book through SMS or USSD. The bank processes the request and sends the cheque book to the registered address.
- **Block/Unblock Cards:** In case of a lost or stolen card, users can block the card instantly by sending a specific SMS command. Similarly, they can unblock the card when it is found.
- **Loan Applications:** Some banks offer the option to apply for loans via SMS or USSD. Users can initiate the application process and receive updates on the status of their application.
- **Security Concerns and Solutions** While SMS and USSD-based banking offer several benefits, they also pose certain security risks. It is major to implement sturdy security measures to protect users' financial data and make certain the safe execution of transactions. Here we examine the

security concerns associated with these banking methods and the solutions to mitigate them.

## *99# USSD Service

The *99# USSD service, introduced by the National Payments Corporation of India (NPCI), is a revolutionary platform that allows users to access banking services without the need for internet connectivity. Launched under the umbrella of the Unified Payments Interface (UPI), the *99# service provides a user-friendly interface for basic banking operations, making it accessible even to those who do not own smartphones.

### Features and Functionality

The *99# USSD service operates by dialing *99# from any mobile phone. Users are presented with a menu of options that include balance inquiry, mini statements, money transfers, and more. The service supports multiple languages, catering to the diverse linguistic population of India. The *99# service works across all telecom operators and is available to users of participating banks.

### Benefits

*Accessibility:* The *99# service does not require an internet connection, making it accessible to users in remote areas with limited digital infrastructure.

*Security:* The service uses two-factor authentication (2FA), with a combination of a mobile number and a Mobile Money Identifier (MMID) or UPI PIN, safeguarding secure transactions.

*Convenience:* Users can access banking services anytime and anywhere, without needing to visit a bank branch or ATM.

# 4.3 Digital Wallets and UPI

The advent of digital wallets and the Unified Payments Interface (UPI) has revolutionized the way transactions are conducted in India. These platforms have made payments more convenient, secure, and accessible, leading to a notable shift from traditional cash-based transactions to digital modes. We now turn to the system of digital wallets and UPI in India, focusing on popular digital wallets, their business models, and revenue streams. The Digital wallets are typically linked to the bank provided accounts to load money. Though they are part of the advanced payment mechanisms, they tend to operate with the help of banking being the backbone.

### 4.3.1 Digital Wallet Business Models and Revenue Streams

Digital wallets, also known as e-wallets, are mobile applications that allow users to store money and make payments electronically. They have gained immense popularity in India due to their ease of use, speed, and widespread acceptance across a number of merchants. Some of the most prominent digital wallets in India include Paytm, PhonePe, and Google Pay.

- **PhonePe:** Introduced in 2016, PhonePe quickly gained popularity as a UPI-based digital wallet. It offers a broad set of services, including bill payments, recharges, insurance, mutual funds, and gold investments. PhonePe's UPI integration allows users to link their bank accounts and make payments directly from their account without the need for a separate wallet balance.

- **Google Pay:** Google Pay, formerly known as Tez, entered the Indian market in 2017. It is a UPI-based app that allows users to send and receive money, pay bills, recharge, and make purchases online and in-store. Google Pay's unique selling point is its frictionless integration with Google's ecosystem, offering a user-friendly experience with additional features like rewards and cashback.

- **Paytm:** Launched in 2010, Paytm is one of the largest digital wallets in India. It started as a mobile recharge platform and has since expanded into a broad financial services app, offering services like bill payments, online shopping, ticket booking, and investment options. Paytm also provides a UPI platform, allowing effortless money transfers between bank accounts.

- **Other Wallets:** Other notable digital wallets in India include Amazon Pay, Mobikwik, and Freecharge. These platforms offer similar services, with a focus on simplifying payments and providing additional features like discounts, cashback, and rewards.

Digital wallets in India operate on diverse business models and generate revenue through streams. The primary business models include:

- **Transaction Fees:** Digital wallets earn revenue by charging a small fee for each transaction. This fee can be a percentage of the transaction value or a flat fee, depending on the type of transaction and the parties involved. For instance, wallets may charge merchants for accepting payments through their platform.

- **Merchant Services:** Many digital wallets offer value-added services to merchants, such as point-of-sale (POS) systems, payment gateways, and analytics tools. These services help merchants manage their business more smoothly and increase customer satisfaction. Wallets earn revenue by charging merchants for these services.

- **Partnerships and Collaborations:** Digital wallets often collaborate with banks, financial institutions, and other service providers to offer exclusive deals and discounts. These partnerships can include co-branded credit and debit cards, insurance products, and investment options. Wallets earn revenue through commissions and referral fees from these partnerships.

- **Advertising and Promotions:** Digital wallets employ their large user base to offer advertising and promotional services to businesses. They can run targeted campaigns, display ads, and offer sponsored content to generate additional revenue.

- **Interest on Wallet Balances:** Some digital wallets offer users the option to store money in their wallet for future transactions. The wallet provider may earn interest on these balances by depositing them in a bank or investing in short-term financial instruments.

- **Financial Services:** In addition to payments, many digital wallets offer financial services such as loans, insurance, and investment products. These services are often provided in collaboration with banks and financial institutions. The wallet providers earn revenue through commissions, referral fees, and interest margins.

## 4.3.2 UPI: Architecture and Functionality

As discussed in earlier chapters, Unified Payments Interface (UPI) has revolutionized the Indian payment ecosystem by providing a smooth and secure platform for instant money transfers. Developed by the National Payments Corporation of India (NPCI), UPI integrates multiple bank accounts into a single mobile application, merging several banking features, frictionless fund routing, and merchant payments under one roof. This section covers architecture and functionality of UPI, highlighting NPCI's role and the UPI transaction flow.

The UPI architecture refers to the underlying framework that enables effortless and secure digital transactions between stakeholders, including users, banks, and the National Payments Corporation of India (NPCI). Here's an overview of the UPI architecture and how it supports the functionality of the system:

**UPI Architecture**

- **User Interface Layer:**

*Mobile Applications:* The user interface layer comprises mobile applications developed by banks, fintech companies, and other service providers. These apps offer user-friendly interfaces for customers to perform transactions. Popular UPI-enabled apps include Google Pay, PhonePe, Paytm, BHIM, and individual bank apps.

*Virtual Payment Address (VPA):* Users create a unique identifier called a VPA, which acts as an alias for their bank account. The VPA eliminates the need to share sensitive information like bank account numbers or IFSC codes, boosting security and convenience.

- **Application Programming Interface (API) Layer:**

*UPI APIs:* The UPI system uses a set of standardized APIs that enable smooth communication between many stakeholders. These APIs handle functions such as payment initiation, authentication, authorization, fund transfer, and transaction status updates.

*Interoperability:* The API layer secures interoperability between different UPI apps and bank systems. It allows users to link multiple bank accounts, make payments, and receive funds through any UPI-enabled app, regardless of the bank or service provider.

- **Switching and Routing Layer:**

*NPCI's UPI Switch:* At the core of the UPI architecture is NPCI's UPI switch, which acts as a central hub for processing and routing transactions. When a user initiates a payment, the UPI switch routes the request to the respective banks for authorization and settlement.

*Transaction Processing:* The switch handles real-time transaction processing, guaranteeing that payments are executed quickly and securely. It manages the flow of information between the payer's bank (issuing bank) and the payee's bank (acquiring bank).

- **Banking Systems:**

*Issuing Bank:* The issuing bank is the bank that holds the sender's account. When a UPI transaction is initiated, the issuing bank verifies the sender's credentials, checks for sufficient funds, and debits the account.

*Acquiring Bank:* The acquiring bank is the bank that holds the recipient's account. Upon receiving a transaction request, the acquiring bank credits the recipient's account with the specified amount.

- **Security and Compliance Layer:**

*Two-Factor Authentication (2FA):* UPI mandates two-factor authentication for all transactions. Users must authenticate transactions using a combination of their mobile device (registered mobile number) and UPI PIN, securing secure access.

*Encryption:* All data transmitted through the UPI system is encrypted, safeguarding user information and transaction details. NPCI uses advanced encryption protocols to protect against unauthorized access and data breaches.

- **Clearing and Settlement Layer:**

*Clearing:* Once a transaction is authorized, the UPI system clears the payment by reconciling the debit and credit entries between the issuing and acquiring banks.

*Settlement:* The final settlement of funds occurs between banks through NPCI's clearing and settlement system. This process involves the transfer of funds between banks' accounts with the Reserve Bank of India (RBI) or other designated settlement agencies.

## 4.3.3 NPCI's Role

The National Payments Corporation of India (NPCI) is the umbrella organization for operating retail payments and settlement systems in India. NPCI contributes to the development and management of UPI, safeguarding its smooth operation and widespread adoption. As the central authority, NPCI's responsibilities include:

*Development and Maintenance:* NPCI developed UPI as a strong and scalable platform to ease frictionless inter-bank transactions. It continuously maintains and upgrades the system to incorporate new features, improve security, and support the growing volume of transactions.

*Regulation and Compliance:* NPCI sets the rules and guidelines for UPI's operation, guaranteeing compliance with regulatory requirements. It collaborates with the Reserve Bank of India (RBI) to align UPI's functioning with the broader financial ecosystem.

*Security and Risk Management:* NPCI is responsible for securing the security and integrity of the UPI platform. It implements reliable security protocols, including two-factor authentication and encryption, to protect users' data and prevent fraud. NPCI also monitors transactions to detect and mitigate any fraudulent activities.

***Interoperability and Standards:*** NPCI safeguards the interoperability of UPI with different banks and financial institutions. It establishes technical standards and protocols that allow effortless integration of UPI with several banking systems, mobile applications, and payment gateways.

***Promotion and Adoption:*** NPCI actively promotes UPI through awareness campaigns, partnerships with banks, and collaborations with fintech companies. It works to increase the adoption of UPI among consumers, merchants, and businesses, promoting a digital payment culture in India.

## 4.3.4 Interoperability Among Wallets and Banks

The concept of interoperability among digital wallets and banks in India aims to create a smooth and integrated payment ecosystem where users can effortlessly transfer funds across different platforms and institutions. This initiative increases user convenience, promotes financial inclusion, and builds a competitive market environment.

### RBI Guidelines on Interoperability

The Reserve Bank of India (RBI) has factored into promoting interoperability among digital wallets and banks. Recognizing the fragmented nature of the payment field, the RBI issued guidelines to guarantee that digital wallets and banks can interoperate, allowing users to make transactions across different platforms without friction.

- **Mandate for Interoperability:** The RBI mandated that all prepaid payment instruments (PPIs), such as digital wallets, should enable interoperability with banks and other PPIs. This directive aimed to eliminate the silos that existed within the payment ecosystem, allowing users to transfer funds between wallets and bank accounts without friction.

- **Timeline and Phased Implementation:** The RBI introduced a phased implementation approach to secure a smooth transition towards interoperability. Initially, the focus was on enabling wallet-to-wallet and wallet-to-bank transactions. Subsequently, the scope was expanded to include other functionalities such as cash withdrawals and fund transfers via UPI.

- **Compliance and Penalties:** The RBI set clear deadlines for compliance, with strict penalties for non-adherence. Digital wallet providers and banks were required to upgrade their systems and infrastructure to support interoperability. The RBI closely monitored the progress and ensured that all stakeholders met the regulatory requirements.

- **Customer Protection Measures:** To safeguard consumers' interests, the RBI emphasized the need for solid customer protection measures. This included clear disclosure of transaction fees, transparent communication of terms and conditions, and the provision of grievance redressal mechanisms. The RBI also mandated that all interoperable transactions adhere to the same security standards as traditional banking transactions.

**Technical Standards for Interoperability**

Interoperability requires a sturdy technical infrastructure to safeguard frictionless communication and data exchange between different platforms. The RBI, in collaboration with the National Payments Corporation of India (NPCI) and other stakeholders, established technical standards and protocols to help interoperability.

- **Unified Payments Interface (UPI) Protocol:** UPI serves as a backbone for interoperability, providing a standardized interface for fund transfers. It enables users to link multiple bank accounts to a single UPI ID, allowing them to transact with any bank or wallet that supports UPI. The protocol includes features like real-time settlement, two-factor authentication, and secure data encryption.

- **Common API Standards:** The RBI and NPCI developed common API standards to make certain compatibility between different platforms. These standards define how digital wallets and banks should communicate with each other, including message formats, data structures, and transaction workflows. The use of common APIs simplifies integration and reduces the technical burden on service providers.

- **QR Code Standards:** To support effortless payments at merchant outlets, the RBI introduced standardized QR code specifications. This standardization allows merchants to generate a single QR code that can be scanned by any UPI-enabled app, regardless of the user's bank or wallet provider. The Bharat QR and UPI QR codes are examples of this standardization.

- **Security Protocols:** The RBI emphasized the importance of security in interoperable systems. It mandated the implementation of advanced security protocols, such as end-to-end encryption, tokenization, and secure socket layer (SSL) encryption. All transactions must comply with the Payment Card Industry Data Security Standard (PCI-DSS) to protect sensitive cardholder data.

- **Testing and Certification:** To guarantee the reliability and security of interoperable systems, the RBI established a rigorous testing and certification process. All digital wallets and banks were required to undergo testing by certified agencies to verify compliance with technical standards and security protocols. Only certified entities were allowed to participate in the interoperable ecosystem.

- **System Upgrades and Maintenance:** The RBI recognized the need for continuous system upgrades and maintenance to accommodate technological advancements and emerging threats. It encouraged service providers to invest in latest technologies, such as artificial intelligence (AI) and machine learning (ML), for fraud detection and risk management.

## 4.3.5 Regulatory Aspects of Digital Wallets in India

The rise of digital wallets in India has revolutionized the way transactions are conducted, offering a convenient and cashless mode of payment. As these platforms gained popularity, the need for a strong regulatory framework became evident to secure the security and integrity of financial transactions, protect consumer interests, and prevent misuse. The Reserve Bank of India (RBI), as the central regulatory authority, has laid down full guidelines to govern the functioning of digital wallets. This section covers regulatory aspects of digital wallets in India, focusing on Know Your Customer (KYC) requirements, transaction limits, and fund transfer restrictions.

### KYC Requirements

Know Your Customer (KYC) is a critical regulatory requirement in the financial sector, including digital wallets. The primary purpose of KYC is to verify the identity of customers, prevent money laundering, and safeguard the security of financial transactions. In India, the RBI mandates KYC compliance for all digital wallet providers, known as Prepaid Payment Instrument (PPI) issuers.

- **Types of KYC:** The RBI has outlined two types of KYC processes for digital wallets: minimum KYC and full KYC. Minimum KYC involves basic identification verification, typically using a one-time password (OTP) sent to the customer's registered mobile number. This level of KYC allows users to perform limited transactions. Full KYC, on the other hand, requires a more thorough verification process, including the submission of official documents such as Aadhaar, PAN card, passport, or voter ID.

- **Aadhaar-based KYC:** Aadhaar, India's biometric identification system, contributes to the KYC process for digital wallets. Aadhaar-based KYC offers a smooth and effective way to verify customer identities. It can be done through e-KYC, where customers authorize the wallet provider to access their Aadhaar details online, or through physical KYC, where customers submit a copy of their Aadhaar card. The Supreme Court's judgment on the usage of Aadhaar has, however, placed certain restrictions on its mandatory use, requiring wallet providers to offer alternative identification options.

- **KYC Update and Revalidation:** The RBI mandates that digital wallet providers periodically update and revalidate customer KYC information to make certain accuracy and compliance. This includes verifying any changes in customer details and updating expired documents. Providers must notify customers of the need to update their KYC information and provide a convenient process for doing so.

- **Consequences of Non-compliance:** Customers who do not complete the KYC process face restrictions on their wallet usage. For instance, wallets with only minimum KYC completed have lower transaction limits and are restricted from performing certain types of transactions, such as cross-border transfers. Non-compliance with KYC norms can also lead to account deactivation or freezing of funds.

## Transaction Limits and Fund Transfer Restrictions

Transaction limits are a central regulatory aspect governing digital wallets in India, set by the RBI to prevent misuse, manage risk, and guarantee compliance. The RBI classifies digital wallets into two categories: small PPIs and full-KYC PPIs, each with different transaction limits based on the account's KYC status.

- **Small PPIs:** With minimal KYC, the maximum wallet balance and total monthly transaction limit are capped at INR 10,000. These limits minimize misuse, focusing on small, everyday transactions.

- **Full-KYC PPIs**: These offer higher limits due to greater trust and security. The maximum balance can reach INR 2,00,000, with no monthly transaction cap.
- **Specific Transaction Limits**: Cash withdrawals and international transfers are subject to additional restrictions, including daily limits and heightened scrutiny.

**Fund Transfer Restrictions**

RBI guidelines govern fund transfers between wallets, bank accounts, and other payment instruments to prevent fraud and unauthorized use.

- **P2P Transfers**: Allowed within and across wallet providers, subject to transaction limits. Full-KYC wallet users face fewer restrictions than those with minimal KYC.
- **Bank Account Transfers**: Wallets are often linked to bank accounts, with transfers needing to comply with transaction limits and KYC norms.
- **Cross-border Transfers**: Permitted only for full-KYC wallets, with strict adherence to RBI and government regulations.
- **Merchant Payments**: Digital wallets are commonly used for online and offline merchant payments. RBI guidelines secure these transactions are secure, requiring measures like two-factor authentication.
- **Monitoring and Reporting**: Digital wallet providers must monitor and report suspicious transactions, especially those deviating from usual behavior or involving large amounts.

## 4.4 Cybersecurity and Risk Management

The digitalization of banking has brought unprecedented convenience and productivity to financial transactions. However, it has also introduced a new set of challenges and vulnerabilities, particularly in cybersecurity. As financial institutions increasingly rely on digital platforms, they become prime targets for cyberattacks. Safeguarding the security and integrity of financial systems has become critical, requiring reliable cybersecurity measures and effective risk management strategies. This section explores common cyber threats in banking, focusing on phishing, malware, and social engineering, and outlines the measures employed by banks to mitigate these risks.

### 4.4.1 Common Cyber Threats in Banking

Cyber threats in banking are diverse and constantly evolving. Cybercriminals employ sophisticated techniques to exploit vulnerabilities in systems and deceive users. The most prevalent threats include phishing, malware, and social engineering, each posing substantial risks to the security of financial institutions and their customers.

**Phishing**

Phishing is one of the most common and effective cyber threats targeting the banking sector. It involves fraudulent attempts to obtain sensitive information, such as usernames, passwords, and credit card details, by masquerading as a trustworthy entity in electronic communications. Phishing attacks can take a number of forms, including emails, text messages, and even phone calls, and are designed to trick recipients into divulging confidential information.

*Email Phishing:* Email phishing is the most traditional form of phishing. Attackers send emails that appear to come from legitimate sources, such as banks or well-known companies. These emails often contain urgent messages, such as account suspension notices or security alerts, prompting the recipient to click on a link or download an attachment. The link typically leads to a fake website that mimics the appearance of a legitimate site, where the victim is asked to enter sensitive information.

*Spear Phishing:* Spear phishing is a more targeted version of phishing, where attackers tailor their messages to specific individuals or organizations. This type of phishing often involves extensive research on the target to craft a convincing message. Spear phishing attacks are particularly dangerous because they are more likely to deceive the recipient due to the personalized nature of the communication.

*Smishing and Vishing:* Smishing (SMS phishing) and vishing (voice phishing) are variations of phishing that use text messages and phone calls, respectively. In smishing, attackers send messages that appear to be from a bank or service provider, asking the recipient to click on a link or call a number. Vishing involves fraudulent phone calls where the attacker pretends to be a bank representative or tech support agent, coercing the victim into providing sensitive information.

Phishing attacks can have severe consequences, including financial loss, identity theft, and unauthorized access to accounts. To combat phishing, banks implement security measures, such as email filters, multi-factor authentication, and user education programs that teach customers how to recognize and avoid phishing attempts.

## Malware

Malware, or malicious software, is a broad category of cyber threats that includes viruses, worms, trojans, ransomware, and spyware. These malicious programs are designed to infiltrate computer systems, steal information, disrupt operations, or extort money from victims. In the banking sector, malware can compromise the security of both individual users and financial institutions.

***Trojans and Banking Trojans:*** Trojans are malicious programs that disguise themselves as legitimate software to trick users into installing them. Once installed, they can perform harmful actions, such as stealing sensitive information or creating backdoors for remote access. Banking trojans specifically target online banking users, capturing login credentials and other confidential information. These trojans can be spread through phishing emails, malicious websites, or infected software downloads.

***Ransomware:*** Ransomware is a type of malware that encrypts a victim's data and demands a ransom payment in exchange for the decryption central. Ransomware attacks can disrupt the operations of financial institutions, prevent access to critical data, and result in major financial losses. Attackers often demand payment in cryptocurrencies, making it difficult to trace the transactions.

***Spyware and Keyloggers:*** Spyware is designed to secretly monitor and collect information from a victim's device. Keyloggers are a type of spyware that records keystrokes, allowing attackers to capture usernames, passwords, and other sensitive data. This information can then be used to gain unauthorized access to online banking accounts and commit fraud.

To protect against malware, banks employ a range of cybersecurity measures, including antivirus software, firewalls, intrusion detection systems, and regular security updates. Banks educate their customers on safe online practices, such as avoiding suspicious links and keeping their software up to date.

## Social Engineering

Social engineering is a technique used by cybercriminals to manipulate individuals into divulging confidential information or performing actions that compromise security. Unlike other cyber threats that exploit technical vulnerabilities, social engineering targets the human element, exploiting trust, curiosity, or fear to deceive victims. In the banking sector, social engineering can lead to unauthorized access to accounts, financial fraud, and data breaches.

***Pretexting:*** Pretexting involves creating a fabricated scenario or pretext to obtain information from the victim. The attacker often pretends to be someone in a position of authority or trust, such as a bank employee, law enforcement officer, or IT support technician. By gaining the victim's trust, the attacker can persuade them to reveal sensitive information, such as account numbers or login credentials.

***Baiting:*** Baiting involves offering something enticing to the victim, such as free software, music, or a gift card, in exchange for their personal information. This technique exploits the victim's curiosity or desire for a reward. For example, an attacker might leave a USB drive labeled "Confidential" in a public place, hoping that someone will pick it up and insert it into their computer, inadvertently installing malware.

***Quid Pro Quo:*** Quid pro quo involves offering a service or benefit in exchange for information or access. In a banking context, an attacker might pose as a customer service representative offering assistance with an account issue. The victim, believing they are receiving help, may provide sensitive information or grant access to their account.

***Tailgating:*** Tailgating, also known as piggybacking, is a physical social engineering technique where an attacker gains unauthorized access to a secure area by following an authorized person. In the banking industry, this could involve gaining access to a secure facility or data center. Once inside, the attacker can steal sensitive information or install malicious devices.

To defend against social engineering attacks, banks implement strict security protocols, such as identity verification procedures and access controls. Employee training is also necessary, as it raises awareness about the tactics used by social engineers and teaches staff how to recognize and respond to suspicious behavior. Also, banks encourage customers to verify the identity of anyone requesting sensitive information and to report any suspicious

## 4.4.2 Security Measures and Protocols

As the banking sector increasingly relies on digital infrastructure, implementing solid security measures and protocols is important to safeguard sensitive information and maintain the integrity of financial transactions. Cybersecurity in banking involves a complete approach that includes preventive, detective, and corrective measures. This section explores primary security measures and protocols employed by banks, focusing on firewalls and intrusion detection systems, data encryption, and secure coding practices.

### Firewalls and Intrusion Detection Systems

**Firewalls** and **Intrusion Detection Systems (IDS)** are components of a bank's cybersecurity infrastructure. They act as the first line of defense against unauthorized access and potential cyber threats.

**Firewalls**: A firewall is a network security device that monitors and controls incoming and outgoing network traffic based on predetermined security rules. Firewalls establish a barrier between trusted internal networks and untrusted external networks, such as the internet. They can be hardware-based, software-based, or a combination of both.

- **Packet Filtering**: Firewalls analyze packets of data as they travel across the network, determining whether they should be allowed through based on source and destination IP addresses, port numbers, and protocols. Packet filtering firewalls are effective at blocking unwanted traffic but may not provide deep inspection of packet contents.

- **Stateful Inspection**: More advanced firewalls use stateful inspection, which tracks the state of active connections and makes decisions based on the context of the traffic. This type of firewall provides a higher level of security by maintaining a table of active connections and guaranteeing that incoming packets correspond to an outgoing request.

- **Next-Generation Firewalls (NGFW)**: NGFWs combine traditional firewall capabilities with advanced features such as application awareness, deep packet inspection, and intrusion prevention. They provide thorough protection against all sorts of cyber threats, including malware, phishing, and data breaches.

**Intrusion Detection Systems (IDS)**: IDS are designed to detect and respond to potential security breaches or attacks. They monitor network traffic, system logs, and other sources of information to identify suspicious activities. IDS can be classified into two types:

**Network-based IDS (NIDS)**: NIDS monitors network traffic for signs of malicious activity. It analyzes packet data and compares it against known attack signatures or patterns of abnormal behavior. When a potential threat is detected, the IDS generates an alert, allowing security personnel to take appropriate action.

**Host-based IDS (HIDS)**: HIDS operates on individual hosts or devices, monitoring system logs, file integrity, and other indicators of compromise. It provides a more granular view of security events on specific systems and can detect unauthorized changes or suspicious behavior.

**Intrusion Prevention Systems (IPS)**: An extension of IDS, IPS not only detects potential threats but also takes proactive measures to prevent them. IPS can block malicious traffic, terminate suspicious sessions, and quarantine compromised devices. This capability is critical for real-time threat mitigation.

Firewalls and IDS/IPS are needed tools for maintaining the security of a bank's network infrastructure. They provide continuous monitoring, filtering, and analysis of network traffic, helping to prevent unauthorized access, data breaches, and other cyber incidents.

## Data Encryption

Data encryption is a fundamental security measure used to protect sensitive information from unauthorized access and disclosure. It involves converting plaintext data into a coded format, known as ciphertext, which can only be read by individuals who possess the correct decryption principal. Encryption is major for securing data both at rest and in transit.

***Encryption of Data at Rest***: Data at rest refers to data stored on physical media, such as hard drives, databases, and backup tapes. Encrypting data at rest guarantees that even if physical storage devices are compromised, the data remains unreadable without the decryption. Banks use many encryption algorithms, such as Advanced Encryption Standard (AES), to secure data stored on their servers and devices.

***Encryption of Data in Transit***: Data in transit refers to data being transmitted over a network. Encryption of data in transit protects information from interception and tampering during transmission. Secure communication protocols, such as Transport Layer Security (TLS) and Secure Sockets Layer (SSL), are commonly used to encrypt data exchanged between clients and servers, securing the confidentiality and integrity of the data.

***Public Infrastructure (PKI)***: PKI is a framework that uses cryptographic techniques to secure digital communications and transactions. It involves the use of public and private main pairs, digital certificates, and certificate authorities (CAs) to authenticate and encrypt data. PKI is widely used in banking for secure email communication, digital signatures, and secure web transactions.

***Tokenization***: As earlier discussed in previous chapters, It is a process that replaces sensitive data, such as credit card numbers, with a unique identifier or token. The token has no intrinsic value and cannot be used outside the specific context in which it was generated. Tokenization is commonly used in payment systems to protect sensitive payment information during transactions.

Data encryption is a component of a bank's cybersecurity strategy. It secures that sensitive information remains secure, even if accessed by unauthorized parties. Banks implement encryption protocols for several types of data, including customer information, financial transactions, and communication channels.

## Secure Coding Practices

**Secure coding practices** are necessary for developing software applications that are resistant to security vulnerabilities and attacks. Banks rely heavily on software systems for a number of functions, including online banking, mobile banking, and payment processing. Secure coding involves adhering to best practices and guidelines to minimize the risk of software vulnerabilities that could be exploited by attackers.

***Input Validation***: Input validation is an aspect of secure coding. It involves checking and sanitizing user inputs to safeguard they are within expected parameters. This prevents common vulnerabilities, such as SQL injection and cross-site scripting (XSS), which can occur when untrusted input is allowed to interact with the application's backend systems.

***Authentication and Authorization***: Secure coding practices include implementing strong authentication and authorization mechanisms. Authentication safeguards that only authorized users can access the system, while authorization determines the level of access granted to each user. Techniques such as multi-factor authentication (MFA) and role-based access control (RBAC) are commonly used to strengthen security.

***Secure Session Management***: Session management involves maintaining the state of a user's interaction with an application. Secure coding practices make certain that session tokens are generated securely, stored safely, and invalidated after use. This prevents session hijacking and other attacks that exploit session vulnerabilities.

***Error Handling and Logging***: Proper error handling and logging are critical for identifying and responding to security incidents. Secure coding practices involve creating detailed and meaningful error messages without revealing sensitive information. Logging mechanisms should record security-relevant events for monitoring and auditing purposes.

***Code Reviews and Testing***: Regular code reviews and security testing are components of secure coding practices. Code reviews involve manually inspecting the source code for potential security issues, while security testing includes techniques such as static code analysis, dynamic application security testing (DAST), and penetration testing. These practices help identify and remediate vulnerabilities before software deployment.

***Secure Development Lifecycle (SDL)***: The SDL is a process that integrates security considerations into every phase of the software development lifecycle. It includes requirements gathering, design, implementation, testing, deployment, and maintenance. The SDL guarantees that security is prioritized throughout the development process, resulting in more secure software products.

Secure coding practices are central for developing and maintaining secure banking applications. By adhering to these practices, banks can minimize the risk of software vulnerabilities and guarantee the security and reliability of their digital services.

### 4.4.3 Customer Education and Awareness

In the digital age, where cyber threats are becoming increasingly sophisticated, educating customers about security best practices and fraud prevention is central for safeguarding the safety of their financial information. Banks and financial institutions are involved in raising awareness and providing guidance to help customers protect themselves from cyber threats and fraudulent activities. This section covers central security best practices for customers and needed tips for fraud prevention.

**Security Best Practices for Customers**

To safeguard their personal and financial information, customers should adopt a set of security best practices. These practices help minimize the risk of falling victim to cyber attacks, identity theft, and other malicious activities. Some primary best practices include:

*Strong Passwords and Two-Factor Authentication*:

**Use Strong Passwords**: Customers should create strong, unique passwords for their online banking and other digital accounts. A strong password typically includes a combination of uppercase and lowercase letters, numbers, and special characters. It should be at least eight characters long and should not contain easily guessable information, such as birthdates or common words.

**Enable Two-Factor Authentication (2FA)**: Two-factor authentication adds an extra layer of security by requiring users to provide a second form of verification in addition to their password. This could be a code sent to their mobile phone, a biometric factor like a fingerprint, or a hardware token. 2FA notably reduces the likelihood of unauthorized access, even if the password is compromised.

*Regularly Update Software and Devices*:

**Keep Software Updated**: Customers should secure that their operating systems, browsers, and other software applications are up to date. Software updates often include security patches that address vulnerabilities, reducing the risk of exploitation by attackers.

**Secure Devices**: It is necessary to secure devices, such as computers, smartphones, and tablets, with the latest security features. Using antivirus software, enabling firewalls, and avoiding downloading apps from untrusted sources can help protect devices from malware and other threats.

*Protect Personal Information*:

**Be Cautious with Personal Information**: Customers should be mindful of the information they share online and over the phone. Personal details, such as Social Security numbers, bank account numbers, and passwords, should never be shared with unknown parties. Banks typically do not ask for sensitive information through email or phone calls, so customers should be wary of such requests.

**Use Secure Websites**: When conducting online transactions, customers should safeguard that the website is secure. Secure websites have URLs that begin with "https://" and display a padlock icon in the address bar. These indicators signify that the website uses encryption to protect data during transmission.

*Monitor Accounts Regularly*:

**Check Account Statements**: Customers should regularly review their bank account and credit card statements for any unauthorized transactions. Promptly reporting any suspicious activity to the bank can help prevent further fraud and mitigate potential losses.

**Set Up Account Alerts**: Many banks offer account alert services that notify customers of specific account activities, such as large transactions or changes in account settings. Setting up alerts can help customers stay informed and quickly detect unusual activity.

*Secure Communication Channels*:

**Use Secure Communication Channels**: When communicating with the bank or conducting transactions, customers should use secure channels. For instance, they should avoid using public Wi-Fi networks for online banking and prefer using their mobile data or a trusted private network. If public Wi-Fi must be used, employing a Virtual Private Network (VPN) can provide an additional layer of security.

## Fraud Prevention Tips

Fraud prevention is an aspect of maintaining financial security. Cybercriminals employ tactics to deceive individuals and gain access to their accounts. By being aware of these tactics and following fraud prevention tips, customers can better protect themselves from becoming victims of fraud.

*Recognize Phishing Attempts*:

**Identify Phishing Emails**: Phishing is a common cybercrime where attackers impersonate legitimate organizations to steal sensitive information. Customers should be cautious of unsolicited emails, especially those that ask for personal information or contain suspicious links and attachments. Phishing emails often have spelling errors, generic greetings, and a sense of urgency to trick recipients into responding quickly.

**Verify the Source**: Before clicking on links or providing information, customers should verify the authenticity of the communication. They can do this by contacting the organization directly using official contact information, rather than relying on the contact details provided in the suspicious message.

*Beware of Phone Scams*:

**Identify Caller Fraud**: Fraudsters may call individuals, posing as bank representatives, government officials, or tech support agents, to extract sensitive information. Customers should be cautious of unsolicited phone calls and never disclose personal or financial information over the phone unless they initiated the call to a verified number.

**Use Caller ID and Call Blocking**: Using caller ID and call-blocking features can help identify and prevent unwanted or fraudulent calls. If in doubt, customers should hang up and contact the organization directly using a verified number.

*Guard Against Social Engineering*:

**Understand Social Engineering Tactics**: Social engineering involves manipulating individuals into divulging confidential information. This can include pretexting (pretending to be someone else), baiting (offering something enticing), and tailgating (following someone into a restricted area). Customers should be aware of these tactics and avoid sharing personal information with strangers or individuals who cannot be verified.

**Question Unusual Requests**: If someone asks for unusual access or information, customers should question the request's legitimacy. They should not hesitate to verify the person's identity and purpose before complying.

*Secure Mobile Devices*:

**Lock Devices**: Customers should use PINs, passwords, or biometric authentication to lock their mobile devices. This prevents unauthorized access in case the device is lost or stolen.

**Be Cautious with Mobile Apps**: When downloading mobile apps, customers should only use official app stores and avoid third-party sources. They should also review app permissions and be cautious of apps that request access to sensitive information without a valid reason.

*Use Strong Security Questions and Backup Options*:

**Choose Secure Security Questions**: When setting up security questions for account recovery, customers should choose questions with answers that are difficult to guess. Avoiding common questions or using unconventional answers can add an extra layer of security.

**Set Up Backup Options**: Customers should set up backup authentication methods, such as secondary email addresses or phone numbers, for account recovery. This secures they can regain access to their accounts even if their primary method is compromised.

*Report Suspected Fraud Immediately*:

**Notify the Bank**: If customers suspect fraudulent activity on their accounts, they should immediately contact their bank's fraud department.

Quick reporting can help prevent further unauthorized transactions and initiate the process of recovering any lost funds.

**File a Complaint**: In addition to notifying the bank, customers should file a complaint with relevant authorities, such as the Federal Trade Commission (FTC) or local law enforcement. This can assist in tracking down the perpetrators and preventing future incidents.

### 4.4.4 Regulatory Guidelines on Cybersecurity

In India, the regulatory framework for cybersecurity in the banking sector is designed to make certain the safety and integrity of financial transactions and data. The Reserve Bank of India (RBI) is involved in shaping and enforcing these guidelines, focusing on creating a resilient cybersecurity infrastructure that can withstand the evolving threats in the digital sector. This section looks at aspects of the RBI's cybersecurity framework, incident reporting mechanisms, and the broader regulatory environment.

*Risk Assessment and Management*: The RBI mandates that banks conduct regular risk assessments to identify and evaluate potential cyber threats and vulnerabilities. This includes assessing the risks associated with new technologies, third-party vendors, and the evolving threat system. Based on the assessment, banks are required to implement appropriate risk management strategies, including preventive and detective controls.

*Governance and Oversight*: The framework emphasizes the importance of strong governance and oversight structures. Banks must establish a dedicated cybersecurity policy, approved by the Board of Directors, outlining the institution's approach to managing cyber risks. The policy should define the roles and responsibilities of stakeholders, including the Chief Information Security Officer (CISO), who is responsible for overseeing cybersecurity initiatives and reporting to senior management.

*Security Operations and Incident Management*: Banks are required to set up Security Operations Centers (SOCs) to monitor, detect, and respond to cybersecurity incidents. The SOCs must be equipped with advanced threat detection and response capabilities, including real-time monitoring tools, intrusion detection systems, and incident response protocols. The framework also mandates regular testing and validation of incident response plans through drills and simulations.

*Data Protection and Privacy*: Protecting customer data is a component of the RBI's cybersecurity framework. Banks must implement sturdy data protection measures, including encryption, secure data storage, and access controls. The framework also requires banks to comply with data privacy regulations, such as the Personal Data Protection Bill, to guarantee that customer information is handled with the utmost confidentiality and integrity.

***Training and Awareness***: The RBI emphasizes the need for continuous training and awareness programs for bank employees. These programs should cover the latest cybersecurity threats, best practices for data protection, and the bank's incident response procedures. Banks are also encouraged to educate their customers about safe online banking practices and the risks associated with phishing, malware, and other cyber threats.

***Third-Party Risk Management***: Banks often rely on third-party vendors and service providers for many IT and cybersecurity functions. The RBI's framework requires banks to conduct thorough due diligence and risk assessments of third-party entities. This includes evaluating the vendor's security controls, incident response capabilities, and compliance with relevant regulations. Banks must also include cybersecurity requirements in their contracts with third-party providers and regularly monitor their performance.

***Regulatory Compliance and Reporting***: Compliance with regulatory requirements is an aspect of the RBI's cybersecurity framework. Banks are required to submit regular reports to the RBI, detailing their cybersecurity posture, incidents, and the measures taken to address identified risks. The RBI conducts periodic audits and inspections to secure that banks adhere to the prescribed cybersecurity standards and guidelines.

## Incident Reporting Mechanisms

Timely and accurate reporting of cybersecurity incidents is important for mitigating the impact of cyber attacks and preventing their recurrence. The RBI has established specific incident reporting mechanisms that banks must follow in the event of a cybersecurity breach. These mechanisms are designed to safeguard that regulatory authorities are promptly informed and can take appropriate actions to safeguard the financial system.

***Immediate Notification***: In the event of a considerable cybersecurity incident, banks are required to notify the RBI immediately, within a specified timeframe. The notification should include preliminary details about the incident, such as the nature of the attack, the systems affected, and the initial assessment of the impact. This allows the RBI to assess the severity of the incident and coordinate a response, if necessary.

***Detailed Incident Report***: Following the initial notification, banks must submit a detailed incident report to the RBI within a stipulated period. The report should provide broad information about the incident, including the timeline of events, the methods used by the attackers, and the data or systems compromised. It should also outline the steps taken by the bank to contain and remediate the incident, as well as any measures implemented to prevent similar occurrences in the future.

***Root Cause Analysis***: As part of the incident reporting process, banks are required to conduct a root cause analysis to identify the underlying factors that contributed to the incident. The analysis should focus on uncovering any weaknesses in the bank's cybersecurity controls, policies, or procedures. The findings of the root cause analysis should be documented and shared with the RBI, along with recommendations for addressing the identified issues.

***Coordination with Law Enforcement***: In cases where a cybersecurity incident involves criminal activity, such as hacking, data theft, or fraud, banks are encouraged to cooperate with law enforcement agencies. The RBI's guidelines recommend that banks file a formal complaint with the relevant authorities and provide them with the necessary information and support to investigate the incident. Cooperation with law enforcement is necessary for tracking down cybercriminals and preventing further attacks.

***Communication with Customers and Stakeholders***: Transparency and effective communication are components of incident management. The RBI's framework advises banks to inform affected customers and stakeholders about the incident in a timely manner. This communication should include information about the nature of the incident, the potential impact on customer data, and the steps being taken to protect their information. Providing guidance on how customers can safeguard their accounts and report suspicious activities is also recommended.

***Post-Incident Review and Reporting***: After the resolution of a cybersecurity incident, banks are required to conduct a post-incident review to evaluate the effectiveness of their response and identify areas for improvement. The review should assess the bank's incident detection, response, and recovery capabilities, as well as the performance of the SOC and other relevant teams. The findings of the post-incident review should be documented and shared with the RBI as part of the final incident report.

***Continuous Monitoring and Reporting***: The RBI's cybersecurity framework emphasizes the importance of continuous monitoring and reporting of cybersecurity activities. Banks are required to maintain logs and records of all cybersecurity events, including unsuccessful attempts and minor incidents. These logs should be regularly reviewed and analyzed to detect patterns and trends that could indicate potential threats. Banks are also encouraged to participate in information-sharing initiatives with other financial institutions and regulatory bodies to boost their situational awareness and preparedness.

# Chapter 5
# The Role of Technology in Payment Systems

Technology has revolutionized the field of payment systems, fundamentally altering the way transactions are conducted. From the development of simple electronic funds transfer systems to the emergence of sophisticated digital payment platforms, technological advancements have enabled faster, safer, and more convenient payment solutions. This chapter revisits some of the earlier covered aspects in Payment Systems point of view, and at the same time the aspects like UPI which directly fall under the PSS and are critically discussed in association with banking earlier are not repeated here, highlighting the interlinkage between both the entities.

**Payment System Operators (PSOs)** are organizations authorized by the Reserve Bank of India to operate payment systems in the country. These entities are responsible for the governance, management, and operation of systems that enable fund transfers, settlement, and clearing services. PSOs contribute to maintaining the infrastructure that supports several payment methods and safeguards their smooth functioning.

**Payment Service Providers (PSPs),** on the other hand, are entities that offer payment services directly to end-users, including consumers and merchants. PSPs encompass a span of organizations, from traditional banks to new fintech companies. They ease the processing of digital payments through a number of channels and instruments, making it easier for individuals and businesses to conduct financial transactions.

**Institute for Development & Research in Banking Technology (IDRBT),** established by the Reserve Bank of India in 1996, serves as the foundation for banking technology research and development in India. As an autonomous center, IDRBT has been driving developing modern technologies and solutions for the banking sector. Its primary mandate includes conducting research, providing consultancy services, and offering training programs to banking professionals. The institute has contributed to incubating fintech startups, building breakthrough, and bridging the gap between academia and the banking industry. One of IDRBT's most notable contributions has been the development of the **Indian Financial Network**

**(INFINET)**, a closed user group network for the banking and financial sector. This network has been instrumental in supporting secure communication and data exchange among banks and financial institutions. IDRBT has also been instrumental in developing standards for banking operations, including the Structured Financial Messaging System (SFMS), which has become the backbone of financial messaging in India.

**Indian Financial Technology and Allied Services (IFTAS)**, a wholly-owned subsidiary of IDRBT, was established in 2015 to focus on the operational aspects of financial technologies. While IDRBT continues to drive research and advance, IFTAS takes charge of implementing and managing the technologies developed. This separation of roles has allowed for more quick and focused operations in both research and implementation domains. IFTAS's primary responsibilities include managing and operating critical financial infrastructures, providing technology services to banks and financial institutions, and developing and maintaining main financial networks and systems. By taking over the operational aspects, IFTAS has allowed IDRBT to focus more intensively on research and development, leading to a more dynamic and novel financial technology ecosystem in India. Developed by IDRBT and IFTAS, SFMS is a secure messaging standard developed specifically for the Indian financial system. It is involved in enabling inter-bank and intra-bank communication, enabling secure electronic fund transfers, and supporting payment and settlement systems in India.

The importance of SFMS cannot be overstated. It has replaced the need for paper-based communication in inter-bank transactions, markedly reducing the time and cost involved in these processes. SFMS guarantees standardization and interoperability in financial messaging, allowing for smooth communication between different banks and financial institutions. This standardization has been central in the implementation of many payment systems, including RTGS (Real Time Gross Settlement) and NEFT (National Electronic Funds Transfer). SFMS has boosted the security of financial transactions by using advanced encryption techniques. This has been instrumental in building trust in electronic financial transactions among both institutions and consumers. The system's ability to handle large volumes of transactions quickly has been necessary in supporting the growth of digital payments in India. The collaborative efforts of IDRBT, IFTAS, and the implementation of SFMS have greatly contributed to the modernization of India's banking and payment systems. They have enabled the sector to keep pace with global technological advancements while addressing India-specific challenges and requirements.

These entities and systems have contributed to supporting the government's digital India initiative and the push towards a less-cash economy. They have provided the technological backbone for initiatives like the Unified Payments Interface (UPI), which has revolutionized digital payments in India.

## 5.1 Payment Gateways and Processors

Payment processors and payment gateways are needed components of the electronic payment ecosystem, each serving distinct but interconnected roles in easing transactions. As discussed in earlier chapters, a payment processor acts as an intermediary between merchants, customers, and banks, handling the verification and transfer of funds during a transaction. It communicates with the issuing and acquiring banks to make certain smooth fund transfers, verifies transaction details, and manages aspects like chargebacks and disputes. On the other hand, a payment gateway is the front-end technology that captures and securely transfers payment data from the customer to the payment processor. It encrypts sensitive information, routes transaction details, authorizes or declines transactions based on risk factors, and supports several payment methods. While payment processors focus on the back-end communication with financial institutions to complete transactions, payment gateways provide the secure interface for customers to enter their payment information. Together, these two components enable businesses to accept electronic payments securely and effectively in both online and physical store environments.

### 5.1.1 Architecture

The architecture is designed to handle many payment methods, including credit cards, debit cards, digital wallets, and direct bank transfers. It can be divided into three components: front-end systems, back-end systems, and integration with bank networks. Each component helps with guaranteeing the smooth and secure processing of transactions.

***Front-end Systems***

Front-end systems are the customer-facing components of payment gateways. They are responsible for collecting payment information from customers and transmitting it securely to the back-end systems. The functions of front-end systems include:

**User Interface (UI)**: The UI is the component that interacts with customers, providing them with a frictionless and intuitive experience when entering their payment details. This includes the web page or mobile app screen where customers input their card information, such as card number, expiration date, and CVV. The UI must be designed to be user-friendly, accessible, and compliant with industry standards, such as the Payment Card Industry Data Security Standard (PCI DSS).

**Data Encryption**: To protect sensitive payment information, front-end systems employ encryption techniques to secure data during transmission. Encryption secures that the information is unreadable to unauthorized parties, thus safeguarding against data breaches and fraud. Technologies like Transport Layer Security (TLS) are commonly used to encrypt data between the customer's device and the payment gateway.

**Tokenization**: Tokenization is a security process that replaces sensitive payment information with a unique identifier called a token. The token is used to process the payment without exposing the actual card details. This reduces the risk of data theft, as the token cannot be reverse engineered to obtain the original information. Tokenization is widely used in mobile wallets and online payment platforms.

**Fraud Detection and Prevention**: Front-end systems are equipped with fraud detection and prevention tools to identify and mitigate suspicious activities. These tools analyze a number of factors, such as the customer's location, transaction history, and device information, to assess the risk of fraud. If a transaction is flagged as potentially fraudulent, additional verification steps, such as two-factor authentication (2FA), may be required.

### Back-end Systems

Back-end systems are the components of payment gateways that handle the processing and authorization of transactions. They are responsible for securely transmitting payment data to the appropriate financial institutions and securing that transactions are completed successfully. The functions of back-end systems include:

**Transaction Routing**: Back-end systems route payment information to the correct acquiring bank or payment processor. This involves determining the appropriate payment network (e.g., Visa, Mastercard) based on the card type and routing the transaction accordingly. The routing process is optimized to guarantee quick and smooth processing, minimizing transaction times.

**Authorization and Authentication**: The authorization process involves verifying the customer's payment details and checking for sufficient funds or credit availability. Back-end systems communicate with the issuing bank to authenticate the transaction, safeguarding that the payment information is valid and that the cardholder has authorized the transaction. If the authorization is successful, an approval code is generated, and the transaction proceeds.

**Clearing and Settlement**: Once a transaction is authorized, back-end systems manage the clearing and settlement processes. Clearing involves the exchange of transaction information between the acquiring and issuing banks, while settlement refers to the actual transfer of funds from the customer's account to the merchant's account. These processes are typically completed within one to two business days, depending on the payment method and network.

**Data Management and Reporting**: Back-end systems store transaction data and generate reports for merchants and financial institutions. These reports provide insights into transaction volumes, payment methods, and other metrics, helping businesses analyze their sales and financial performance. Data management also includes maintaining compliance with regulatory requirements, such as data retention and privacy laws.

### Integration with Bank Networks

Integration with bank networks is an aspect of payment gateway architecture. It enables effortless communication between payment gateways, acquiring banks, and issuing banks, supporting the effective processing of transactions. The integration process involves several components:

**Application Programming Interfaces (APIs)**: APIs are the primary means of communication between payment gateways and bank networks. They provide a standardized way for different systems to interact, exchange data, and execute transactions. APIs enable payment gateways to connect with multiple banks and payment processors, offering merchants a broad set of payment options. The use of APIs also allows for real-time transaction processing and status updates.

**Payment Networks and Schemes**: Payment networks, such as Visa, Mastercard, and American Express, are involved in the payment ecosystem. They establish the rules and standards for processing transactions, including security protocols, interchange fees, and dispute resolution procedures. Payment gateways must comply with these standards and integrate with the networks to help transactions. Payment gateways may connect with domestic payment schemes, such as RuPay in India, to support local payment methods.

**Interchange Fees and Settlement**: Interchange fees are the fees charged by the issuing bank to the acquiring bank for processing a transaction. These fees are a component of the payment processing cost and vary based on factors such as card type, transaction size, and risk level. Payment gateways must account for interchange fees when calculating the total cost of a transaction. The settlement process involves reconciling transactions and guaranteeing that funds are transferred from the issuing bank to the acquiring bank, and ultimately to the merchant's account.

**Compliance and Security**: Integration with bank networks requires adherence to strict security and compliance standards. Payment gateways must comply with PCI DSS, which sets the requirements for securing cardholder data. Also, payment gateways must follow regulations related to anti-money laundering (AML), know your customer (KYC), and data protection. Compliance safeguards that payment gateways operate within legal and regulatory frameworks, protecting both customers and businesses.

**Redundancy and Failover Mechanisms**: To secure the reliability and availability of payment services, payment gateways implement redundancy and failover mechanisms. This includes maintaining multiple connections to bank networks and data centers to handle high transaction volumes and minimize downtime. In the event of a system failure or network outage, failover mechanisms automatically switch to backup systems, securing that transactions can still be processed without disruption.

## 5.1.2 Major Payment Processors in India

The payment processing sector in India has evolved considerably over the years, with a dynamic mix of domestic and international players. These payment processors are necessary intermediaries in the digital payment ecosystem, enabling transactions between merchants and consumers through secure and quick platforms. Here we examine the major payment processors in India, categorizing them into domestic and international players, and explores into the competitive environment, market share, and the factors driving their growth.

### *Domestic Players*

India's domestic payment processors have was involved in the rapid adoption of digital payments across the country. These processors cater to all sorts of payment methods, including card payments, UPI, mobile wallets, and net banking. The domestic players include:

- **Razorpay**: Founded in 2014, Razorpay has quickly become one of India's leading payment processors. It offers a full suite of payment solutions, including payment gateway services, payment links, subscriptions, and more. Razorpay supports multiple payment methods, such as credit/debit cards, UPI, net banking, and mobile wallets. Its user-friendly interface, strong developer support, and focus on development have made it a popular choice among businesses of all sizes.

- **PayU India**: PayU India is a prominent payment processor that has been serving the Indian market since 2011. It provides payment gateway services and other financial solutions, including merchant lending and buy now, pay later (BNPL) options. PayU supports a span of payment methods, including cards, UPI, and mobile wallets. The company's strong focus on security and compliance has helped it establish a strong presence in the market.

- **BillDesk**: Established in 2000, BillDesk is one of India's oldest and most trusted payment processors. It offers a variety of payment solutions, including bill payments, utility payments, and online payment gateways. BillDesk's extensive network and partnerships with banks and financial institutions have made it a player in the Indian payment ecosystem. It supports multiple payment methods, including cards, net banking, and UPI.

- **CCAvenue**: CCAvenue, founded in 2001, is a leading payment gateway provider in India. It offers a complete range of payment solutions, including multi-currency processing, EMI options, and digital wallets. CCAvenue supports a vast array of payment methods, making it a versatile option for businesses looking to expand their payment acceptance capabilities. The company's reliable security measures and smooth integration options have contributed to its success.

- **Instamojo**: Instamojo is a popular payment processor that caters to small and medium-sized enterprises (SMEs) in India. Launched in 2012, Instamojo offers a simple and user-friendly platform for businesses to accept payments online. It provides payment links, online stores, and digital goods sales options. Instamojo supports payment methods, including cards, UPI, and wallets, making it an accessible choice for entrepreneurs and small businesses.

In addition to domestic players, several international payment processors have made marked inroads into the Indian market. These global companies bring with them advanced technologies, international expertise, and many payment solutions. The main international players include:

- **PayPal**: PayPal is a globally recognized payment processor that has been operating in India since 2017. It offers a secure and convenient platform for online payments, enabling users to send and receive money domestically and internationally. PayPal supports multiple payment methods, including cards, bank transfers, and its own digital wallet. Its strong brand presence and focus on security have made it a popular choice for cross-border transactions.

- **Stripe**: Stripe, a leading payment processing company based in the United States, entered the Indian market in 2019. Stripe offers a thorough suite of payment solutions, including payment gateway services, subscription billing, and global payouts. The company's solid API and developer-friendly platform have made it a preferred choice for technology-driven businesses. Stripe supports a broad set of payment methods, including cards, UPI, and digital wallets.

- **Square**: Square, another prominent payment processor from the United States, has gradually expanded its presence in India. Square offers a range of payment solutions, including point-of-sale (POS) systems, online payment gateways, and invoicing services. The company's user-friendly platform and integration capabilities have made it a popular choice for small businesses and retail merchants. Square supports payment methods, including cards and mobile payments.

- **Worldline**: Worldline is a global payment processor that entered the Indian market through its acquisition of Ingenico. Worldline offers all sorts of payment solutions, including payment terminals, online payment gateways, and mobile payment solutions. The company's extensive experience in the payment industry and its focus on breakthrough have helped it establish a strong presence in India. Worldline supports multiple payment methods, including cards, UPI, and digital wallets.

- **Adyen**: Adyen is a Dutch payment processor that provides a unified platform for global payment acceptance. Adyen's presence in India has grown steadily, offering businesses a broad suite of payment solutions, including payment gateway services, risk management, and fraud prevention. Adyen supports a span of payment methods, including cards, UPI, and local payment methods. The company's focus on frictionless cross-border transactions has made it a popular choice for international businesses operating in India.

### Market Share and Competition

The Indian payment processing market is highly competitive, with both domestic and international players vying for market share. The competition is driven by factors such as technological advance, customer service, security, and pricing. Several central trends and dynamics shape the competitive system:

- **Technological Development**: Technological advancements help with differentiating payment processors in India. Companies invest heavily in developing new features, such as real-time payments, artificial intelligence (AI)-driven fraud detection, and effortless integration capabilities. The introduction of UPI has been a game-changer, allowing payment processors to offer instant and secure transactions, further intensifying competition.

- **Customer Service and User Experience**: Customer service and user experience are factors in gaining and retaining market share. Payment processors that offer intuitive interfaces, easy onboarding, and smooth customer support tend to attract more merchants and consumers. Companies also focus on providing full analytics and reporting tools, enabling businesses to track and optimize their payment processes.

- **Security and Compliance**: Security is a top priority for payment processors, given the increasing prevalence of cyber threats and data breaches. Companies invest in advanced security measures, such as encryption, tokenization, and multi-factor authentication, to protect sensitive payment information. Compliance with regulations, such as PCI DSS and AML/KYC norms, is also important for maintaining trust and credibility.

- **Pricing and Fees**: Pricing is a primary competitive factor in the Indian payment processing market. Payment processors offer many pricing models, including flat-rate fees, interchange-plus pricing, and tiered pricing. Competitive pricing, coupled with transparent fee structures, can be a substantial differentiator. Companies may offer discounts, incentives, and promotional offers to attract new customers.

- **Partnerships and Ecosystem Integration**: Partnerships with banks, financial institutions, and technology providers are necessary for expanding the reach and capabilities of payment processors. Companies collaborate with banks to offer co-branded solutions, integrate with e-commerce platforms, and provide value-added services, such as lending and financial management. Ecosystem integration improves the overall customer experience and provides additional revenue streams.

- **Market Share Dynamics**: The market share of payment processors in India is influenced by several factors, including brand reputation, product offerings, and target customer segments. Domestic players, such as Razorpay and PayU India, have a strong presence in the SME and startup segments, while international players, such as PayPal and Stripe, cater to global businesses and cross-border transactions. The UPI ecosystem has also created opportunities for new entrants and fintech companies, leading to increased competition.

### 5.1.3 Integration with E-commerce Platforms

The integration of payment gateways and processors with e-commerce platforms is a component of the online shopping experience. It guarantees that transactions are smooth, secure, and user-friendly, allowing customers to pay for goods and services smoothly. This integration can be achieved through several methods, each offering features and benefits. In this section, we explore the principal integration methods used by payment processors and e-commerce platforms, focusing on API-based integration, hosted payment pages, and checkout SDKs.

*API-based Integration*

API-based integration is one of the most popular and flexible methods for integrating payment gateways with e-commerce platforms. It involves the use of Application Programming Interfaces (APIs) that allow developers to connect the payment processor's system directly with the e-commerce website or mobile app.

**Features and Benefits:**

**Customization**: API-based integration offers a high degree of customization, allowing businesses to tailor the payment process to their specific needs. Merchants can design their checkout flow, implement custom user interfaces, and control the entire transaction experience.

**Smooth User Experience**: Since the payment process is integrated directly into the e-commerce platform, customers can complete transactions without being redirected to external sites. This frictionless experience can increase customer satisfaction and reduce cart abandonment rates.

**Security**: API-based integration allows merchants to implement sturdy security measures, such as tokenization and encryption, to protect sensitive payment information. Payment processors typically provide APIs that comply with industry standards, such as PCI DSS, safeguarding secure transactions.

**Advanced Features**: APIs enable the implementation of advanced payment features, such as recurring billing, subscriptions, and split payments. Merchants can also access real-time transaction data and analytics through API endpoints, helping them make informed business decisions.

**Challenges**:

**Development Complexity**: Implementing API-based integration requires technical expertise and resources. Developers must manage the integration, testing, and maintenance of the API, which can be complex and time-consuming.

**Compliance and Security**: Merchants must safeguard that their systems comply with regulatory requirements and maintain high security standards. This includes regular audits, security patches, and adherence to data protection regulations.

### *Hosted Payment Pages*

Hosted payment pages are an alternative integration method that involves redirecting customers to a secure, external payment page hosted by the payment processor. This method simplifies the integration process for merchants and provides a secure environment for handling payment transactions.

**Features and Benefits**:

**Simplicity**: Hosted payment pages are easy to implement, requiring minimal technical expertise. Merchants can quickly set up payment processing without extensive development work.

**Security**: Since the payment process is handled by the payment processor, merchants do not need to store or manage sensitive payment information. This reduces the risk of data breaches and simplifies compliance with security standards like PCI DSS.

**Customization Options**: While not as flexible as API-based integration, hosted payment pages often offer some customization options. Merchants can typically add their branding elements, such as logos and color schemes, to maintain a consistent user experience.

**Fraud Prevention**: Payment processors that provide hosted payment pages often include built-in fraud detection and prevention tools. This can help merchants minimize fraudulent transactions and chargebacks.

**Challenges**:

**Limited Control**: Hosted payment pages offer less control over the checkout process compared to API-based integration. Merchants may not be able to customize the user experience to the same extent, which can be a limitation for businesses with specific branding or functionality requirements.

**Redirection**: The process of redirecting customers to an external payment page can sometimes lead to higher cart abandonment rates. Customers may feel uneasy about leaving the e-commerce site to complete their transaction, which can impact conversion rates.

## Checkout SDKs

Checkout SDKs (Software Development Kits) provide a middle-ground solution between API-based integration and hosted payment pages. SDKs offer pre-built components and tools that developers can use to integrate payment processing features directly into their e-commerce platforms.

**Features and Benefits**:

**Ease of Integration**: Checkout SDKs simplify the integration process by providing pre-built code libraries and components. Developers can quickly integrate payment functionality without building it from scratch, reducing development time and effort.

**Customization and Control**: SDKs offer a balance between customization and ease of use. Merchants can customize the payment flow and user interface while tapping the pre-built components provided by the SDK.

**Security**: Payment processors that offer checkout SDKs typically make certain that the SDKs comply with security standards, such as PCI DSS. This helps merchants maintain a secure payment environment without extensive security management.

**Cross-Platform Compatibility**: Many checkout SDKs are designed to work across different platforms, including web and mobile. This allows merchants to offer a consistent payment experience across multiple channels.

**Challenges**:

**Dependence on SDK Provider**: Merchants rely on the SDK provider for updates, support, and security patches. Any issues with the SDK can impact the payment experience and require prompt resolution from the provider.

**Customization Limitations**: While SDKs offer some customization options, they may not provide the same level of flexibility as fully custom-built solutions. Merchants may need to work within the constraints of the SDK's features and capabilities.

The integration of payment gateways and processors with e-commerce platforms is an aspect of the digital payment field. The choice of integration method, whether API-based integration, hosted payment pages, or checkout SDKs, depends on a number of factors, including the level of customization required, technical expertise available, and security considerations. Each method offers advantages and challenges, and businesses must carefully evaluate their specific needs and resources to choose the most suitable option. As e-commerce continues to grow, the importance of effortless and secure payment integration will only increase, making it needed for businesses to stay updated with the latest technologies and trends in payment systems.

## 5.1.4 Security Standards (PCI-DSS)

The Payment Card Industry Data Security Standard (PCI-DSS) is a complete set of security standards introduced by the Payment Card Industry Security Standards Council (PCI SSC). The PCI SSC, established in 2006 by major payment card brands including Visa, MasterCard, American Express, Discover, and JCB, aims to improve global payment account security by setting standards and supporting services that promote education, awareness, and effective implementation among stakeholders.

### *Compliance Requirements*

Compliance with PCI-DSS is mandatory for any organization that handles payment card data. The standards are designed to protect cardholder data and mitigate the risks of breaches and fraud. The PCI-DSS comprises six objectives, divided into these requirements:

1. Build and Maintain a Secure Network and Systems: This involves creating a strong infrastructure that can withstand potential security threats.
2. Install and maintain firewall configurations: Firewalls act as a barrier between trusted internal networks and untrusted external networks.

3. Avoid vendor-supplied defaults for passwords and security parameters: Default settings are often weak and widely known, making them easy targets for attackers.

4. Protect Cardholder Data: This secures that sensitive payment information is safeguarded against unauthorized access or theft.

5. Secure stored data: Any cardholder data that is kept on file must be protected through encryption or other security measures.

6. Encrypt data transmission across public networks: This prevents interception of data as it travels across the internet or other public networks.

7. Maintain a Vulnerability Management Program: This involves regularly checking for and addressing potential weaknesses in the system.

8. Regularly update anti-virus software: This helps protect against the latest malware and cyber threats.

9. Develop and maintain secure systems and applications: This safeguards that all software used in the payment process is designed with security in mind.

10. Implement Strong Access Control Measures: This limits who can access sensitive data and systems.

11. Restrict access based on business need: Only those who require access to perform their job should have it.

12. Identify and authenticate system access: This guarantees that only authorized individuals can access the system.

13. Limit physical access to cardholder data: This prevents unauthorized individuals from physically accessing servers or other hardware storing sensitive data.

14. Regularly Monitor and Test Networks: This helps detect any unusual activity or potential breaches.

15. Track and monitor all network access: This creates an audit trail of who accessed what and when.

16. Test security systems and processes regularly: This secures that security measures are working as intended.

17. Maintain an Information Security Policy: This provides guidelines for all employees on how to handle sensitive information and maintain security.

*Data Security Measures*

To comply with PCI-DSS, organizations must implement reliable data security measures, including:

1. Encryption: This is the process of encoding information to protect its confidentiality.

2. Data at Rest: Encrypt sensitive cardholder data stored in databases, files, or other storage media. This safeguards it remains inaccessible to unauthorized users even if storage systems are compromised.

3. Data in Transit: Use strong encryption protocols such as Transport Layer Security (TLS) to secure data transmission over open, public networks. This protects information as it travels between systems or over the internet.

4. Tokenization: Replace sensitive card data with a unique identifier (token) that cannot be reverse-engineered. This minimizes the amount of sensitive data handled and stored, reducing potential exposure.

5. Access Control: Implement multi-factor authentication (MFA) and role-based access control (RBAC). These measures guarantee that only authorized individuals can access cardholder data, adding layers of security beyond simple passwords.

6. Monitoring and Logging: Maintain thorough logs of all access to network resources and cardholder data. This eases the detection of and response to security incidents by creating an audit trail of system activities.

7. Physical Security: Implement physical security controls to protect facilities housing sensitive data. This includes surveillance systems, secure access points, and secure storage, preventing unauthorized physical access to data.

8. Vulnerability Management: Regularly update and patch systems, use anti-virus software, and conduct vulnerability assessments and penetration testing. This proactive approach helps identify and address potential weaknesses before they can be exploited.

*Auditing and Certification Process*

The PCI-DSS compliance process includes thorough auditing and certification to secure organizations meet the necessary standards:

1. Scope Definition: Identify all system components involved in storing, processing, or transmitting cardholder data. This step guarantees that all relevant parts of the system are included in the compliance process.

2. Self-Assessment or External Audit: Organizations may complete a Self-Assessment Questionnaire (SAQ) or undergo an external audit by a

Qualified Security Assessor (QSA). The choice depends on the organization's size and transaction volume, guaranteeing appropriate scrutiny.

3. Assessment and Remediation: Review security measures and address any non-compliance issues identified during the assessment. This step is important for closing security gaps and improving overall system protection.

4. Report on Compliance (ROC) and Attestation of Compliance (AOC): Compile a ROC detailing the assessment findings and complete an AOC to confirm compliance with PCI-DSS requirements. These documents provide formal evidence of the organization's compliance status.

5. Certification and Ongoing Compliance: Achieve certification of compliance and maintain it through continuous monitoring, regular assessments, and adherence to PCI-DSS standards. This secures ongoing protection as threats evolve.

6. Incident Response and Reporting: Have an incident response plan in place to address security breaches. This includes notifying affected parties and conducting forensic investigations, important for minimizing damage and preventing future incidents.

## 5.2 Blockchain and Cryptocurrencies

Blockchain technology and cryptocurrencies have revolutionized the digital sector, offering new ways of conducting transactions, storing data, and creating decentralized applications. This technology is characterized by its distributed nature, cryptographic security, and potential to transform industries. In this section, we will explore the basics of blockchain technology, including the concept of distributed ledgers, consensus mechanisms, and smart contracts, as well as their implications and applications.

### 5.2.1 Basics of Blockchain Technology

*Distributed Ledger Concept*

At the core of blockchain technology lies the concept of a distributed ledger, a digital record of transactions or data that is maintained across a network of computers, known as nodes. Unlike traditional centralized databases, where data is stored on a single server or a group of servers under the control of a single entity, a distributed ledger is decentralized. This means that no single party has complete control over the entire system, improving transparency and security.

Each node in a blockchain network maintains a copy of the entire ledger, and updates are made through a consensus process, securing that all copies are identical and up-to-date. The data in a blockchain is structured in blocks, which are linked together in a chronological chain. Each block contains a set of transactions or data entries, a timestamp, and a cryptographic hash of the previous block, creating a secure and immutable record.

The distributed nature of blockchain technology offers several benefits:

- **Decentralization**: No single point of control or failure, reducing the risk of data tampering, censorship, and outages.

- **Transparency**: All transactions are visible to network participants, promoting accountability and trust.

- **Security**: The use of cryptographic techniques and consensus mechanisms makes it difficult for malicious actors to alter the ledger.

### Consensus Mechanisms

Consensus mechanisms are protocols used to achieve agreement among nodes in a blockchain network on the state of the ledger. They are central for safeguarding the integrity and security of the blockchain. Several consensus mechanisms have been developed, each with its own advantages and trade-offs.

### Smart Contracts

Smart contracts are self-executing contracts with the terms of the agreement directly written into code. They automatically enforce and execute the terms of the contract when predefined conditions are met, without the need for intermediaries. Smart contracts are a fundamental feature of blockchain platforms like Ethereum, enabling many decentralized applications (dApps) and services.

The characteristics of smart contracts include:

- **Automation**: Smart contracts automate the execution of contract terms, reducing the need for manual intervention and minimizing the risk of human error.

- **Transparency**: The code and execution of smart contracts are transparent and accessible to all participants in the blockchain network, guaranteeing that the terms are clear and verifiable.

- **Immutability**: Once deployed on the blockchain, smart contracts cannot be altered, securing the integrity and trustworthiness of the contract.

- **Effectiveness**: Smart contracts speed up processes by removing intermediaries, reducing costs and delays associated with traditional contracts.

Smart contracts have applications across industries, including finance, supply chain management, real estate, and healthcare. For example, in the finance sector, smart contracts can automate the settlement of financial derivatives, enforce lending agreements, and support tokenized asset transactions. In supply chain management, they can track the movement of goods, verify the authenticity of products, and safeguard timely payments.

Despite their potential, smart contracts also present challenges, such as the difficulty of coding complex legal agreements into smart contract code, the risk of coding errors or vulnerabilities, and the need for a reliable oracle system to provide external data inputs.

## 5.2.2 Potential Applications in Banking and Payments

Blockchain technology has far-reaching implications for the banking and payments sectors, offering fresh solutions to longstanding challenges. Its applications can strengthen speed, security, and transparency in many financial processes. We now turn to the potential of blockchain in cross-border payments, trade finance, and Know Your Customer (KYC) processes.

### Cross-border Payments

Cross-border payments have traditionally been complex, costly, and slow, often involving multiple intermediaries and facing challenges related to currency conversion, compliance, and transparency. Blockchain technology offers a promising solution by enabling faster, cheaper, and more transparent transactions across borders.

### Trade Finance

Trade finance involves several financial products and services that enable international trade, such as letters of credit, trade credits, and invoice financing. The traditional trade finance process is often paper-intensive, time-consuming, and prone to errors and fraud. Blockchain technology can transform trade finance by digitizing and automating processes, strengthening transparency, and reducing risks.

- **Digitization and Automation**:
Blockchain can digitize trade documents, such as bills of lading, invoices, and letters of credit, making them easily accessible and shareable among parties. Smart contracts can automate the execution of trade agreements,

triggering payments or releasing goods upon the fulfillment of predefined conditions. This reduces the need for manual intervention and speeds up the trade finance process.

**Transparency and Trust**:

Blockchain provides a shared and immutable ledger that all participants in the trade finance ecosystem can access. This transparency helps build trust among buyers, sellers, banks, and other intermediaries, as each party can verify the authenticity and status of trade documents. It also reduces the risk of double financing and other fraudulent activities.

**Risk Reduction**:

Blockchain's ability to provide real-time visibility into the supply chain can help mitigate risks associated with delays, disputes, and non-payment. It allows for better monitoring and tracking of goods, safeguarding that they are delivered as agreed.

**Examples and Initiatives**:

Several blockchain-based trade finance platforms have been developed, such as Marco Polo and we.trade. These platforms enable banks and corporates to conduct trade transactions more smoothly and securely, using blockchain technology to simplify processes and reduce costs.

### *Know Your Customer (KYC) Processes*

KYC processes are necessary for financial institutions to verify the identity of their customers and assess their risk profile. However, traditional KYC processes are often cumbersome, costly, and repetitive, as customers must submit the same documentation to multiple institutions. Blockchain technology offers a more effective and secure solution for KYC processes.

**Simplifying and Standardization**:

Blockchain can create a secure and standardized digital identity for customers, which can be shared with multiple financial institutions. Once a customer's identity is verified and recorded on the blockchain, other institutions can access this information without needing to repeat the verification process. This speeds up the KYC process, reduces duplication of effort, and saves time and resources for both customers and financial institutions.

**Data Security and Privacy**:

Blockchain's cryptographic features make certain the secure storage and sharing of sensitive customer information. Customers have control over their data and can grant or revoke access to specific institutions, boosting privacy.

The decentralized nature of blockchain also reduces the risk of a single point of failure or data breach.

**Cost Reduction**:

By eliminating redundant processes and manual verification, blockchain can notably reduce the costs associated with KYC compliance. Financial institutions can share the cost of maintaining a shared KYC platform, reducing the financial burden on individual institutions.

**Regulatory Compliance**:

Blockchain's immutable ledger provides a transparent and auditable record of KYC processes, making it easier for financial institutions to demonstrate compliance with regulatory requirements. This can reduce the risk of non-compliance penalties and improve the overall productivity of regulatory reporting.

**Examples and Initiatives**:

Several blockchain-based KYC solutions have been developed, such as KYC-Chain and SelfKey. These platforms enable customers to manage their digital identities securely and provide financial institutions with a simplified and quick KYC process.

## 5.2.3 Overview of Cryptocurrencies

Cryptocurrencies represent a major breakthrough in the financial environment, drawing on blockchain technology to create decentralized digital assets. Unlike traditional fiat currencies issued by governments, cryptocurrencies operate on decentralized networks, offering new possibilities for transactions and asset management. This section provides an overview of major cryptocurrencies, the processes of mining and transaction validation, and the role of cryptocurrency exchanges.

**Bitcoin, Ethereum, and Other Major Cryptocurrencies**

*Bitcoin (BTC)*:

Bitcoin, introduced in 2009 by the pseudonymous entity Satoshi Nakamoto, is the first and most well-known cryptocurrency. It operates on a decentralized blockchain, enabling peer-to-peer transactions without the need for intermediaries like banks. Bitcoin's limited supply of 21 million coins and its decentralized nature have made it a popular choice as a digital store of value, often referred to as "digital gold."

*Ethereum (ETH)*:

Ethereum, launched in 2015 by Vitalik Buterin and others, is a decentralized platform that enables the creation of smart contracts and decentralized applications (dApps). Unlike Bitcoin, which primarily serves as a digital currency, Ethereum's blockchain supports a programmable platform where developers can build and deploy their own applications. Ether (ETH) is the native cryptocurrency of the Ethereum network and is used to pay for transaction fees and computational services on the network.

*Other Major Cryptocurrencies*:

**Ripple (XRP)**: Ripple focuses on easing real-time cross-border payments and remittances. Unlike Bitcoin and Ethereum, Ripple uses a consensus ledger and does not require mining. Its network is designed to enable fast and low-cost international transactions.

**Litecoin (LTC)**: Created by Charlie Lee in 2011, Litecoin is often considered the "silver to Bitcoin's gold." It offers faster transaction confirmation times and a different hashing algorithm, making it a popular choice for smaller transactions.

**Cardano (ADA)**: Cardano is a blockchain platform that aims to provide a more secure and scalable infrastructure for developing dApps and smart contracts. It uses a proof-of-stake consensus mechanism and emphasizes a research-driven approach to development.

**Binance Coin (BNB)**: Initially launched as a utility token for the Binance cryptocurrency exchange, BNB has evolved to power the Binance Smart Chain, a platform for dApps and smart contracts.

## Mining and Transaction Validation

Cryptocurrency mining and transaction validation are critical processes that maintain the security and integrity of blockchain networks. These processes vary depending on the consensus mechanism used by the network. Here is the real time discussion of the mining process.

- **Proof of Work (PoW):** This consensus mechanism is used by Bitcoin and other cryptocurrencies. Miners solve complex mathematical puzzles to validate transactions and add them to the blockchain, with the first to solve being rewarded. While resource-intensive, PoW is secure due to the high cost of controlling the network's majority computational power.

- **Proof of Stake (PoS):** An energy-smooth alternative to PoW, PoS selects validators based on the number of coins they're willing to "stake" as collateral. This reduces energy consumption but can lead to centralization if a few entities control a large portion of coins.

- **Delegated Proof of Stake (DPoS):** A variant of PoS where stakeholders elect delegates to validate transactions and create blocks. DPoS is more effective and scalable than PoW and PoS but relies on the trustworthiness of elected delegates.

- **Practical Byzantine Fault Tolerance (PBFT):** Designed for permissioned blockchain networks with known and trusted nodes, PBFT allows consensus even if some nodes act maliciously or fail. It's fast and quick, making it suitable for enterprise applications.

- **Proof of Authority (PoA):** Used in permissioned networks, PoA relies on a limited number of trusted nodes (authorities) to validate transactions and create blocks. It's smooth and secure but depends on the reputation and reliability of the authorities.

## Cryptocurrency Exchanges

Cryptocurrency exchanges are platforms that ease the buying, selling, and trading of cryptocurrencies. They factor into the cryptocurrency ecosystem by providing liquidity and enabling price discovery. There are several types of cryptocurrency exchanges, each serving different needs.

### *Centralized Exchanges (CEXs)*:

Centralized exchanges are the most common type of cryptocurrency exchange. They act as intermediaries between buyers and sellers, providing a secure platform for trading. Users deposit their funds into the exchange's custody and trade cryptocurrencies using the exchange's order book. CEXs offer a range of trading pairs, advanced trading tools, and features like margin trading and futures contracts. However, they require users to undergo KYC (Know Your Customer) verification and often hold custody of users' funds, which can be a risk if the exchange is hacked or becomes insolvent. Major centralized exchanges include Binance, Coinbase, and Kraken.

### *Decentralized Exchanges (DEXs)*:

DEXs operate without a central authority, allowing users to trade directly with each other in a peer-to-peer manner. They typically use smart contracts to automate the trading process and do not require users to deposit funds into a centralized account. DEXs offer greater privacy and control over funds but may lack the liquidity and user experience of centralized exchanges. They also present challenges in terms of regulatory compliance and customer support.

Examples of DEXs include Uniswap, SushiSwap, and PancakeSwap.

### *Hybrid Exchanges*:

Hybrid exchanges combine features of both centralized and decentralized exchanges. They aim to offer the security and control of DEXs with the liquidity and ease of use of CEXs. Hybrid exchanges often provide users with the option to trade through a decentralized protocol or a centralized platform.

### *Over the Counter (OTC) Trading*:

OTC trading involves the direct exchange of cryptocurrencies between parties, typically facilitated by a broker. This type of trading is often used for large transactions that may not be feasible on public exchanges due to liquidity constraints. OTC desks provide a discreet and effective way to execute large trades without affecting the market price.

### *Security and Regulation*:

Cryptocurrency exchanges must implement solid security measures to protect users' funds and data. Common security practices include multi-factor authentication, cold storage for assets, and regular security audits. Regulatory compliance is also a consideration, as exchanges must adhere to local laws and regulations regarding KYC, anti-money laundering (AML), and consumer protection.

### *Challenges and Future Developments*:

The cryptocurrency exchange system is evolving rapidly, with new technologies and regulatory frameworks shaping the future of trading. The rise of decentralized finance (DeFi) and non-fungible tokens (NFTs) has expanded the scope of what exchanges can offer. However, challenges such as regulatory uncertainty, security risks, and market volatility remain considerable concerns for both users and operators.

Cryptocurrencies, blockchain technology, and related financial advances are reshaping the global financial field. With Bitcoin and Ethereum leading the way, a wide array of cryptocurrencies and blockchain applications are emerging, offering new possibilities for transactions, asset management, and financial services. The growth of cryptocurrency exchanges and the development of sturdy security measures are major to the continued expansion and adoption of these technologies. As the ecosystem evolves, it will be important to address the challenges and opportunities presented by this major shift in finance.

## 5.2.4 Regulatory Stance on Cryptocurrencies in India

The regulation of cryptocurrencies in India has been a topic of considerable debate and evolving perspectives. The government and the Reserve Bank of India (RBI) have expressed varying levels of concern and caution regarding the use of cryptocurrencies. This section covers regulatory stance in India, covering the RBI's concerns and actions, the government's position and proposed regulations, and the taxation of cryptocurrency transactions.

### RBI's Concerns and Actions in chronological order

### Concerns About Financial Stability and Consumer Protection:

The RBI has consistently expressed concerns about the potential risks associated with cryptocurrencies, including their volatility, lack of intrinsic value, and potential use in illicit activities such as money laundering and terrorist financing. The decentralized and anonymous nature of cryptocurrencies can make them difficult to regulate and monitor, posing challenges to the financial system's integrity and consumer protection.

### 2013 and 2017 Warnings:

In December 2013, the RBI issued its first public advisory, warning users of the potential financial, operational, legal, and security-related risks associated with virtual currencies. The advisory highlighted the lack of regulatory oversight and the potential loss of funds due to cyber attacks or fraud.

In December 2017, as cryptocurrency trading gained notable traction in India, the RBI reiterated its concerns and cautioned users, holders, and traders of virtual currencies. The advisory stressed that virtual currencies were not legal tender and that individuals dealing in them did so at their own risk.

### Banking Ban (2018):

In April 2018, the RBI took a more assertive stance by prohibiting regulated financial institutions from providing services to individuals or businesses dealing in virtual currencies. This effectively cut off the cryptocurrency exchanges and traders from the banking system, making it challenging for them to operate. The RBI's directive was challenged in the Supreme Court of India, and after nearly two years of legal proceedings, the Supreme Court overturned the ban in March 2020, citing it as disproportionate and unconstitutional.

**RBI's Position Post-Supreme Court Ruling**:

After the Supreme Court's decision, the RBI clarified that its earlier circular prohibiting banks from dealing with cryptocurrencies was no longer valid. However, the RBI continued to express caution, emphasizing the need for a balanced approach that considers both advance and risk management.

**Government's Position and Proposed Regulations**

**Inter-Ministerial Committee (IMC) Report (2019)**:

In July 2019, the IMC, constituted by the Ministry of Finance, submitted a report recommending a complete ban on private cryptocurrencies in India. The report proposed the introduction of a draft bill titled "Banning of Cryptocurrency and Regulation of Official Digital Currency Bill, 2019." The bill sought to prohibit the mining, generation, holding, sale, trade, issuance, disposal, or use of cryptocurrencies in India, with provisions for penalties and imprisonment for violations.

**Proposed Regulation of Official Digital Currency**:

While proposing a ban on private cryptocurrencies, the IMC report also recommended the introduction of an official digital currency issued by the RBI. This central bank digital currency (CBDC) would be a legal tender and function as a sovereign digital currency, complementing the existing monetary system.

**Draft Cryptocurrency and Regulation of Official Digital Currency Bill (2021)**:

In 2021, the government introduced a new bill with the same name, indicating a possible change in its stance towards regulating rather than banning cryptocurrencies. The bill proposed the creation of a framework for the introduction of a CBDC while allowing for certain exceptions to promote blockchain and its applications.

**Public Consultation and Industry Feedback**:

The government has also sought feedback from stakeholders, including industry experts, investors, and the public, to shape the regulatory framework. This consultation process aims to balance development and economic growth with financial stability and consumer protection.

**Taxation of Cryptocurrency Transactions**

*Income Tax*:

In India, income from cryptocurrency transactions is subject to taxation under the Income Tax Act, 1961. The classification of income from cryptocurrencies depends on the nature of the transaction and the individual's intent. Profits from trading cryptocurrencies may be treated as capital gains or business income, depending on the frequency and nature of transactions.

***Capital Gains Tax***:

If cryptocurrencies are held as investments, profits from their sale are considered capital gains. The taxation rate varies based on the holding period.

***Business Income***:

For individuals or entities engaged in cryptocurrency trading as a business, the profits are treated as business income and taxed at applicable income tax rates. The expenses incurred in the course of trading, such as transaction fees, may be deducted from the total income.

***Goods and Services Tax (GST)***:

The applicability of GST on cryptocurrency transactions remains a grey area. While there is no specific provision under the GST law for cryptocurrencies, the government may levy GST on services provided by cryptocurrency exchanges, such as trading fees.

***Reporting Requirements***:

Taxpayers dealing in cryptocurrencies are required to disclose their holdings and transactions in their income tax returns. The government has taken steps to increase transparency and compliance by mandating disclosure of foreign assets, including cryptocurrencies held outside India.

***Future Taxation Framework***:

As the regulatory sector for cryptocurrencies evolves, the government may introduce specific provisions for their taxation. This could include a detailed framework for the treatment of different types of cryptocurrency transactions, reporting requirements, and compliance obligations.

The regulatory stance on cryptocurrencies in India reflects a cautious approach, balancing the potential benefits of blockchain technology and digital assets with concerns over financial stability, consumer protection, and illegal activities. The RBI and the Indian government have taken marked steps to regulate the sector, including proposing broad legislation and enforcing tax regulations. As the market matures and global trends influence domestic policy, India's regulatory framework for cryptocurrencies is likely to evolve, shaping the future of digital assets in the country.

# 5.3 Central Bank Digital Currency (CBDC)

Central Bank Digital Currency (CBDC) is a new concept that has gained considerable attention from central banks worldwide. As the digital counterpart to traditional fiat currencies, CBDCs aim to modernize the monetary system, providing a secure, quick, and inclusive means of payment. Unlike decentralized cryptocurrencies, CBDCs are issued and regulated by a central bank, guaranteeing state control over the currency supply. This section looks at concept, a number of types of CBDCs, including wholesale and retail variants, and the distinctions between account-based and token-based models.

## 5.3.1 Concept and Types of CBDCs

CBDCs represent the digital form of a country's official currency, issued and backed by the central bank. They are intended to function as legal tender, providing the same level of trust and acceptance as physical currency. The development of CBDCs is driven by multiple factors, including the need to improve payment system effectiveness, reduce reliance on cash, boost financial inclusion, and maintain control over the monetary system amidst the rise of private digital currencies.

The potential benefits of CBDCs include faster and cheaper transactions, particularly for cross-border payments, greater financial transparency, and improved monetary policy transmission. However, their implementation poses substantial challenges, such as securing privacy, preventing cyber threats, and managing the impact on existing financial institutions. Central banks must carefully design CBDCs to balance these benefits and challenges.

### Wholesale vs. Retail CBDC

CBDCs can be categorized into two types: wholesale and retail, each serving different purposes and audiences.

**Wholesale CBDC**: Wholesale CBDCs are designed for financial institutions and other entities within the banking and financial ecosystem. These digital currencies help large-value transactions and settlements, typically between banks or between a central bank and financial institutions. Wholesale CBDCs aim to improve the speed and security of interbank payments, reducing settlement times and costs associated with current systems.

AN advantage of wholesale CBDCs is their potential to speed up cross-border transactions. By eliminating the need for correspondent banks and reducing the complexity of currency exchanges, wholesale CBDCs can markedly lower transaction costs and time. They can increase the central bank's ability to monitor and control the flow of money, helping to prevent illicit activities such as money laundering and terrorism financing.

**Retail CBDC**: Retail CBDCs are intended for use by the general public in everyday transactions. They provide a digital alternative to physical cash, allowing individuals and businesses to make payments and store value electronically. Retail CBDCs can be accessed through digital wallets, mobile apps, or other electronic devices, offering a convenient and secure payment method.

One of the primary motivations for developing retail CBDCs is to improve financial inclusion. In many regions, especially in developing countries, a major portion of the population lacks access to traditional banking services. Retail CBDCs can provide these individuals with a safe and reliable means of saving and transacting money, thereby integrating them into the formal financial system.

Retail CBDCs also offer potential benefits in terms of monetary policy. By providing a direct channel for distributing stimulus payments or other government benefits, central banks can guarantee that funds reach their intended recipients quickly and quickly. The data generated by CBDC transactions can offer valuable insights into economic activity, helping policymakers to better understand and respond to economic trends.

## Account-based vs. Token-based Models

The implementation of CBDCs can follow two primary models: account-based and token-based, each with distinct operational and security characteristics.

**Account-based CBDC**: In an account-based CBDC model, digital currency is tied to an individual's or entity's account maintained by the central bank or authorized financial institutions. This model requires a centralized ledger system to record ownership and transactions. Users access their CBDC holdings through digital accounts, with the central bank or an intermediary verifying their identity and maintaining the account balance.

The account-based model is similar to the current banking system, where accounts are identified and transactions are authorized based on the account holder's identity. This model offers a high level of security and accountability, as it allows for stringent verification processes and compliance with anti-money laundering (AML) and counter-terrorism financing (CTF) regulations. It also enables the central bank to have direct oversight of the money supply and transactional data, supporting more effective monetary policy implementation.

However, the account-based model may raise concerns regarding privacy and data security, as the central bank or intermediaries would have access to detailed information about individuals' financial activities. To address these concerns, strong data protection measures and clear regulations on data access and use would be necessary.

**Token-based CBDC**: In contrast, a token-based CBDC model operates on the principle of digital tokens that represent the digital currency. Ownership of the CBDC is transferred through the exchange of these tokens, similar to the transfer of physical cash. The system's security relies on the ability to authenticate the tokens rather than the identity of the transacting parties.

Token-based CBDCs can be implemented using blockchain or other distributed ledger technologies, enabling decentralized or partially decentralized networks. This model provides greater anonymity and privacy for users, as transactions can be conducted without directly linking them to an individual's identity. It also allows for peer-to-peer transactions, reducing the need for intermediaries and potentially lowering transaction costs.

However, token-based CBDCs also present challenges, particularly in terms of preventing illicit activities. The pseudonymous nature of transactions can make it more difficult to trace and prevent money laundering, tax evasion, and other financial crimes. Also, safeguarding the security and integrity of the tokens themselves is critical, as the loss or theft of tokens could result in irreversible losses for users.

The introduction of CBDCs represents a far-reaching development in the global financial environment. By tapping digital technologies, central banks can offer more smooth, secure, and inclusive monetary systems. The choice between wholesale and retail CBDCs, as well as account-based versus token-based models, depends on the specific objectives, infrastructure, and regulatory environment of each country.

Wholesale CBDCs offer advantages for interbank settlements and cross-border transactions, while retail CBDCs provide a digital alternative to cash, promoting financial inclusion and enabling direct government interventions. The account-based model offers reliable security and regulatory compliance, while the token-based model provides greater privacy and decentralization.

As central banks around the world continue to explore and experiment with CBDCs, it is needed to carefully consider the design and implementation aspects to balance the benefits and risks. The future of CBDCs will likely see a blend of these models, tailored to the unique needs of each economy, ultimately reshaping the way we understand and use money in the digital age.

### 5.3.2 RBI's Plans for Digital Rupee

The Reserve Bank of India (RBI) has moved from exploring to actively piloting a Central Bank Digital Currency (CBDC), known as the "Digital Rupee" (e₹). The wholesale pilot (e₹-W) was launched on 1 November 2022 for the settlement of secondary-market government-securities transactions, and the retail pilot (e₹-R) was launched on 1 December 2022 within a closed user group of customers and merchants. The retail Digital Rupee has since been made interoperable with UPI, broadening its reach.

**Pilot Project and Trials**

The RBI launched live pilot projects for the Digital Rupee in both the wholesale and retail segments in late 2022, and these pilots remain ongoing, testing features such as creation, distribution, programmability, offline use, and cross-border settlement.

The RBI collaborated with commercial banks, technology firms, and payment service providers to conduct these trials, guaranteeing a full evaluation. The pilot projects were conducted in controlled environments, allowing the RBI to monitor and analyze the outcomes closely. Initial results indicated successful transactions and secure processing, with participants providing valuable feedback for further refinement.

**Architecture and Design**

The architecture and design of the Digital Rupee are central to its development and implementation. The RBI has opted for a "intermediated CBDC" model, where the central bank issues the digital currency to intermediaries, primarily commercial banks, which then distribute it to the public. This model employs the existing banking infrastructure and expertise in customer management, thereby reducing the operational burden on the RBI.

**Technological Infrastructure**: The RBI explored both centralized and decentralized ledger technologies to support the Digital Rupee. While centralized systems offer simplicity and control, decentralized ledger technology (DLT), such as blockchain, provides improved security and transparency. The RBI chose a hybrid approach that combines the strengths of both systems, securing robustness and scalability.

**Operational Framework**: In the intermediated/indirect CBDC model, the RBI issues Digital Rupees to commercial banks, which then distribute them to individuals and businesses. This framework uses digital wallets provided by the banks, enabling users to hold and transact in Digital Rupees. The digital currency can be used for transactions, including payments, remittances, and investments.

The RBI is considering many features for the Digital Rupee, such as offline transactions and programmable payments. These features are designed to cater to diverse use cases, safeguarding broad usability and acceptance.

**Implementation Roadmap**

The implementation of the Digital Rupee follows a phased approach, encompassing research, pilot testing, policy formulation, infrastructure development, and public awareness.

**Research and Development**: The RBI's research phase involved extensive studies and experiments, focusing on the feasibility, security, and economic implications of the Digital Rupee. Collaboration with academic institutions and technology experts was important in identifying technical, legal, and regulatory challenges.

**Pilot Testing and Evaluation**: Following the research phase, the RBI conducted pilot testing to assess the Digital Rupee's performance in several scenarios. These tests evaluated the digital currency's integration with existing systems, security protocols, and user experience. Feedback from these trials was used to refine the design and address potential issues.

**Policy Formulation and Regulatory Framework**: The RBI formulated policies and established a regulatory framework to govern the Digital Rupee. This framework includes guidelines on issuance, distribution, usage, consumer protection, data privacy, and cybersecurity. The RBI worked closely with other regulatory bodies to secure complete oversight.

**Infrastructure Development and Integration**: The RBI and commercial banks developed the necessary infrastructure, including digital wallets, data centers, and payment gateways. The RBI also focused on guaranteeing the Digital Rupee's interoperability with existing payment systems, enabling smooth transactions across different platforms.

**Public Awareness and Education**: To safeguard smooth adoption, the RBI launched public awareness campaigns to educate the public about the

Digital Rupee's features, benefits, and usage. These initiatives aimed to build trust and confidence among potential users, addressing any concerns or misconceptions.

**Full-Scale Deployment and Adoption**: The final phase involves the full-scale deployment of the Digital Rupee. The RBI, in collaboration with commercial banks, made the digital currency available to the public, allowing them to access and use it for a number of transactions. The RBI continues to monitor the Digital Rupee's performance, making adjustments as needed to optimize its functionality.

The RBI's careful planning and phased implementation make certain that the Digital Rupee is secure, effective, and inclusive. By using existing banking infrastructure, the RBI aims to create a digital currency that meets the needs of the modern economy. As India moves towards a cashless society, the Digital Rupee holds the potential to reshape the way transactions are conducted, offering a safer, faster, and more convenient payment option for all.

### 5.3.3 Potential Impact on Monetary Policy and Banking

The introduction of the Digital Rupee, India's Central Bank Digital Currency (CBDC), presents marked implications for monetary policy, commercial banking, and cross-border transactions. As a new form of digital money issued by the Reserve Bank of India (RBI), the Digital Rupee has the potential to reshape the financial system, affecting aspects of the economy and financial system. Here we examine the potential impact on monetary policy, commercial banking, and cross-border transactions and remittances.

**Implications for Money Supply**

The issuance of the Digital Rupee could have profound implications for the money supply in India. As a digital representation of sovereign currency, the Digital Rupee will coexist with physical cash and other forms of digital money, such as bank deposits. The impact on money supply will depend on the extent to which the Digital Rupee replaces other forms of money and how it is integrated into the overall monetary system.

**Money Supply Measurement**: The introduction of the Digital Rupee may necessitate revisions to traditional measures of money supply, such as M0 (currency in circulation), M1 (currency plus demand deposits), and M2 (M1 plus savings deposits). The Digital Rupee, being a central bank liability, would likely be included in M0 and could alter the composition and dynamics of these aggregates.

**Velocity of Money**: The velocity of money, which measures the frequency at which money circulates in the economy, could be affected by the Digital Rupee's adoption. If the Digital Rupee strengthens transaction effectiveness and reduces the demand for cash, it could increase the velocity of money. However, if it primarily substitutes for other forms of digital payments, the impact may be neutral.

**Central Bank Control**: The Digital Rupee could provide the RBI with greater control over the money supply. The central bank could potentially adjust the supply of digital currency more precisely than physical cash, responding quickly to economic conditions. The Digital Rupee could offer real-time data on transaction volumes and flows, improving the accuracy of monetary policy assessments.

**Interest Rate Implications**: The introduction of a Digital Rupee could also influence interest rates. If the Digital Rupee offers an alternative to bank deposits, it could affect the demand for deposits and, consequently, the deposit rates offered by banks. The RBI's ability to set interest rates on the Digital Rupee could serve as an additional tool for monetary policy, influencing the broader interest rate environment.

## Effects on Commercial Banking

The Digital Rupee's implementation could have substantial effects on the commercial banking sector, altering the traditional roles and functions of banks. These effects could be both positive and negative, depending on how the Digital Rupee is integrated into the financial system.

**Deposit Mobilization**: The Digital Rupee could impact banks' ability to mobilize deposits. If consumers and businesses choose to hold Digital Rupees instead of bank deposits, it could reduce the overall deposit base of commercial banks. This, in turn, could affect banks' ability to lend and generate interest income. However, the impact may be mitigated if the Digital Rupee is primarily used for transactional purposes rather than as a store of value.

**Payment Services**: The Digital Rupee could boost the speed and reach of payment services. Banks could integrate the Digital Rupee into their digital banking platforms, offering frictionless and secure payment options to customers. This could reduce the reliance on traditional payment methods, such as cheques and physical cash, and increase the overall payment ecosystem.

**Credit Creation**: Commercial banks contribute to credit creation by lending out deposits. The introduction of the Digital Rupee could potentially alter this dynamic. If the Digital Rupee leads to a shift away from bank deposits, it could constrain banks' ability to create credit. However, the impact would depend on the extent of the shift and how banks adapt to the new environment.

**Operational Changes**: The adoption of the Digital Rupee may require banks to make operational changes, including upgrading their IT infrastructure and systems to support digital currency transactions. Banks may also need to develop new products and services tailored to the Digital Rupee, such as digital wallets and payment solutions.

**Competition and Breakthrough**: The introduction of the Digital Rupee could increase competition in the financial sector, particularly from fintech companies and non-bank payment service providers. Banks may need to innovate and differentiate their offerings to retain and attract customers. This could lead to new financial products, strengthened customer experiences, and greater financial inclusion.

## Cross-border Transactions and Remittances

The Digital Rupee could have a major impact on cross-border transactions and remittances, offering faster, cheaper, and more secure alternatives to traditional methods. The potential benefits extend to both individuals and businesses, improving the productivity of international trade and financial flows.

**Faster Transactions**: The Digital Rupee could support real-time cross-border transactions, reducing the time required for settlements compared to traditional methods, such as wire transfers. This could benefit businesses engaged in international trade, enabling them to manage their cash flows more effectively and reduce settlement risk.

**Reduced Costs**: The use of the Digital Rupee for cross-border transactions could lower costs by eliminating intermediaries and reducing fees associated with currency conversion and correspondent banking. This could make remittances more affordable for individuals sending money abroad, particularly to countries with large Indian diaspora communities.

**Improved Transparency**: The Digital Rupee's digital nature could improve the transparency and traceability of cross-border transactions. This could help reduce instances of fraud and money laundering, as transactions would be recorded on a secure digital ledger. The increased transparency could also enable regulatory oversight and compliance with anti-money laundering (AML) and counter-terrorism financing (CTF) regulations.

**Regulatory Considerations**: The cross-border use of the Digital Rupee would require coordination and cooperation between central banks and regulators in different jurisdictions. This includes addressing issues related to exchange controls, capital flows, and regulatory harmonization. The RBI would need to work closely with international organizations, such as the Financial Action Task Force (FATF) and the Bank for International Settlements (BIS), to establish frameworks for cross-border CBDC transactions.

**Currency Competition**: The introduction of the Digital Rupee could influence the global currency field, particularly if other countries adopt CBDCs. It could potentially increase competition among national currencies for cross-border trade and investment. The ease of use and effectiveness of the Digital Rupee could strengthen its attractiveness for international transactions, potentially impacting the dominance of established currencies like the US dollar and the euro.

## 5.3.4 Challenges and Considerations in CBDC Implementation

The implementation of a Central Bank Digital Currency (CBDC) such as the Digital Rupee presents a unique set of challenges and considerations. While CBDCs offer many potential benefits, such as increased speed and financial inclusion, their implementation is complex and requires careful planning and consideration of factors. We now turn to the challenges and considerations in CBDC implementation, focusing on technology infrastructure requirements, privacy and data protection concerns, and financial inclusion aspects.

**Technology Infrastructure Requirements**

**Solid and Scalable Infrastructure**: The introduction of a CBDC necessitates a sturdy and scalable technology infrastructure capable of handling a large volume of transactions smoothly and securely. The infrastructure must be designed to accommodate peak loads, guarantee high availability, and provide real-time processing capabilities. This requires major investment in data centers, network infrastructure, and transaction processing systems.

**Interoperability**: A necessary aspect of CBDC implementation is securing interoperability with existing payment systems, both domestically and internationally. The CBDC system must be compatible with traditional banking systems, digital payment platforms, and other CBDCs. This interoperability is necessary for effortless transactions and to prevent fragmentation of the payment ecosystem.

**Cybersecurity and Resilience**: The CBDC infrastructure must be highly secure to protect against cyber threats, such as hacking, data breaches, and fraud. This requires implementing advanced cybersecurity measures, including encryption, multi-factor authentication, and intrusion detection systems. The infrastructure must be resilient to withstand potential attacks and disruptions, safeguarding the continuous availability of the CBDC system.

**Scalability and Future-Proofing**: The CBDC infrastructure must be scalable to accommodate future growth in transaction volumes and user adoption. It should be designed to support new functionalities and technological advancements, such as smart contracts and programmable money. Future-proofing the infrastructure involves selecting flexible and adaptable technologies that can evolve with the changing sector of digital currencies and financial services.

## Privacy and Data Protection Concerns

**Data Privacy**: The implementation of a CBDC raises considerable privacy concerns, as digital transactions can potentially be tracked and monitored by central authorities. Guaranteeing the privacy of users while maintaining transparency and regulatory oversight is a delicate balance. The CBDC system must incorporate privacy-preserving technologies, such as zero-knowledge proofs and cryptographic techniques, to protect user identities and transaction details.

**Data Security**: Protecting the data associated with CBDC transactions is foremost. This includes securing sensitive information, such as account details, transaction histories, and personal data. The CBDC system must adhere to stringent data protection regulations and standards, such as the General Data Protection Regulation (GDPR) and India's Personal Data Protection Bill. Implementing strong data security measures, such as encryption and secure data storage, is important to prevent unauthorized access and data breaches.

**Regulatory Compliance**: The CBDC system must comply with existing regulations related to data protection, anti-money laundering (AML), and counter-terrorism financing (CTF). This includes implementing know-your-customer (KYC) procedures and transaction monitoring systems to detect and prevent illicit activities. The regulatory framework must be clear and thorough, providing guidelines for data collection, processing, and sharing while safeguarding user rights and privacy.

**User Trust and Acceptance**: Building user trust is critical for the successful adoption of a CBDC. Users must be confident that their privacy is protected and that their data will not be misused. Transparent communication about data usage policies, security measures, and user rights is needed to build trust and encourage adoption. Also, the CBDC system must provide users with control over their data, including the ability to manage permissions and consent.

### Financial Inclusion Aspects

**Accessibility**: One of the objectives of a CBDC is to boost financial inclusion by providing access to digital financial services for underserved and unbanked populations. The CBDC system must be accessible to all segments of the population, including those in remote and rural areas. This requires addressing barriers such as lack of internet access, digital literacy, and affordable technology. Securing that the CBDC can be accessed via basic mobile phones and offline mechanisms is major for broad-based adoption.

**Affordability**: To promote financial inclusion, the costs associated with using the CBDC must be minimized. This includes reducing transaction fees, account maintenance charges, and the cost of accessing digital infrastructure. The central bank and other stakeholders must work together to provide affordable solutions that do not disproportionately burden low-income individuals and small businesses.

**Education and Awareness**: Educating the public about the benefits and usage of the CBDC is necessary for widespread adoption. Financial literacy programs should be implemented to raise awareness about digital currencies, including how to use them safely and effectively. This includes providing information about transaction processes, security measures, and consumer protection mechanisms. Targeted outreach efforts are needed to reach marginalized communities and address their specific concerns.

**Inclusion of Marginalized Groups**: Special consideration must be given to including marginalized groups, such as women, elderly individuals, and persons with disabilities, in the CBDC ecosystem. This involves designing inclusive policies and services that cater to their unique needs and challenges. For example, providing user-friendly interfaces, voice-assisted technologies, and alternative authentication methods can help secure that these groups can participate fully in the digital economy.

**Mitigating Risks of Exclusion**: While the CBDC has the potential to promote financial inclusion, there is also a risk of exclusion if not implemented carefully. The transition to digital currency may inadvertently exclude those who are less technologically savvy or lack access to digital devices. To mitigate this risk, a hybrid model that includes both digital and physical forms of currency should be considered. Partnerships with community organizations and financial intermediaries can help bridge the digital divide and safeguard that everyone benefits from the CBDC.

## 5.4 Fintech Developments

The rapid evolution of financial technology, or fintech, has fundamentally transformed the banking and financial services industry. Fintech advances have introduced new products, services, and business models, offering greater convenience, productivity, and personalized experiences for consumers. Among the areas of fintech advance, artificial intelligence (AI) and machine learning (ML) have emerged as far-reaching technologies, greatly impacting many aspects of banking operations and customer interactions. This section covers role of AI and ML in banking, focusing on their applications in chatbots and virtual assistants, credit scoring models, fraud detection systems, and personalized financial advice.

### 5.4.1 AI and Machine Learning in Banking

Artificial intelligence and machine learning have revolutionized the banking sector by enabling automation, data analysis, and decision-making processes. These technologies use vast amounts of data to identify patterns, make predictions, and optimize operations, thereby strengthening the effectiveness and effectiveness of banking services. The integration of AI and ML in banking has led to the development of novel solutions that improve customer service, risk management, and financial planning.

*Credit Scoring Models*

**Data-Driven Credit Assessment**: Traditional credit scoring models rely on a limited set of data points, such as credit history, income, and employment status. AI and ML have expanded the scope of credit assessment by incorporating alternative data sources, including social media activity, online behavior, and transaction patterns. This data-driven approach provides a more broad view of a borrower's creditworthiness, enabling banks to make more informed lending decisions.

**Real-Time Credit Scoring**: AI-powered credit scoring models can process and analyze data in real time, allowing banks to assess credit applications quickly and accurately. This real-time capability boosts the speed and speed of the lending process, reducing the time required for loan approvals and disbursements. It also enables banks to respond to changing financial conditions and customer needs more effectively.

**Improved Risk Assessment**: Machine learning algorithms can identify patterns and correlations in large datasets, helping banks detect early warning signs of potential defaults. By continuously learning from new data, these algorithms can refine their predictions and improve the accuracy of risk assessment. This proactive approach enables banks to mitigate credit risk and reduce the likelihood of bad loans.

**Financial Inclusion**: AI-driven credit scoring models have the potential to promote financial inclusion by evaluating creditworthiness for individuals with limited or no credit history. By considering non-traditional data, these models can provide access to credit for underserved populations, such as freelancers, small business owners, and gig economy workers. This inclusivity can help bridge the gap between traditional banking and unbanked or underbanked individuals.

*Fraud Detection Systems*

**Anomaly Detection**: Fraud detection is a critical application of AI and ML in banking. Machine learning algorithms can analyze transaction data to identify unusual patterns and anomalies that may indicate fraudulent activity. These systems can detect several types of fraud, including identity theft, account takeover, and payment fraud. By flagging suspicious transactions in real time, banks can take immediate action to prevent financial losses.

**Behavioral Analytics**: AI-powered fraud detection systems use behavioral analytics to create profiles of typical customer behavior. These profiles include information about transaction frequency, amounts, and locations. When a transaction deviates from the established pattern, the system triggers an alert for further investigation. This approach helps banks identify potential fraud while minimizing false positives.

**Predictive Analytics**: Predictive analytics is another powerful tool for fraud detection. Machine learning models can predict the likelihood of fraud based on historical data and known fraud patterns. By continuously updating these models with new data, banks can stay ahead of evolving fraud tactics and emerging threats. Predictive analytics also enables banks to allocate resources more quickly, focusing on high-risk cases.

**Collaboration and Data Sharing**: AI-driven fraud detection systems benefit from collaboration and data sharing among financial institutions. By pooling anonymized data, banks can gain insights into broader fraud trends and patterns. This collective intelligence increases the effectiveness of fraud detection efforts and strengthens the overall security of the financial ecosystem.

### *Personalized Financial Advice*

**Customized Financial Planning**: AI-powered financial advisory services provide personalized financial advice to customers based on their unique financial goals, risk tolerance, and life stages. These services use data analytics and algorithms to create customized investment portfolios, retirement plans, and savings strategies. By offering tailored recommendations, AI-driven advisors help customers make informed financial decisions.

**Robo-Advisors**: Robo-advisors are a popular application of AI in wealth management. These digital platforms use algorithms to manage investment portfolios with minimal human intervention. Robo-advisors assess a customer's risk profile, investment goals, and time horizon to create and manage a diversified portfolio. They offer automated rebalancing, tax optimization, and portfolio monitoring, making wealth management accessible to a broader audience.

**Proactive Recommendations**: AI-driven financial advisors can provide proactive recommendations based on market conditions and changes in a customer's financial situation. For example, they can suggest adjustments to investment strategies during market volatility or recommend saving plans for upcoming expenses. This proactive approach helps customers stay on track with their financial goals and adapt to changing circumstances.

**Boosted Customer Engagement**: AI-powered financial advisory services increase customer engagement by providing personalized insights and education. These services can generate reports, visualizations, and simulations to help customers understand their financial position and potential outcomes. By making financial planning more interactive and engaging, AI-driven advisors enable customers to take control of their financial future.

## 5.4.2 Robotic Process Automation (RPA)

Robotic Process Automation (RPA) has emerged as a major technology in the banking and financial services industry, offering a solution to automate repetitive, rule-based tasks that were traditionally performed by humans. RPA uses software robots or "bots" to mimic human actions within digital systems, enabling banks to improve operational productivity, reduce costs, and improve accuracy. This section looks at use cases of RPA in banking operations, explores the benefits and challenges associated with its implementation, and examines the integration of RPA with legacy systems.

**Use Cases in Banking Operations**

RPA has a broad set of applications in banking, from back-office operations to customer-facing processes. Some of the primary use cases include:

***Account Opening and KYC Compliance:*** The process of opening a new bank account involves multiple steps, including data entry, verification of customer documents, and compliance checks. RPA can automate these tasks, speeding up the account opening process and safeguarding compliance with Know Your Customer (KYC) regulations. Bots can extract information from customer documents, cross-reference data with internal and external databases, and flag any discrepancies for further review.

***Loan Processing:*** Loan processing is another area where RPA can be highly effective. The loan application process often involves data collection, credit scoring, document verification, and underwriting. RPA bots can automate data extraction from application forms, validate customer information, and perform credit checks. By automating these steps, banks can reduce processing times and strengthen the accuracy of loan approvals.

***Anti-Money Laundering (AML) Compliance:*** Banks are required to monitor transactions for suspicious activity to comply with AML regulations. RPA can assist in this process by automating the monitoring of transactions, flagging unusual patterns, and generating alerts for potential money laundering activities. Bots can cross-reference transactions against watchlists and perform risk assessments, helping banks stay compliant with regulatory requirements.

***Payment Processing:*** RPA can simplify payment processing by automating tasks such as payment initiation, reconciliation, and exception handling. Bots can extract payment details from a number of sources, validate the information, and initiate payments through the appropriate channels. They can also reconcile payment records, identify discrepancies, and generate reports for audit purposes.

***Customer Service and Support:*** In customer service, RPA can be used to automate routine inquiries and service requests. Bots can handle tasks such as password resets, account balance inquiries, and transaction history requests. By automating these processes, banks can free up customer service agents to focus on more complex issues, improving overall service quality.

***Regulatory Reporting:*** Banks are required to submit reports to regulatory authorities, including financial statements, risk assessments, and compliance reports. RPA can automate the compilation and submission of these reports, guaranteeing accuracy and timeliness. Bots can extract data from multiple systems, perform calculations, and generate the required reports, reducing the risk of errors and penalties.

***Reconciliation and Data Management:*** RPA can be used to automate data reconciliation tasks, such as matching transactions across different systems or accounts. This includes reconciliation of bank statements, general ledger accounts, and interbank transfers. By automating these processes, banks can improve data accuracy and reduce manual effort.

## Benefits and Challenges of RPA Implementation

## Benefits of RPA Implementation:

***Cost Savings:*** RPA can considerably reduce operational costs by automating repetitive tasks that would otherwise require human labor. This cost effectiveness comes from reducing the need for additional staff and minimizing errors that could lead to financial losses.

***Increased Speed:*** Bots can operate 24/7 without breaks, handling tasks quickly and consistently. This leads to faster processing times and the ability to scale operations during peak periods without additional staffing.

***Improved Accuracy:*** RPA reduces the risk of human error in data entry and processing. Bots follow predefined rules and logic, securing that tasks are completed accurately and consistently.

***Compliance and Risk Management:*** RPA can boost compliance by safeguarding that processes adhere to regulatory requirements. Bots can generate audit trails, document every action taken, and provide evidence for compliance audits.

*Scalability and Flexibility:* RPA systems are highly scalable and can be quickly adjusted to handle increased workloads. Banks can deploy additional bots to manage higher volumes of transactions or scale down during off-peak times.

*Improved Customer Experience:* By automating routine tasks, banks can provide faster and more quick services to customers. This leads to improved customer satisfaction and loyalty.

**Challenges of RPA Implementation:**

*Initial Investment:* The implementation of RPA requires a notable initial investment in technology, infrastructure, and training. Banks need to allocate resources for bot development, deployment, and maintenance.

*Change Management:* Introducing RPA can lead to resistance from employees who may fear job displacement. Effective change management strategies are needed to address concerns, provide training, and reassign employees to higher-value tasks.

*Complexity in Integration:* Integrating RPA with existing systems and processes can be complex, especially in banks with legacy systems. Guaranteeing smooth integration and data flow between bots and existing applications is important for successful implementation.

*Data Security and Privacy:* RPA bots handle sensitive customer and financial data, raising concerns about data security and privacy. Banks must implement reliable security measures to protect data and make certain compliance with data protection regulations.

*Maintenance and Monitoring:* RPA systems require ongoing maintenance and monitoring to guarantee they function correctly. Bots need to be updated and tested regularly to adapt to changes in business processes and regulatory requirements.

*Limitations in Cognitive Tasks:* While RPA excels in rule-based tasks, it has limitations in handling complex decision-making and cognitive tasks that require human judgment. Banks need to combine RPA with other technologies, such as AI, to address these limitations.

**Legacy Systems**

Legacy systems refer to outdated or older computer systems, software, or technologies that are still in use within an organization. These systems were often built with specific technologies and architectures that are no longer considered modern or smooth. Despite being outdated, legacy systems may still be operational because they perform functions that are difficult or costly to replace.

**Challenges with Legacy Systems:**

1. **Integration Difficulties:** Legacy systems often lack the flexibility and compatibility needed to integrate with modern technologies and platforms. This can make it challenging to implement new features or connect with other systems, such as APIs in Open Banking.

2. **Maintenance and Support:** Maintaining legacy systems can be expensive and complex. As these systems age, finding qualified personnel who understand the technology becomes more difficult, and the cost of maintenance increases.

3. **Security Vulnerabilities:** Legacy systems may have outdated security measures, making them vulnerable to cyberattacks. They may not support modern encryption standards or security protocols, posing risks to sensitive data.

4. **Limited Scalability:** Legacy systems may not be designed to handle the growing volume of data and transactions that modern businesses require. This limitation can hinder an organization's ability to scale and adapt to new market demands.

## API Integration:

For legacy systems that support APIs, RPA bots can interact with these systems through API calls. This method allows bots to retrieve and update data without the need for direct access to the underlying systems. API integration provides a secure and effective way to connect RPA with legacy applications.

### *Screen Scraping and Optical Character Recognition (OCR):*

In cases where legacy systems do not support APIs, RPA can use screen scraping and OCR technologies to extract data from the user interface. Bots can handle through screens, extract information, and perform actions based on visual elements. While this method can be effective, it may be less reliable than API integration due to changes in the user interface.

### *Middleware Solutions:*

Middleware solutions can act as intermediaries between RPA and legacy systems, providing a layer of abstraction. These solutions can ease data exchange, transformation, and routing, enabling RPA bots to interact with legacy systems without direct integration. Middleware can also provide additional functionalities, such as error handling and monitoring.

### Data Migration and Transformation:

When integrating RPA with legacy systems, banks may need to migrate data from older systems to newer platforms. This process involves data transformation, cleansing, and validation to secure data accuracy and consistency. RPA can automate parts of this process, reducing the manual effort involved.

### Testing and Validation:

Integration with legacy systems requires thorough testing and validation to safeguard that RPA bots function correctly and do not disrupt existing processes. Banks must conduct end-to-end testing, simulate scenarios, and validate data accuracy to mitigate risks.

### Continuous Monitoring and Maintenance:

Once integrated, RPA systems require continuous monitoring and maintenance to make certain they function as expected. Banks need to establish monitoring frameworks, set up alert mechanisms, and regularly review bot performance. Any issues or changes in legacy systems must be addressed promptly to prevent disruptions.

***Robotic Process Automation (RPA)*** has become a basis of digital transformation in banking, offering several benefits, such as cost savings, increased productivity, and improved accuracy. By automating repetitive and rule-based tasks, RPA enables banks to speed up operations, increase customer experiences, and guarantee compliance with regulatory requirements. However, the implementation of RPA also presents challenges, including initial investment costs, change management, data security concerns, and integration complexities with legacy systems.

Despite these challenges, the potential of RPA in banking is immense. As technology continues to evolve, RPA is expected to play an increasingly role in reshaping banking operations, enabling banks to adapt to changing customer expectations and market conditions. The future of banking will likely see greater integration of RPA with other advanced technologies, such as AI and machine learning, further boosting the capabilities and scope of automation in the financial services industry.

### 5.4.3 Big Data Analytics in Risk Management and Customer Service

Big Data Analytics has revolutionized the banking industry by providing new ways to understand customer behavior, assess risks, and make real-time decisions. This section looks at role of Big Data Analytics in customer segmentation and targeting, predictive analytics for risk assessment, and real-time decision-making in banking.

**Customer Segmentation and Targeting**

Customer segmentation is an aspect of banking that allows financial institutions to tailor their products and services to specific customer groups. Big Data Analytics enables banks to segment their customer base more accurately and effectively by analyzing vast amounts of data from many sources, including transaction history, social media interactions, demographic information, and more.

***Strengthened Personalization:*** Big Data Analytics allows banks to create detailed customer profiles, identifying characteristics and preferences. This data-driven approach enables banks to offer personalized products and services, such as customized credit card offers, personalized investment advice, and tailored loan products. By understanding customer needs and preferences, banks can increase customer satisfaction and loyalty.

**Targeted Marketing Campaigns**: With detailed customer segmentation, banks can design targeted marketing campaigns that resonate with specific customer segments. For instance, a bank can identify customers who are likely to be interested in home loans based on their search history and spending patterns. This targeted approach not only improves the effectiveness of marketing efforts but also reduces costs associated with broad-based advertising.

***Customer Lifetime Value (CLV) Analysis:*** Big Data Analytics helps banks calculate the Customer Lifetime Value (CLV) by analyzing past transactions, customer behavior, and demographic data. CLV analysis enables banks to identify high-value customers and develop strategies to retain them. By focusing on customers with high CLV, banks can optimize their resources and maximize profitability.

***Cross-selling and Upselling:*** Banks can use Big Data Analytics to identify cross-selling and upselling opportunities. For example, if a customer has a mortgage with the bank, analytics can reveal whether they are likely to be interested in home insurance or investment products. By drawing on these insights, banks can increase their revenue through additional product offerings.

***Predictive Analytics for Risk Assessment:*** Predictive analytics is a powerful tool that allows banks to assess and manage several types of risks, including credit risk, market risk, and operational risk. By analyzing historical data and identifying patterns, predictive models can forecast future events and behaviors, helping banks make informed decisions.

***Credit Risk Assessment:*** Predictive analytics helps banks evaluate the creditworthiness of potential borrowers by analyzing their financial history, spending habits, and other relevant data. Advanced algorithms can predict the likelihood of default, enabling banks to set appropriate credit limits and interest rates. This proactive approach reduces the risk of bad loans and improves portfolio quality.

***Fraud Detection and Prevention:*** Banks face a marked challenge in detecting and preventing fraudulent activities. Big Data Analytics can analyze vast datasets in real-time to identify unusual patterns and anomalies that may indicate fraud. For example, predictive models can detect atypical transaction patterns or unusual account activities, triggering alerts for further investigation. By identifying potential fraud early, banks can mitigate losses and protect their customers.

***Market Risk Management:*** Predictive analytics also helps with managing market risk. By analyzing historical market data, economic indicators, and financial trends, banks can forecast potential market movements and adjust their investment strategies accordingly. This allows banks to hedge against market volatility and make informed trading decisions.

***Compliance and Regulatory Risk:*** Big Data Analytics helps banks secure compliance with regulatory requirements by monitoring transactions and identifying suspicious activities. Predictive models can assess the likelihood of regulatory breaches and generate alerts for potential violations. This proactive approach helps banks avoid penalties and maintain their reputation.

***Real-time Decision Making:*** The ability to make real-time decisions is critical in the fast-paced banking environment. Big Data Analytics enables banks to process and analyze data in real-time, allowing them to respond quickly to emerging opportunities and challenges.

***Dynamic Pricing and Offers:*** Real-time analytics allows banks to offer dynamic pricing and real-time offers to customers. For example, a bank can provide instant loan approvals with personalized interest rates based on the customer's credit profile and current market conditions. This flexibility strengthens the customer experience and increases the likelihood of conversion.

***Real-time Risk Monitoring:*** Banks can use real-time analytics to monitor a number of risks continuously. For instance, in the trading environment, real-time data analysis can help identify sudden market shifts, allowing traders to adjust their positions accordingly. In retail banking, real-time monitoring of transactions can detect potential fraud and trigger immediate actions, such as freezing the account or notifying the customer.

***Personalized Customer Interactions:*** Real-time analytics can improve customer interactions by providing relevant information and insights during customer service engagements. For example, when a customer contacts the bank, the customer service representative can access real-time data on the customer's recent activities, preferences, and inquiries. This information allows the representative to provide personalized assistance and resolve issues more effectively.

***Operational Effectiveness:*** Big Data Analytics enables banks to optimize their operations by analyzing real-time data on branch performance, ATM usage, and online transactions. This data-driven approach allows banks to allocate resources effectively, reduce operational costs, and improve service delivery. For instance, real-time analytics can identify underperforming branches or ATMs, enabling the bank to take corrective actions.

***Sentiment Analysis and Customer Feedback:*** Real-time sentiment analysis allows banks to gauge customer sentiment and feedback from channels, including social media, customer reviews, and surveys. By analyzing this data, banks can identify emerging issues, address customer concerns promptly, and improve their products and services. This proactive approach helps banks build a positive brand image and strengthen customer satisfaction.

Big Data Analytics has become an indispensable tool in the banking industry, transforming how banks manage risks, engage with customers, and make decisions. By tapping advanced analytics techniques, banks can gain valuable insights into customer behavior, predict potential risks, and respond swiftly to changing market conditions. The integration of Big Data Analytics into banking operations not only boosts speed and profitability but also improves the overall customer experience.

As the volume and complexity of data continue to grow, the role of Big Data Analytics in banking will only become more critical. Banks must invest in advanced analytics infrastructure, talent, and technology to harness the full potential of Big Data. They must address challenges related to data privacy, security, and regulatory compliance to safeguard the responsible and ethical use of data.

### 5.4.4 Open Banking and APIs

The advent of Open Banking and the implementation of Application Programming Interfaces (APIs) have revolutionized the banking industry by encouraging development, competition, and customer-centricity. This new paradigm allows third-party developers to build applications and services around a financial institution, enabling more tailored and diversified offerings.

**Account Aggregation Services**

Account aggregation services are one of the most prominent features of Open Banking, providing customers with a consolidated view of their financial data across multiple accounts and institutions. These services draw on APIs to securely access and aggregate information from bank accounts, investment portfolios, credit cards, and other financial products.

**Full Financial Overview:**

Account aggregation services allow customers to gain a complete view of their financial situation by consolidating data from different accounts. This unified dashboard helps users track their spending, monitor account balances, and manage investments more effectively. It also enables better financial planning by providing insights into cash flow, savings, and liabilities.

**Personalized Financial Insights:**

By analyzing aggregated data, account aggregation services can offer personalized financial insights and recommendations. For instance, they can identify spending patterns, highlight potential savings opportunities, and suggest investment strategies. These insights equip customers to make informed financial decisions and achieve their financial goals.

**Simplified Account Management:**

With account aggregation, customers no longer need to log in to multiple banking portals to access their accounts. They can view all their financial information in one place, simplifying account management and reducing the hassle of managing multiple logins. This convenience increases the overall user experience and encourages customer loyalty.

**Boosted Security and Privacy:**

Account aggregation services use secure APIs and advanced encryption methods to protect sensitive financial data. Customers must provide explicit consent for their data to be accessed and shared, securing compliance with privacy regulations. Also, many aggregation services offer multi-factor authentication and other security features to safeguard user accounts.

**Third-party Service Integrations**

Open Banking has opened the door for third-party providers (TPPs) to integrate their services with banks and financial institutions. This integration enables the creation of fresh financial products and services that cater to specific customer needs.

- **Payment Initiation Services:**

  One of the principal applications of third-party integrations is payment initiation services. TPPs can initiate payments directly from a customer's bank account with their consent, offering an alternative to traditional payment methods like credit cards or bank transfers. This service simplifies the payment process, reduces transaction costs, and provides a frictionless payment experience.

- **Fintech Collaborations:**

  Banks are increasingly collaborating with fintech companies to offer a range of value-added services. These include budgeting tools, investment platforms, lending marketplaces, and insurance services. By integrating these third-party solutions, banks can expand their product offerings and provide customers with more choices and personalized experiences.

- **Data-driven Financial Products:**

  Third-party integrations also help the development of data-driven financial products. For example, TPPs can use transaction data to offer personalized lending solutions, such as pre-approved loans or customized credit cards. Similarly, investment platforms can use aggregated data to recommend tailored investment portfolios based on a customer's risk profile and financial goals.

- **Customer-centric Developments:**

The integration of third-party services promotes customer-centric advances, such as loyalty programs, rewards schemes, and personalized offers. For instance, a bank could partner with a retail platform to offer discounts on purchases made using the bank's payment methods. These collaborations boost customer engagement and drive business growth.

## Regulatory Framework for Open Banking

The regulatory framework for Open Banking is major in safeguarding a secure and transparent environment for data sharing and third-party integrations. Regulators are involved in setting standards and guidelines to protect consumer interests and maintain financial stability.

- **Data Protection and Privacy:**

Regulators have established strict data protection and privacy regulations to safeguard customer information. For instance, the General Data Protection Regulation (GDPR) in the European Union mandates that personal data be processed lawfully, fairly, and transparently. Similar regulations in other jurisdictions make certain that customers have control over their data and that their privacy is protected.

- **Licensing and Authorization:**

To operate in the Open Banking ecosystem, third-party providers must obtain the necessary licenses and authorizations from regulatory authorities. This includes payment initiation service providers (PISPs) and account information service providers (AISPs). Licensing requirements guarantee that TPPs meet the necessary standards for security, compliance, and financial stability.

- **API Standards and Interoperability:**

Regulators often mandate the use of standardized APIs to secure interoperability and security in the Open Banking ecosystem. Standardized APIs enable effortless data sharing between banks and TPPs, reducing integration costs and improving the customer experience. For example, the Open Banking Implementation Entity (OBIE) in the UK has developed a set of standards for secure API implementation.

- **Consumer Consent and Transparency:**

A fundamental principle of Open Banking is that customers must provide explicit consent for their data to be accessed and shared. Regulators require that consent be obtained transparently, with clear information about the data being shared, the purpose of sharing, and the entities involved. Customers should also have the ability to revoke consent at any time.

- **Dispute Resolution and Liability:**

Regulatory frameworks often include provisions for dispute resolution and liability in the event of data breaches or unauthorized transactions. These provisions outline the responsibilities of banks, TPPs, and other parties involved in the Open Banking ecosystem. They also establish mechanisms for customers to seek redress and compensation for losses.

- **Risk Management and Cybersecurity:**

Regulators emphasize the importance of solid risk management and cybersecurity practices in the Open Banking ecosystem. This includes implementing strong authentication measures, monitoring for suspicious activities, and conducting regular security assessments. Regulatory guidelines often require banks and TPPs to have complete cybersecurity frameworks to protect customer data and safeguard the integrity of financial transactions.

## Chapter 6
# Interlinkage Between Banks and Payment Systems

The interlinkage between banks and payment systems is a fundamental aspect of the modern financial ecosystem, creating a smooth network that supports all sorts of economic activities. This interconnection allows for the quick flow of funds, supports commerce, and provides individuals and businesses with reliable access to financial services. Understanding this interlinkage involves examining the infrastructure, operations, and roles that banks and payment systems play in conjunction with each other.

As we have seen all through the previous chapters we can understand, banks are players in the payment systems environment. They act as intermediaries between customers and many payment systems, providing the necessary infrastructure and services to support transactions. Banks issue payment instruments such as debit cards, credit cards, and electronic payment systems, allowing customers to access their funds and make payments smoothly. These instruments are not only tools for accessing money but also serve as central links to broader payment systems. Debit cards, for example, are directly linked to a customer's bank account, enabling real-time debits during transactions. Credit cards offer a line of credit, allowing customers to make purchases and settle payments later. Electronic payment systems, including online banking platforms and mobile apps, enable frictionless electronic transfers and payments, strengthening convenience for users.

In addition to providing payment instruments, banks help with the settlement and clearing of transactions. When a payment is initiated, banks are responsible for guaranteeing that funds are transferred from the payer's account to the payee's account. This involves verifying transaction details, checking account balances, and easing the actual transfer of funds. Banks participate in clearinghouses and settlement systems, such as the National Payments Corporation of India (NPCI) and the Clearing Corporation of India Limited (CCIL), to manage the clearing and settlement of interbank transactions. These systems make certain that transactions are processed quickly and that funds are settled accurately, maintaining the integrity and reliability of the payment ecosystem.

The integration of banks and payment systems also encompasses the management of risks and the implementation of security measures. With the increasing complexity and volume of digital transactions, banks have a critical responsibility to safeguard customer data and financial assets. They employ sturdy security protocols, such as encryption and two-factor authentication, to protect against unauthorized access and cyber threats. Also, banks must comply with regulatory frameworks and industry standards, like the Payment Card Industry Data Security Standard (PCI-DSS), to guarantee the secure processing of payment transactions. These measures help mitigate risks associated with fraud, data breaches, and other cyber threats, thereby boosting customer trust and confidence in the banking system.

Banks and payment systems work together to innovate and improve the productivity of financial transactions. The development and deployment of technologies like contactless payments, QR code-based payments, and blockchain have revolutionized the way payments are made. Banks have been instrumental in adopting and integrating these technologies into their services, enabling faster, more secure, and more convenient payment options for consumers. This collaboration has led to the proliferation of digital wallets, UPI (Unified Payments Interface), and other digital payment solutions that have transformed the financial system in India and beyond. In this chapter, we will also highlight the critical overlapping's between banking and payment systems, focusing on intersections from previous chapters.

## 6.1 Integration of Banking and Payment Infrastructure

The integration of banking and payment infrastructure is central for the smooth functioning of financial systems. Banks and payment systems are deeply intertwined, as banks provide the foundational infrastructure and support for several payment mechanisms. This symbiotic relationship safeguards effortless transactions, improves customer convenience, and supports economic activities.

### Interbank Networks

Interbank networks are central to the integration of banks and payment systems. They enable different banks to communicate, process transactions, and settle payments effectively. These networks form the backbone of the financial ecosystem, securing that payment systems can function smoothly across different banking entities.

**National Financial Switch (NFS)**

The National Financial Switch (NFS) is an interbank network that connects the ATMs of different banks across India. Managed by the National Payments Corporation of India (NPCI), NFS enables the interoperability of ATMs, allowing customers of one bank to use the ATMs of another. This network's integration with banks is critical as it relies on the infrastructure and security measures provided by banks to enable transactions.

Banks factor into NFS by issuing ATM cards, maintaining customer accounts, and safeguarding the secure processing of transactions. They also provide the necessary infrastructure, such as ATMs and core banking systems, which interface with the NFS network. This interlinkage guarantees that customers have access to their funds from any ATM within the network, improving the convenience and reach of banking services. The participation of banks in the NFS network also involves sharing transaction data and adhering to regulatory standards set by the RBI and NPCI. This collaboration secures that all transactions are processed smoothly, securely, and in compliance with the law.

## 6.1.1 Role of Core Banking Systems in Payments

Core Banking Systems (CBS) are the backbone of banking operations, being involved in the processing and management of financial transactions. As the financial field evolves, CBS has become increasingly intertwined with payment systems, enabling banks to offer smooth, effective, and secure payment services. Core banking is a centralized system that connects multiple branches of a bank to deliver operations like loan management, withdrawals, deposits, and payments in real-time.

**Integration with Payment Gateways**

The integration of Core Banking Systems with payment gateways is fundamental to enabling a span of payment services. Payment gateways act as intermediaries between merchants, customers, and banks, supporting the authorization and processing of electronic transactions. By integrating with payment gateways, CBS can provide real-time access to customer accounts, authenticate transactions, and secure that funds are available before completing a transaction.

This integration typically involves the use of APIs (Application Programming Interfaces) that allow payment gateways to communicate with the bank's CBS. These APIs ease the secure exchange of information, such as transaction details, account balances, and customer credentials. For example, when a customer initiates an online payment, the payment gateway sends a request to the bank's CBS to verify the customer's account details and confirm the availability of funds. The CBS then responds with a confirmation or rejection based on the account status, enabling the gateway to proceed with the transaction.

The integration with payment gateways also supports a number of payment methods, including credit and debit cards, net banking, and digital wallets. It allows banks to offer a unified platform for processing payments, providing customers with a frictionless experience across different channels. This integration strengthens security by enabling real-time fraud detection and monitoring, guaranteeing that transactions are secure and compliant with regulatory standards.

**Real-time Transaction Processing**

Real-time transaction processing is a feature of modern Core Banking Systems, enabling banks to process and settle transactions instantly. This capability is important for payment systems, including Immediate Payment Service (IMPS), Unified Payments Interface (UPI), and Real-Time Gross Settlement (RTGS). Real-time processing safeguards that transactions are completed without delays, providing immediate confirmation to customers and merchants.

The real-time processing capability of CBS is facilitated by a strong infrastructure that supports high-speed data transmission and processing. It involves a real-time core engine that handles transaction requests, updates account balances, and triggers necessary actions, such as fund transfers or payments. This engine is designed to handle large volumes of transactions simultaneously, securing scalability and reliability.

Real-time transaction processing also involves the integration of components, including authentication systems, fraud detection mechanisms, and risk management tools. These components work together to verify the identity of customers, assess the risk of transactions, and detect any suspicious activities. For instance, the CBS may use multi-factor authentication (MFA) and biometric verification to authenticate customers, while employing machine learning algorithms to detect and prevent fraud.

The benefits of real-time transaction processing are manifold. It boosts customer satisfaction by providing instant access to funds and services, reduces the risk of payment delays and errors, and supports the quick management of liquidity for banks. Real-time processing enables banks to offer new payment services, such as instant credit transfers, bill payments, and mobile payments, catering to the growing demand for fast and convenient financial services.

## Reconciliation and Settlement

Reconciliation and settlement are critical processes in the functioning of payment systems, safeguarding the accuracy and completeness of financial transactions. Core Banking Systems help with these processes, providing the tools and capabilities needed to reconcile transaction data, manage settlements, and resolve discrepancies.

Reconciliation involves the comparison of transaction records from different sources, such as payment gateways, merchant systems, and the bank's CBS. The goal is to safeguard that all transactions are accurately recorded, authorized, and settled. CBS supports reconciliation by maintaining detailed transaction logs, which include information on transaction amounts, timestamps, account details, and status. These logs are used to cross-check transactions against external records, identify discrepancies, and take corrective actions.

The reconciliation process is automated in modern CBS, using algorithms and rules to match transactions and flag any inconsistencies. This automation reduces the risk of human errors, speeds up the reconciliation process, and increases the accuracy of financial reporting. CBS provides real-time reconciliation capabilities, allowing banks to monitor transactions continuously and address issues as they arise.

Settlement refers to the finalization of transactions, where funds are transferred between accounts to complete a payment. Core Banking Systems help settlement by updating account balances, transferring funds, and generating settlement reports. In the case of interbank transactions, CBS coordinates with payment systems, such as RTGS or Automated Clearing House (ACH), to settle funds between banks. The system guarantees that settlements are conducted in a timely and secure manner, minimizing settlement risk and maintaining the integrity of the payment system.

CBS also supports the management of liquidity during the settlement process. It provides real-time information on account balances, cash flows, and liquidity positions, enabling banks to optimize their liquidity management strategies. For instance, CBS can trigger liquidity adjustments, such as interbank borrowing or collateral transfers, to make certain that banks have sufficient funds to meet their settlement obligations.

**SWIFT Network for Cross-border Transactions**

The SWIFT (Society for Worldwide Interbank Financial Telecommunication) network as earlier stated is a global messaging system that eases cross-border transactions between banks. In India, banks use the SWIFT network to send and receive payment instructions for international transactions, such as trade finance, foreign exchange, and remittances. The interlinkage between banks and the SWIFT network is critical for the execution of international payments. Banks are responsible for maintaining correspondent banking relationships with other financial institutions worldwide. Through these relationships, banks can settle cross-border transactions on behalf of their customers. The SWIFT network acts as a secure communication channel, guaranteeing that payment instructions are transmitted accurately and promptly. Banks' integration with SWIFT also involves complying with international standards and regulations, such as anti-money laundering (AML) and counter-terrorism financing (CTF) laws. This compliance is needed to maintain the integrity and security of the global financial system. Also, banks use SWIFT's many services, such as SWIFT gpi (Global Payments Breakthrough), to provide improved transparency and speed in cross-border transactions.

## 6.1.2 Payment System Access for Non-bank Entities

The involvement of non-bank entities in payment systems has become increasingly prominent, reflecting the evolving sector of financial services. Traditionally, banks were the primary participants in payment systems, but the rise of fintech companies and other non-bank entities has expanded the ecosystem. Here we examine the mechanisms through which non-bank entities access payment systems, the regulatory frameworks governing their participation, and the risk management considerations associated with their involvement.

**Direct and Indirect Participation Models**

Non-bank entities can access payment systems through either direct or indirect participation models. In the direct participation model, non-bank entities, such as payment service providers (PSPs), e-money issuers, and fintech companies, are granted direct access to payment system infrastructures. This means they can directly initiate and settle transactions without relying on intermediary banks. Direct participation allows these entities to offer a wider range of financial services, including real-time payments, cross-border transfers, and digital wallets.

In contrast, the indirect participation model involves non-bank entities partnering with banks to access payment systems. These entities do not have direct access to the payment infrastructure but instead operate through a sponsoring bank. The bank acts as an intermediary, processing transactions on behalf of the non-bank participant. This model is commonly used by smaller fintech companies and PSPs that may not have the regulatory standing or infrastructure to participate directly. The indirect model offers a viable pathway for non-bank entities to enter the payment systems market, using the infrastructure and regulatory compliance of their partner banks.

**Regulatory Requirements for Access**

The participation of non-bank entities in payment systems is subject to stringent regulatory requirements designed to guarantee the integrity, security, and stability of the financial system. Regulatory bodies, such as the Reserve Bank of India (RBI), set the rules and guidelines for non-bank entities seeking access to payment systems. These regulations cover several aspects, including licensing, capital adequacy, operational standards, and compliance with anti-money laundering (AML) and know-your-customer (KYC) norms.

To participate directly in payment systems, non-bank entities must obtain the necessary licenses from regulatory authorities. For example, in India, entities seeking to offer payment aggregation services or issue prepaid payment instruments (PPIs) must be registered with the RBI and comply with specific guidelines. These guidelines may include requirements related to minimum capital requirements, data security, customer grievance redressal mechanisms, and periodic reporting. The regulatory framework secures that non-bank participants operate transparently, securely, and responsibly within the payment systems.

## 6.1.3 Risk Management for Non-bank Participants

The inclusion of non-bank entities in payment systems introduces new risks that must be managed effectively to safeguard the financial ecosystem. These risks include operational risks, cybersecurity threats, liquidity risks, and reputational risks. Non-bank participants must implement reliable risk management frameworks to identify, assess, and mitigate these risks.

Operational risks arise from the potential for system failures, processing errors, or disruptions in service. Non-bank entities must have contingency plans, business continuity measures, and disaster recovery protocols to minimize the impact of operational disruptions. Cybersecurity threats, such as hacking, phishing, and data breaches, pose substantial risks to payment systems. Non-bank participants must invest in advanced security technologies, conduct regular security audits, and adhere to data protection regulations to safeguard sensitive customer information.

Liquidity risks pertain to the ability of non-bank entities to meet their financial obligations, especially in real-time payment environments. Non-bank participants must maintain sufficient liquidity reserves and have access to emergency funding sources to manage liquidity shocks. Reputational risks can arise from regulatory non-compliance, security breaches, or poor customer service. Non-bank entities must uphold high standards of governance, compliance, and customer service to maintain their reputation and trust in the market.

## 6.2 Impact on Financial Stability and Effectiveness

The interlinkage between banks and payment systems factors into maintaining financial stability and strengthening the speed of the financial ecosystem. The integration of these systems affects how risks are managed and mitigated, and how quickly transactions are processed.

### Systemic Risk Considerations

Systemic risk in the context of payment systems refers to the potential for a failure in one part of the system to trigger a chain reaction, affecting the entire financial network. Given the high volume and value of transactions processed through payment systems, any disruption can have major repercussions on financial stability.

### Interdependencies in Payment Systems

The interdependencies among payment systems, banks, and other financial institutions create a complex network where the failure of one component can have cascading effects. For instance, if a major bank experiences technical difficulties or a liquidity shortfall, it can delay the settlement of transactions, affecting other banks and payment systems. This interconnectedness means that the health of the payment infrastructure is closely tied to the overall stability of the financial system.

Such interdependencies are particularly evident in Real-Time Gross Settlement (RTGS) systems, where high-value transactions are settled in real time. The failure of a participant in a RTGS system to meet its obligations can lead to a liquidity crunch, affecting the timely settlement of other transactions. Similarly, disruptions in systems like SWIFT or domestic networks like RuPay can impact cross-border and domestic payments, respectively.

## Risk Mitigation Measures

To mitigate systemic risks, several measures are implemented within payment systems and the broader financial ecosystem. A critical approach can be the establishment of solid risk management frameworks by central banks and regulatory authorities. These frameworks often include guidelines for liquidity management, credit risk, and operational risk.

Liquidity management is necessary in securing that banks have sufficient funds to meet their payment obligations. Central banks often provide intraday credit facilities or liquidity support mechanisms to prevent payment gridlocks. For example, the Reserve Bank of India (RBI) offers liquidity adjustment facilities to help banks manage short-term liquidity needs.

Another main measure is the implementation of collateral requirements for participants in payment systems. By requiring participants to post collateral, payment systems can reduce the risk of default and secure that there are sufficient resources to cover potential losses. Payment systems often employ netting arrangements, where multiple transactions are consolidated into a single net payment obligation, reducing the overall liquidity requirements.

Operational risk is addressed through stringent security protocols, including encryption, access controls, and fraud detection systems. Payment systems must comply with international standards such as the Payment Card Industry Data Security Standard (PCI-DSS) and ISO 27001 to safeguard data integrity and prevent unauthorized access.

## Regulatory Oversight and Stress Testing

Regulatory oversight is major in maintaining the integrity and stability of payment systems. Central banks and regulatory bodies set rules and guidelines that govern the functioning of payment systems, safeguarding compliance with legal and operational standards. They also conduct regular inspections and audits to assess the risk profiles of participants and the overall system.

Stress testing is a tool used by regulators to evaluate the resilience of payment systems under a number of adverse scenarios. These tests simulate extreme conditions, such as a considerable drop in liquidity, cyber-attacks, or the failure of a major participant. The results of stress tests help identify potential vulnerabilities and guide the implementation of corrective measures.

In addition to regulatory oversight, payment systems often have their governance structures that include risk management committees and audit functions. These bodies are responsible for monitoring compliance, assessing risks, and implementing policies to increase system stability.

## Productivity Gains from Integrated Systems

The integration of banking and payment systems has brought about notable effectiveness gains, transforming the way financial transactions are conducted. This integration speeds up processes, reduces operational costs, and improves the overall customer experience. We now turn to the aspects of these speed gains, focusing on straight-through processing, reduction in settlement times, and cost savings for both banks and customers.

## Straight-through Processing

Straight-through processing (STP) is a component of modern financial systems, enabling automated transaction processing without the need for manual intervention. STP uses advanced technologies such as electronic data interchange (EDI), automated clearing houses (ACH), and real-time gross settlement (RTGS) systems to support effortless transaction flows. The objective of STP is to minimize errors, reduce processing time, and increase the productivity of financial transactions.

In the context of integrated banking and payment systems, STP allows for the automatic validation, approval, and execution of transactions. For instance, in securities trading, STP enables the end-to-end automation of trade execution, clearing, and settlement. Similarly, in payments, STP allows for the direct transfer of funds between bank accounts, guaranteeing that payments are processed quickly and accurately.

The benefits of STP extend beyond effectiveness gains. By reducing manual intervention, STP minimizes the risk of human error, boosting the accuracy and reliability of transactions. It also supports greater transparency, as all transaction details are electronically recorded and easily traceable. Also, STP strengthens compliance with regulatory requirements, as automated systems can be programmed to enforce compliance checks and controls.

## Reduction in Settlement Times

The integration of payment systems and banking infrastructure has led to a marked reduction in settlement times, a factor in the financial industry's speed.

Historically, the settlement of transactions, especially in cross-border payments, could take several days due to the involvement of multiple intermediaries and complex processes. However, with advancements in payment systems, settlement times have been dramatically reduced.

For example, the implementation of real-time payment systems such as Immediate Payment Service (IMPS) and Unified Payments Interface (UPI) in India has enabled instant fund transfers. These systems allow transactions to be completed within seconds, providing customers with immediate access to funds. Similarly, the adoption of real-time gross settlement (RTGS) systems for high-value transactions has ensured the immediate settlement of funds, reducing the risk of settlement delays and improving liquidity management.

The reduction in settlement times has several benefits for banks and customers. For banks, faster settlement times improve cash flow management and reduce the need for extensive liquidity buffers. For customers, quick access to funds boosts their ability to make timely payments and manage their finances effectively. Also, faster settlements reduce the counterparty risk, as the time frame for potential default or non-payment is minimized.

## Cost Savings for Banks and Customers

The integration of banking and payment systems also leads to substantial cost savings for both banks and customers. One of the primary sources of these savings is the automation and digitization of processes, which reduce the need for manual intervention and paperwork. For banks, this translates into lower operational costs, as fewer resources are required to process transactions. The reduction in manual processing also decreases the likelihood of errors, further lowering costs associated with error resolution and corrections.

For customers, the cost savings are reflected in lower transaction fees and charges. For instance, digital payment systems like UPI and mobile banking apps often offer low or no-cost transactions, making them a cost-effective alternative to traditional payment methods such as cheques or cash. The convenience of digital payments eliminates the need for physical visits to bank branches, saving customers time and travel expenses.

The adoption of digital wallets and mobile banking solutions provides customers with a more flexible and accessible banking experience. They can manage their accounts, make payments, and access financial services from anywhere and at any time, reducing the opportunity cost associated with traditional banking methods. This convenience increases customer satisfaction and loyalty, which can lead to long-term benefits for banks in terms of customer retention and increased usage of banking services.

Integrated systems enable banks to tap data analytics and artificial intelligence (AI) to optimize their operations and offer personalized services to customers. By analyzing transaction data, banks can identify cost-saving opportunities, simplify their services, and offer targeted products and services that meet the specific needs of their customers. This data-driven approach not only improves operational productivity but also creates value for customers by providing them with tailored financial solutions.

## 6.3 Role in Economic Growth

The integration of banks and payment systems factors into supporting and accelerating economic growth. These systems not only improve the effectiveness of financial transactions but also provide the infrastructure necessary for the smooth functioning of trade, commerce, and economic activities. This section explores how the interlinkage between banks and payment systems enables trade and commerce, focusing on B2B payment solutions, international trade payments, and supply chain finance.

### Enabling Trade and Commerce

In a modern economy, the ability to conduct transactions effectively and securely is central for businesses of all sizes. The integration of banks and payment systems eases trade and commerce by providing reliable and smooth payment solutions, enabling businesses to manage their finances effectively and engage in commercial activities with ease.

### B2B Payment Solutions

Business-to-business (B2B) payment solutions are necessary for the smooth exchange of goods and services between companies. These solutions include a range of payment methods such as electronic funds transfers (EFTs), wire transfers, corporate credit cards, and automated clearing house (ACH) transactions. The integration of banks and payment systems enables businesses to automate their payment processes, reducing the reliance on manual methods such as cheques.

Automated B2B payment solutions speed up the invoicing and payment processes, reducing the time and effort required to settle transactions. This speed is particularly important for businesses that deal with high volumes of transactions, as it helps them manage their cash flow more effectively. Digital payment solutions offer strengthened security features, such as encryption and multi-factor authentication, securing that transactions are secure and reducing the risk of fraud.

## International Trade Payments

The globalization of trade has led to an increase in cross-border transactions, making international trade payments a component of the global economy. Today, in any formal cross border trade we cannot imagine payment systems without banks as intermediaries providing businesses with the necessary infrastructure to conduct international transactions securely and smoothly.

The element of international trade payments is the use of SWIFT (Society for Worldwide Interbank Financial Telecommunication) for secure communication between banks. SWIFT enables the transmission of payment instructions and other financial messages between banks across different countries. This standardized messaging system safeguards that international payments are processed accurately and quickly, reducing the risk of errors and delays.

In addition to SWIFT, banks also offer a range of trade finance products, such as letters of credit, trade credit insurance, and documentary collections. These products help mitigate the risks associated with international trade, such as non-payment and currency fluctuations. By providing these financial instruments, banks support businesses in managing their trade risks and securing payment for their goods and services.

The advent of digital payment systems has further simplified international trade payments. Digital platforms enable businesses to conduct cross-border transactions in multiple currencies, offering competitive exchange rates and lower transaction fees. These platforms also provide real-time tracking and reporting, giving businesses greater visibility into their international transactions.

## Supply Chain Finance

Supply chain finance is a set of solutions that optimize the management of working capital and liquidity in supply chain processes. It involves the financing of trade receivables, payables, and inventory, providing businesses with access to short-term credit. The integration of banks and payment systems contributes to easing supply chain finance, enabling businesses to manage their cash flow more effectively and maintain a healthy supply chain.

One of the components of supply chain finance is factoring, where businesses sell their accounts receivable to a financial institution at a discount. This provides immediate cash flow, allowing businesses to meet their operational expenses and invest in growth opportunities. The integration of banks and payment systems enables the effective processing of factoring transactions, safeguarding that businesses receive funds promptly. Another aspect of supply chain finance is reverse factoring, also known as supplier financing. In this arrangement, a financial institution pays the suppliers on behalf of the buyer, allowing the buyer to extend their payment terms. This benefits both parties, as the supplier receives payment earlier, while the buyer gains more time to manage their cash flow. The integration of banks and payment systems simplifies this process, providing transparency and productivity in the payment settlement.

Also, digital payment solutions and blockchain technology have introduced new avenues for supply chain finance. Blockchain-based platforms offer secure and transparent tracking of goods and payments, reducing the risk of fraud and disputes. These platforms also enable smart contracts, which automatically execute payment transactions when certain conditions are met, further strengthening the effectiveness of supply chain finance.

**Boosting Financial Intermediation**

The integration is behind the major improvements in financial intermediation, which refers to the process of channelling funds from savers to borrowers. This interlinkage improves the speed and accessibility of financial services, supporting better fund flow, increased credit availability, and the emergence of alternative lending models. The following sections explore these aspects in detail.

**Improved Fund Flow in the Economy**

Traditionally, financial transactions involved considerable time lags due to manual processing and physical movement of cash or cheques. However, with the advent of digital payment systems and real-time settlements, the transfer of funds has become instantaneous, leading to a more dynamic and responsive financial system.

Real-time gross settlement (RTGS) systems, immediate payment services (IMPS), and unified payments interfaces (UPI) have notably reduced the time required for funds to move between accounts. This immediate availability of funds strengthens liquidity in the economy, enabling individuals and businesses to manage their finances more effectively. For instance, businesses can pay suppliers and receive payments from customers in real-time, optimizing their cash flow management and reducing the need for short-term borrowing.

The increased velocity of money circulation due to faster fund transfers contributes to overall economic growth. With funds available promptly, consumers can make purchases more readily, and businesses can invest in new projects, hire additional staff, and expand their operations. This acceleration in economic activity is a direct result of the improved interlinkage between banks and payment systems.

## Credit Availability Through Digital Channels

The digitalization of banking and payment systems has greatly expanded access to credit, particularly for underserved segments of the population. Digital channels, such as online banking platforms, mobile apps, and digital lending platforms, have made it easier for individuals and businesses to apply for and receive loans. This ease of access has democratized the availability of credit, making it possible for more people to participate in the financial system.

The benefit of digital channels is the ability to provide instant credit approvals. By drawing on data analytics, machine learning algorithms, and alternative data sources, digital lenders can assess the creditworthiness of applicants quickly and accurately. This enables the rapid disbursement of loans, which is particularly beneficial for small businesses and individuals in need of immediate financial support.

Digital credit platforms also offer customized loan products tailored to the specific needs of borrowers. For instance, small-ticket loans, payday loans, and microloans are available to cater to the short-term financial needs of individuals. Similarly, businesses can access working capital loans, invoice financing, and merchant cash advances through digital platforms. The flexibility and convenience of these products make them attractive options for borrowers.

The digital footprint generated through online transactions, social media activity, and other digital behaviors provides valuable insights into the creditworthiness of individuals and businesses. This data can be used to develop alternative credit scoring models, enabling lenders to extend credit to those who may not have a traditional credit history. As a result, more people can access formal credit, reducing their reliance on informal and often exploitative sources of finance.

## Alternative Lending Models

The integration of banks and payment systems has facilitated the emergence of alternative lending models, which have disrupted traditional banking practices and expanded the range of financing options available to borrowers. These models employ technology and data analytics to offer novel financial products and services, catering to the diverse needs of consumers and businesses. A prominent alternative lending model is peer-to-peer (P2P) lending. P2P lending platforms connect individual lenders with borrowers, enabling the direct transfer of funds without the involvement of traditional financial institutions. These platforms use advanced algorithms to match lenders and borrowers based on their risk profiles and investment preferences. P2P lending offers competitive interest rates and flexible terms, making it an attractive option for both parties. For borrowers, it provides access to credit without the stringent requirements of traditional banks, while lenders can earn higher returns on their investments.

Another emerging model is crowdfunding, which allows individuals and businesses to raise funds from a large number of investors through online platforms. Crowdfunding can take forms, including donation-based, reward-based, equity-based, and debt-based models. This approach is particularly popular among startups and small businesses, as it provides a means to secure funding for fresh projects and ventures. Crowdfunding platforms often use digital payment systems to enable the collection and distribution of funds, guaranteeing a smooth and transparent process.

Digital lending platforms also offer pay-as-you-go financing models, which are especially useful for consumers and businesses with irregular income streams. For example, some platforms offer "buy now, pay later" (BNPL) services, allowing consumers to make purchases and pay for them in instalments. This model has gained popularity in the retail sector, providing consumers with greater flexibility in managing their expenses. Similarly, businesses can access revenue-based financing, where repayments are linked to their monthly sales, making it easier to manage cash flow.

## Supporting Government Initiatives (Direct Benefit Transfers)

This integration phenomenon has was involved in supporting government initiatives, particularly within Direct Benefit Transfers (DBT). The DBT scheme is designed to simplify the delivery of government subsidies and welfare benefits, securing that they reach the intended beneficiaries smoothly and transparently. This section covers many aspects of DBT, focusing on the Jan Dhan-Aadhaar-Mobile (JAM) Trinity, productivity in subsidy disbursement, and the impact on financial inclusion.

## Jan Dhan-Aadhaar-Mobile (JAM) Trinity

The JAM Trinity represents the convergence of three components: Jan Dhan Yojana, Aadhaar, and Mobile. This initiative has been instrumental in transforming India's payment environment by integrating banking, digital identity, and mobile connectivity. The Jan Dhan Yojana aims to provide every household with a basic savings bank account, enabling access to financial services. Aadhaar, as a unique biometric identification system, guarantees accurate identification and authentication of beneficiaries. Mobile connectivity supports instant communication and financial transactions.

The JAM Trinity has been a game-changer in the implementation of DBT. By linking bank accounts with Aadhaar and mobile numbers, the government has been able to create a unified platform for the direct transfer of benefits. This system minimizes the risk of fraud and leakage by safeguarding that subsidies and welfare payments are credited directly to the beneficiaries' bank accounts. The frictionless integration of these three elements has markedly reduced the administrative burden and delays associated with traditional modes of benefit distribution.

Also, the JAM Trinity has facilitated the development of a sturdy digital payments infrastructure, which includes mobile banking apps, UPI, and digital wallets. This infrastructure has made it easier for beneficiaries to access their funds, make payments, and manage their finances. The widespread adoption of digital payment methods has also contributed to the formalization of the economy, as more transactions are recorded and monitored.

## Effectiveness in Subsidy Disbursement

Payment systems with help of banks have greatly boosted the speed of subsidy disbursement under the DBT scheme. Before the implementation of DBT, subsidies were often disbursed in-kind or through intermediaries, leading to inefficiencies, corruption, and delays. The DBT system, enabled by the JAM Trinity, has addressed these challenges by providing a direct and transparent mechanism for transferring funds.

Under the DBT framework, subsidies for several welfare schemes, such as LPG, fertilizer, and food subsidies, are directly credited to the bank accounts of eligible beneficiaries. This direct transfer mechanism secures that the subsidies reach the intended recipients without any intermediaries. The use of Aadhaar-based authentication further safeguards that only genuine beneficiaries receive the benefits, reducing the scope for duplicate and fake entries.

The productivity of the DBT system is further improved by the use of electronic payment systems. Digital payment platforms, such as UPI and mobile banking apps, allow beneficiaries to access their funds instantly and conveniently. The real-time nature of these platforms guarantees that payments are processed quickly, minimizing delays and providing immediate relief to beneficiaries. The electronic trail of transactions helps in monitoring and auditing the disbursement process, guaranteeing transparency and accountability.

The DBT system has also led to notable cost savings for the government. By eliminating intermediaries and reducing administrative overheads, the government has been able to channel more funds towards actual benefits rather than operational costs. The smooth process has also reduced the time required for processing and disbursing subsidies, allowing for more timely and quick delivery of welfare benefits. The most marked achievements of the DBT initiative are the widespread opening of bank accounts under the Pradhan Mantri Jan Dhan Yojana (PMJDY). As of 2023, over 430 million Jan Dhan accounts have been opened, providing individuals with access to basic banking services. These accounts have not only facilitated the direct transfer of subsidies but have also enabled individuals to save, invest, and access credit.

**Micro-ATMs and Business correspondents**

Micro-ATMs and business correspondents have emerged as components in bridging the financial inclusion gap in rural areas. These solutions address the challenges posed by the lack of traditional banking infrastructure in remote locations, offering basic banking services to those who would otherwise be excluded from the formal financial system.

Micro-ATMs are portable devices that allow business correspondents to perform basic banking transactions, such as cash deposits, withdrawals, and balance inquiries, in areas without traditional ATMs or bank branches. These devices are connected to the bank's core banking system, enabling real-time transactions. The biometric authentication feature, often integrated with Aadhaar, secures secure and accurate identification of customers. Micro-ATMs have been particularly useful in disbursing government benefits, pensions, and subsidies, as they can reach beneficiaries in their villages, reducing the need for travel and long waits at bank branches.

Business correspondents are individuals or entities authorized by banks to provide banking services on their behalf. They factor into extending financial services to underserved areas, acting as the last-mile connection between the bank and the customer. BCs are typically local residents, which helps in building trust and understanding the specific needs of the community. They offer a range of services, including account opening, cash deposits and withdrawals, loan applications, and remittance services.

The integration of micro-ATMs and business correspondents has greatly expanded the reach of the banking system in rural India. These initiatives have not only increased the accessibility of banking services but have also contributed to the formalization of the rural economy. By providing a convenient and secure means of conducting transactions, they have encouraged rural populations to save, invest, and access credit, thereby promoting economic growth and development.

## 6.4 Challenges and Opportunities

The interlinkage between banks and payment systems presents a complex system of challenges and opportunities, especially in the context of India's fast-changing financial ecosystem. Let us now see, the technological challenges, including scalability, interoperability, and cybersecurity concerns, and discuss how these issues create both obstacles and avenues for growth and advance.

### Technological Challenges

As the digital economy expands and the volume of transactions increases, the banking and payment systems infrastructure must scale accordingly. Scalability is a substantial concern, as systems need to handle a growing number of transactions quickly without compromising performance or security. The challenge lies in securing that infrastructure can be scaled up to meet demand without causing delays or system failures.

Banks and payment service providers must continuously upgrade their systems to accommodate higher transaction volumes, which involves major capital expenditure. This includes expanding server capacities, improving network bandwidth, and optimizing databases to safeguard fast and reliable transaction processing. Maintaining high availability and redundancy is major to prevent downtime, which can disrupt services and erode customer trust.

Another aspect of scalability is the ability to handle peak transaction periods, such as during festivals or sales events, when transaction volumes can surge dramatically. Banks and payment systems must have strong load balancing and traffic management mechanisms to manage these spikes effectively. Failure to do so can result in service disruptions, leading to financial losses and customer dissatisfaction.

**Interoperability Issues**

Interoperability refers to the ability of different systems and platforms to work together without friction. In the context of banks and payment systems, interoperability is critical for enabling smooth transactions across a number of channels, such as cards, digital wallets, UPI, and traditional bank accounts. However, achieving interoperability can be challenging due to differences in technology standards, protocols, and regulations.

The primary barrier could be the lack of a common standard across different payment systems. For instance, different banks may use proprietary systems for processing transactions, making it difficult for these systems to communicate with each other. This can lead to fragmented payment experiences, where customers face difficulties in transferring funds between accounts or using different payment methods.

Regulatory frameworks also contribute to shaping interoperability. In India, the Reserve Bank of India (RBI) and other regulatory bodies have introduced guidelines to promote interoperability among payment systems. For example, the RBI's mandate for interoperability among prepaid payment instruments (PPIs) has enabled customers to transfer funds between different digital wallets. However, the implementation of such regulations can be complex and require considerable coordination among stakeholders, including banks, payment service providers, and technology vendors.

Technological advancements, such as the adoption of open APIs and the development of common standards like ISO 20022, have the potential to address interoperability challenges. Open APIs enable different systems to interact with each other, allowing for the effortless exchange of data and services. ISO 20022, a global standard for electronic data interchange between financial institutions, provides a common language for financial messaging, easing interoperability across different platforms. However, the transition to these standards requires substantial effort and investment from all parties involved.

**Cybersecurity Concerns**

Cybersecurity is a critical concern in the digital payment ecosystem, given the sensitive nature of financial data and the increasing sophistication of cyber threats. As banks and payment systems become more interconnected and reliant on digital technologies, they become more vulnerable to cyberattacks. Safeguarding the security of these systems is central to protecting customer information, maintaining trust, and preventing financial losses.

To protect customer's data banks and payment service providers must implement reliable encryption and data protection measures to secure sensitive information, such as account numbers, personal identification numbers (PINs), and transaction details. The adoption of secure encryption protocols, such as SSL/TLS for data transmission and AES for data storage, is important for safeguarding data against unauthorized access.

Another aspect of cybersecurity is the detection and prevention of fraud. Cybercriminals use methods, such as phishing, malware, and social engineering, to steal customer information and commit fraud. Banks and payment systems must employ advanced security technologies, such as artificial intelligence (AI) and machine learning (ML), to detect and prevent fraudulent activities in real-time. AI and ML algorithms can analyze transaction patterns and identify anomalies that may indicate fraud, allowing for swift action to mitigate risks.

Regulatory compliance is also a consideration in cybersecurity. In India, the RBI has established guidelines for the cybersecurity framework in banks, which outline the minimum standards for information security. Compliance with these guidelines is mandatory for banks and payment service providers, and failure to adhere to them can result in penalties and reputational damage. Also, global regulations, such as the General Data Protection Regulation (GDPR), have implications for data protection and privacy, requiring organizations to implement stringent measures to protect customer data.

While cybersecurity presents notable challenges, it also offers opportunities for development and growth. The demand for secure and reliable payment solutions has led to the emergence of new technologies and business models. For example, the rise of biometric authentication methods, such as fingerprint and facial recognition, has strengthened security and convenience for customers. The development of blockchain technology offers the potential for secure and transparent transactions, reducing the risk of fraud and improving trust in the financial system.

## Regulatory Balancing Act

As the banking and payment systems field continues to evolve rapidly, regulators face the challenging task of balancing breakthrough with stability, guaranteeing consumer protection in an increasingly digital environment, and achieving harmonization across borders. The regulatory framework must support technological advancements and new business models while safeguarding the financial system's integrity and protecting consumers' rights. This balancing act is central for building a secure, smooth, and inclusive financial ecosystem.

## Advance vs. Stability

The rapid pace of development in the financial sector, particularly in digital payments, has led to the emergence of new technologies and business models that challenge traditional regulatory frameworks. Regulators must strike a balance between encouraging breakthrough and maintaining financial stability. On one hand, encouraging advance is needed for improving effectiveness, strengthening customer experience, and expanding access to financial services. On the other hand, unregulated development can introduce new risks, such as systemic risks and market instability.

To manage this delicate balance, regulators often adopt a flexible and adaptive approach. For instance, regulatory sandboxes allow fintech companies to test new products and services in a controlled environment under the regulator's supervision.

Another aspect of balancing breakthrough and stability is the regulation of cryptocurrencies and blockchain technology. These technologies offer marked potential benefits, such as increased speed, transparency, and security. However, they also pose unique challenges, including volatility, potential for illicit activities, and lack of consumer protection. Regulators worldwide are grappling with how to regulate cryptocurrencies in a way that harnesses their benefits while mitigating their risks. In India, the RBI and the government have taken a cautious approach, focusing on understanding the technology's implications and exploring the potential for a Central Bank Digital Currency (CBDC).

## Cross-border Regulatory Harmonization

The global nature of modern payment systems necessitates cross-border regulatory harmonization. As financial transactions increasingly transcend national borders, differing regulatory standards can create challenges for international trade and commerce. Disparities in regulations can lead to compliance burdens, increased costs, and inefficiencies for businesses operating across multiple jurisdictions.

To address these challenges, regulators worldwide are working towards harmonizing regulations and standards. This involves collaboration and coordination among regulatory bodies, standard-setting organizations, and international institutions. For example, the Financial Action Task Force (FATF) sets global standards for anti-money laundering (AML) and combating the financing of terrorism (CFT), which member countries, including India, adopt and implement. These standards help make certain consistency in regulatory approaches and ease cross-border cooperation in preventing financial crimes.

Harmonization is particularly important in the context of cross-border payments and remittances. The SWIFT network, which enables international wire transfers, operates under a set of standardized messaging formats and security protocols. This standardization enables effective and secure cross-border transactions. However, the rise of digital currencies and blockchain-based solutions presents new challenges and opportunities for cross-border payments. Regulators must work together to develop frameworks that address these emerging technologies' legal, regulatory, and operational aspects.

In India, the RBI collaborates with international counterparts through many forums and agreements to align its regulatory framework with global standards. This includes participation in international organizations such as the Bank for International Settlements (BIS) and the International Monetary Fund (IMF). Through these engagements, the RBI contributes to and adopts international best practices, securing that India's financial system remains solid and resilient in the face of global challenges.

## Competition from Non-bank Players

The sector of financial services has been considerably altered by the entry of non-bank players, particularly fintech companies and big tech firms. These entities have introduced new products and services, tapping technology to provide more quick, user-friendly, and accessible financial solutions. As they continue to grow and capture market share, they present both opportunities and challenges for traditional banks and regulators. This section looks at impact of fintech disruption, the entry of big tech into financial services, and concerns related to regulatory arbitrage.

## Fintech Disruption

Fintech companies, which blend financial services with technology, have rapidly transformed several aspects of the banking and payment systems. These startups and emerging companies have introduced novel solutions in areas such as digital payments, peer-to-peer lending, robo-advisory, and personal finance management. Their agility, customer-centric approach, and use of advanced technologies like artificial intelligence (AI) and blockchain have enabled them to quickly adapt to market needs and disrupt traditional banking models.

One of the most substantial disruptions caused by fintech has been in the payments sector. Mobile wallets, digital payment platforms, and peer-to-peer payment apps have made transactions faster, more convenient, and often cheaper than traditional banking channels. For instance, companies like Paytm, PhonePe, and Google Pay have gained widespread adoption in India, offering a range of services from bill payments to booking services, all within a single app. These platforms have also integrated with the Unified Payments Interface (UPI), further simplifying the payment process and making it more accessible to the masses.

In lending, fintech companies have used advanced analytics and alternative data sources to assess creditworthiness, enabling them to extend loans to individuals and small businesses that may have been underserved by traditional banks. Peer-to-peer (P2P) lending platforms and digital lending apps offer quick loan approvals and disbursements, providing a viable alternative to conventional bank loans. This has particularly benefited customers who lack a traditional credit history but possess a digital footprint that fintech companies can analyze.

## Big Tech Entry into Financial Services

Big tech companies, such as Google, Amazon have also made major inroads into the financial services sector. Using their vast user bases, technological expertise, and data capabilities, these firms have introduced a range of financial products and services, including payments. Their entry into the financial domain has intensified competition and raised questions about data privacy, market dominance, and the potential for monopolistic behavior.

Big tech's advantage lies in its ability to integrate financial services into its existing ecosystem smoothly. For example, Google Pay and Amazon Pay are integrated with their respective parent companies' e-commerce platforms, offering a convenient checkout process for users. Facebook has introduced payment features within its messaging apps, such as WhatsApp Pay, enabling users to send money as easily as sending a message. Apple has ventured into the credit card business with the Apple Card, offering a unique combination of features and benefits that use its ecosystem.

The data advantage of big tech firms cannot be overstated. They possess vast amounts of user data, ranging from purchasing habits to social interactions, which can be used to tailor financial products and services. This data-driven approach allows for more personalized offerings, potentially increasing customer satisfaction and loyalty. However, it also raises concerns about data privacy and the potential misuse of sensitive information.

## Regulatory Arbitrage Concerns

The entry of non-bank players, including fintech and big tech companies, into the financial services sector has led to concerns about regulatory arbitrage. Regulatory arbitrage occurs when companies exploit gaps or differences in regulatory frameworks to gain a competitive advantage. This can result in an uneven playing field, where traditional banks are subject to stricter regulations while non-bank players operate under less stringent oversight.

One area where regulatory arbitrage is evident is in the differing levels of capital and compliance requirements. Traditional banks are subject to rigorous capital adequacy norms, liquidity requirements, and prudential regulations to guarantee financial stability. In contrast, many fintech companies and big tech firms are not subject to the same level of scrutiny, potentially allowing them to operate with lower costs and take on higher risks. This discrepancy can lead to competitive imbalances and increase systemic risk.

Another concern is the oversight of data protection and cybersecurity. While banks are required to adhere to stringent data security standards and reporting requirements, fintech and big tech companies may not be subject to the same level of regulation. This is particularly concerning given the vast amounts of sensitive financial and personal data these companies handle. The lack of a consistent regulatory framework can result in vulnerabilities and pose risks to consumer protection and financial stability.

Regulators face the challenge of developing a cohesive regulatory framework that addresses these issues without stifling advance. This involves extending regulatory oversight to non-bank players, safeguarding they meet similar standards for consumer protection, data security, and financial stability as traditional banks. It also requires international cooperation to address cross-border regulatory arbitrage, given the global nature of many big tech companies.

## Opportunities for Development and Collaboration

The evolving environment of financial services offers opportunities for breakthrough and collaboration, particularly between traditional banks and emerging fintech companies. As technology continues to advance, the integration of new solutions and collaborative efforts can notably strengthen the productivity, security, and inclusivity of financial systems. Here we examine the potential for bank-fintech partnerships, the use of sandbox approaches for testing new technologies, and the implementation of blockchain and distributed ledger technology (DLT)-based solutions.

## Bank-Fintech Partnerships

One of the most promising opportunities for advance lies in the collaboration between traditional banks and fintech companies. These partnerships can draw on the strengths of both parties: banks bring established customer bases, regulatory expertise, and financial stability, while fintechs contribute agility, technological development, and a customer-centric approach.

Banks and fintechs can collaborate in a number of areas, including payments, lending, wealth management, and customer service. For instance, banks can integrate fintech solutions to boost their digital payment offerings, providing smooth and secure payment experiences. Similarly, fintechs specializing in data analytics and machine learning can partner with banks to improve credit scoring models and risk assessment processes, thereby extending credit to underserved segments.

One example of successful bank-fintech collaboration is the integration of digital lending platforms with traditional banking systems. Banks can use these platforms to expedite loan processing, offer customized loan products, and reach a wider audience. By drawing on fintech capabilities, banks can also reduce operational costs and increase customer engagement.

Fintech partnerships enable banks to innovate at a faster pace. Fintechs can develop and test new technologies and services more quickly than banks can internally, allowing for rapid deployment and iteration. This collaborative model not only accelerates breakthrough but also helps banks stay competitive in a rapidly changing market.

## Sandbox Approaches for Testing New Technologies

To support advance while managing risks, regulators and financial institutions are increasingly adopting sandbox approaches. A regulatory sandbox is a controlled environment where fintech startups and other financial service providers can test new products, services, and business models under regulatory supervision. This approach allows innovators to experiment with new technologies and solutions without the full burden of regulatory compliance.

The sandbox approach offers several benefits. First, it enables regulators to gain insights into emerging technologies and their potential impact on the financial system. By observing sandbox experiments, regulators can better understand the risks and benefits of new solutions, informing future regulatory frameworks. Second, it provides fintechs with a safe space to test their developments, helping them refine their offerings and secure compliance with regulatory standards.

In India, the Reserve Bank of India (RBI) has introduced a regulatory sandbox framework to encourage development in the fintech space. The framework covers sectors, including payments, lending, insurance, and capital markets. Through the sandbox, fintechs can pilot their products and services, engage with regulators, and receive feedback on compliance and risk management.

The sandbox approach also promotes collaboration between regulators, financial institutions, and fintechs. By working together in a controlled environment, these stakeholders can identify potential regulatory and operational challenges early on, supporting smoother integration of new technologies into the broader financial system.

## Blockchain and DLT-based Solutions

Blockchain and distributed ledger technology (DLT) represent another considerable opportunity for breakthrough and collaboration in the financial sector. These technologies offer a decentralized and transparent way to record transactions, potentially transforming aspects of banking and payment systems.

The most promising applications of blockchain is in cross-border payments. Traditional cross-border transactions can be slow, expensive, and prone to errors. Blockchain can speed up this process by enabling near-instantaneous settlement, reducing costs, and boosting transparency. Several banks and fintechs are exploring blockchain-based solutions for cross-border payments, tapping the technology's ability to help secure and smooth transfers.

Trade finance is another area where blockchain can make a substantial impact. The trade finance process involves multiple parties, including exporters, importers, banks, and insurers, and often requires the exchange of many documents. Blockchain can digitize and automate this process, reducing paperwork, lowering the risk of fraud, and improving effectiveness. By providing a single, immutable record of transactions, blockchain can improve trust among parties and simplify the verification process. In addition to payments and trade finance, blockchain has potential applications in areas such as identity verification, asset management, and smart contracts. For example, blockchain-based identity solutions can provide a secure and effective way to verify customer identities, reducing the reliance on physical documents and minimizing the risk of identity theft. The adoption of blockchain and DLT-based solutions presents several challenges, including regulatory uncertainties, scalability issues, and the need for industry-wide standards. However, these challenges also offer opportunities for collaboration among banks, fintechs, and regulators. By working together, these stakeholders can address technical and regulatory barriers, develop interoperable solutions, and promote the adoption of blockchain technology in the financial sector.

The idea of detaching payment systems from banks may seem like a progressive move towards decentralization or technological advance, but it carries notable risks and drawbacks that could undermine the stability and speed of the financial system. Here's why payment systems should remain integrated with banks, and why detachment could be detrimental.

**Loss of Trust and Security**

Banks have been the bedrock of financial transactions for centuries, building trust with their customers through regulation, oversight, and a proven track record of handling money responsibly. Payment systems detached from banks would lack this inherent trust and security. Banks operate under stringent regulations and are backed by government guarantees, such as deposit insurance, which assures customers that their money is safe. Independent payment systems would likely not have the same level of regulatory oversight, increasing the risk of fraud, hacking, and financial instability.

## Undermining Financial Stability

Banks contribute to maintaining the stability of the financial system. They manage liquidity, provide credit, and serve as intermediaries in the financial markets. If payment systems detach from banks, it could disrupt the delicate balance of the financial ecosystem. Banks rely on payment systems for the smooth transfer of funds between accounts, and this integration safeguards that the flow of money within the economy remains stable. Detachment could lead to fragmentation, where multiple payment systems operate independently, leading to inefficiencies, delays, and increased costs.

## Erosion of Central Bank Control

Central banks use the banking system to implement monetary policy, control inflation, and manage economic growth. Payment systems detached from banks would weaken the central bank's ability to monitor and influence money supply and demand. For example, central banks use interest rates, reserve requirements, and open market operations to guide the economy. If payment systems operate independently of banks, central banks would struggle to control the flow of money, leading to potential economic instability. This erosion of control could result in higher inflation, reduced economic growth, and financial crises.

## Increased Risk of Money Laundering and Terrorism Financing

Banks are subject to strict anti-money laundering (AML) and counter-terrorism financing (CTF) regulations. They are required to monitor transactions, report suspicious activities, and safeguard that their systems are not being used for illegal purposes. Detached payment systems might not have the same level of scrutiny, making them more vulnerable to exploitation by criminals and terrorists. This could lead to an increase in illicit activities, undermining global efforts to combat financial crime.

## Impact on Financial Inclusion

Banks have been instrumental in promoting financial inclusion, especially in developing countries. They provide access to savings accounts, loans, and other financial services that enable individuals and businesses. Payment systems detached from banks could hinder these efforts by creating barriers to access. For example, if a payment system operates independently of banks, it may require users to have access to technology or services that are not widely available, especially in rural or underserved areas. This could exacerbate financial exclusion, leaving millions without access to necessary financial services.

## Disruption of Credit and Lending Systems

Banks provide credit by lending money to individuals and businesses, which fuels economic growth. Payment systems that are detached from banks would lack the ability to provide such credit. This detachment would disrupt the traditional lending system, as payment systems would not have the necessary infrastructure, risk assessment capabilities, or capital reserves to offer loans.

## Complications in Regulatory Compliance

Banks operate within a well-established regulatory framework that guarantees the stability, security, and integrity of the financial system. Detached payment systems would fall outside this framework, creating challenges for regulators. Guaranteeing compliance with financial regulations, such as Know Your Customer (KYC) and AML, would become more complex and difficult to enforce. This lack of regulatory oversight could lead to a proliferation of unregulated payment systems, increasing the risk of financial instability and consumer harm.

## Reduction in Consumer Protection

Consumers are protected by many regulations that govern banking operations, including safeguards against fraud, errors, and unfair practices. Banks are required to adhere to these regulations, providing a layer of protection for their customers. Payment systems operating independently of banks might not be subject to the same regulations, leaving consumers vulnerable to fraud, loss of funds, and poor service.

## Loss of Integrated Financial Services

Banks offer many financial services beyond payments, including savings, investments, insurance, and financial planning. The integration of payment systems with these services provides convenience and productivity for consumers. Detaching payment systems from banks would lead to a fragmented financial experience, where consumers must manage multiple accounts and services across different platforms. This lack of integration could result in a disjointed financial experience, reducing the overall value that consumers derive from their financial service providers.

## Potential for Increased Costs

Detached payment systems would likely result in higher costs for consumers and businesses, as these systems would need to develop their infrastructure, compliance mechanisms, and customer support independently. These increased costs could be passed on to consumers in the form of higher fees, making financial services less affordable and accessible. The detachment of payment systems from banks is not just an undesirable outcome; it is a potentially dangerous one that could have far-reaching consequences for the global financial system. The integration of payment systems with banks provides trust, security, stability, and effectiveness that cannot be replicated by independent systems. Hence, detaching these systems would undermine financial stability, reduce consumer protection, complicate regulatory compliance, and increase the risk of financial crime. It would also disrupt credit and lending systems, hinder financial inclusion, and lead to higher costs for consumers. For these reasons, along with advancements in these areas, payment systems has to be ensured to remain firmly integrated with banks, securing that they continue to contribute positively to the economy and society.

# Chapter 7
# Financial Inclusion and Banking Accessibility

Financial inclusion and banking accessibility are critical pillars of a modern, equitable society, helping with promoting economic development and social stability. They encompass the availability and accessibility of important financial services, such as savings accounts, credit facilities, insurance, and investment products, to all individuals and businesses, regardless of their income level or geographical location. In a world where financial services are increasingly digital, safeguarding that these services are accessible to everyone, including the traditionally underserved and unbanked populations, is more important than ever.

The concept of financial inclusion goes beyond mere access to banking services; it also involves the ability to use these services effectively and responsibly. It aims to equip people with the tools and knowledge they need to manage their financial lives, protect themselves against economic shocks, and seize economic opportunities. By promoting financial inclusion, governments and financial institutions can help reduce income inequality, support small business growth, and stimulate overall economic activity.

In many developing countries, including India, the drive towards financial inclusion has been a major focus of policy and development. Initiatives such as the expansion of digital banking, microfinance, and government-backed schemes have helped with bringing millions into the formal financial system. As the system of financial services continues to evolve with technological advancements, the challenge lies in guaranteeing that these advances are inclusive and accessible to all.

## 7.1 Importance of Financial Inclusion

### Definition and Scope of Financial Inclusion

Financial inclusion refers to the process of securing that individuals and businesses have access to useful and affordable financial products and services that meet their needs, transactions, payments, savings, credit, and insurance, delivered in a responsible and sustainable way. It is a component of economic development, promoting equitable growth and financial stability by bringing underserved populations into the financial fold.

## Access to Banking Services

Access to basic banking services is a fundamental aspect of financial inclusion. It involves providing individuals and businesses with the ability to open bank accounts, conduct transactions, and use payment systems. In many developing countries, a marked portion of the population remains unbanked, lacking access to even the most basic financial services. This exclusion can result from several factors, including geographic barriers, lack of financial literacy, inadequate infrastructure, and socioeconomic challenges.

Efforts to strengthen access to banking services include the expansion of physical banking infrastructure, such as branches and ATMs, and the development of digital banking channels. In India, initiatives like the Pradhan Mantri Jan Dhan Yojana (PMJDY) have aimed to provide every household with at least one bank account, offering access to needed banking services like savings accounts, direct benefit transfers, and overdraft facilities. The proliferation of mobile banking and digital wallets has further facilitated financial inclusion, allowing individuals to access banking services via smartphones and other digital devices.

## Credit Availability

Credit availability is another element of financial inclusion. Access to credit allows individuals and businesses to invest in opportunities, manage risks, and smooth out consumption patterns. For low-income households and small businesses, credit can be a tool for economic empowerment, enabling them to improve their livelihoods, expand operations, and respond to emergencies.

However, in many regions, access to credit remains limited due to stringent lending criteria, lack of collateral, and high transaction costs. Microfinance institutions (MFIs) and self-help groups (SHGs) have factored into bridging this gap, providing small loans to individuals and micro-entrepreneurs who may not qualify for traditional bank loans. The emergence of digital lending platforms has facilitated easier access to credit, using technology to assess creditworthiness and disburse loans quickly and smoothly. In India, the Mudra Yojana initiative has been instrumental in extending credit to the non-corporate, non-farm small and micro-enterprises. The scheme offers loans under three categories, Shishu, Kishor, and Tarun, catering to different stages of business growth, thus supporting a wide spectrum of credit needs.

**Insurance and Investment Products**

Beyond banking and credit, financial inclusion also encompasses access to insurance and investment products. Insurance is involved in financial security, helping individuals and businesses manage risks associated with health, accidents, natural disasters, and other unforeseen events. However, insurance penetration remains low in many developing countries, often due to a lack of awareness, affordability issues, and limited availability of suitable products. To address these challenges, governments and financial institutions have introduced a number of microinsurance products tailored to the needs of low-income populations. These products offer coverage at lower premiums, making insurance accessible to a broader segment of society. In India, schemes like the Pradhan Mantri Suraksha Bima Yojana (PMSBY) and Pradhan Mantri Jeevan Jyoti Bima Yojana (PMJJBY) provide affordable insurance cover for accidental death and disability, and life insurance, respectively.

Investment products are another aspect of financial inclusion, providing opportunities for wealth accumulation and long-term financial planning. However, many individuals, especially in rural and low-income segments, lack access to formal investment channels due to barriers such as limited financial literacy, geographic isolation, and lack of trust in formal financial institutions.

Efforts to improve investment access have included the promotion of mutual funds, government savings schemes, and pension plans. Initiatives like the Atal Pension Yojana (APY) in India aim to provide a guaranteed pension to workers in the unorganized sector, encouraging long-term savings and financial security. The increasing adoption of digital platforms has also facilitated greater participation in capital markets, with mobile and internet-based trading platforms making it easier for individuals to invest in stocks, bonds, and other financial instruments.

## 7.1.1 Economic and Social Benefits

**Poverty Reduction**

Financial inclusion serves as a powerful tool in the fight against poverty. By providing access to basic financial services such as savings accounts, credit, and insurance, individuals and families can manage risks, smooth consumption, and invest in opportunities that lead to improved livelihoods. The availability of credit allows people to invest in education, start or expand businesses, and improve their homes, thus lifting them out of poverty. Savings accounts offer a safe place to store money, helping families build reserves for emergencies, thus preventing them from falling into poverty traps due to unexpected expenses or economic shocks.

In many developing countries, including India, a substantial portion of the population has traditionally been excluded from the formal financial sector. This exclusion has perpetuated cycles of poverty, as those without access to banking services are often forced to rely on informal and often exploitative financial services. These include moneylenders who charge exorbitant interest rates, leading to debt traps. Financial inclusion initiatives, such as microfinance and mobile banking, have provided a more affordable and secure alternative, enabling the poor to participate in the economy more effectively and break free from the cycle of poverty.

**Economic Growth**

Financial inclusion is a driver of economic growth. By broadening access to financial services, countries can harness the full potential of their population, leading to increased economic activity and higher GDP growth rates. Access to credit and other financial products enables businesses to invest in productive activities, expand operations, and create jobs. Small and medium-sized enterprises (SMEs), which are often the backbone of developing economies, benefit markedly from improved access to finance. This leads to greater breakthrough, diversification of the economy, and boosted competitiveness in the global market.

Financial inclusion eases the quick allocation of resources, as it allows savers and investors to channel their funds into productive uses. This, in turn, boosts capital formation and infrastructure development. For example, individuals with access to formal banking services are more likely to save and invest their money, leading to higher levels of domestic investment. This can fund large-scale projects in sectors such as agriculture, manufacturing, and services, further stimulating economic growth.

The digitalization of financial services, including mobile payments and digital wallets, has also contributed to promoting economic growth. These technologies have reduced transaction costs, increased the speed and security of payments, and broadened access to financial services in rural and remote areas. As a result, even the most marginalized populations can now participate in the formal economy, contributing to overall economic growth and stability.

**Social Empowerment**

Beyond its economic benefits, financial inclusion also has profound social implications. It equips individuals and communities by providing them with the tools and resources needed to take control of their financial lives. Access to financial services builds a sense of security and confidence, as individuals can better plan for their future, manage risks, and protect themselves against economic uncertainties. This empowerment is particularly considerable for women, who have historically been marginalized in financial systems worldwide.

In many cultures, women face barriers to accessing financial services, such as lack of collateral, limited financial literacy, and societal norms that restrict their economic activities. Financial inclusion initiatives that target women, such as microfinance programs and women's savings groups, have been instrumental in breaking down these barriers. By providing women with access to credit, savings, and insurance, these initiatives enable them to invest in income-generating activities, improve their families' living standards, and gain greater autonomy and decision-making power. As a result, financial inclusion contributes to gender equality and the overall empowerment of women.

Also, financial inclusion promotes social cohesion by reducing income inequality and building a more inclusive society. When individuals and communities have access to financial services, they are better able to participate in economic and social activities, contributing to a more equitable distribution of wealth and resources. This, in turn, reduces social tensions and promotes a sense of belonging and inclusion.

In the broader context, financial inclusion can also support social initiatives, such as education and healthcare. For example, access to microinsurance can provide low-income families with financial protection against health emergencies, safeguarding they can afford necessary medical treatments. Similarly, access to education loans can enable students from disadvantaged backgrounds to pursue higher education, breaking the cycle of poverty and opening up new opportunities for social mobility.

## 7.1.2 Global Perspective on Financial Inclusion

**World Bank Initiatives**

The World Bank has been leading global financial inclusion efforts, recognizing its importance for poverty reduction and shared prosperity. Through initiatives and partnerships, the World Bank aims to provide universal access to affordable financial services by 2030. Central initiatives include the Financial Inclusion Support Framework (FISF), which offers technical assistance and funding to countries working to improve financial inclusion. The World Bank also collaborates with the International Finance Corporation (IFC) to promote responsible financial services and strengthen financial infrastructure in developing countries. One of the World Bank's notable contributions is the Global Findex database, a thorough source of data on how adults around the world use financial services. The database tracks primary indicators of financial inclusion, such as account ownership, savings, credit, and payment behaviors. This data helps policymakers, researchers, and financial institutions understand the barriers to financial inclusion and design targeted interventions to address them.

The World Bank's Universal Financial Access 2020 initiative aimed to enable 1 billion people to gain access to a transaction account, through which they can store money, send and receive payments, and manage their financial lives. Although the initiative has faced challenges, it underscores the World Bank's commitment to guaranteeing that financial inclusion remains a global priority.

**G20 Financial Inclusion Action Plan**

The G20 has was involved in promoting financial inclusion as a means to encourage inclusive growth and stability. The G20 Financial Inclusion Action Plan, launched in 2010, outlines a framework for advancing financial inclusion across its member countries and beyond. The plan emphasizes the importance of creating an enabling environment, drawing on technology, and developing fresh financial services to reach underserved populations.

The G20 has established the Global Partnership for Financial Inclusion (GPFI), a platform that coordinates actions among G20 countries and other stakeholders, including the private sector and international organizations. The GPFI works on several fronts, including improving data collection, promoting digital financial services, and supporting the development of national financial inclusion strategies. It also focuses on consumer protection and financial literacy, recognizing that access to financial services must be accompanied by the knowledge and skills to use them effectively. One notable outcome of the G20's efforts is the development of the G20 High-Level Principles for Digital Financial Inclusion. These principles provide a framework for countries to harness digital technologies to expand access to financial services, particularly for marginalized and vulnerable populations. The principles cover areas such as digital infrastructure, financial and digital literacy, and cybersecurity, securing an all-round approach to digital financial inclusion.

**Sustainable Development Goals (SDGs)**

Financial inclusion is a component of the United Nations' Sustainable Development Goals (SDGs), a set of 17 goals adopted in 2015 to address global challenges such as poverty, inequality, and climate change.

While financial inclusion is not a SDG on its own, it is recognized as a principal enabler for achieving several goals, particularly those related to poverty reduction, gender equality, and economic growth. For instance, SDG 1, which aims to end poverty in all its forms, is closely linked to financial inclusion. Access to financial services enables individuals to save, invest, and manage risks, thus providing a pathway out of poverty. Similarly, SDG 5, which focuses on achieving gender equality, highlights the importance of financial inclusion in enabling women. By providing women with access to credit, savings, and insurance, financial inclusion can boost their economic independence and decision-making power.

SDG 8, which promotes sustained, inclusive, and sustainable economic growth, also underscores the role of financial inclusion. By enabling access to credit and other financial services, financial inclusion can support entrepreneurship, job creation, and advance. Also, financial inclusion contributes to reducing inequalities (SDG 10) by providing underserved populations with opportunities to participate in the formal economy and improve their livelihoods. The global community, through the UN and other international organizations, has recognized the far-reaching potential of financial inclusion. Efforts to integrate financial inclusion into the SDGs have led to increased investment and collaboration among governments, development agencies, and the private sector. Initiatives such as the Better Than Cash Alliance and the United Nations Capital Development Fund (UNCDF) focus on promoting digital payments and inclusive finance, further aligning financial inclusion with the broader sustainable development agenda.

## 7.2 Government Initiatives and Schemes

The Indian government has launched initiatives and schemes to promote financial inclusion and make certain that every citizen has access to basic financial services. These initiatives are aimed at reducing poverty, promoting economic growth, and safeguarding social justice by enabling all sections of society, especially the marginalized and underprivileged, to participate in the financial system. Among these, as discussed earlier, the Pradhan Mantri Jan Dhan Yojana (PMJDY) stands out as a flagship initiative.

### 7.2.1 Pradhan Mantri Jan Dhan Yojana (PMJDY)

The Pradhan Mantri Jan Dhan Yojana (PMJDY), launched on 28 August 2014, is one of the world's largest financial-inclusion programmes. It gives every household access to a basic, zero-balance bank account, each linked to a RuPay debit card and basic mobile banking. Accounts carry a built-in overdraft facility and bundled insurance, accidental cover of ₹2 lakh through the RuPay card and, for early account holders, a life cover of ₹30,000, and act as the rails for Direct Benefit Transfers of government subsidies. Account opening uses simplified, Aadhaar-based KYC and is paired with financial-literacy support. The impact has been substantial: hundreds of millions of new accounts, most of them in rural areas and a large share held by women, advancing both financial inclusion and the wider goals of poverty reduction and a less-cash economy.

### 7.2.2 Direct Benefit Transfer (DBT)

The Direct Benefit Transfer (DBT) initiative, launched in 2013, routes government subsidies and welfare payments directly into beneficiaries' Aadhaar-linked bank accounts, cutting out intermediaries and reducing leakage. It spans subsidy schemes (food grains, fertilizers, LPG), welfare and social-security programmes, and wage and employment payments such as MGNREGA. Aadhaar is central to the system: it gives each beneficiary a unique identity, enables real-time authentication, links bank accounts, and lets benefits travel with the person across the country, improving transparency and curbing duplicate or 'ghost' claims. Implementation has faced real hurdles: uneven banking infrastructure and digital literacy in rural areas, Aadhaar authentication failures, weak grievance redressal, and the need to coordinate many government departments. The heavy reliance on Aadhaar has also drawn data-privacy and security concerns. Even so, DBT remains a scalable backbone of India's welfare delivery.

### 7.2.3 Financial Literacy Programs

Financial-literacy programmes underpin India's inclusion efforts by helping people use financial services responsibly. The National Strategy for

Financial Education (NSFE) provides the overarching framework, raising awareness, embedding financial education in schools, encouraging sound financial behaviour, building the capacity of educators and providers, and monitoring outcomes. As digital finance has grown, the focus has widened to digital financial literacy through initiatives such as the Digital Saksharta Abhiyan (DISHA), nationwide campaigns, school programmes, public-private partnerships, and online resources, with growing attention to online security and privacy.

## 7.3 Microfinance and Rural Banking

Microfinance and rural banking are involved in India's financial field, particularly in promoting financial inclusion and providing needed banking services to underserved populations. Microfinance institutions (MFIs) and rural banks are players in this ecosystem, offering a range of financial products and services that cater to the unique needs of low-income households and rural communities. This section covers role of MFIs, their business models, regulatory framework, and the impact on rural credit access.

### 7.3.1 Role of Microfinance Institutions

Microfinance institutions (MFIs) are specialized financial entities that provide financial services to low-income individuals who lack access to traditional banking services. MFIs aim to equip economically disadvantaged groups by offering them credit, savings, insurance, and other financial products. The core mission of MFIs is to alleviate poverty, promote entrepreneurship, and improve the overall quality of life for their clients.

**Business Models**

MFIs operate through business models, each designed to cater to the specific needs of their target clientele. The most common business models include:

- **Self-Help Groups (SHGs):** This model involves the formation of small groups of individuals, typically women, who come together to pool their savings and lend money to each other. SHGs serve as a platform for members to access credit and build financial discipline. Banks and MFIs often extend loans to SHGs, using the group's collective responsibility as collateral.
- **Joint Liability Groups (JLGs):** In the JLG model, small groups of borrowers come together and jointly guarantee each other's loans. This

shared liability reduces the risk for the lender and safeguards better loan repayment rates. JLGs are commonly used for agricultural and small business loans in rural areas.

- **Individual Lending:** Some MFIs offer loans directly to individual borrowers without the need for group formation. This model is suitable for clients with established credit histories or those engaged in individual enterprises. MFIs assess the borrower's creditworthiness and ability to repay before disbursing loans.

- **Microfinance Banks:** These are specialized banks that focus on providing financial services to low-income customers. Microfinance banks offer all sorts of products, including microloans, savings accounts, and insurance products. They operate under a banking license and are regulated by the central bank.

- **Non-Governmental Organizations (NGOs):** Many NGOs engage in microfinance activities as part of their development programs. They provide microloans, training, and capacity-building services to marginalized communities. NGOs often work in collaboration with other financial institutions to extend their reach.

**Regulatory Framework for MFIs**

The regulation of MFIs in India is governed by a combination of legal and regulatory frameworks designed to guarantee the stability and integrity of the sector. regulatory aspects include:

- **Reserve Bank of India (RBI) Guidelines:** The RBI is the primary regulator of MFIs in India. It issues guidelines on capital adequacy, asset classification, provisioning, and interest rate caps. The RBI's regulations aim to secure the financial soundness of MFIs and protect the interests of borrowers.

- **Microfinance Institutions (Development and Regulation) Bill:** This bill, proposed by the Indian government, seeks to provide a full legal framework for the regulation and development of the microfinance sector. It aims to promote financial inclusion, protect customers' interests, and safeguard transparency in MFI operations.

- **Self-Regulatory Organizations (SROs):** SROs, such as the Microfinance Institutions Network (MFIN) and Sa-Dhan, are involved in regulating MFIs. They establish codes of conduct, promote best practices, and resolve disputes within the sector. SROs also collaborate with the RBI and other regulatory bodies to make certain compliance.

- **Priority Sector Lending (PSL) Norms:** The RBI's PSL norms mandate that banks allocate a portion of their lending to sectors that have a positive impact on the economy, including microfinance. This regulation guarantees that MFIs have access to funding from mainstream financial institutions.

- **Client Protection Principles:** The regulation of MFIs also includes guidelines on client protection, securing that borrowers are treated fairly and with dignity. This includes transparent pricing, appropriate product design, and mechanisms for addressing customer grievances.

**Impact on Rural Credit Access**

MFIs have had a profound impact on rural credit access in India. By providing small, collateral-free loans to low-income households, MFIs have empowered individuals to pursue income-generating activities, invest in agriculture, and improve their living standards. The impacts of MFIs on rural credit access include:

- **Financial Inclusion:** MFIs have factored into promoting financial inclusion by extending financial services to underserved and unbanked populations. They have reached remote areas where traditional banks are absent, providing access to credit, savings, and insurance products.

- **Empowerment of Women:** A major proportion of MFI clients are women. By providing them with access to credit and financial services, MFIs have empowered women to start businesses, contribute to household income, and improve their social status. This has led to greater gender equality and economic independence for women.

- **Support for Agriculture:** MFIs have been instrumental in supporting agricultural activities by providing loans for purchasing seeds, fertilizers, and equipment. This has increased agricultural productivity, improved food security, and strengthened the livelihoods of rural farmers.

- **Promotion of Entrepreneurship:** MFIs have facilitated the growth of micro and small enterprises by providing the necessary capital for startup and expansion. This has created employment opportunities, stimulated local economies, and contributed to economic development.

- **Reduction of Informal Lending:** By providing formal financial services, MFIs have reduced the reliance on informal moneylenders who often charge exorbitant interest rates. This has helped prevent the exploitation of low-income borrowers and promoted fair lending practices.

- **Social Impact:** Beyond financial services, MFIs often provide non-financial services such as financial literacy training, health education, and skill development programs. These initiatives have had a positive impact on the overall well-being of rural communities.

Despite the positive impact of MFIs, challenges remain in the sector. Issues such as over-indebtedness, aggressive lending practices, and the need for better regulation continue to pose risks. However, the sector's potential for promoting financial inclusion and economic development remains considerable, making it a component of India's financial system.

## 7.3.2 Self-Help Groups (SHGs) and Their Impact

Self-Help Groups (SHGs) have emerged as a powerful tool for promoting financial inclusion and socioeconomic development in India. These small, informal groups, typically comprising 10 to 20 members, predominantly women, come together with the common goal of improving their economic and social conditions. SHGs function on the principles of self-help, mutual trust, and collective decision-making. They help with providing access to financial services, enabling women, and encouraging community development. This section looks at SHG-Bank Linkage Programme, the impact of SHGs on women's empowerment, and the challenges and success factors associated with these groups.

**SHG-Bank Linkage Programme**

The SHG-Bank Linkage Programme, initiated by the National Bank for Agriculture and Rural Development (NABARD) in 1992, is a landmark initiative aimed at linking SHGs with formal financial institutions. The programme seeks to provide SHGs with access to credit, savings, and other banking services, thereby integrating them into the formal financial system. It has become one of the world's largest microfinance programmes, considerably contributing to financial inclusion in India.

**Features of the SHG-Bank Linkage Programme:**

- **Formation and Capacity Building:** SHGs are formed at the grassroots level, often with the assistance of NGOs, government agencies, or other facilitators. The groups undergo capacity-building exercises, including training in financial literacy, bookkeeping, and group management. This helps members understand the importance of savings, financial planning, and credit management.

- **Savings Mobilization:** Members of SHGs regularly contribute small amounts to a common savings pool. These savings are used to provide loans to members for purposes, such as starting a business, meeting emergency needs, or funding children's education. The group maintains detailed records of all transactions, promoting financial discipline among members.

- **Credit Linkage:** Once a SHG demonstrates a good track record of savings and internal lending, it becomes eligible for a loan from a bank. The credit provided by banks is generally collateral-free and can be used for income-generating activities. The loan amount depends on the group's savings, repayment capacity, and the nature of the proposed activity. Banks may offer loans to individual members or to the group as a whole.

- **Repayment and Monitoring:** The SHG collectively decides the terms of loans, including interest rates and repayment schedules. The group's mutual accountability and peer pressure guarantee high repayment rates. Banks closely monitor the performance of linked SHGs and provide guidance as needed. The SHG-Bank Linkage Programme has maintained a high repayment rate, attributed to the group's collective responsibility.

- **Government Support:** The Indian government has supported the SHG-Bank Linkage Programme through many schemes and policies. For instance, the Deendayal Antyodaya Yojana-National Rural Livelihood Mission (DAY-NRLM) provides financial support, capacity-building assistance, and marketing support to SHGs. The programme also supports the formation of federations of SHGs at the village, block, and district levels, providing a platform for collective action and advocacy.

**Women Empowerment Through SHGs**

One of the most notable impacts of SHGs has been the empowerment of women. In many parts of India, women face socio-economic barriers that limit their access to education, employment, and financial services. SHGs have provided a platform for women to come together, share experiences, and collectively work towards their economic and social betterment.

**Aspects of Women Empowerment Through SHGs:**

- **Economic Independence:** SHGs have enabled women to save money, access credit, and start income-generating activities. This economic independence has improved their standard of living and reduced their dependence on male family members. Many women have used SHG loans to start small businesses, such as tailoring, handicrafts, and livestock farming, contributing to household income.

- **Skill Development:** Participation in SHGs has equipped women with valuable skills, including financial literacy, entrepreneurship, and leadership. Women receive training in several trades and crafts, as well as in soft skills like communication and negotiation. These skills strengthen their employability and entrepreneurial capabilities.

- **Social Empowerment:** SHGs have provided a platform for women to voice their opinions, participate in decision-making, and engage in community activities. The collective strength of the group has enabled women to challenge social norms, address issues like domestic violence and gender discrimination, and advocate for their rights. SHGs have also facilitated access to government schemes and services, such as healthcare and education.

- **Leadership and Governance:** Many women in SHGs have taken on leadership roles within their groups and in larger federations. This experience has empowered them to take part in local governance, such as Panchayati Raj Institutions (PRIs). The involvement of women in governance has led to greater accountability and responsiveness to community needs.

- **Social Capital:** SHGs have fostered a sense of solidarity and social capital among women. The trust and mutual support within the group have strengthened social bonds and networks. This social capital has extended beyond the SHG, benefiting the broader community.

### 7.3.3 Regional Rural Banks and Their Significance

Regional Rural Banks (RRBs) help with the Indian banking sector, particularly in promoting rural banking and financial inclusion. Established with the aim of providing credit and other financial services to the rural population, RRBs have a unique structure and operational focus. Here we examine the ownership structure of RRBs, their performance and challenges, and their future role in rural banking.

## Ownership Structure

RRBs were established under the Regional Rural Banks Act, 1976, as government-sponsored, regionally based rural lending institutions. The ownership structure of RRBs is distinctive, as it involves a tripartite arrangement among the Central Government, the concerned State Government, and a sponsoring commercial bank. As discussed in the first chapter, the capital share is distributed in the ratio of 50:15:35 among these three entities.

- **Central Government:** The Central Government holds the majority share, providing half of the capital. This involvement secures that RRBs align with national policies and development goals.

- **State Government:** The concerned State Government contributes 15% of the capital, supporting the alignment of RRB activities with state-level developmental objectives and local needs.

- **Sponsoring Bank:** A designated commercial bank, often a public sector bank, holds 35% of the capital. The sponsoring bank provides managerial and operational support, including staff training, technological infrastructure, and strategic guidance.

This tripartite ownership structure is designed to combine local knowledge and responsiveness with national policy directives and the operational expertise of commercial banks. It enables RRBs to function effectively in rural areas, addressing the specific needs of their clients.

## Performance and Challenges

Over the years, RRBs have made marked contributions to rural banking in India. They have been instrumental in extending banking services to remote and underserved areas, promoting agricultural credit, and supporting rural development initiatives. However, the performance of RRBs has been mixed, with several challenges affecting their operations.

## Performance Achievements:

- **Financial Inclusion:** RRBs have helped with improving financial inclusion by providing banking services to the rural population. They have extended credit to small and marginal farmers, artisans, and small enterprises, thereby contributing to rural economic development.

- **Credit Delivery:** RRBs have been a substantial source of credit for agriculture and allied activities. They offer a number of loan products, including crop loans, term loans for farm equipment, and loans for rural non-farm enterprises. This support has been necessary for sustaining and promoting rural livelihoods.

- **Deposit Mobilization:** RRBs have also been effective in mobilizing rural savings. By offering deposit schemes, such as savings accounts, fixed deposits, and recurring deposits, they have encouraged the habit of saving among the rural populace.

## Challenges in Rural Banking

- ○ **Operational Inefficiencies:** Many RRBs have faced operational inefficiencies due to outdated technology, inadequate infrastructure, and a lack of skilled staff. These inefficiencies have hindered their ability to compete with other financial institutions and deliver quality services.

- **Financial Viability:** Several RRBs have struggled with financial viability due to a high level of non-performing assets (NPAs), low recovery rates, and limited income from non-interest sources. The high cost of operations in rural areas, coupled with limited business opportunities, has further strained their financial health.

- **Regulatory and Governance Issues:** The governance structure of RRBs, with multiple stakeholders, sometimes leads to conflicts of interest and delays in decision-making. The regulatory framework for RRBs, while providing necessary oversight, can also impose restrictions that limit their operational flexibility.

- **Competition from Other Institutions:** RRBs face competition from other financial institutions, including commercial banks, cooperative banks, and microfinance institutions (MFIs). This competition has intensified with the advent of digital banking and fintech solutions, which offer convenient and cost-effective services.

## Future Role in Rural Banking

Despite the challenges, RRBs remain a component of the rural banking sector in India. Their future role will likely involve a strategic shift towards greater speed, digital transformation, and a broader service portfolio. The following aspects highlight the potential future role of RRBs in rural banking:

- **Digital Transformation:** Embracing digital banking solutions is necessary for RRBs to boost their operational productivity and service delivery. Adopting core banking systems, mobile banking, and internet banking can help RRBs reach a wider audience and provide convenient services. The integration of digital payment systems, such as UPI and Aadhaar-enabled payment systems, can further increase financial inclusion.

- **Diversification of Services:** To remain competitive, RRBs may need to diversify their product and service offerings. Beyond traditional credit and deposit products, RRBs can explore areas like insurance, investment products, and remittance services. Offering tailored financial products, such as microloans and financial planning services, can meet the specific needs of rural customers.

- **Strengthening Governance and Risk Management:** Improving governance structures and strengthening risk management practices are critical for the sustainable growth of RRBs. Strengthening internal controls, improving credit appraisal processes, and implementing strong risk assessment frameworks can help mitigate risks and improve financial stability.

- **Partnerships and Collaborations:** RRBs can benefit from partnerships with fintech companies, MFIs, and non-governmental organizations (NGOs) to tap technology and expand their outreach. Collaborations can also provide access to new customer segments, particularly in remote and underserved areas.

- **Focus on Financial Literacy and Inclusion:** RRBs can factor into promoting financial literacy and inclusion. Conducting financial literacy programs, offering advisory services, and enabling access to government schemes can enable rural communities. RRBs can also actively participate in government initiatives, such as the Pradhan Mantri Jan Dhan Yojana (PMJDY) and the Pradhan Mantri MUDRA Yojana (PMMY), to promote financial inclusion.

- **Policy Support and Reforms:** Continued policy support and reforms are important for the growth and development of RRBs. The government and regulatory authorities can provide incentives for digital adoption, offer financial support for capacity building, and speed up regulations to strengthen the operational flexibility of RRBs. Encouraging mergers and consolidations can also create stronger and more viable RRBs.

# 7.4 Challenges and Opportunities

The journey toward complete financial inclusion in India is fraught with both challenges and opportunities. The diverse and vast rural environment presents unique hurdles that must be overcome to secure that banking and financial services reach every corner of the country. This section turns to specific challenges related to last-mile connectivity and explores potential solutions and opportunities to bridge these gaps.

**Last-mile Connectivity Issues**

One of the most critical challenges in achieving full financial inclusion is last-mile connectivity. This term refers to the final segment of delivering services to end-users, which is often the most difficult and resource-intensive part. In the context of rural banking, last-mile connectivity involves the challenges associated with delivering banking services to remote, rural, and underserved areas. The following subsections explore the aspects of last-mile connectivity issues.

**Physical Infrastructure Gaps**

Physical infrastructure gaps pose a considerable barrier to the provision of banking services in rural India. These gaps encompass the lack of needed infrastructure such as roads, electricity, and banking outlets, which are central for the smooth operation of banking services.

***Roads and Transportation:*** Many rural areas lack adequate road networks, making it difficult for people to access banking facilities. Poor transportation infrastructure not only hinders the movement of customers but also affects the ability of banks to transport cash and other banking supplies. In some regions, especially during monsoon seasons, roads become impassable, further isolating these communities from banking services.

***Electricity:*** Reliable electricity is a prerequisite for the functioning of ATMs, bank branches, and digital banking services. However, many rural areas suffer from frequent power outages or lack electricity altogether. This inconsistency can disrupt banking operations, making it challenging to maintain regular banking hours and services. The lack of electricity also hampers the adoption of digital banking, as electronic devices and systems require a stable power supply.

***Banking Outlets:*** The scarcity of bank branches and ATMs in rural areas is another major issue. While initiatives like the expansion of Regional Rural

Banks (RRBs) and the introduction of Business Correspondents (BCs) have improved the situation, many villages still do not have easy access to physical banking outlets. The limited number of branches often results in overcrowding and long wait times, discouraging people from using formal banking channels.

## Digital Connectivity Challenges

In addition to physical infrastructure, digital connectivity is necessary for the delivery of modern banking services. The digital divide between urban and rural areas remains a notable challenge, affecting the adoption and effectiveness of digital banking solutions.

***Internet Access:*** The penetration of high-speed internet in rural areas is relatively low compared to urban regions. Many villages either lack internet connectivity or have access to slow and unreliable connections. This digital divide limits the ability of rural residents to use online banking services, digital wallets, and other internet-based financial services. The high cost of internet access and the lack of digital literacy contribute to the underutilization of digital banking platforms.

***Mobile Connectivity:*** Mobile phones have emerged as a tool for financial inclusion, especially through mobile banking and payment services. However, in rural areas, mobile network coverage is often patchy and unreliable. The quality of mobile service can vary notably, affecting the accessibility and usability of mobile banking apps. Also, the affordability of smartphones and data plans can be a barrier for low-income households.

***Digital Literacy:*** The adoption of digital banking services is also hindered by the lack of digital literacy among rural populations. Many people in these areas are unfamiliar with digital devices and platforms, making them hesitant to adopt online and mobile banking services.

This lack of familiarity can lead to a lack of trust in digital transactions and a preference for cash-based transactions.

## Solutions (Mobile Banking Vans, Satellite Connectivity)

To address the challenges associated with last-mile connectivity, new solutions have been proposed and implemented. These solutions aim to overcome the physical and digital barriers that hinder access to banking services in rural areas.

***Mobile Banking Vans:*** Mobile banking vans are a novel solution designed to bring banking services directly to remote and underserved areas. These vans are equipped with the necessary technology and equipment to provide a range of banking services, including account opening, cash deposits and withdrawals, and loan applications. Mobile banking vans can visit different villages on a scheduled basis, providing a convenient and flexible banking option for rural residents. They also serve as a means of financial education, helping to raise awareness about banking services and products.

***Satellite Connectivity:*** In areas where traditional internet infrastructure is lacking, satellite connectivity can provide a viable alternative. Satellite internet can deliver high-speed connectivity to remote locations, enabling the use of digital banking services. This technology can support the operation of ATMs, point-of-sale (POS) terminals, and mobile banking services, even in the most isolated regions. While satellite internet can be expensive, advancements in technology and the increasing demand for connectivity are driving down costs, making it a more feasible option for rural banking.

***Digital Financial Literacy Programs:*** To bridge the digital literacy gap, many stakeholders, including banks, government agencies, and non-governmental organizations, have launched digital financial literacy programs. These initiatives aim to educate rural populations about the benefits and uses of digital banking services. They provide training on how to use ATMs, mobile banking apps, and digital payment platforms. By improving digital literacy, these programs help build trust in digital transactions and encourage the adoption of formal banking services.

***Public-Private Partnerships (PPPs):*** Collaboration between the government and private sector can contribute to boosting last-mile connectivity. Public-Private Partnerships (PPPs) can support the development of infrastructure, such as internet and mobile networks, in rural areas. These partnerships can also support the deployment of mobile banking vans and the implementation of digital literacy programs. By drawing on the strengths and resources of both sectors, PPPs can accelerate the reach and effectiveness of financial inclusion initiatives.

***Regulatory Support:*** The government and regulatory bodies are involved in supporting last-mile connectivity initiatives. Policies that promote the expansion of banking infrastructure, such as the requirement for banks to open branches in rural areas, can help increase access to banking services. Regulatory frameworks that encourage the use of digital channels and protect consumers' interests are necessary for building trust and confidence in digital banking.

**Barriers to Digital Banking Adoption**

Despite the rapid growth of digital banking services in India, several barriers continue to impede their widespread adoption, particularly in rural and semi-urban areas. These barriers include:

- **Lack of Digital Literacy:** A marked portion of the Indian population, especially in rural areas, lacks basic digital literacy skills. Many individuals are unfamiliar with digital devices, such as smartphones and computers, and are unaware of how to use online banking platforms. This lack of knowledge can lead to apprehension and mistrust of digital transactions, making people reluctant to switch from traditional cash-based methods.

- **Limited Access to Digital Devices and Internet:** Access to digital devices like smartphones and reliable internet connections is uneven across the country. While urban areas have higher penetration rates, rural areas often suffer from poor connectivity and limited access to affordable devices. This digital divide hampers the ability of rural residents to engage with digital banking services.

- **Concerns About Security and Privacy:** The fear of cyber fraud and identity theft is a major deterrent for many potential users of digital banking services. Reports of phishing, malware, and other cyber threats have heightened concerns about the security and privacy of digital transactions. This lack of trust in digital platforms is compounded by inadequate consumer protection mechanisms and limited awareness of safe online practices.

- **Complex User Interfaces:** Many digital banking platforms have complex user interfaces that are difficult for first-time users to manage. The lack of user-friendly designs can discourage individuals, particularly those who are less tech-savvy, from using digital banking services. The absence of localized language options further complicates access for non-English speaking populations.

- **Cultural and Behavioral Factors:** In many parts of India, there is a strong cultural preference for cash transactions. The tangible nature of cash is perceived as more secure and reliable than digital money. Behavioural inertia and resistance to change can prevent people from adopting new technologies, even if they offer clear advantages.

Possible solutions are already being implemented through Digital Literacy initiatives by the government through banks and other institutions as discussed earlier and will help in boosting digital adoption, but their implementation effectiveness can only be boosted through intervention and objective evaluation and continuous monitoring.

**Role of Local Language Interfaces**

India is a linguistically diverse country, with a substantial portion of the population speaking regional languages. The availability of digital banking platforms in local languages is important for making these services accessible to non-English speaking users. Local language interfaces can markedly boost the user experience, making digital banking more intuitive and user-friendly.

- **Increased Accessibility:** Local language interfaces allow users to work through digital banking platforms in their native language, reducing the language barrier that often deters people from using these services. This is particularly important in rural areas, where many people may not be proficient in English.

- **Improved User Experience:** User interfaces in regional languages can simplify complex financial terminology, making it easier for users to understand and use digital banking services. This clarity helps build confidence among users, encouraging them to explore and adopt digital platforms.

- **Trust and Familiarity:** Using digital platforms in one's native language can promote a sense of familiarity and trust. Users are more likely to trust a platform that communicates in a language they understand, which can reduce apprehension about using digital banking services.

- **Increased Adoption:** By providing local language options, banks and fintech companies can reach a broader audience, including older adults and less-educated individuals who may not be comfortable with English. This inclusivity can drive higher adoption rates of digital banking services, contributing to greater financial inclusion.

- **Regulatory Support:** The Reserve Bank of India (RBI) and other regulatory bodies encourage the development of digital financial services in local languages. Regulatory guidelines often emphasize the importance of language accessibility to safeguard that digital financial services cater to the diverse linguistic needs of the Indian population.

## 7.4.1 Product Design for Low-income Segments

Designing financial products tailored to the needs of low-income segments is central for improving financial inclusion and safeguarding that the benefits of the financial system reach all layers of society. In India, a major portion of the population resides in low-income segments, where traditional financial products may not be suitable due to affordability constraints or complex terms. We now turn to the several financial products specifically designed for these segments, focusing on no-frills accounts, micro-insurance products, and small-ticket loans.

### No-frills Accounts

No-frills accounts, also known as basic savings bank deposit accounts (BSBDAs), are a type of savings account designed to cater to the financial needs of low-income individuals who may not have access to conventional banking services. These accounts are characterized by their minimal balance requirements and simplified features, making them accessible to the economically weaker sections of society.

- **Minimal or Zero Balance Requirements:** No-frills accounts typically do not require a minimum balance, thereby eliminating a common barrier faced by low-income individuals in maintaining a bank account. This feature makes banking services accessible without the fear of incurring penalties for not maintaining a certain balance.

- **Basic Banking Services:** These accounts offer important banking services, such as deposits, withdrawals, fund transfers, and access to ATMs. They often come with a limited number of free transactions per month, making it easier for customers to manage their finances.

- **Simplified Documentation:** The process of opening a no-frills account is smooth, with minimal documentation requirements. The use of Aadhaar, India's unique identification number, has further simplified the Know Your Customer (KYC) process, enabling easier access to banking services.

- **Accessibility and Inclusion:** No-frills accounts help with financial inclusion by bringing banking services to the unbanked population. They serve as an entry point into the formal financial system, allowing individuals to gradually access more complex financial products as their financial literacy and income levels improve.

- **Regulatory Support:** The Reserve Bank of India (RBI) has actively promoted the use of no-frills accounts as part of its financial inclusion initiatives. The regulatory framework supports the provision of these accounts with minimal charges, guaranteeing that low-income individuals can access basic banking services without financial strain.

## Micro-insurance Products

Micro-insurance products are designed to offer affordable insurance coverage to low-income individuals who are typically underserved by conventional insurance products. These products provide financial protection against specific risks, such as health emergencies, accidents, and death, at a low premium cost. Micro-insurance factors into protecting the financial well-being of low-income households, who are often vulnerable to economic shocks.

- **Affordability:** The feature of micro-insurance products is their low premium cost, making them accessible to low-income individuals. The premiums are often structured to be paid on a flexible basis, such as weekly, monthly, or yearly, to accommodate the irregular income flows of the target demographic.

- **Simple Terms and Conditions:** Micro-insurance products are designed with simplified terms and conditions to make certain that policyholders can easily understand the coverage and claims process. This simplicity helps build trust and encourages the uptake of insurance among low-income segments.

- **Diverse Product Offerings:** Micro-insurance covers a range of risks, including life insurance, health insurance, crop insurance, and property insurance. These products are tailored to meet the specific needs of low-income individuals, providing them with financial security in times of need.

- **Accessibility:** Micro-insurance products are often distributed through a number of channels, including banks, non-governmental organizations (NGOs), microfinance institutions (MFIs), and mobile platforms. This wide distribution network safeguards that even those in remote areas can access insurance services.

- **Government Initiatives:** The Indian government has launched several initiatives to promote micro-insurance, such as the Pradhan Mantri Jeevan Jyoti Bima Yojana (PMJJBY) and the Pradhan Mantri Suraksha Bima

Yojana (PMSBY). These schemes provide life and accidental insurance coverage at affordable premiums, securing that low-income individuals can access basic insurance protection.

**Small-ticket Loans**

Small-ticket loans are credit products designed to meet the financial needs of low-income individuals and small businesses. These loans are characterized by their low principal amounts, short repayment tenures, and flexible terms. Small-ticket loans factor into providing access to credit for those who may not qualify for traditional bank loans due to lack of collateral or credit history.

- **Low Principal Amounts:** Small-ticket loans typically range from a few hundred to a few thousand rupees. The low principal amount makes these loans accessible to low-income borrowers, who may require credit for purposes, such as meeting daily expenses, emergency needs, or small business investments.

- **Flexible Repayment Terms:** The repayment terms of small-ticket loans are designed to be flexible, accommodating the irregular income patterns of low-income borrowers. Repayment schedules may be structured on a daily, weekly, or monthly basis, depending on the borrower's cash flow.

- **Minimal Documentation:** The application process for small-ticket loans is simplified, with minimal documentation requirements. Lenders often rely on alternative credit assessment methods, such as social reputation and group lending models, to evaluate the borrower's creditworthiness.

- **Accessibility:** Small-ticket loans are offered by a variety of financial institutions, including banks, microfinance institutions (MFIs), and non-banking financial companies (NBFCs). The widespread availability of these loans guarantees that low-income individuals and small businesses can access credit even in underserved areas.

- **Government Support:** The Indian government has introduced several schemes to promote small-ticket loans, such as the Pradhan Mantri Mudra Yojana (PMMY). Under this scheme, loans are provided to micro and small enterprises for business purposes, promoting entrepreneurship and economic development at the grassroots level.

### 7.4.2 Fresh Models for Financial Inclusion

India's diverse socio-economic system presents unique challenges and opportunities for financial inclusion. Traditional banking models often struggle to reach remote and underserved areas, where infrastructure is limited, and the population's financial literacy may be low. In response, new models have emerged to bridge the gap, tapping technology and community networks to extend financial services to all corners of the country. This section covers role of business correspondents, mobile money agents, and fintech solutions in strengthening financial inclusion, focusing on their impact, challenges, and future prospects.

## Business Correspondents

As discussed in earlier chapter, the concept of business correspondents (BCs) was introduced in India as part of the Reserve Bank of India's (RBI) efforts to extend banking services to unbanked and underbanked regions. BCs act as intermediaries between banks and rural customers, providing a range of financial services without the need for customers to visit a physical bank branch. This model has been central in bringing banking services to India's vast rural population. Business Correspondents act as an extension of the bank's workforce, providing a full range of banking services, including cash deposits, withdrawals, fund transfers, and more.

Similarly, **Business Facilitators** are appointed by banks to spread awareness about banking services and products. They assist in business generation activities and recovery of bad debts but do not handle cash transactions. Their primary responsibilities include mobilizing business for their link branches, such as savings, current, recurring, and fixed deposit accounts, and loan referrals.

## Mobile Money Agents

Mobile money agents represent another novel model for financial inclusion, particularly in areas with limited banking infrastructure. Using the widespread use of mobile phones, mobile money services allow users to perform financial transactions through their mobile devices. Agents act as the primary interface between the service providers and customers, easing cash-in and cash-out transactions, as well as other services.

- **Mobile Money Ecosystem:** The mobile money ecosystem comprises mobile network operators (MNOs), banks, technology providers, and a network of agents. Mobile money services enable users to store money in digital wallets, transfer funds, pay bills, and purchase goods and services. In India, services like Paytm, PhonePe, and Google Pay have gained considerable traction, offering a span of digital financial services.

- **Agent Network:** Mobile money agents are important to the system's functionality, providing cash-in and cash-out services that enable users to convert cash into digital money and vice versa. These agents are typically small retailers or shop owners who have partnered with MNOs or mobile wallet providers. They factor into onboarding new users, educating them about the services, and safeguarding the liquidity needed for transactions.

- **Impact on Financial Inclusion:** Mobile money services have greatly increased access to financial services in rural and semi-urban areas. They provide a convenient and secure way to conduct transactions without the need for a bank account or physical branch. This is particularly beneficial for the unbanked population, which may lack the documentation or credit history required to open traditional bank accounts.

- **Challenges and Opportunities:** While mobile money has the potential to transform financial inclusion, several challenges remain. Regulatory issues, such as licensing and compliance requirements, can pose barriers to entry for new players. Security concerns, including the risk of fraud and cyberattacks, are also notable. However, the integration of mobile money with other financial services, such as micro-loans and insurance, offers opportunities for further development and expansion.

## Fintech Solutions for Underserved Segments

The fintech industry in India has seen rapid growth, driven by technological advancements and a favorable regulatory environment. Fintech companies are drawing on digital platforms to offer fresh financial products and services, targeting underserved segments of the population. These solutions range from digital lending and savings platforms to investment and insurance products, all designed to meet the specific needs of low-income and unbanked individuals.

- **Digital Lending Platforms:** Digital lending platforms use data analytics and machine learning to assess the creditworthiness of applicants, enabling quick and smooth loan disbursement. These platforms often cater to individuals and small businesses that lack access to traditional credit. By using alternative data sources, such as transaction histories and social media activity, fintech companies can offer personalized credit solutions.

- **Savings and Investment Platforms:** Fintech companies are also providing digital platforms for savings and investments, offering products like micro-savings accounts and robo-advisors. These platforms allow users to start investing with small amounts, making financial planning accessible to a broader audience. The use of digital channels reduces costs and enables users to manage their finances more effectively.

- **Insurtech Solutions:** The insurtech segment focuses on making insurance products more accessible and affordable. By tapping digital platforms, insurtech companies offer tailored insurance products, such as micro-insurance, which provide coverage for specific risks at a lower cost. These solutions are particularly relevant for low-income individuals who may not afford traditional insurance premiums.

- **Digital Payment Solutions:** Fintech firms have contributed to the proliferation of digital payment solutions in India. Services like UPI, mobile wallets, and prepaid payment instruments have transformed how transactions are conducted, making it easier for individuals and businesses to engage in the digital economy. The frictionless integration of these solutions with other financial services has strengthened their utility and adoption.

- **Challenges and Future Prospects:** While fintech solutions offer marked potential for financial inclusion, they face several challenges. Regulatory compliance, data privacy concerns, and cybersecurity risks are critical issues that need to be addressed. The digital divide, characterized by unequal access to digital technology, can limit the reach of fintech solutions in certain areas. However, ongoing developments, such as blockchain technology and artificial intelligence, promise to further transform the financial field, offering new ways to serve underserved segments.

The discussion on Financial Inclusion and Banking Accessibility is strategically placed between our exploration of traditional banking roles and the future of these systems. This placement emphasizes the needed role of financial inclusion in bridging the gap between existing infrastructure and future advances. By integrating financial inclusion into this section, we highlight the importance of considering how banking and payment systems impact all segments of society. Banks have a fundamental responsibility to extend their services to underserved communities, guaranteeing access to necessary financial tools like savings accounts, loans, and credit. This discussion underscores the role banks play in promoting economic equity and inclusion, necessary for sustainable development. It serves as a reminder that technological advancements should not be pursued in isolation from the goal of financial inclusion. The success of future financial technologies will be measured by their ability to reach and serve all segments of the population. In essence, this focus on financial inclusion bridges understanding the current state of banking and payment systems and envisioning their future. It reinforces the idea that progress should be guided by a commitment to inclusivity, securing that advancements contribute to a more equitable and accessible financial sector. Without this focus, the benefits of breakthrough may be unevenly distributed, potentially widening the gap between those with access to financial services and those without. As we explore the future of banking and payment systems, the discussion on financial inclusion reminds us that advancements must be grounded in equity and accessibility. This chapter connects the present with the future, safeguarding that the path forward includes and benefits everyone.

# Chapter 8
# The Future of Indian Banking and Payment Systems

As India stands at the cusp of a digital revolution, the future of its banking and payment systems appears promising and major. The country's financial environment has evolved rapidly over the past decade, driven by technological advancements, regulatory reforms, and a growing focus on financial inclusion. The Indian banking sector, traditionally dominated by public sector banks, has witnessed the entry of private and foreign players, leading to increased competition and advance. Simultaneously, the payment systems in India have undergone a substantial shift, with digital payments gaining widespread acceptance and new technologies like UPI and digital wallets reshaping the way transactions are conducted. In this rapidly changing environment, the future of Indian banking and payment systems will be shaped by several factors, including the adoption of emerging technologies such as artificial intelligence, blockchain, and digital currencies. The rise of fintech companies and the increasing importance of cybersecurity will also contribute to determining the direction of the industry. Also, regulatory frameworks and government policies will continue to evolve to address new challenges and opportunities, guaranteeing the stability and security of the financial system.

As we look ahead, it is important to explore the potential developments and trends that will define the future of banking and payments in India. This chapter examines into the anticipated advancements, challenges, and opportunities in the sector, offering insights into how banks, payment service providers, and regulators can handle this dynamic system. By examining the possible scenarios and strategic imperatives, we aim to provide a thorough outlook on the future of Indian banking and payment systems, highlighting the pathways to a more inclusive, effective, and secure financial ecosystem.

## 8.1 Emerging Trends

### 8.1.1 Artificial Intelligence and Machine Learning Applications

The integration of artificial intelligence (AI) and machine learning (ML) into the banking and payment systems is reshaping the industry. These technologies offer benefits, ranging from personalized customer experiences to advanced security measures. As AI and ML continue to evolve, they are expected to play an even more role in shaping the future of banking and payments in India. This far-reaching impact was extensively covered in Section 5.4 of this book, where we delved into applications such as fraud detection, customer service automation, and personalized financial recommendations. Some of these developments are already in implementation, while others are on the horizon, promising to further increase the speed and inclusivity of India's financial ecosystem.

## 8.1.2 Internet of Things (IoT) in Banking

The Internet of Things (IoT) is gradually transforming the banking and financial services industry by creating a more connected and quick ecosystem. By using IoT technology, banks can offer new services, simplify operations, and improve customer experiences. The application of IoT in banking encompasses a range of areas, including payment systems, smart branch concepts, and risk assessment.

### IoT-based Payment Systems

IoT-based payment systems represent a considerable advancement in the way transactions are conducted. These systems enable devices equipped with IoT technology, such as smartwatches, fitness trackers, and connected cars, to enable payments without friction. For instance, wearable devices can be linked to a customer's bank account or digital wallet, allowing for contactless payments with just a tap. This not only increases convenience for customers but also reduces the reliance on physical cards or cash. In India, the adoption of IoT-based payment systems is gaining traction, especially in urban areas where consumers are increasingly embracing smart technology. The integration of IoT with payment systems also opens up new avenues for businesses to offer personalized and contextual offers to customers based on their real-time location and behavior. For example, a connected car could automatically pay for fuel at a gas station or a parking fee, making transactions more smooth and hassle-free.

## 8.1.3 Smart Branch Concepts

The concept of smart branches is another novel application of IoT in banking. Smart branches employ IoT devices and sensors to create a more interactive and customer-friendly environment. For example, IoT-enabled devices can manage queues by providing real-time updates on waiting times, directing customers to available service counters, or even offering virtual queuing options. In addition, smart branches can use IoT to gather data on customer preferences and behavior, enabling banks to offer personalized services. For instance, smart devices can detect when a customer enters the branch and immediately access their profile, allowing bank staff to greet them by name and provide tailored services. Smart branches can incorporate IoT-enabled devices like smart ATMs and self-service kiosks, which offer a range of banking services without the need for direct human intervention. In India, where banking infrastructure is continually evolving, smart branches can are involved in boosting customer engagement and operational productivity. They can help banks reduce operational costs while providing customers with a modern and convenient banking experience.

### 8.1.4  Risk Assessment Using IoT Data

IoT technology can also contribute to risk assessment and management within the banking sector. IoT devices generate vast amounts of data, which can be harnessed to assess and mitigate many types of risks, including credit, operational, and security risks. For instance, in the context of loan underwriting, IoT data from connected devices can provide real-time insights into a borrower's asset condition, usage patterns, and overall financial behavior.

For example, in agricultural lending, IoT devices can monitor crop health, soil conditions, and weather patterns, providing banks with valuable data to assess the risk associated with lending to farmers. Similarly, in the case of vehicle loans, IoT sensors can track vehicle usage and maintenance, helping banks evaluate the risk of default more accurately. IoT data can strengthen fraud detection and prevention efforts. By continuously monitoring transactions and device activities, banks can identify suspicious patterns that deviate from a customer's typical behavior, allowing for timely intervention. This proactive approach to risk management not only protects the bank's assets but also safeguards customers from potential fraud.

### 8.1.5  Voice-activated Banking Services

The advent of voice-activated banking services marks a notable leap in the evolution of customer interaction within the financial industry. With the growing adoption of smart speakers and voice assistants, banks are increasingly drawing on this technology to offer a more effortless and intuitive banking experience. Voice-activated banking services encompass several functionalities, from conducting transactions to providing personalized financial advice.

## Voice Assistants for Banking Transactions

Voice assistants, powered by artificial intelligence (AI), are transforming the way customers interact with their banks. These virtual assistants can be integrated into smart devices, such as Amazon Alexa, Google Assistant, and Apple's Siri, enabling users to manage their finances through simple voice commands. Voice assistants ease a range of banking transactions, including checking account balances, transferring funds, paying bills, and even making investment decisions. For instance, a customer can ask their voice assistant for the current balance in their checking account, and the assistant will provide the information instantly. Similarly, customers can instruct the assistant to transfer money to a friend's account or pay an outstanding credit card bill, all without the need to log into a mobile app or visit a physical branch. This convenience makes voice banking particularly appealing to tech-savvy consumers who value effectiveness and ease of use. In India, where digital adoption is accelerating, voice assistants are becoming increasingly popular among younger demographics and urban populations. The integration of voice-activated services into banking apps and smart devices offers a hands-free, user-friendly experience that aligns with the growing trend of smart home technologies. Banks are also exploring the use of regional languages in voice interactions to cater to a broader audience, making banking services more accessible to non-English speakers.

## Voice Biometrics for Authentication

As voice-activated services gain traction, the need for secure and reliable authentication methods becomes critical. Voice biometrics has emerged as a promising solution, tapping the characteristics of an individual's voice for identity verification. Voice biometrics analyzes a number of vocal attributes, such as pitch, tone, and rhythm, to create a voiceprint that is unique to each person, similar to a fingerprint. The implementation of voice biometrics in banking offers several advantages. Firstly, it improves security by providing a more secure alternative to traditional authentication methods, such as passwords or PINs, which are susceptible to breaches and theft. Since each person's voice is unique and difficult to replicate, voice biometrics reduces the risk of unauthorized access to accounts.

Secondly, voice biometrics strengthens the user experience by simplifying the authentication process. Customers no longer need to remember complex passwords or go through multiple steps to verify their identity. Instead, they can simply speak a passphrase or answer a security question to authenticate themselves. This ease of use is particularly beneficial for individuals with disabilities or those who prefer a more intuitive form of interaction. In the Indian banking sector, voice biometrics is being explored as a viable option for improving security and customer convenience. Banks are investing in voice recognition technology to offer secure, voice-based authentication for services, including accessing account information, authorizing transactions, and contacting customer support. The adoption of voice biometrics also aligns with the broader trend of biometric authentication in India, where initiatives like Aadhaar have popularized the use of biometric data for identity verification.

### 8.1.6 Personalization and Customer Experience Improvement

In the shifting field of banking, personalization and customer experience have emerged as factors for retaining and attracting customers. As competition intensifies and customer expectations rise, banks are increasingly using advanced technologies and data analytics to offer tailored services and boost the overall customer experience.

**Data-driven Personalization**

Data-driven personalization involves using customer data to tailor banking products, services, and communications to individual preferences and needs. With the proliferation of digital channels and the increasing availability of data, banks have access to a wealth of information about their customers' financial behaviors, preferences, and life stages. By analyzing this data, banks can offer personalized recommendations, promotions, and services that align with each customer's unique financial situation.

For example, by analyzing transaction data, a bank can identify a customer who frequently shops at a particular retailer and offer targeted discounts or cashback offers for purchases at that retailer. Similarly, banks can use data on customers' spending habits and financial goals to offer personalized investment advice, loan offers, or savings plans. This level of personalization not only boosts customer satisfaction but also helps banks build stronger relationships with their customers. In the Indian banking sector, data-driven personalization is becoming increasingly prevalent as banks invest in big data analytics and artificial intelligence (AI) technologies. Banks are developing sophisticated algorithms and machine learning models to segment customers, predict their needs, and deliver personalized experiences across digital and physical channels. This approach not only improves customer engagement but also enables banks to cross-sell and upsell products more effectively.

## Omnichannel Banking Experiences

Omnichannel banking refers to the smooth integration of banking channels, including online, mobile, branch, and customer service, to provide a consistent and unified customer experience. In an omnichannel banking model, customers can start a transaction on one channel and complete it on another without any disruption. This flexibility and convenience are major in today's digital age, where customers expect to interact with their banks through multiple touchpoints. Omnichannel banking experiences are designed to cater to customers' preferences and lifestyles. For instance, a customer may prefer to use a mobile app for routine transactions, visit a branch for complex financial advice, and call customer service for immediate assistance. By offering a cohesive and integrated experience across all these channels, banks can meet customer expectations and build loyalty.

The adoption of omnichannel banking is driven by the increasing penetration of smartphones and the internet, along with the growing demand for digital banking services. Banks are investing in digital platforms and technologies to create frictionless and personalized customer journeys. For example, a customer can apply for a loan online, receive approval via a mobile app, and complete the documentation process at a nearby branch. This integrated approach secures that customers have a consistent and convenient experience, regardless of the channel they choose to use.

## Behavioral Economics in Banking

Behavioral economics, the study of how psychological, social, and emotional factors influence economic decision-making, has marked applications in the banking industry. By understanding the cognitive biases and decision-making processes of customers, banks can design products and services that encourage positive financial behaviors and increase customer satisfaction.One of the applications of behavioral economics in banking is the use of nudges, subtle prompts or suggestions that encourage customers to make better financial decisions. For example, banks can use reminders to encourage customers to save more, pay off debts, or invest in long-term financial products. Nudges can also be used to simplify complex financial decisions, such as choosing the right investment portfolio or insurance plan. Another application is the design of user interfaces and communication strategies that align with customers' cognitive preferences. For example, presenting information in a clear and visually appealing format can help customers better understand their financial options and make informed decisions. Similarly, personalized messaging that resonates with customers' values and goals can increase engagement and drive positive financial behaviors.

Banks in India are increasingly incorporating behavioral economics principles into their customer engagement strategies. For instance, banks use gamification techniques to encourage savings and investment, offering rewards and incentives for achieving financial milestones. They also use data analytics to identify customers' financial habits and preferences, allowing them to tailor nudges and messages accordingly. The integration of behavioral economics into banking not only improves customer experience but also helps banks achieve better business outcomes. By encouraging responsible financial behaviors, banks can reduce defaults, increase savings, and promote long-term financial well-being among their customers.

## 8.2 Impact of Globalization

Globalization has profoundly influenced the banking and payment systems worldwide, creating opportunities and challenges for financial institutions, businesses, and consumers. As borders become increasingly irrelevant in financial transactions, banks and payment service providers have had to adapt to the demands of a globalized economy. This section looks at impact of globalization on cross-border banking and payment services, focusing on instant cross-border payments, global account access, and multi-currency digital wallets.

### 8.2.1 Cross-border Banking and Payment Services

The integration of global economies has led to a substantial increase in cross-border banking and payment services. These services enable businesses and individuals to transact smoothly across international borders, supporting global trade, investment, and remittances. The evolution of technology and regulatory frameworks has further accelerated the growth of cross-border financial services, making them more effective, cost-effective, and accessible.

**Instant Cross-border Payments**

One of the most major developments in cross-border banking is the advent of instant cross-border payments. Traditionally, international payments were slow, costly, and prone to errors due to the involvement of multiple intermediaries and varying regulatory environments. However, advancements in technology, particularly blockchain and distributed ledger technology (DLT), have revolutionized cross-border payments by enabling real-time settlement and reducing transaction costs.

Instant cross-border payments allow funds to be transferred between countries within seconds, providing an effortless experience for businesses and consumers. This is particularly beneficial for global supply chains, where timely payments are important for maintaining smooth operations. For instance, companies can pay suppliers in different countries instantaneously, reducing the risk of supply chain disruptions and improving cash flow management.

Instant cross-border payments are necessary for individuals who need to send remittances to family members abroad. Traditional remittance methods could take several days and incur high fees, but modern instant payment systems offer faster and cheaper alternatives. This has a considerable impact on households in developing countries that rely on remittances for their daily needs.

## 8.2.2 Global Account Access

Globalization has also led to the demand for global account access, where individuals and businesses can manage their finances across multiple countries from a single platform. This concept is particularly relevant for multinational corporations, expatriates, and frequent travelers who require smooth access to banking services in different jurisdictions.

Global account access enables customers to open and manage bank accounts in multiple currencies, making it easier to conduct international transactions and manage foreign exchange risk. For businesses, this means the ability to receive payments in many currencies and hold funds in different accounts to optimize cash management. For individuals, global accounts offer the convenience of accessing funds and making payments worldwide, without the need to maintain multiple accounts in different countries.

Financial institutions have responded to this demand by offering specialized global banking services, including multi-currency accounts, global debit and credit cards, and international money transfer services. These services often come with added features such as competitive exchange rates, low transaction fees, and access to international ATMs, providing a broad solution for global banking needs.

### 8.2.3 Multi-currency Digital Wallets

The rise of digital wallets has transformed the way people store and use money, and the globalization of financial services has extended this convenience to multi-currency digital wallets. These wallets allow users to hold, exchange, and spend multiple currencies within a single app, making them an attractive option for international travelers, freelancers, and online shoppers.

Multi-currency digital wallets offer several advantages over traditional banking products. They provide real-time currency conversion at competitive rates, enabling users to make purchases or withdrawals in foreign currencies without the hassle of currency exchange. Also, these wallets often support peer-to-peer transfers, allowing users to send money to friends and family across borders instantly and at low cost. The convenience and flexibility of multi-currency digital wallets have made them popular among global citizens who require frictionless financial services across different countries. For example, a traveler can load their wallet with multiple currencies before a trip, use the wallet to pay for expenses abroad, and exchange leftover funds back to their home currency upon return. Similarly, freelancers working with international clients can receive payments in different currencies and convert them to their preferred currency at favorable rates.

Also, multi-currency digital wallets are increasingly being integrated with other financial services, such as investment platforms and cryptocurrency exchanges, providing users with a full financial ecosystem. This integration allows users to diversify their portfolios, invest in global markets, and manage their finances from a single platform. The impact of globalization on cross-border banking and payment services is profound, enabling greater financial inclusion, speed, and convenience. The development of instant cross-border payments, global account access, and multi-currency digital wallets has transformed the way businesses and individuals conduct international transactions, breaking down barriers and creating a more connected global economy. As technology continues to evolve and regulatory frameworks adapt to the changing sector, the future of cross-border banking and payment services promises even greater advances and opportunities.

## 8.2.4 International Regulations and Compliance

As the global financial system becomes increasingly interconnected, international regulations and compliance frameworks help with maintaining stability, preventing financial crimes, and securing a level playing field. The complex nature of cross-border transactions necessitates stringent regulatory measures to manage risks and protect the integrity of the financial system. This section explores international regulations, including the Financial Action Task Force (FATF) Recommendations, Basel IV implementation, and the challenges associated with cross-border data sharing and privacy.

## 8.2.5 Cross-border Data Sharing and Privacy

The global nature of banking and payment systems requires the exchange of data across borders, which raises notable challenges related to data sharing and privacy. Financial institutions must manage a complex web of regulations governing the transfer, storage, and use of personal and financial data. These regulations vary widely by jurisdiction, reflecting different legal frameworks, cultural attitudes towards privacy, and national security concerns. One of the primary challenges in cross-border data sharing is compliance with data protection laws, such as the European Union's General Data Protection Regulation (GDPR). The GDPR sets strict rules on data processing and transfer, including requirements for obtaining explicit consent from individuals, safeguarding data minimization, and implementing reliable security measures. For non-EU banks and payment service providers, compliance with the GDPR is mandatory when processing the data of EU citizens, even if the data processing occurs outside the EU. In addition to data protection laws, financial institutions must also adhere to regulations related to financial secrecy and confidentiality. Some jurisdictions have strict banking secrecy laws that restrict the sharing of customer information with foreign authorities or other entities. This can create obstacles for international cooperation in AML/CTF efforts and complicate the detection of cross-border financial crimes. To address these challenges, international organizations and regulatory bodies have developed frameworks for cross-border data sharing and cooperation. For example, the FATF and the Financial Stability Board (FSB) encourage countries to establish legal frameworks that enable the exchange of information for regulatory and supervisory purposes. The Global Forum on Transparency and Exchange of Information for Tax Purposes, established by the Organisation for Economic Co-operation and Development (OECD), promotes international cooperation in tax matters, including the exchange of financial information. Advancements in technology, such as blockchain and secure multiparty computation, offer potential solutions for secure cross-border data sharing. These technologies enable the secure transfer of data without compromising privacy, by allowing multiple parties to collaborate on data analysis without revealing sensitive information. However, the adoption of these technologies is still in its early stages, and their widespread implementation will require overcoming technical, regulatory, and operational challenges.

### 8.2.6 Competition from Global Fintech Players

The entry of global fintech players into the Indian market has considerably reshaped the competitive environment of banking and payment systems. As technology continues to evolve, the distinction between traditional banking and financial technology companies is becoming increasingly blurred. Global fintech players, including tech giants, neobanks, and challenger banks, have introduced fresh business models and customer-centric services that challenge the dominance of conventional banks.

### 8.2.7 Neobanks and Challenger Banks

Neobanks and challenger banks are digital-first financial institutions that operate without physical branches. They offer many banking services through mobile apps and online platforms, providing customers with a convenient and user-friendly banking experience. These banks have gained popularity in India due to their ability to offer new financial products, competitive pricing, and superior customer service. Neobanks, such as Niyo, Jupiter, and RazorpayX, have emerged as players in the Indian fintech ecosystem. They typically partner with traditional banks to offer banking services, drawing on the bank's infrastructure and regulatory licenses while focusing on customer acquisition and experience. Neobanks cater to a tech-savvy customer base, offering features such as instant account opening, real-time transaction notifications, budgeting tools, and personalized financial advice. Challenger banks, like the UK's Revolut and Germany's N26, have also shown interest in entering the Indian market. These banks operate independently and hold their banking licenses, offering a full suite of banking services, including deposits, loans, and foreign exchange. Challenger banks have been successful in other markets by providing low-cost services, novel features, and effortless digital experiences. The rise of neobanks and challenger banks presents a competitive threat to traditional banks, particularly in the areas of customer experience and technological development. These digital-first banks are agile and can quickly adapt to changing customer preferences, offering personalized and data-driven services that appeal to a younger demographic. They have also capitalized on the growing trend of digital payments and the increasing adoption of smartphones in India.

However, the growth of neobanks and challenger banks is not without challenges. These banks face regulatory hurdles, as they must comply with the stringent requirements set by the Reserve Bank of India (RBI) and other regulatory bodies. Building customer trust and achieving profitability remain marked challenges for these digital-only banks. While they have gained traction in urban areas, reaching customers in rural and semi-urban regions, where traditional banks have a strong presence, remains a challenge.

## 8.2.8 Regulatory Challenges for Global Players

The entry of global fintech players into India's financial sector has highlighted the need for a solid regulatory framework to address the unique challenges posed by these new market entrants. The presence of global players brings several regulatory challenges, including data protection, consumer protection, and fair competition. One of the primary regulatory challenges is data protection and privacy. Global fintech players, especially tech giants, collect and process vast amounts of data from their users. Guaranteeing that this data is handled in compliance with India's data protection laws, such as the Personal Data Protection Bill, is central. The bill aims to protect the privacy of individuals and establish guidelines for data processing, storage, and sharing. However, implementing these regulations across different jurisdictions and securing compliance by global players remains a complex task. Another challenge is safeguarding consumer protection in the digital age. With the rise of digital financial services, customers are increasingly vulnerable to cyber threats, fraud, and data breaches. Regulators must guarantee that global fintech players implement sturdy security measures and provide transparent information about their services. Regulators must establish clear guidelines for dispute resolution and customer support, guaranteeing that consumers have access to timely and effective remedies in case of issues.

Fair competition is another area of concern. The entry of global players with substantial financial resources and technological capabilities can potentially distort competition in the market. Regulators must secure that these players do not engage in anti-competitive practices, such as predatory pricing or market monopolization. The Competition Commission of India (CCI) contributes to monitoring and regulating competition in the market, securing a level playing field for all market participants.Furthermore, the global nature of fintech players requires coordination among regulators from different countries. The cross-border operations of these players necessitate collaboration between regulatory bodies to safeguard consistent enforcement of regulations and prevent regulatory arbitrage. This collaboration is particularly important in areas such as anti-money laundering (AML) and counter-terrorist financing (CTF), where international cooperation is major for preventing illicit financial activities.

## 8.2.9 Opportunities for Indian Banks in Global Markets

The globalization of financial services has opened new avenues for Indian banks to expand their presence beyond domestic borders. With a growing Indian diaspora, increasing South-South cooperation, and a booming fintech sector, Indian banks are well-positioned to use these opportunities. Here we examine the potential for Indian banks to serve the Indian diaspora, engage in South-South cooperation, and export fintech solutions, highlighting the strategic benefits and challenges associated with these endeavors.

**Serving Indian Diaspora**

The Indian diaspora is one of the largest and most influential in the world, with millions of Indians residing in countries across the globe. This diaspora not only contributes notably to their host countries' economies but also maintains strong financial and cultural ties with India. Indian banks have long recognized the potential of this demographic, offering several services tailored to their needs, such as Non-Resident Indian (NRI) accounts, remittance services, and investment products.

***NRI Accounts and Services:*** Indian banks offer specialized NRI accounts, including Non-Resident External (NRE) accounts, Non-Resident Ordinary (NRO) accounts, and Foreign Currency Non-Resident (FCNR) accounts. These accounts provide NRIs with the convenience of managing their funds in India, enabling easy repatriation of money, and offering attractive interest rates. The ability to maintain accounts in foreign currencies also helps NRIs hedge against currency fluctuations. Also, Indian banks provide investment options like mutual funds, fixed deposits, and real estate, catering to the diverse financial goals of the diaspora.

***Remittance Services:*** Remittances from the Indian diaspora constitute a major source of foreign exchange for India. Indian banks have developed quick remittance services, partnering with international money transfer operators and tapping digital platforms to make certain quick, secure, and cost-effective money transfers. The introduction of products like the Immediate Payment Service (IMPS) and Unified Payments Interface (UPI) has further smooth the remittance process, making it easier for NRIs to send money home. By offering competitive exchange rates and low transaction fees, Indian banks have positioned themselves as preferred partners for remittances.

***Wealth Management and Advisory Services:*** As the Indian diaspora continues to grow wealthier, there is an increasing demand for wealth management and advisory services. Indian banks can offer tailored wealth management solutions, including portfolio management, estate planning, and tax advisory services. By understanding the unique financial needs and regulatory requirements of different countries, Indian banks can provide personalized advice to help NRIs optimize their investments and tax liabilities.

***Digital Banking Solutions:*** The digitalization of banking services presents a unique opportunity for Indian banks to expand their reach among the diaspora. Mobile banking apps, internet banking platforms, and digital wallets offer NRIs convenient access to their accounts and financial services from anywhere in the world. By investing in strong digital infrastructure and cybersecurity measures, Indian banks can provide smooth and secure banking experiences, catering to the tech-savvy younger generation of NRIs.

## South-South Cooperation in Banking

South-South cooperation, referring to the collaboration between developing countries, has gained momentum in recent years as these nations seek to strengthen economic ties and share knowledge and resources. For Indian banks, South-South cooperation offers a strategic opportunity to expand their footprint in emerging markets, particularly in Africa, Asia, and Latin America.

***Expanding Branch Networks:*** Indian banks have the potential to expand their branch networks in other developing countries, using their expertise in serving diverse customer segments and understanding the unique challenges of emerging markets. By establishing branches and representative offices, Indian banks can tap into local markets, offer tailored financial products, and help trade and investment flows. The presence of Indian banks in these regions can also help Indian companies expand their operations, providing them with the necessary financial support and advisory services.

***Collaborative Ventures and Partnerships:*** Indian banks can explore collaborative ventures and partnerships with local financial institutions in other developing countries. Such partnerships can support knowledge exchange, joint product development, and shared infrastructure, reducing costs and risks. For example, Indian banks can collaborate with local banks to develop digital payment systems, microfinance initiatives, and financial inclusion programs. These partnerships can also improve the credibility and market acceptance of Indian banks in new regions.

### Trade Finance and Investment Banking:

As trade between developing countries continues to grow, there is an increasing demand for trade finance and investment banking services. Indian banks can are involved in easing cross-border trade by offering trade finance products such as letters of credit, trade guarantees, and export credit. Indian banks can provide investment banking services, including advisory on mergers and acquisitions, capital raising, and market entry strategies. By drawing on their experience in handling complex transactions and understanding local market dynamics, Indian banks can support businesses in handling the challenges of cross-border trade and investment.

***Technology Transfer and Capacity Building:*** Indian banks have developed reliable financial technologies and systems that can be exported to other developing countries. By sharing technological expertise and best practices, Indian banks can contribute to the modernization of banking systems in other regions. This includes implementing core banking systems, digital payment platforms, and risk management frameworks. Indian banks can engage in capacity-building initiatives, offering training programs and workshops to strengthen the skills and knowledge of local banking professionals.

### Export of Fintech Solutions

India has emerged as a global fintech hub, with a vibrant ecosystem of startups and established companies developing fresh financial technologies. The country's advancements in digital payments, mobile banking, and blockchain technology have positioned Indian fintech solutions as competitive offerings in the global market. Indian banks and fintech companies have the opportunity to export these solutions to other countries, addressing the growing demand for digital financial services.

***Digital Payment Solutions:*** Indian fintech companies have developed advanced digital payment solutions, including UPI, BharatQR, and a number of mobile wallets. These solutions offer secure, smooth, and user-friendly payment options, making them attractive to other countries looking to boost their digital payment infrastructure. Indian banks can partner with fintech companies to export these solutions, providing technical support, customization, and integration services. By offering scalable and cost-effective payment systems, Indian banks can help other countries accelerate their digital transformation.

## RegTech and Compliance Solutions:

Regulatory technology (RegTech) solutions developed in India can assist financial institutions in other countries with compliance and regulatory reporting. Indian companies have developed tools for real-time monitoring, risk assessment, and reporting, helping banks comply with complex regulatory frameworks. By exporting these solutions, Indian banks can support global financial institutions in managing regulatory risks and safeguarding compliance with international standards.

## Financial Inclusion Technologies:

India's experience in promoting financial inclusion through digital platforms and mobile banking solutions can be leveraged to address similar challenges in other developing countries. Indian banks and fintech companies can export technologies such as micro-lending platforms, digital identity verification systems, and agent banking solutions. By providing affordable and accessible financial services, these technologies can contribute to the economic empowerment of underserved populations in other regions.

## Global Partnerships and Alliances:

Indian banks and fintech companies can establish global partnerships and alliances to increase their market presence and expand their reach. By collaborating with international financial institutions, technology providers, and industry associations, Indian companies can gain access to new markets, share expertise, and co-develop new solutions. These partnerships can also enable knowledge exchange and promote the adoption of best practices in the global fintech ecosystem.

The globalization of financial services presents considerable opportunities for Indian banks to expand their presence in global markets. Serving the Indian diaspora, engaging in South-South cooperation, and exporting fintech solutions are central avenues for growth. However, Indian banks must work through challenges such as regulatory compliance, competition, and market dynamics. By tapping their strengths, building strategic partnerships, and embracing breakthrough, Indian banks can factor into shaping the future of global banking and payment systems.

## 8.3 Policy and Regulatory Outlook

The regulatory system for banking and payment systems in India is poised for notable changes as the industry evolves in response to technological advancements, financial advance, and globalization. We now turn to the anticipated regulatory changes, focusing on new bank licensing policies, fintech regulations, and regulations for Non-bank Financial Companies (NBFCs). These changes aim to build a secure, inclusive, and competitive financial environment while addressing emerging risks and challenges.

### 8.3.1 Anticipated Regulatory Changes

**New Bank Licensing Policies**

As India's financial sector expands, the Reserve Bank of India (RBI) is expected to revisit its policies on bank licensing to encourage greater competition, development, and financial inclusion. The introduction of differentiated banking models, such as payments banks and small finance banks, has already diversified the banking field. Future licensing policies may further liberalize entry requirements for new banks, including universal banks, to improve financial access and cater to diverse customer needs.

***Universal Bank Licenses:*** The RBI may consider issuing new universal bank licenses to both established entities and new entrants, including corporate groups, technology companies, and fintech players. The objective is to introduce more players into the market, building competition and breakthrough. However, stringent eligibility criteria, including capital adequacy, governance standards, and risk management frameworks, will likely be enforced to guarantee financial stability and consumer protection.

***Niche and Specialized Banks:*** The regulator may also focus on promoting niche and specialized banking institutions, such as digital-only banks, green banks, and Islamic banks. These entities can cater to specific market segments and address unique financial needs. For instance, digital-only banks can offer frictionless, cost-effective banking services through digital channels, while green banks can finance sustainable projects and promote environmental stewardship.

***Foreign Bank Participation:*** The policy environment may become more favorable for foreign banks, with potential revisions to entry and operational requirements. By easing restrictions on foreign bank subsidiaries and branches, the RBI could attract more global players, strengthening the diversity and competitiveness of the Indian banking sector. This move could also ease the transfer of global best practices and advanced financial technologies to the Indian market.

## 8.3.2 Fintech Regulations

The rapid growth of fintech companies in India has revolutionized the financial services sector, offering novel solutions in payments, lending, insurance, and wealth management. However, the rise of fintech has also introduced new risks, including data privacy concerns, cybersecurity threats, and regulatory arbitrage. To address these challenges, the Indian regulatory framework is expected to evolve, with a focus on guaranteeing consumer protection, promoting fair competition, and mitigating systemic risks.

***Complete Fintech Framework:*** The RBI and other regulatory bodies may develop a thorough framework for fintech regulation, encompassing licensing requirements, prudential norms, and operational guidelines. This framework could cover fintech activities, including peer-to-peer lending, digital wallets, robo-advisory services, and cryptocurrency trading. By establishing clear regulatory guidelines, the authorities aim to create a level playing field for fintech and traditional financial institutions.

***Data Privacy and Security Regulations:*** Given the increasing reliance on digital channels and data-driven services, regulators are likely to strengthen data privacy and security regulations. The implementation of the Personal Data Protection Bill, once enacted, will impose strict obligations on data controllers and processors, including consent requirements, data localization, and the right to be forgotten. Fintech companies will need to strengthen their data protection measures and comply with these regulations to safeguard customer information and maintain trust.

### 8.3.3 Non-bank Financial Company (NBFC) Regulations

NBFCs contribute to India's financial ecosystem, providing credit to sectors and segments underserved by traditional banks, such as small and medium enterprises (SMEs), microfinance, and consumer finance. However, the rapid growth and increasing interconnectedness of NBFCs have raised concerns about financial stability and regulatory oversight. The RBI has been tightening the regulatory framework for NBFCs to address these concerns, and further reforms are expected in the near future.

### 8.3.4 Specialized NBFC Categories

The regulator may also consider creating specialized categories of NBFCs, such as NBFC-Factors, NBFC-IFCs (Infrastructure Finance Companies), and NBFC-MFIs (Microfinance Institutions), with tailored regulatory frameworks. These specialized NBFCs can cater to specific sectors and market segments, aligning with India's broader economic and social development goals. For example, NBFC-MFIs can focus on providing microcredit to low-income households, while NBFC-IFCs can support infrastructure projects.

### 8.3.5 Strengthening Prudential Norms

The RBI may introduce more stringent prudential norms for NBFCs, including higher capital adequacy requirements, tighter asset classification and provisioning standards, and boosted liquidity management rules. These measures aim to bolster the resilience of NBFCs and reduce their vulnerability to shocks. The adoption of the Liquidity Coverage Ratio (LCR) and Net Stable Funding Ratio (NSFR) could be extended to NBFCs, securing adequate liquidity buffers and stable funding sources.

### 8.3.6 Consolidation and Corporate Governance

To address issues related to fragmented ownership and governance practices, the RBI may encourage consolidation in the NBFC sector. By promoting mergers and acquisitions, the regulator seeks to create larger, more solid entities capable of managing risks effectively. Also, the RBI may introduce stricter corporate governance norms, including the composition of boards, fit and proper criteria for directors, and disclosure requirements. These measures aim to boost transparency, accountability, and risk management within NBFCs.

### 8.3.7 Regulation of Shadow Banking Activities

The RBI is also likely to focus on regulating shadow banking activities within the NBFC sector. Shadow banking refers to credit intermediation activities conducted by non-bank entities, which may not be subject to the same regulatory oversight as traditional banks. To mitigate systemic risks, the RBI may implement measures to monitor and regulate these activities, including broad reporting requirements and restrictions on complex financial products.

### 8.3.8 Data Protection and Privacy Regulations

The protection of personal data and privacy has become a foremost concern in the digital age, especially with the rapid growth of digital banking and financial services. In India, the evolving regulatory environment around data protection and privacy is poised to have a marked impact on the banking sector. The Digital Personal Data Protection Act, 2023 (DPDPA) is a full legislation that aims to protect the personal data of individuals. The Act defines personal data as any information that can be used to identify an individual, such as their name, address, phone number, email address, and financial information. The DPDPA sets out rules for how personal data can be collected, used, and shared, emphasizing the need for consent from individuals before collecting their personal data.

Primary provisions of the DPDPA include:

- **Data Processing and Consent**: The Act requires data controllers to obtain explicit consent from individuals before collecting their personal data.

- **Rights of Data Subjects**: The Act grants several rights to data subjects, including the right to access, rectify, and erase their data, as well as the right to data portability and the right to object to certain data processing activities.

- **Data Localization**: The Act requires critical personal data to be stored and processed within India's borders.

- **Data Protection Authority**: The Act establishes a Data Protection Authority (DPA) to oversee compliance, enforce regulations, and address grievances related to data processing activities.

The DPDPA also addresses cross-border data flows, requiring that sensitive personal data not be transferred outside India except under specific conditions. The Act aims to balance the need for data protection with the operational benefits of global data integration, safeguarding that data transferred to foreign jurisdictions adheres to the DPDPA's protection standards. The implementation of the DPDPA will have substantial implications for banking operations in India, affecting how banks handle customer data, design their systems, and interact with customers. Banks will need to make substantial adjustments to comply with the new regulations, including obtaining explicit consent from customers, implementing mechanisms to allow customers to exercise their rights, boosting data security measures, and complying with data localization requirements.

## 8.3.9 Open Banking Initiatives

The concept of open banking represents a major shift in the financial services system, enabling greater transparency, competition, and advance. In India, the open banking framework is being developed with a focus on improving customer control over financial data, promoting financial inclusion, and encouraging a more competitive ecosystem. We now examine the components of open banking initiatives in India, including the Account Aggregator Framework, API Standardization, and Consent Management Systems.

**Account Aggregator Framework**

The Account Aggregator (AA) framework is a critical pillar of India's open banking initiative, designed to help effortless and secure data sharing among financial institutions, customers, and third-party service providers. The framework allows individuals and businesses to consolidate and manage their financial data from multiple sources in a single platform, providing a complete view of their financial status.

**Features of the AA Framework:**

***Data Aggregation:*** The AA framework enables the aggregation of financial data from financial institutions, including banks, insurance companies, mutual funds, pension funds, and tax authorities. This aggregated data can be accessed by customers through an AA, which acts as a data intermediary without storing the data.

*__User Consent:__* A principle of the AA framework is user consent. Customers have complete control over who can access their financial data and for what purpose. AAs can only share data with third parties with explicit customer consent, guaranteeing privacy and data security.

*__Interoperability:__* The AA framework promotes interoperability among different financial institutions, allowing data to be exchanged without friction. This interoperability is achieved through standardized data formats and protocols, enabling easy integration with many financial service providers.

The AA framework is regulated by the Reserve Bank of India (RBI) and other sectoral regulators, securing compliance with data protection and privacy laws. The initiative is expected to equip customers by giving them greater control over their financial data, improve financial planning and management, and support access to a broader range of financial products and services.

## API Standardization

Application Programming Interfaces (APIs) are involved in open banking by enabling the secure and effective exchange of financial data between banks, third-party providers, and customers. API standardization is a component of open banking initiatives, safeguarding that APIs are consistent, secure, and interoperable across the industry.

### Importance of API Standardization:

*__Security and Compliance:__* Standardized APIs secure that data is exchanged securely, adhering to industry best practices and regulatory requirements. This standardization helps prevent data breaches and unauthorized access, protecting customer data.

*__Interoperability:__* With standardized APIs, financial institutions and third-party providers can easily integrate their systems, supporting smooth data sharing and service delivery. This interoperability increases customer experiences by allowing access to a broad set of financial services through a single platform.

*__Development and Competition:__* API standardization encourages a more competitive environment by lowering entry barriers for new market players, including fintech startups. It enables these players to offer fresh financial products and services, driving industry growth and customer satisfaction.

In India, the implementation of standardized APIs is guided by regulatory bodies such as the RBI and the National Payments Corporation of India (NPCI). These standards are designed to align with international best practices, promoting a globally competitive and secure open banking ecosystem.

**Consent Management Systems**

Consent Management Systems (CMS) are central to the open banking framework, providing a secure and transparent mechanism for obtaining, managing, and auditing customer consent for data sharing. These systems safeguard that customer data is only accessed and used with explicit consent, in compliance with data protection laws and regulations.

**Components of Consent Management Systems:**

***Consent Collection:*** CMS enables customers to grant or revoke consent for specific data-sharing activities. This process is typically facilitated through digital interfaces, such as mobile apps or web portals, where customers can view and manage their consent preferences.

***Consent Management:*** Once consent is granted, CMS manages the permissions associated with data access and sharing. This includes defining the scope, duration, and purpose of data usage, as well as the entities involved in data processing.

***Audit and Compliance:*** CMS provides an audit trail of all consent-related activities, guaranteeing transparency and accountability. This auditability is major for regulatory compliance, allowing financial institutions and regulators to verify that data-sharing practices align with customer consent and legal requirements.

The implementation of CMS in India's open banking framework is driven by the need to protect customer data and make certain compliance with the Personal Data Protection Bill and other regulatory mandates. The system improves customer trust by providing transparency and control over personal data, promoting a more secure and customer-centric financial ecosystem.

## 8.3.10 AI and ML Governance in Banking

Artificial Intelligence (AI) and Machine Learning (ML) have the potential to transform banking by automating processes, strengthening customer experiences, and improving risk management. However, the adoption of these technologies also raises ethical, legal, and regulatory concerns, such as bias in decision-making, transparency, and accountability.

**Aspects of AI and ML Governance:**

*Bias and Fairness:* AI and ML models can inadvertently perpetuate biases present in the training data, leading to unfair outcomes in areas like credit scoring, loan approvals, and fraud detection. Regulators must establish guidelines to guarantee that AI systems are fair, transparent, and non-discriminatory. This may include requirements for regular audits of AI systems, transparency in model design, and mechanisms for redressal of grievances.

*Explainability and Transparency:* One of the challenges with AI and ML models is their "black-box" nature, where the decision-making process is not easily understandable. Regulators may require financial institutions to adopt explainable AI (XAI) techniques, which provide clear explanations of how AI models arrive at their decisions. This transparency is important for building trust with consumers and securing compliance with regulatory standards.

*Accountability and Responsibility:* As AI systems take on more roles in decision-making, there is a need to clarify accountability. Regulators must secure that financial institutions remain accountable for the actions of their AI systems. This accountability includes establishing clear lines of responsibility, safeguarding human oversight of AI systems, and implementing sturdy governance frameworks.

The RBI and other regulatory bodies in India have recognized the far-reaching potential of AI and ML in banking. In recent years, they have issued guidelines and circulars addressing the ethical and governance aspects of AI adoption. These guidelines emphasize the need for transparency, fairness, and accountability in AI systems. Regulators encourage financial institutions to adopt AI governance frameworks that align with global best practices.

## 8.4 Future Challenges and Opportunities

As the Indian banking and payment systems continue to evolve, they face a range of future challenges and opportunities. These arise from changing customer expectations, technological advancements, regulatory landscapes, and socio-economic developments. In this section, we explore the challenges and opportunities associated with changing customer expectations, including the shift towards digital-first banking, the demand for instant and frictionless services, and the growing importance of ethical and sustainable banking.

## 8.4.1 Changing Customer Expectations

### Digital-first Banking

The digital revolution has dramatically transformed the banking field, leading to the emergence of digital-first banking. Customers increasingly prefer digital channels over traditional brick-and-mortar branches, expecting effortless and quick services through their smartphones and computers. This shift presents both challenges and opportunities for banks and financial institutions.

**Challenges:**

- **Technology Infrastructure:** Banks must invest in strong and scalable technology infrastructure to support digital banking services. This includes upgrading legacy systems, guaranteeing cybersecurity, and integrating new digital platforms.

- **Digital Literacy:** While urban and younger populations have readily adopted digital banking, there remains a considerable portion of the population, especially in rural areas, that lacks digital literacy. Banks need to bridge this gap by offering user-friendly interfaces and educational initiatives.

- **Customer Trust:** The digital space is vulnerable to cyber threats, making data security and privacy central. Banks must safeguard reliable security measures to build and maintain customer trust.

**Opportunities:**

- **Cost Productivity:** Digital-first banking can markedly reduce operational costs by minimizing the need for physical branches and manual processes. This cost-saving can be passed on to customers through lower fees and better interest rates.

- **Personalization:** Digital platforms allow banks to offer personalized services by analyzing customer data. This includes tailored product recommendations, customized financial advice, and personalized customer experiences.

- **Expansion of Reach:** Digital banking allows financial institutions to expand their reach to previously underserved areas, promoting financial inclusion and enabling access to banking services for a larger population.

## Instant and Smooth Services

In the age of instant gratification, customers expect immediate and frictionless banking services. The demand for real-time transactions, quick account access, and smooth customer experiences has never been higher. Meeting these expectations requires notable investments in technology and process optimization.

**Challenges:**

- **Real-time Processing:** Offering real-time transaction processing, such as instant payments and real-time account updates, requires sophisticated technology and infrastructure. Banks must make certain their systems can handle high transaction volumes with minimal latency.

- **Interoperability:** Effortless services often require interoperability between different banking systems, payment gateways, and financial platforms. Achieving this interoperability can be complex and requires standardization across the industry.

- **Customer Support:** With the increase in digital interactions, the need for smooth and responsive customer support has also grown. Banks must offer multi-channel support, including chatbots, call centers, and in-app assistance, to resolve customer issues promptly.

**Opportunities:**

- **Improved Customer Experience:** Providing instant and smooth services can greatly increase customer satisfaction and loyalty. Features like instant fund transfers, real-time notifications, and quick loan approvals cater to customers' need for speed and convenience.

- **New Product Offerings:** The demand for instant services drives breakthrough in product offerings. This includes features like instant credit, real-time investment options, and on-the-spot insurance coverage, which cater to the modern customer's expectations.

- **Increased Transaction Volumes:** As customers increasingly prefer digital and instant services, transaction volumes through digital channels are likely to grow, offering banks additional revenue streams through transaction fees and value-added services.

## Ethical and Sustainable Banking

The growing awareness of social, environmental, and ethical issues has led to a rising demand for ethical and sustainable banking practices. Customers increasingly expect banks to operate responsibly, not only in terms of financial practices but also in their environmental and social impact.

**Challenges:**

- **Integration of ESG Factors:** Banks face the challenge of integrating environmental, social, and governance (ESG) factors into their business strategies. This includes evaluating the sustainability impact of lending practices, investments, and corporate governance.

- **Transparency and Reporting:** As customers and regulators demand greater transparency, banks must improve their reporting on ESG initiatives and guarantee clear communication about their sustainability efforts and progress.

- **Balancing Profitability and Responsibility:** Banks must balance the pursuit of profitability with their commitment to ethical and sustainable practices. This requires careful decision-making and potentially rethinking traditional business models.

**Opportunities:**

- **New Market Segments:** Ethical and sustainable banking opens up new market segments, including green financing, sustainable investment products, and socially responsible banking services. These offerings cater to environmentally and socially conscious customers.

- **Brand Differentiation:** Adopting ethical and sustainable practices can differentiate a bank's brand in a competitive market. It can attract customers who prioritize values and ethics, building long-term loyalty and trust.

- **Regulatory Compliance and Risk Management:** Proactively adopting ESG principles can help banks stay ahead of regulatory requirements and mitigate risks associated with environmental and social issues. It can also attract ESG-focused investors and improve access to capital.

## 8.4.2 Technological Disruptions

The banking and payment systems sector is undergoing marked transformations due to rapid advancements in technology. As we look to the future, several technological disruptions are poised to reshape the industry, offering both unprecedented opportunities and challenges. This section covers impact of quantum computing and augmented and virtual reality (AR/VR) on the banking and payment systems.

## Quantum Computing in Banking

Quantum computing represents a paradigm shift in computational power and capabilities. Unlike classical computers, which use bits as the smallest unit of information, quantum computers use quantum bits or qubits. This allows quantum computers to perform complex calculations at unprecedented speeds, potentially transforming the banking sector.

**Potential Applications:**

- **Risk Analysis and Portfolio Optimization:** Quantum computing can improve risk modeling and portfolio optimization by processing vast amounts of data and performing complex calculations faster than traditional computers. This can lead to more accurate risk assessments and investment strategies.

- **Cryptography and Security:** Quantum computers have the potential to break existing cryptographic systems, which are the backbone of digital security. As a result, the banking industry must develop quantum-resistant cryptographic algorithms to secure sensitive financial data and transactions.

- **Fraud Detection:** Quantum computing can improve fraud detection by quickly analyzing large datasets to identify patterns and anomalies. This can help banks detect fraudulent activities in real-time, reducing the risk of financial losses.

**Challenges:**

- **High Cost and Complexity:** The development and maintenance of quantum computers are currently costly and complex. Banks will need substantial investments in infrastructure and expertise to draw on quantum computing effectively.

- **Security Concerns:** The potential to break existing cryptographic systems poses a major security threat. Banks must stay ahead of the curve by developing quantum-resistant security measures to protect customer data and transactions.

## Augmented and Virtual Reality in Banking

Augmented Reality (AR) and Virtual Reality (VR) technologies offer new ways for banks to engage with customers and strengthen their service offerings. These immersive technologies can transform the customer experience and offer new opportunities for financial education and training.

**Potential Applications:**

- **Virtual Branches:** VR can create virtual bank branches, allowing customers to interact with bank representatives and access services from the comfort of their homes. This can be particularly useful for providing personalized financial advice and support.

- **Immersive Financial Education:** AR and VR can offer immersive financial education experiences, helping customers understand complex financial products and services. For example, customers can use AR to visualize investment portfolios or loan repayment schedules.

- **Strengthened Customer Service:** AR can boost in-person customer service by providing bank employees with real-time information about customers, such as account details and transaction history. This can help employees provide more personalized and effective service.

**Challenges:**

- **Adoption and Accessibility:** The adoption of AR and VR technologies may be limited by the availability and affordability of the necessary hardware, such as VR headsets. Banks must consider the accessibility of these technologies for all customers.

- **Technical Limitations:** While AR and VR technologies have great potential, they are still in the early stages of development. Technical limitations, such as resolution, latency, and user comfort, must be addressed to secure a smooth and effective experience.

### 8.4.3 Cybersecurity Threats

In the evolving environment of banking and payment systems, cybersecurity remains a critical concern. As digital technologies advance, so do the methods employed by cybercriminals. This section explores two major cybersecurity threats, Advanced Persistent Threats (APTs) and AI-powered cyberattacks, that pose considerable risks to the financial sector.

**Advanced Persistent Threats (APTs)**

*Definition and Characteristics:* Advanced Persistent Threats (APTs) refer to prolonged and targeted cyberattacks in which an intruder gains access to a network and remains undetected for an extended period. The objective of APTs is not just to cause immediate damage but to steal data, monitor activity, or manipulate systems over time. These attacks are often sophisticated, using a combination of tactics, techniques, and procedures (TTPs) to evade detection and maintain access.

***Modus Operandi:*** APTs typically involve multiple stages, including reconnaissance, initial compromise, establishment of a foothold, escalation of privileges, internal reconnaissance, lateral movement, data exfiltration, and maintenance of persistence. Attackers may use several methods such as spear-phishing, exploiting vulnerabilities, and deploying malware to achieve their objectives.

***Impact on Banks and Payment Systems:*** APTs pose a notable risk to banks and payment systems due to the sensitive nature of financial data. Attackers can steal customer information, financial records, and intellectual property, leading to financial losses, reputational damage, and regulatory penalties. APTs can disrupt operations by sabotaging systems or altering data.

***Countermeasures:*** To defend against APTs, financial institutions must adopt a multi-layered security approach. This includes implementing advanced threat detection systems, network segmentation, solid access controls, and regular security assessments. Continuous monitoring, threat intelligence sharing, and incident response planning are also central for identifying and mitigating APTs.

## AI-powered Cyberattacks

***Emergence of AI in Cyberattacks:*** Artificial Intelligence (AI) has revolutionized many industries, including cybersecurity. However, it has also become a tool for cybercriminals. AI-powered cyberattacks tap machine learning algorithms to increase the sophistication, speed, and scale of attacks. These attacks can adapt to defenses, making them more challenging to detect and counter.

### Types of AI-powered Cyberattacks:

- **Automated Phishing:** AI can generate convincing phishing emails by mimicking writing styles and creating personalized messages. Machine learning models can analyze social media profiles and online behavior to craft targeted phishing attempts.

- **Malware Evasion:** AI algorithms can modify malware to evade detection by traditional security systems. This includes changing signatures, adapting behaviors, and learning from defensive measures to avoid triggering alarms.

- **Deepfake and Social Engineering Attacks:** AI can create realistic deepfake videos and audio recordings, which can be used for social engineering attacks. For instance, attackers can impersonate executives to authorize fraudulent transactions.

***Implications for Financial Institutions:*** AI-powered cyberattacks can lead to data breaches, financial fraud, and identity theft. The speed and accuracy of these attacks can overwhelm traditional security systems, making it difficult for financial institutions to respond in real-time. The use of AI in cyberattacks raises concerns about the scale and automation of such threats, potentially leading to widespread and simultaneous attacks.

***Defensive Strategies:*** To combat AI-powered cyberattacks, banks and payment systems must improve their cybersecurity frameworks with AI-driven defense mechanisms. This includes using machine learning for anomaly detection, behavioral analysis, and threat intelligence. Also, investing in AI research and development for cybersecurity can help institutions stay ahead of emerging threats. Collaboration with other financial institutions, regulatory bodies, and cybersecurity firms is needed for sharing knowledge and best practices.

## Quantum-resistant Cryptography

The advent of quantum computing presents both opportunities and challenges for a number of industries, including banking and payment systems. Quantum computers have the potential to solve complex mathematical problems at unprecedented speeds, posing a threat to current cryptographic protocols. As a result, the development and implementation of quantum-resistant cryptography have become necessary to securing the security and integrity of financial systems.

***Post-Quantum Cryptography:*** Quantum-resistant cryptography, also known as post-quantum cryptography (PQC), involves developing cryptographic algorithms that are secure against quantum attacks. These algorithms are based on mathematical problems that are believed to be hard for both classical and quantum computers to solve. Areas of research include lattice-based cryptography, hash-based cryptography, code-based cryptography, and multivariate polynomial cryptography.

***Lattice-based Cryptography:*** Lattice-based cryptography is one of the most promising approaches for quantum-resistant algorithms. It relies on the hardness of lattice problems, such as the Shortest Vector Problem (SVP) and

Learning With Errors (LWE). These problems are computationally challenging even for quantum computers. Lattice-based schemes provide a foundation for cryptographic primitives, including encryption, digital signatures, and primary exchange.

***Hash-based Cryptography:*** Hash-based cryptography uses hash functions to create digital signatures. It includes algorithms like the Merkle Signature Scheme (MSS) and the eXtended Merkle Signature Scheme (XMSS). Hash-based methods offer strong security guarantees based on the collision resistance of hash functions, making them resistant to quantum attacks.

***Code-based Cryptography:*** Code-based cryptography is based on the difficulty of decoding random linear codes. The McEliece and Niederreiter cryptosystems are well-known examples. These systems offer a high level of security, but they often require large principal sizes, which can be a limitation in practical applications.

***Multivariate Polynomial Cryptography:*** Multivariate polynomial cryptography involves solving systems of multivariate polynomial equations. The complexity of these problems, particularly in large fields, provides security against quantum attacks. Schemes like the Unbalanced Oil and Vinegar (UOV) and Hidden Field Equations (HFE) are examples of this approach.

## The Threat of Quantum Computing

***Quantum Computing Capabilities:*** Quantum computers employ the principles of quantum mechanics, using qubits instead of classical bits. Qubits can exist in multiple states simultaneously, enabling quantum computers to perform parallel computations. This property allows them to solve certain problems much faster than classical computers, such as factoring large numbers, which is the basis of many cryptographic algorithms like RSA.

***Impact on Cryptography:*** Current public-cryptography, including RSA and elliptic curve cryptography (ECC), relies on the difficulty of factoring large integers and solving discrete logarithm problems. Quantum computers, particularly those using Shor's algorithm, can effectively solve these problems, rendering traditional encryption methods vulnerable to decryption. This potential capability poses a marked risk to the confidentiality and security of sensitive financial data.

***Implementation and Standardization:*** The transition to quantum-resistant cryptography requires a thorough evaluation of new algorithms and their implementation in existing systems. The US National Institute of

Standards and Technology (NIST) has initiated a process to standardize post-quantum cryptographic algorithms. This effort involves selecting the most secure and quick algorithms for widespread adoption. Financial institutions and payment system operators must begin preparing for the integration of quantum-resistant solutions, safeguarding a smooth transition when quantum computers become viable.

***Challenges and Considerations:*** While quantum-resistant cryptography offers promising solutions, it also presents challenges. The increased computational and storage requirements of some post-quantum algorithms can impact system performance. The implementation of new cryptographic standards requires substantial changes to existing infrastructure, software, and protocols. Financial institutions must carefully evaluate these factors and plan for the long-term security of their systems.

## 8.4.4 Sustainable and Green Banking

As global awareness of environmental issues grows, the banking and financial sectors are increasingly focusing on sustainable and green banking practices. These practices aim to promote environmentally friendly and socially responsible initiatives, aligning financial activities with the goals of sustainability and climate action. This section explores green financing initiatives, Environmental, Social, and Governance (ESG) risk assessment in lending, and the overall impact of sustainable banking on the industry.

### Green Financing Initiatives

***Definition and Importance:*** Green financing refers to the allocation of capital towards projects and businesses that contribute to environmental sustainability. This includes investments in renewable energy, energy effectiveness, sustainable agriculture, water conservation, and pollution reduction. Green financing initiatives are critical in supporting the transition to a low-carbon economy and addressing the challenges posed by climate change.

***Green Bonds:*** Green bonds are a prominent green financing instrument. They are fixed-income securities issued to raise capital for projects with environmental benefits. Green bonds offer investors a way to support sustainable initiatives while receiving financial returns. The proceeds from green bonds are earmarked for specific projects, guaranteeing transparency and accountability. The market for green bonds has grown rapidly, with both public and private sector issuers participating.

***Sustainable Investment Funds:*** Sustainable investment funds, also known as ESG funds, invest in companies that meet specific environmental, social, and governance criteria. These funds assess the ESG performance of companies, considering factors such as carbon footprint, labor practices, board diversity, and ethical governance. By investing in ESG-compliant companies, sustainable investment funds aim to generate long-term financial returns while promoting positive societal impact.

***Green Loans and Sustainability-linked Loans:*** Green loans are similar to traditional loans but are specifically designated for environmentally sustainable projects. These loans often come with favorable terms, such as lower interest rates, to incentivize borrowers to engage in green activities. Sustainability-linked loans, on the other hand, are tied to the borrower's overall ESG performance. The loan terms may vary based on the achievement of specific sustainability targets, such as reducing carbon emissions or improving energy speed.

***Role of Development Banks:*** Development banks, both national and international, help with promoting green financing. Institutions like the World Bank, Asian Development Bank, and the Green Climate Fund provide funding and technical assistance for climate-resilient projects. These banks often offer concessional financing, grants, and guarantees to support green initiatives in developing countries, enabling sustainable development.

***Challenges and Opportunities:*** While green financing offers many benefits, it also faces challenges. The lack of standardized definitions and criteria for green projects can lead to "greenwashing," where projects are falsely marketed as environmentally friendly. The higher perceived risk and lower returns of green projects can deter investors. However, the growing demand for sustainable investments and the increasing regulatory focus on ESG factors present considerable opportunities for the expansion of green financing.

## ESG Risk Assessment in Lending

***Importance of ESG Risk Assessment:*** Environmental, Social, and Governance (ESG) risk assessment is a part of sustainable banking. It involves evaluating the potential environmental, social, and governance risks associated with lending and investment decisions. ESG risk assessment helps financial institutions identify and manage risks that could impact their financial performance, reputation, and compliance with regulatory standards.

***Environmental Risk Factors:*** Environmental risks include issues related to climate change, resource depletion, pollution, and biodiversity loss. For example, lending to industries with high carbon emissions or those involved in deforestation can expose banks to reputational and regulatory risks. Assessing environmental risks involves analyzing the borrower's environmental impact, carbon footprint, and compliance with environmental regulations.

***Social Risk Factors:*** Social risks encompass issues related to labor practices, human rights, community relations, and social equity. Financial institutions must consider the social implications of their lending decisions, such as the treatment of workers, supply chain practices, and community engagement. For instance, lending to companies with poor labor practices or those involved in controversial projects can lead to social backlash and reputational damage.

***Governance Risk Factors:*** Governance risks pertain to the quality and integrity of corporate governance structures. This includes factors such as board diversity, executive compensation, transparency, and accountability. Poor governance practices can lead to financial mismanagement, fraud, and legal liabilities. Banks assess governance risks by examining the corporate governance frameworks and ethical standards of borrowers.

***Integration of ESG Factors in Credit Analysis:*** Integrating ESG factors into credit analysis involves assessing the potential impact of these factors on the borrower's financial health and ability to repay loans. This includes evaluating the borrower's ESG performance, identifying material ESG risks, and incorporating these risks into credit ratings and pricing. By considering ESG factors, banks can make more informed lending decisions and mitigate potential risks.

***Regulatory and Industry Standards:*** The growing emphasis on ESG factors has led to the development of regulatory and industry standards for ESG risk assessment. For example, the Equator Principles provide a risk management framework for assessing environmental and social risks in project finance. Also, the Task Force on Climate-related Financial Disclosures (TCFD) provides guidelines for disclosing climate-related risks and opportunities. Adherence to these standards strengthens transparency and accountability in ESG risk assessment.

***Opportunities for Banks:*** ESG risk assessment presents opportunities for banks to differentiate themselves in the market and attract ESG-conscious investors and customers. By offering green financing products, banks can tap into the growing demand for sustainable investments. Banks that proactively manage ESG risks can strengthen their reputation, build customer trust, and create long-term value.

## Carbon Footprint Reduction in Banking Operations

As the global conversation around climate change intensifies, industries across the board are being called upon to reduce their carbon footprints. The banking sector, while not typically associated with high emissions, has a role to play in this transition. Banks not only influence carbon emissions through their lending and investment choices but also through their operational activities. This section looks at strategies and measures banks can implement to reduce their carbon footprint, contributing to broader environmental sustainability goals.

### Reducing Energy Consumption in Bank Branches

***Energy Productivity in Buildings:*** One of the areas where banks can reduce their carbon footprint is through energy effectiveness in their physical branches and office buildings. This includes the adoption of energy-smooth lighting, heating, ventilation, and air conditioning (HVAC) systems. By installing LED lighting, using motion sensors to control lights, and optimizing HVAC systems, banks can considerably cut down on energy consumption.

***Green Building Certifications:*** Pursuing green building certifications, such as LEED (Leadership in Energy and Environmental Design) or BREEAM (Building Research Establishment Environmental Assessment Method), can further boost a bank's sustainability efforts. These certifications encourage the use of sustainable building materials, effective water use, and renewable energy sources. Banks can retrofit existing buildings to meet these standards or construct new branches with green design principles.

***Use of Renewable Energy:*** Shifting to renewable energy sources, such as solar, wind, or geothermal, is another effective strategy for reducing carbon emissions. Banks can install solar panels on their rooftops or partner with renewable energy providers to source green electricity. This not only lowers the carbon footprint but also reduces reliance on fossil fuels and can provide long-term cost savings.

### Green Data Centers and IT Infrastructure

***Energy-quick Data Centers:*** As banks increasingly rely on digital services, the demand for data processing and storage has surged, making data centers a marked source of energy consumption. To mitigate their environmental impact, banks can invest in energy-smooth data centers. This includes using energy-effective servers, implementing advanced cooling systems, and optimizing data storage and processing.

***Green Cloud Computing:*** Cloud computing offers a sustainable alternative to traditional data centers. By migrating to cloud services provided by companies with strong environmental commitments, banks can use shared resources and reduce the need for on-premises servers. Cloud providers often have the scale to implement more energy-quick technologies and renewable energy sources, thus lowering the overall carbon footprint.

***Virtualization and Server Optimization:*** Virtualization technology allows banks to run multiple virtual servers on a single physical server, maximizing resource use and reducing energy consumption. Similarly, server optimization techniques, such as load balancing and dynamic resource allocation, can improve the speed of IT operations, leading to lower energy use and carbon emissions.

### Sustainable Procurement and Supply Chain Management

***Green Procurement Policies:*** Banks can implement green procurement policies that prioritize environmentally friendly products and services. This includes selecting office supplies made from recycled materials, energy-smooth electronic devices, and sustainable furniture. By working with suppliers who share their commitment to sustainability, banks can reduce the environmental impact of their procurement processes.

***Sustainable Vendor Management:*** Beyond procurement, banks can influence their entire supply chain by engaging with vendors on sustainability issues. This includes assessing the carbon footprint of suppliers, setting environmental performance criteria, and encouraging the adoption of green practices. Sustainable vendor management not only helps banks reduce their indirect emissions but also promotes sustainability across the industry.

### Employee Engagement and Awareness

***Sustainability Training and Awareness:*** Educating employees about the importance of sustainability and how they can contribute to reducing the bank's carbon footprint is major. Banks can conduct training sessions, workshops, and awareness campaigns to highlight energy-saving practices, waste reduction, and sustainable commuting options.

***Green Office Practices:*** Encouraging green office practices, such as recycling, reducing water usage, and minimizing single-use plastics, can further lower the carbon footprint. Banks can also implement policies that promote remote work and flexible working hours, reducing the need for commuting and the associated carbon emissions.

***Employee Incentives for Sustainability:*** To motivate employees to adopt sustainable practices, banks can offer incentives such as rewards for using public transport, carpooling, or cycling to work. They can also establish green teams or sustainability committees to drive initiatives and monitor progress towards environmental goals.

This textbook has provided a broad exploration of the Indian banking system and payment systems, offering deep and broad insights into their interconnectedness. Understanding these two domains together is important, as they form the dual pillars that uphold the country's financial infrastructure. The Indian banking system is the foundation of the country's financial stability, managing capital flow, providing credit, and securing market liquidity. Banks factor into economic development by easing investment, consumption, and savings, driving overall economic growth. This textbook has detailed how banks, through their services, are central to the economy's functioning. Payment systems, on the other hand, are the backbone that keeps the economy moving. In today's digital era, the productivity, speed, and security of payment systems are critical. The discussions within this book have highlighted how these systems have evolved from traditional methods to advanced digital platforms, enabling instantaneous transactions globally. Payment systems enable money transfers, making it possible for businesses to operate smoothly, consumers to access goods and services, and governments to collect taxes and disburse welfare benefits. Understanding the relationship between banks and payment systems is critical, as it provides a complete view of how financial transactions are conducted in a complex economy like India. These two components are interdependent, with banks relying on effective payment systems and payment systems depending on the banking infrastructure. This interdependence means that changes or disruptions in one domain can have substantial repercussions in the other. Reading about Indian banking and payment systems together offers valuable insights into how these systems contribute to broader economic goals, such as financial inclusion. By bringing more people into the formal financial system, banks and payment systems can help reduce poverty, increase economic stability, and promote sustainable development. As we conclude this book, it's clear that banking and payment systems in India are closely tied. The future of these systems holds tremendous potential and rapid change, with the continued convergence of these two domains likely to bring about further developments that improve the effectiveness, accessibility, and security of financial services.

**Disclaimer**

This textbook is intended to provide readers with relevant content in one place, aiming to support learning and understanding. Portions of the text were drafted using generative AI tools (ChatGPT and Claude) for content synthesis and formatting, under the author's supervision. The author has reviewed, edited, and verified the content and assumes full responsibility for its accuracy.

If any discrepancies or errors are found, readers are encouraged to share feedback at: **vijaykiranslp@gmail.com.** Suggestions and corrections are welcome.